FAITH IN REASON

Series Editors:
Susan Frank Parsons and Laurence Paul Hemming

Inspired by the challenge of the papal encyclical *Fides et ratio*, (1998), to consider anew the relation of faith and reason, this series is dedicated to paying generous heed to the questions that lie within this goal. The series comprises monographs by a wide range of international and ecumenical authors, edited collections and translations of significant texts, with appeal both to an academic community, and more broadly to all those on whom the apologetic task impinges. The studies it encompasses are informed by a desire for the mutual engagement of the disciplines of theology and philosophy in the problematic areas of current debate at the highest and most serious level of scholarship. May they serve to illuminate the foundations of faith as lived in one's contemporary cultural context and thus constitute an ecumenical renewal of the work of philosophical theology. The series is promoted by the Society of St Catherine of Siena, in the spirit of its commitment to the renewal of the intellectual apostolate of the Catholic Church. http://www.caterinati.org.uk/

PUBLISHED

Restoring Faith in Reason
A new translation of the Encyclical Letter *Faith and Reason*
of Pope John Paul II together with a commentary and discussion
Laurence Paul Hemming and Susan Frank Parsons (editors)

Contemplating Aquinas
On the Varieties of Interpretation
Fergus Kerr OP (editor)

The Politics of Human Frailty
A Theological Defence of Political Liberalism
Christopher J. Insole

Postmodernity's Transcending
Devaluing God
Laurence Paul Hemming

Corpus Mysticum
The Eucharist and the Church in the Middle Ages
– historical survey
Henri Cardinal de Lubac SJ

Redeeming Truth:
Considering Faith and Reason
Laurence Paul Hemming and Susan Frank Parsons (editors)

The Liturgical Subject

Subject, Subjectivity, and the Human Person in Contemporary Liturgical Discussion and Critique

Edited by
James G. Leachman, OSB

University of Notre Dame Press
Notre Dame, Indiana

Copyright © 2009 James G. Leachman, O.S.B.

First published in 2008 by SCM Press
9–17 St. Albans Place, London n1 0nx

Published in the United States in 2009
by the University of Notre Dame Press
Notre Dame, Indiana 46556
www.undpress.nd.edu

All Rights Reserved

Published in the United States of America

Library of Congress Cataloging-in-Publication Data

The liturgical subject : subject, subjectivity, and the human person in contemporary liturgical discussion and critique / edited by James G. Leachman.

   p. cm. — (faith in reason)
   Includes bibliographical references and index.
   isbn-13: 978-0-268-03410-8 (pbk. : alk. paper)
   isbn-10: 0-268-03410-9 (pbk. : alk. paper)
 1. Catholic Church--Liturgy. 2. Liturgical reform. I. Leachman, James G.
bx1970.L4926 2009
264′.02—dc22

                                             2009023273

CUI EX OCCIDENTE ROMAM EMISSO
STUDIIS OMNINO PERFECTIS
SIT LITURGIAE DOCENDAE MUNUS
CONFISUM

CUIQUE PLURIMI APPROPINQUARINT
LITURGIAE SCIENTIAE AD RATIONEM
TRADENDAM
UT CULTO DOCTORI PATRIQUE AMATO

DOMINO EPHREM CARR OSB

HOC MUNUSCULUM
RECEPTI HAUD IMMEMOR BENEFICII
DEDICAT DICIPULUS

Contents

Acknowledgements   ix

Contributors   xi

Editor's Preface   xv

1. The Liturgical Subject   1
   Laurence Paul Hemming

2. The Liturgical Self: An Exploration of Christian Anthropology in Light of the Liturgy   17
   Robert Barron

3. Liturgical Polarity and Symbolic Hermeneutics   32
   Ângelo Manuel dos Santos Cardita

4. What does the 'Roman Rite' Denominate?   57
   László Dobszay

5. Eucharistic Personalism   74
   Eduardo J. Echeverria

6. Liturgies within the Liturgy   114
   Bruce E. Harbert

7. The Human Person at Play: A Model for Contemporary Liturgical Understanding   132
   Zsolt Ilyés

8. St Thomas Aquinas on Eucharistic Ecstasy   154
   Peter A. Kwasniewski

9. The Formation of the Ecclesial Person Through Baptismal Preparation and the Celebrations in the RCIA: the Collects for the Scrutinies   172
   James G. Leachman OSB and
   Daniel P. McCarthy OSB

10　The influence of Anthropology on the development of Baptismal Rites: up to and including the Mystagogical Catechists of the Fourth Century　201
　　Enrico Mazza

11　The Holy Trinity and the Liturgical Subject　226
　　Simon Oliver

12　Communio, Truth and the Preaching of John Henry Newman　242
　　Denis Robinson OSB

Index of Names　263

Index of Scriptural References　267

Acknowledgements

The inspiration for this seventh volume in the Faith and Reason series was sown by Dr Laurence Hemming and Dr Susan Parsons of the Society of St Catherine of Siena when, in the Spring of 2003, they asked me to edit a collection of essays which would respond in the broadest way to the very suggestive remarks in the then Cardinal Joseph Ratzinger's reflection on the Sacred Liturgy, that thought be given and a means be found, 'daß die maßlose Übersteigerung des Subjekts überwunden und wieder erkannt wird, daß gerade die Beziehung auf den am Anfang stehenden Logos auch das Subjekt, nämlich die Person, rettet und sie zugleich in die wahre Beziehung der Gemeinschaft hineinversetzt, die letztlich in der trinitarischen Liebe gründet'.[1]

The positive responses of those I invited to collaborate in the project were encouraging to me. The Society of St Catherine of Siena subsequently held a one-day international colloquium on the Encyclical Letter *Ecclesia de Eucharistia* on 11 February 2004 which was co-sponsored by and held at Heythrop College, University of London, where the dialogue helped me to further develop this project. The editors are most grateful to the Principal, the Revd Dr John McDade SJ, for the hospitality of the College on the occasion, to the Revd Dr Aidan Nichols OP for presiding at the Mass with which the day began, to His Eminence the Cardinal Archbishop of Westminster for sending a greeting to the conference, and to all the speakers and participants for their co-operation in making this a well-attended, lively and serious event.

Soon after the Heythrop colloquium, the Holy Father followed his Encyclical Letter *Ecclesia de Eucharistia* by announcing that the Synod of Bishops to be held in October 2005 would reflect on the Eucharist. This prompted the Society to organize a series of further studies on various aspects of the Eucharist and the Sacred Liturgy of the Church: theological, philosophical, historical, æsthetic, musicological, pastoral,

---

[1] Joseph Cardinal Ratzinger, *Der Geist der Liturgie: eine Einführung*, Freiburg, Herder, 2000, p. 133 f. 'to overcome the boundless superiority of the [philosophical] subject and to recognize once more that a relationship with the Logos, who is from the beginning, saves the subject, that is the person, and at the same time puts us into a true relation of communality which is ultimately grounded in the Trinitarian life'.

ACKNOWLEDGEMENTS

linguistic, hermeneutical and ecumenical, to which series this volume contributes.

The editors would like to thank those who helped produce this volume, those who generously accepted the invitation to submit papers, and those who worked on translating and editing. The contribution of Ângelo Cardita was translated from Portuguese with funding generously offered by the late Mrs Josette Willmott, and further revised and edited by Miguel S. Vieira, a postgraduate student at Heythrop College. The contribution of László Dobszay, composed in Hungarian and translated by the author was further edited by Henry St John Broadbent, a postgraduate student at Heythrop College and a trustee of the Society of St Catherine of Siena. The contributions of Zsolt Ilyés was translated from Italian and edited for content by Daniel McCarthy OSB, who also translated the contribution of Enrico Mazza, also originally in Italian.

Finally our thanks go to the external reader for valuable insights and advice, and to Mary Matthews and Barbara Laing at SCM-Canterbury Press and Chuck van Hof at the University of Notre Dame Press for their help in its production.

Contributors

Revd Dr Laurence Paul Hemming is a Deacon of the Archdiocese of Westminster and a co-founder of the Society of St Catherine of Siena. He is the author of *Heidegger's Atheism: The Refusal of a Theological Voice* (Notre Dame University Press, 2002); *Postmodernity's Transcending: Devaluing God* (SCM Press and Notre Dame University Press in the Faith in Reason series, 2005); a short book on Pope Benedict XVI; and, most recently, *Worship as a Revelation: The Past, Present and Future of Catholic Liturgy* (Continuum, 2008).

Fr Robert Barron is professor of systematic theology at the University of St Mary of the Lake/Mundelein Seminary. He has a Doctorate in Sacred Theology from the Institut Catholique de Paris and is the author of seven books, including *And Now I See: A Theology of Transformation* (Crossroad, 1998); *Thomas Aquinas: Spiritual Master* (Crossroad, 1996); *Bridging the Great Divide* (Rowman and Littlefield, 2004); and *The Priority of Christ: Toward a Postliberal Catholicism* (Brazos, 2007).

Dr Ângelo Cardita studied theology in Evora and Porto in Portugal and at the Istituto Superior de Barcelona, before completing his doctorate in the Theology Faculty at Sant'Anselmo, Rome. He is now a visiting professor at the Istituto Superior de Barcelona.

Professor László Dobszay is professor at the Liszt Ferenc Academy of Music, State University, Budapest, Hungary. He has written *The Bugnini-Liturgy and the Reform of the Reform* (Catholic Church Music Associates, 2003).

Professor Eduardo J. Echeverria is Associate Professor of Philosophy at Sacred Heart Major Seminary, Detroit, Michigan, USA. He received his doctorate from the Vrije Universiteit of Amsterdam and has contributed articles to various scholarly journals, including *The Thomist, Logos, Philosophia Reformata* and *Revista Portuguesa de Filosofia*.

CONTRIBUTORS

Monsignor Bruce Harbert is Secretary of the International Commission on English in the Liturgy (ICEL) and Executive Director of the Secretariat of ICEL.

Fr Zsolt Ilyés, a priest of the Hungarian Diocese of Alba Iulia, Romania, earned a Licence in Theology in Budapest and a Licence in Liturgy from the Pontifical Liturgical Institute, Sant'Anselmo, Rome. He is currently the spiritual director of the diocesan seminary of Alba Iulia, and a professor of liturgy in the theological institute there.

Dr Peter Kwasniewski is Assistant Academic Dean and Associate Professor of Philosophy and Theology at Wyoming Catholic College. His articles have appeared in many journals, including *Mediaeval Studies, Communio, Angelicum, The Thomist, The Modern Schoolman,* and *Nova & Vetera.* His translation of portions of St Thomas Aquinas's *Commentary on the Sentences of Peter Lombard,* is forthcoming from the Catholic University of America Press.

Fr James Leachman OSB is a monk of St Benedict's Abbey, Ealing, London, Professor of Liturgical Spirituality and Professor of Liturgy of the Churches of the Reformation at the Pontifical Liturgical Institute, Rome. He has written articles on the Liturgy of the Church of England in *Ecclesia Orans,* and on the sources and theology of RCIA in *Studia Liturgica.*

Fr Daniel McCarthy OSB is a monk of St Benedict's Abbey, Atchison, Kansas, has recently defended his doctorate at the Pontifical Liturgical Institute, Rome and been appointed Professor of Liturgy at the Beda College, Rome. The volume *Appreciating the Collect: An Irenic Methodology,* edited by Leachman and McCarthy, is forthcoming from St Michael's Abbey Press.

Monsignor Enrico Mazza is Professor of Liturgical History in the Faculty of Letters and Philosophy at the Catholic University of Milan and Professor of History of the Eucharist at The Pontifical Liturgical Institute, Rome. He is author of *Le odierne preghiere eucaristiche,* (1984), trans. *The Eucharistic Prayers of the Roman Rite* (Pueblo, 1986) and *La Mistagogia: una teologia della liturgia in epoca patristica* (CLV, 1988), trans. *Mystagogy: A Theology of Liturgy in the Patristic Age* (Pueblo, 1989).

Dr Simon Oliver is an Anglican systematic theologian, currently Senior Lecturer in Theology at the University of Wales, Lampeter, and author of *Philosophy, God and Motion* (Routledge, 2005).

CONTRIBUTORS

Fr Denis Robinson OSB is a monk of St Meinrad Archabbey, Indiana, USA, has recently defended his doctorate in Systematic Theology at the Catholic University of Leuven and is a member of the international research project: Orthodoxy, Process and Product. He has published *The Mother of Wisdom: Exploring the Parabolic Imperative of the Anglican Sermons of John Henry Newman* (Louvain Studies, 2002) and *Imagination and Theological Pluralism* (Peeters, 2003).

Editor's Preface

In the heat of the summer of 2003 in Rome, at the beginning of this editorial project, after over 30 years I read once again a fascinating short article, written soon after the close of the Second Vatican Council, by the Anglican existentialist and systematic theologian John M. Macquarrie (1919–2007).[1] At this time Macquarrie was still the Professor of Systematic Theology in Union Theological Seminary, New York, and the article was called 'Subjectivity and objectivity in theology and worship.'[2] It is to my mind not only a measured consideration of the history of English-language theology in the first two-thirds of the twentieth century, but also a warning of future trends and pitfalls and an encouragement to his readers to 'hold the line' in the face of the theological tendencies then prevalent.

In his article Macquarrie describes the pendulum swing which he saw occurring at that time. It was a swing away from objectivity, tradition and authority towards subjectivity and towards an attenuation of the faith in doctrine, morals and worship. Macquarrie writes in this 1967 article that,

> The trouble is that at different epochs in its history theology tends to allow its language to become one-sided. The unique reality of God gets lost, and sometimes he is allowed to degenerate in our thought into one object among others in the world, while sometimes he is dissolved into our subjective ideals and imaginings.[3]

We have also seen the pendulum swing back and forth in Catholic theology and liturgy during the twentieth century and so we ask whether the Church can come in the twenty-first century to discern with sufficient insight the ever-moving balance point of the pendulum in its course between two extremes?

---

[1] John M. Macquarrie died on 28 May 2007.
[2] J. M. Macquarrie, 'Subjectivity and objectivity in theology and worship', *Worship* 41 (1967), pp. 152–60.
[3] Macquarrie, 'Subjectivity', p. 154.

EDITOR'S PREFACE

Some consider that the Second Vatican Council's message of hope and renewal, given to a tired and anxious Church and world after the Second World War and at the beginning of the Cold War, was wildly over-optimistic concerning human nature, and that this exaggerated confidence may in fact have propelled the Church (in the West) into a prolonged crisis of self-identity and purpose from which she does not seem to have yet emerged. Perhaps the Council fathers were indeed over-confident about the Church's ability to 'read the signs of the times'[4] accurately and to steer a straight course ahead. Certainly they were unaware of the cultural shifts – relativism, globalization, neo-paganism, consumerism and excessive materialism – that were about to occur in the places where Catholicism was then strong: Europe, America and Australia. Almost immediately after the conclusion of the Council, the worldwide cultural phenomenon now popularly known as the 'sixties' happened. This amounted to nothing less than a frontal assault on forms of authority in the Church as well as in society. Subjectivity, feelings and personal judgement were espoused as the new touchstones of authenticity, reality and power.

Macquarrie continued,

> In contemporary theology, then, subjectivism is on the upswing. In this situation, the duty of the sane theologian, as I see it, is to hold the line and stress the objective truths of the Christian faith in the face of this flood. In doing so, he will above all try to make known the presence and reality of God . . . [A]t the present time, with the overwhelming drift towards subjectivism, those who stress the sacraments are helping to maintain a healthy balance, not only in the church's life but in the theology that gets shaped by that life, and then shapes it in turn.[5]

This volume is intended to offer to church philosophers, liturgists and theologians of different schools a forum for conversation on issues of liturgy, theology and church philosophy and to enable a greater appreciation of the wealth of theologies in current Catholic writing. The potential of the Church's ministry in the world is diminished to the degree that internal dialogue is limited; more robust conversation *ad intram* could only strengthen the theological community in its service to the whole Church for her service to the world.

'Subject, subjectivity and the human person in contemporary liturgical

---

4 *The Documents of Vatican II*, tr. W. Abbot (London: Chapman, 1966), pp. 201–2. *Gaudium et Spes* n. 4. '. . . the Church has always had the duty of scrutinizing the signs of the times and of interpreting them in the light of the gospel.'
5 Macquarrie, 'Subjectivity', p. 157.

discussion and critique' aims to promote this internal dialogue by presenting a variety of approaches to the topic. What seems most helpful and of service is to present various points of reference and different scenarios in order to encourage an internal dialogue, so that the Church may further discern and develop her mission.

The risks of refusing to engage in such a conversation with others in the Church-in-the-world are great. We only have to look at the polarization and enervation in the English-language theological tradition to see the dangers and the consequences. Exaggerating the role of subjectivity in theology and worship can tend to entice practitioners of both theology and liturgy away from tradition and the transcendent. Macquarrie himself elsewhere avoids this danger by carefully using a subjective approach consistent with Catholic theology when he writes that the human experience of 'being' is 'graceful', provided that resources can be found to bring order and pattern into one's human life.[6]

Consequently, we must not forget that undervaluing the role of Christian experience can also weaken the connection between doctrine and life. We can understand something of the basis of the current reliance upon subjectivity if we recall the development of theology in the earlier part of the last century. Karl Barth (1886–1968) protested against the shallowness of nineteenth-century religious liberalism and its association with culture. In its place he created a theology which had a weakened cultural and rational substructure. Religion was rejected, and so was any human means to objective proof, and so disastrously 'when this substructure ... [is] ... swept away and only the arbitrary appeal to revelation is left, then if ever a doubt arises about this revelation, there is no way of dealing with it'.[7]

This radical tendency has been carried to extremes among other protestant theologians who have proclaimed the death of God (and therefore, surely, of theology). Among these was numbered John Robinson (1919–83), one of the main exponents of this kind of theology for a British audience, especially in his *Honest to God* first published in 1963 by SCM Press.

Many of the trends of thought found in such 'subjectivist and liberal' circles stem from Bonhoeffer (1906–45) particularly from his *Letters and Papers from Prison*, where he in turn draws on ideas of Kierkegaard (1813–55) and suggests the image of the man come of age, who has matured beyond childish expectations and is no longer naïve, but who still cannot show any visible evidence for what is believed with total inward conviction. Correspondingly there arises the idea that we now live

---

6 Macquarrie, *Principles of Christian Theology* (London: SCM Press, 1977), pp. 73, 87.

7 Macquarrie, 'Subjectivity', p. 154.

in a world without God, as though God were at the centre of everything though totally inaccessible.

Such terminologies suggested to theologians the possibility of a secular theology, a theology without God. The main US proponent of this is Thomas J. J. Altizer (1927–), who coined the phrase 'death of God theology'. Then, during the 1980s and 1990s the writings of Don Cupitt (1934–) picked up the theme more fully and prolifically in the 'Sea of Faith' material and the various conferences his ideas inspired. By the 1990s this movement was appearing tired and was looking like liberalism in yet another guise.

Already, by the 1980s and 1990s there were signs that the theological and cultural pendulum had swung to an extreme position. More recently Gavin Hyman has offered a critique of the threat of both Cupitt's *non-realism* and of Milbank and Loughlin's *radical orthodoxy* to theological liberalism, and in the same volume Steve Bruce's chilling sociological tailpiece gives the liberal theologian few grounds for hope.[8]

Such developments inevitably led many away from the central tradition of Western and ecumenical theology past a point where God becomes just a name for the subjective depths and longings of our all too human nature and further on into the borderlands of the nihilism of post-modernity and relativism. This theological trend has been especially typical of the Anglo-Saxon, German and Scandinavian theological worlds and, being now a part of the cultural air that the West breathes, was visible also in many of the church traditions that had sprung from the Reformation; of course it also permeated the Catholic Church.

By the end of Paul VI's pontificate, enthusiasms and anxieties in the field of liturgical study and practice had become inflamed and polarized. Worries grew about the dissolution of the integral unity of the Roman rite focused on an overly hasty inculturation and the translation of Latin texts using the method of dynamic equivalence indicating that from some perspectives an extreme position had been reached and necessitated a correction.

Eleven years after Macquarrie's article, the newly elected Pope John Paul II offered his developed personalist philosophy, born from his studies and experience during and after World War Two, to reinvigorate the conversation on traditional questions such as truth, revelation and authority. Though 'post-modernisms' are now the air we breathe and the worlds we live in, John Paul II recognized that the human subject, wherever he or she is found and whoever he or she is, continues to search for eternal values, love and truth, and endeavours to live them out in daily life. While he affirmed that each human person is a 'subject', he also

---

8 Mark Chapman (ed.), *The Future of Liberal Theology* (London: Ashgate, 2002); review by Stephen Platten, *Theology* 106 (2003), pp. 208–9.

sought to contextualize the human person as a member of diverse and overlapping communities and cultures, a person who struggles, thinks and hopes for meaning, purpose and self-esteem all through life. A consideration of 'Subject, subjectivity, and the human person in contemporary liturgical discussion and critique' is offered in this volume as a way of enlarging the constituency of this conversation on Faith and Reason in the Church. Pope John Paul II clearly saw that there was a need, in Macquarrie's words, to 'hold the line' in the face of rapid change and attenuation of the faith.

Later on in Pope John Paul II's papacy the 1998 document *Fides et Ratio* helped liturgists, among many others, to consider the identity of the human subject in the church, the liturgy and in the world today. *Ecclesia de Eucharistia* of 2003,[9] like so many documents produced during that busy pontificate of John Paul II, has added a further dimension of liturgical and sacramental theology to the broad conversation. There is a tension in this document between the profoundly visionary theology of Teilhard de Chardin (1881–1955), when Pope John Paul II speaks of offering the sacrifice of the Mass on the altar of the world, and the rubrical elimination of abuses. The section of this encyclical on the elimination of abuses in the celebration of the liturgy brings to the reader's awareness the need for a recognized voice of authority in the regulation of Catholic worship. The church has recently also published documents aimed at correcting perceived abuses or warning of dangers to the faithful (*Liturgiam Authenticam*,[10] *On the New Age*,[11] and *Redemptoris Sacramentum*[12]).

This volume as we originally conceived it sprang from the very suggestive remarks in the then Cardinal Ratzinger's little book, *The Spirit of the Liturgy*. Specifically in relation to music, the book notes, 'The cosmic character of liturgical music stands in opposition to the two tendencies of the modern age that we have described: music as pure subjectivity, music as the expression of mere will', and on the same page continues:

> Let us have one last brief look at our own times. The dissolution of the subject, which coincides for us today with radical forms of subjectivism, has led to 'deconstructionism' – the anarchistic theory of art. Perhaps this will help us to overcome the unbounded inflation of

---

9 John Paul II, *Ecclesia de Eucharistia*, 17 April 2003 (London: CTS, 2003).

10 Congregation for Divine Worship and the Discipline of the Sacraments, *Liturgiam Authenticam*, 7 May 2001 (London: CTS, 2001).

11 Pontifical Council for Culture–Pontifical Council for Interreligious Dialogue, *Jesus Christ the Bearer of the Water of Life: A Christian Reflection on the 'New Age'*, 21 February 2003 (London: CTS, 2003).

12 Congregation for Divine Worship and the Discipline of the Sacraments, *Redemptionis Sacramentum*, 25 March 2004 (London: CTS, 2004).

subjectivity and to recognize once more that a relationship with the Logos, who was at the beginning, brings salvation to the subject, that is, to the person. At the same time it puts us into a true relationship of communion that is ultimately grounded in Trinitarian love.'[13]

In this volume we have tried to gather a collection of articles that would examine understandings of the subject, of subjectivity and of the human person which lie behind both contemporary liturgical discussion and critique. In his pontificate so far Pope Benedict XVI has added to these insights in his encyclical letters *Deus Caritas Est*[14] and *Spe Salvi*,[15] and his own reflection on the person of Jesus of Nazareth.[16]

There is today, perhaps even more than any time since the Second Vatican Council, greater need for a forum for discussion among those of different schools who are awaiting this next pendulum swing, and who see their duty as 'holding the line' and even as the restoration of truths forgotten or overlooked. In fact the purpose of this series of books entitled 'Faith and Reason' is to follow or push the pendulum back towards a more centred focus of discussion on faith and reason, towards a renewed valuing of revelation, clear doctrine and traditional worship.

This seventh volume in the Faith and Reason series, centred round the understanding of the human person in contemporary liturgical discussion and critique, presents a collection of articles that aim at furthering this important conversation. This wide range of approaches to the different issues that have arisen from the then Cardinal Ratzinger's statement on the liturgy gives a reasonably accurate picture of current discussion on 'the liturgical subject'. I hope that it may act as a springboard for further patient research, irenic conversation and scientific publication among and by those whose joy is appreciating the liturgy.

It has been a pleasure to meet and work with this varied and distinguished group of contributors from such different theological perspectives; and an honour to be able to offer these papers on 'Subject, subjectivity, and the human person in contemporary liturgical discussion and critique' to a wider audience.

James Leachman OSB

---

13 Joseph Cardinal Ratzinger, *The Spirit of the Liturgy*, tr. John Saward (San Francisco: Ignatius Press, 2000), from *Einführung in den Geist der Liturgie* (Frankfurt: Herder, 2000).

14 Benedict XVI, Encyclical letter, *Deus Caritas Est*, 25 December 2005 (London: CTS, 2006).

15 Benedict XVI, Encyclical letter, *Spe Salvi*, 30 November 2007 (London: CTS, 2007).

16 Benedict XVI, *Jesus of Nazareth* (San Francisco: Ignatius Press, 2007).

I

The Liturgical Subject
Introductory Essay

LAURENCE PAUL HEMMING

This book is called 'the liturgical subject' for all the reasons suggested in the ambiguity of that phrase. If one subject can be said to have vexed the peace of Catholics in the past century it is the manner, character and status of Catholic worship. And yet this vexatious subject concerns the very means of our salvation – and nothing less than that. This same century has seen the rise (and fall) of the description of, and debate concerning, the philosophical subject – subjectivity as such. Is modern man the man for the sake of whom Catholic liturgy became a vexation, so that the Second Vatican Council decided to advance the (already far-reaching) process of liturgical reform 'better to accommodate [it] to the requirements of the age'?[1] Understood like this, precisely because the liturgy was adapted to the requirements of a changed mankind, the contemporary understanding of the subjectivity of the subject became the subject of the liturgy, because the subject is that one for whom, and against whom, everything is measured, including the liturgy itself. In 2000, in his book translated into English as *The Spirit of the Liturgy*, the future Pope Benedict XVI spoke of 'the boundless superiority of the subject' which characterizes contemporary liturgical life,[2] the philosophical conception of the human person that has arisen after Descartes, after Nietzsche, and that still holds sway even now.

Or is the real subject of the liturgy – the one underpinning it and making it possible – none other than Christ himself, as the tradition itself has from ancient times taught and held? How are these three areas of enquiry (liturgical reform, the subjectivity of the subject, the person and place of Christ in Catholic worship) to be held together? Few theologians, let

---

1 Cf. Vatican Council II, Dogmatic Constitution on the Sacred Liturgy *Sacrosanctum Concilium*, 1963, §1, when it speaks of those aspects of the liturgy capable of being changed 'ad nostræ ætatis necessitates melius accomodare'.

2 Benedict XVI, *Der Geist der Liturgie: eine Einführung* (Freiburg: Herder, 2000), p. 133, 'die maßlose Übersteigerung des Subjekts'.

alone liturgical experts, have addressed the question put here, of what unfolds – and what clash is unleashed – in the interrelationship of modern humanity with the liturgical life of the Church and with Christological reflection: in other words few contemporary *liturgical* theologians have thought it their business to ask what the impact of their surrounding world has been on their methods, and their assumptions, as they have undertaken their work. Few enough theologians have been philosophically self-reflexive or self-aware, and few enough have therefore attended to the dangers inherent in the age, as they busily adapted themselves and their activity to its requirements. Yet the unfolding conceptions of philosophical subjectivity have unfolded a revolution – literally a turning over and inside-out of the understanding of the human person. This book attempts to examine that transformation in its effects, from a broad range of perspectives.

How is this transformation to be understood, and what are its effects? To give just one example, it has become a persistent feature of contemporary discussion to argue that liturgical action makes God present to man. When Mgr Robert Sokolowski says 'the Eucharist reenacts [the] sacrifice [of Calvary]' he leaves unclarified an ambiguity which exactly encapsulates this thought.[3] If Sokolowski means by this that *each* eucharistic celebration re-enacts Calvary (rather than the Eucharist as such), then indeed we would have to say that the Eucharist brings God here, makes God present. This idea was developed extensively by Dom Odo Casel OSB in the course of the Liturgical Movement, and yet it runs quite counter to the understanding found in Catholic theology prior to the Enlightenment. It encapsulates, almost without thinking, the way that human subjectivity has become the standard by which all other things are measured.

Each particular Eucharist does not bring God, or the divine presence, to us. Rather through the action of the Eucharist are we moved to enter the divine conspection. *We*, by uttering God's name are *moved* to the blessing presence in which the name can be heard: this is what liturgy as *performance* and *performative* does: we are made present to the one and single sacrifice of Calvary, a sacrifice which is at the same time the heavenly banquet of the eternal liturgy, of the self-offering of the Divine lamb to the Father (the Eucharist as such). Most of all: by virtue of our having been moved by God's having opened our mouth to utter prayer and thanksgiving, the one single sacrifice of Christ (and by analogy the Hours and all our other prayers and devotions) is extended through the Eucharist in its effects to where we are now, and in fact to all times and all places. What this means, and what the direction of human movement

---

3 R. Sokolowski, *Eucharistic Presence: A Study in the Theology of Disclosure* (Washington DC: Catholic University of America Press, 1994), p. 88f.

is in worship, is one of the issues that any serious liturgical theology has to address. If it is we who are to move, how did it come about that we thought we could move the impassable *God*?

Speaking to a conference of the Catholic University of Louvain in 2001, the Jesuit Paul Verdeyen noted that 'the Holy Scriptures never mention a possible divorce between theology and spirituality',[4] adding 'the writings of the first Christian millennium do not know our distinctions between dogmatic and sacramental life, between morals and canon law, between ascesis and mysticism'.[5] Verdeyen suggests that the 'real origins of the gap can be found in the conflict in which the Cistercians Bernard and William were opposed to the premier dialectician, Peter Abelard'.[6] The meaning of this gap is that 'for several centuries, scholasticism has occupied the entire field of theology'.[7] Yet the return of the study of 'spirituality', a discipline in the newly created departments of 'pastoral' or 'practical' theology, has not overcome the gap Verdeyen names, but rather has given rise to a post-modern intensification whereby the acts and æsthetic empirica of faith – separated even from the rigorous standards of evidence and logical or philosophical requirements of a 'merely' intellectual theology – have become the matter of study for 'styles' of prayer or belief.

The gap Verdeyen identifies is as old as faith itself: this is not his point. In Abelard it took on a concrete form (rather than being understood as a deviancy from sainthood) and is supplied with a legitimacy that initiates an eclipse of the self-understanding of Christian life which, by the end of the twentieth century, gives rise to the effective transvaluation of the whole of the Catholic, let alone the wider Christian, tradition. For the sake of a provocation and for brevity, as an inflexible rule (even when the opposite is believed to be the case) faith has in too much theological discussion begun to follow society and not the other way round. The Scottish Catholic philosopher John Haldane recently commented that 'those who celebrate and explore the Catholic cultural tradition seem more concerned with ethical, social and political issues. These are certainly important, but the difficulty seems to me that Catholic contributions

---

4 P. Verdeyen SJ, 'La séparation entre théologie et spiritualité: Origine, conséquences et dépassement de ce divorce', in J. Haers SJ and P. De May, *Theology and Conversation* (Leuven: Peeters, 2003), pp. 674–88, p. 674. 'Vous savez tous que les divines Écritures ne mentionnent nulle part un divorce possible entre théologie et spiritualité.'

5 Verdeyen, 'La séparation entre théologie et spiritualité', p. 674. 'Les écrits du premier millénaire chrétien ne connaissent pas nos distinctions entre dogmatique et vie sacramentelle, entre morale et droit canonique, entre ascèse et mystique.'

6 Verdeyen, 'La séparation entre théologie et spiritualité', p. 674. 'En plus, on pourrait trouver la vraie origine du divorce dans le conflit qui a opposé les cisterciens Bernard et Guillaume au premier maître de la dialectique, Pierre Abélard.'

7 Verdeyen, 'La séparation entre théologie et spiritualité', p. 679. 'Plusieurs siècles durant, la scolastique occupait tout le terrain de la théologie.'

seem mere echoes of notions acceptable to the secular world, and familiar because of it.'[8] Earlier centuries had understood things differently. We have become products of what Verdeyen calls Scholasticism and its subsequent deformations.

To illustrate Verdeyen's gap we could do worse than begin with the phrase, all too familiar in current liturgical discussion, *lex orandi, lex credendi*. Normally translated into English as 'the law of prayer is the law of belief', it asserts that what is prayed – and here liturgical, public, prayer is specified – defines and lays out the terms for what is taught, and so believed. Critics of much contemporary liturgical theology have pointed out, however, that the phrase taken like this is ambiguous. For it suggests a possible instrumentalization of the Sacred Liturgy *to* the theological. If the law of prayer is tied to the law of belief in this way, then *when* theology changes, the textual and ritual form of the Sacred liturgy must be altered together with it. If we live in Verdeyen's gap, where theology and the practices of sanctity are understood to be separated, this danger is ever-present. If you are a theologian who works hard in his teaching and attends well to his subject, but because he is so consumed with the business of theology only just makes it to Holy Mass and cannot remember the words of the Collect or Opening Prayer of that day's Mass on his return to his desk, you are living in Verdeyen's gap. St Dominic's injunction to the friars to celebrate the Sacred Liturgy 'with simplicity and moderation' has often been interpreted as encouraging just this, and yet it is far from what he intended.[9]

The critics who notice the ambiguity of *lex orandi, lex credendi* often point to the discussion of this very phrase in Pope Pius XII's 1947 Encyclical Letter *Mediator Dei* which, arguably more than *Sacrosanctum Concilium*, inaugurated the processes of liturgical reform in the Catholic Church.[10] Pius XII exploits this ambiguity when he absolutely reverses the order of prayer and matters concerning belief (by which, therefore, is meant theology) in the encyclical letter. He says 'But inasmuch as we desire to differentiate and describe the relationship between faith and the sacred liturgy in absolute and general terms, it is perfectly correct to say, "Lex credendi legem statuat supplicandi" – let the rule of belief determine the rule of prayer.'[11] As an aside one should note

---

8 J. Haldane, 'The Waiting Game', *The Tablet*, 5 February 2005, p. 9.

9 Cf. Order of Preachers, *Constitutions*, §65: To the contrary, however, Ventura of Verona, a companion of St Dominic says of the saint that even when travelling 'with great devotion he celebrated the whole night and day Office at the prescribed hours so that he omitted nothing'.

10 See, for example, G. Hull, *The Banished Heart: The Origins of Heteropraxis in the Catholic Church* (Sydney: Spes Nova, 1995), esp. p. 39. The reference to *Mediator Dei* given in note 20 is in fact to be found at §48 of the encyclical.

11 Pius XII, Encyclical Letter of 20th November 1947 *Mediator Dei* in *Acta Apostolicæ*

that this exemplifies Pius XII's fundamental radicalism – this supposed 'arch-conservative' in fact ends up in perfect agreement with all those who argue that the Sacred Liturgy is subordinate and instrumentalized to the decisions and conclusions of theology, which was certainly not his original intention. Did Pius XII initiate this attitude? Or did he not rather authenticate an inevitability that was already possible because of the gap that Verdeyen identifies, a gap that had worked centuries of subtle transformation within the tradition as a whole? And Pius XII said this *because* of his confidence in the certitude of the positive results of (especially twentieth-century) Catholic theology, a certitude to which he witnessed in a papacy almost constructed from out of the possibilities of post-war philosophical (I hasten to add, *not* theological) high modernism. Pius XII believed that so objective and certain were the positive results of theological research that they could not but be consonant with the *lex orandi*.

Now inasmuch as theology has been overcome by its subordination to philosophy (as it has been since the Enlightenment, but Catholics were a while in catching up), Pius XII, his critics argue, opened the flood-gates for an entirely rationalistic reconstruction of the Sacred Liturgy that the eighteenth-century Italian bishop Scipio dei Ricci and the disgraced council of Pistoia could hardly have dared hope for.[12] The certitude in which he placed his hope has subsequently collapsed, especially in the wake of the upheavals of the Second Vatican Council. This has led a later pope, Benedict XVI, to speak of a need for a 'hermeneutic of continuity' in understanding how the tradition itself is to be interpreted. In a speech to the whole Roman curia in December 2005 Benedict XVI suggested that there is a fundamental division in the Church between those who interpreted the Second Vatican Council theologically within a 'hermeneutic of rupture', by which he meant that they interpret Vatican II as having made a conscious break with the whole past tradition of the Church, and those who seek a theological 'hermeneutic of continuity', whereby Vatican II can only be understood and implemented in continuity with the whole of the Church's past history and tradition. On this occasion he spoke of how for those who stressed the 'spirit of the Council', 'a vast margin was left open for the question on how this

---

Sedis [AAS] (Vatican: Typis Polyglottis Vaticanis, 1947), vol. 14, pp. 521-95; p. 541. 'Quodsi volumus eas, quæ inter fidem sacramque Liturgiam intercedunt, rationes absoluto generalique modo internoscere ac determinare, iure meriotque dici potest: "Lex credendi legem statuat supplicandi"'.

12 For an account of the Synod, see C. A. Bolton, *Church Reform in 18th Century Italy* (The Hague: Martinus Nijhoff, 1969), esp. pp. 55-114. See also Fr Aidan Nichol's discussion of the eighteenth-century intrusion of rationalism into Catholic worship in A. Nichols OP, *Looking at the Liturgy: A Critical View of its Contemporary Form* (San Francisco: Ignatius Press, 1996), pp. 16-38.

spirit should subsequently be defined, and room was consequently made for every whim'.[13] It is possible to see how if, on the one hand, an iron continuity guarantees the equation of *lex orandi, lex credendi* irrespective of the order in which they appear (which was Pius XII's hope and understanding), any rupture in the order of *credendi* will *also* transform what is prayed and how, especially if the order of precedence has been reversed so that *credendi* takes precedence over *orandi*.

Contemporary theology has become driven by, and subordinated to, an *essential* rationalism: the drive to synthesize reason with faith underwent in the Enlightenment a most devastating reversal: inasmuch as it became impossible to synthesize certain of the claims of faith with reason, reason was taken as the standard and the measure by which faith must be reformed. When that rationalism is exposed and itself undergoes radical decay, the question emerges – if theology is no longer to be driven by reason, then by what exactly, and what indeed will drive prayer, if 'reason' as the motor force of theology is gone? If theology now drives prayer, and theology itself loses its ground, what then will become of our prayers to God?

How are we to understand the Sacred Liturgy in the light of these developments, all in consequence of the uprising and triumph of the claims of subjectivity? Recent attempts to reinstate the sublime as a passageway to the 'supersensible' aspect of the what the liturgy points towards have emphasized the recovery of the aesthetic forms of liturgical practice. Liturgy is made to function in the region of philosophical aesthetics – as performance, as mediating a sublime moment in the life of the believer. Kant's account of the sublime appears to support this view by providing access to the divine presence through exalted moments of feeling: here, we could say, is grounded the concern both for intelligibility in liturgical forms, and for 'participation' understood as 'intellectual concentration'. By approaching an openly intelligible liturgy in the right mind, with the heart also opened to instruction and exaltation, then an 'experience' of God must, surely, be guaranteed. It would be churlish to suggest that the Protestant and pietistic Kant seems poorly equipped to instruct in such matters, or that Kant's description of the sublime referred primarily to events in nature rather than in art or performative form.

The aesthetic understanding of sublimity has in any case already moved on. The Flemish scholar Yves De Maeseneer has noted that Adorno 'reinterprets Kant's account of the sublime and indicates how the Kantian sublime involves an experience in which the subject is initially overpowered, but that Kant subsequently turns this overpowerment of

---

13 Benedict XVI, Allocution to the Curia of 22nd December 2005 in *Acta Apostolicæ Sedis*, Vatican, vol. 98 (2006), pp. 44–5.

the subject into an affirmation of the subject'.¹⁴ Whereas for Kant 'the transcendental subject discovers itself as superior over nature, because it is gifted with reason', for Adorno 'the experience of the sublime confronts the subject with a negation of the subject, and this negation cannot be overcome by the subject' and so leads to 'an annihilation of the self in front of art'.¹⁵ This is the essentially *interpellative* moment of modern subjectivity, also described by Althusser, which leads, Adorno says, to 'the tears of pain, the crying of the subject, bears witness to its bodiliness: the subject is a body'.¹⁶

Here is exactly the contemporary theological attitude: we emphasize the embodiments of the assembly, the believer, as the basis for, and accomplishment of, the sublime, especially liturgically, in worship. What we find here is the devaluation of the uppermost values and the revaluation of all values precisely as Nietzsche's reinscription of the Kantian sublime: instead of the sublime indicating the subjective relation to the supersensible, the sublime returns the subject to embodiment *because there is nothing else beyond the subject*. The subject reads himself *against* and *from out of* what is given in sublimity, so that what is given is a scandal – precisely because it is essentially self-denying of the subject. The marks of the Sacred Liturgy, that it is hierarchical, performed by ones distinct and not typical in the ranks of men (bishops, priests and clerics), 'exclusive', elitist, hieratic, clerical, mean that it must constantly be depotentiated to become democratic, inclusive, and accessible to all (intelligibility becomes inclusivity). Inculturation, which first arose as a concept in the evangelization of non-Western peoples whose social and symbolic practices were far detached from those of the European Church, has now become a focus of alteration for the liturgy even in the West, in order to overcome the 'exclusion' of those formed in a supposedly entirely secularized world. Almost before we have realized it, we are more concerned with the sociological consequences of liturgical acts – the consequences arising from our embodiment – than with the liturgy's capacity to make *us* present to God.

Kant understood the sublime moment to be one of negation, where the subject, provoked by an essential *vision*, an experience above all in sight, was lifted beyond that vision to the divine 'beyond', the 'transcendent'. It is a feature of much contemporary liturgical theology to understand the liturgy as an art-form, above all visual, and comprising additional performative, and ritual aspects. Adorno again marks a further transition

---

14 Y. De Maeseneer, 'The Subject's Destruction: A Note on Adorno's *Sublime*', in De Maeseneer (ed.) *God out of Place? Ars Disputandi* Supplement Series, vol. 3 (Utrecht: Ars Disputandi, 2005), p. 84.

15 De Maeseneer, 'The Subject's Destruction', p. 84, quoting Adorno.

16 De Maeseneer, 'The Subject's Destruction', p. 90, quoting Adorno.

in the Kantian sublime when he remarks that 'the encounter with art involves the "self-negation of the viewer, who virtually vanishes in the work"'.[17] The consequence of this is that in its self-negation the self is at one and the same time liberated: in this view 'art is not so much about self-productive representation, but about a process of negation, which allows the subject for a purgatorial movement of self-destruction'[18] which inevitably means the subject must reassert itself *through* its liberative self-negation. It attains to a new horizon of selfhood *through* a self-abolition which provides the basis for a renewed self-assertion on the basis of the subject's rediscovered embodiment. The very negation which *once* threw us off to the theological sublime, *now* functions as an entirely human self-referentiality, precisely because there is no 'beyond' or 'transcendent' out to toward which one can be drawn.[19]

The way is therefore prepared for a further extension of Pius XII's transformation of the phrase *lex orandi, lex credendi*. If the law of prayer follows the law of belief, and if the liturgy is seen as an essentially sociological arena within which the subject attains to a certain kind of *self*-understanding, then theology may *rearrange* the self-understanding of the subject through the reconstruction of the liturgical event. Hence the drive for a busied *actuosa participatio* because there is never a level at which the subject is sufficiently participative in what (as Adorno demonstrates) essentially annihilates him. The only recourse, for the theologian who wishes to overcome this annihilation, is constant rearrangement of the liturgy and of its concomitant ecclesial structures to reaccommodate the negated subject. Here, at the altar, the tolling of Nietzsche's bell rings out. Here is the reason for the reduction of a hitherto sacred place to an entirely *human* ethics.

Is it possible to overcome the subordination of the liturgy to an understanding driven entirely by philosophical subjectivity in its latest forms? Too little has been said concerning the character of intentionality in the understanding of the liturgy. The idea – well known in the East – that the entire liturgy must be fulfilled, but that it is impossible for any one person to fulfil it alone, was superseded in the West by the idea that every priest must complete the Office and Mass daily and in full, which

---

17 De Maeseneer, 'The Subject's Destruction', p. 85: T. W. Adorno ed. G. Adorno And R. Tiedemann, *Ästhetische Theorie*, in *Gesammelte Schriften*, vol. 7 (Frankfurt a. M.: Suhrkamp, 1970), p. 396. 'Selbstnegation des Betrachtenden, der im Werk virtuell erlischt.'

18 De Maeseneer, 'The Subject's Destruction', p. 85.

19 Despite what would appear to be the obvious implications of this understanding, Adorno is keen to stress that negations of the encounter with the aesthetic in no way invalidate the formal order of reality. On the contrary 'By rejecting reality – and this is not a form of escapism but an inherent quality of art – art vindicates reality' (Adorno, *Ästhetische Theorie*, p. 10).

after Vatican II was extended, at least as a possibility, to the laity as well. An attitude that developed as early as the appearance and growth of the mendicant orders, liturgy has increasingly come to be understood as something that I can accomplish 'for myself' rather than something which the whole local Church – monastic house, diocese, and so forth – has to distribute across its membership and life. Far better than truncating the rites to fit in with the demands of everyday life is the idea that if I am dispensed from, or fail in, any part or Office of the Church's sacred worship, then I owe a debt to God and to the Church which is nevertheless repaid through the work of others. Immediately in this understanding *I* as the worshipping person am taken out of the stranglehold where the subject of liturgy become liturgy *for* the (Cartesian) subject.

The idea that a single self can consummate in itself the entire meaning of every particular liturgical act as it is enacted – this is the real meaning toward which to many contemporary definitions of *actuosa participatio* have been driven – is foreign and indeed corrosive to the interior character of a complex and centuries-long symbolic language which uses the *differentiatedness* of humanity to mediate the drama of our salvation. The sense of the sacred is actually the way in which the hiddenness of God the Father is disclosed. This hiddenness of the Father is disclosed by making manifest where *I* cannot go, or where I cannot have access to without great difficulty (it is grounded, for Christians, in the difficulty I have in ascending the Cross on Calvary: only Christ can ascend the Cross – I may witness this ascent but *I* cannot undertake it).[20] This is the reason why the liturgy relies on hierarchy, mystery, limitations (who may and may not go where, and when, and why). Traditionally the Sacred Liturgy has explained this by exhibiting through its performativity how even the priest or his ministers are barely able to ascend the altar steps, and then only to undertake those rites which make manifest the Lord himself. Remaining only at the top of those steps for as long as it takes to effect these rites, he too must return to the foot. When *I* am present to this (which means share by being present, in its enaction, as a liturgical phenomenon), only then will I understand that only after much preparation and in certain circumstances may this individual approach the altar of God, and so will I understand what it will take for *me also* to enter the divine presence. To see this as so much clericalism is the

---

20 The idea is derived from the structure of the Temple in Jerusalem itself – different parts of the Temple were reserved, successively to different persons who were hierarchically ordered to the work of atonement, up to the absolute separateness of the 'holy of holies', the part of the Temple which signified the *Shekinah* or divine presence itself, into which the High Priest, and he alone, could only enter on the Day of Atonement itself (and only then), after long ritual preparation. The same structure is repeated in the classical structure of Christian churches, either by means in the East of the Iconostasis (or dais), or in the West the sanctuary and the step before the altar (predella).

way in which subjectivity reduces the alterity of the actions and functions of others solely to myself. It is to emphasize my 'exclusion' without understanding that the exclusion is precisely a gateway, an opportunity for me to understand *how* and by what means I should enter. Above all the failure here has been to present the liturgy as – in totality, and in its minutiae – text, a text which is to be read, and one which, in being read, is available to my understanding but which transforms my understanding by its being primarily addressed not to me but God.

Modern Cartesian subjectivity teaches us that everyone is implicitly the same: anyone may implicitly perform any task in the social, political, religious or moral sphere (irrespective of age, gender, disposition or preparedness) but ancient philosophy never taught this, and the liturgy could for centuries take for granted an understanding of the human person far richer and deeper than that which we are now accustomed to take for granted as true. With that understanding's long collapse, the liturgy must go in one of two ways – it must either continue to assert this richer understanding in the face of contemporary incomprehension, or, as I have shown, it must in the eyes of others be altered and modified to reflect the modern requirement.

Even much of the critique of the contemporary philosophy of subjectivity takes place from within the philosophy of subjectivity itself. Paradoxically, in theological discourse, Descartes' *cogito* and its effects is accorded higher status than is the authorization which God's self-disclosure of himself to men and women to whom he imparts the gift of faith.

But if philosophy – even at the level of phenomenological description – is not to provide the authorization of Christian worship, whence will authority derive? Surely, this authorization is given to us through divine revelation itself. The Sacred Liturgy has traditionally implicitly taught that who each of us is can be understood not through a self-declaration, a mental act presupposed in every other mental act (the meaning of *cogito, ergo sum*), but *with respect to the altar*. It is the symbolic body of Christ, the divine Christ in his embodied full humanity, who reveals to us who we are and at the same time constitutes us in relation to his Father *through* the divinity which is *manifested by his body*, above all through the meaning that is disclosed by what happens to that body *in* and *after* its crucifixion. Symbolically the body of Christ is manifested in the structure of a church and in the liturgy through the altar itself, through the crucifix upon it, and of course through the presence in the tabernacle.

It is for this reason that traditionally the Mass and the other sacred actions of the liturgy are filled with actions that *defer to the altar*, and defer to its crucifix. Even when, in the pre-conciliar rites, the sacred ministers and those in choir bow to each other in rank of precedence they do so with respect to the altar. In other words, even when we acknowledge differences between us – say between bishop, priest, deacon, etc. – we do so only with respect to, and so in a way derived from, the sacred body of Christ, which demonstrates that who we are – who each of us is – is constituted only sacramentally and mysteriously through the relational character of baptism, which gives us a right to consider ourselves in some sense related to, and identical with, Christ.[21] This is the most radical challenge to our self-constitution in its description in the Cartesian *cogito*. There is no prior 'self' which is *then* redeemed, such that I am one who cannot other than, as thinking, exist, and once I know I exist, I then discover my need to be redeemed. Rather my entire identity is received *from* and *with respect to* Christ, symbolically manifest in sacrament and altar, and in whose risen being I am then related to the Father. The identity I receive from Christ is not absolute, but *precisely relative* to what redeemed me – namely the sacrifice of the Cross (which is at the same time the sacrifice of the altar). The theological point is this: that the meaning of the body of Christ disclosed through the Liturgy supersedes and completes any understanding of the human being arrived at by philosophy, and *not* the other way round.

The Sacred Liturgy first, foremost, and only, is oriented around the body of Christ. In this sense its proper expression is normatively with respect to a consecrated altar (the symbolic presence of the Lord's body in our midst). Sacramentally (which here means symbolically and mysteriously) understood, the life, death, and resurrection of the body of Christ is unfolded with respect to the altar. The altar authorizes and makes possible every sacred action of the liturgy, which means shows who the author and subject is of every sacred action, and the embodied means by which those sacred actions are made available to us. All sacred actions are drawn from and return to the altar.

The meaning of this is disclosed for us in Scripture – it is the Apostolic activity par excellence which is explained by St Paul in the Acts of the Apostles in the following way: 'For passing by and seeing your idols, I found an altar also, on which was written: To the Unknown God. What therefore you worship without knowing it, that I preach to you'.[22] The verb here translated as 'I preach' is in Greek καταγγνλλω. St Paul, when he speaks of preaching, much more frequently uses the verbs κηρύσσω

---

[21] The theology here is directly from St Paul's letter to the Romans 6.4–5. 'For we are buried together with him by baptism into death: that, as Christ is risen from the dead by the glory of the Father, so we also may walk in newness of life. For if we have been planted together in the likeness of his death, we shall be also in the likeness of his resurrection.'

[22] Acts 17.23. ιερχόμενος γὰρ καὶ ἀναθεωρῶν τὰ σεβάσματα ὑμῶν εὗρον καὶ βωμὸν ἐν ᾧ ἐπεγέγραπτο, Ἀγνώστῳ θεῷ. ὃ οὖν ἀγνοοῦντες εὐσεβεῖτε, τοῦτο ἐγὼ καταγγέλλω ὑμῖν.

(I proclaim) or εὐαγγελίζω (well do I bring news). Καταγγνλλω is a word less commonly used by the Apostle, and does not really mean preach or announce as such, but rather that the message to be laid out (αγγέλλειν) is κατά, 'with respect to some which'. Precisely in this passage of St Paul, the 'with respect to' is the altar. The Apostles and their successors lay out the meaning of the God who is unknown to us. We are moved by the message the Apostles bring from the unknown to what of God is to be known (in faith, with respect to the altar and to what it brings, do we take knowledge that is knowledge of God). The meaning of an altar by which the unknown God is made known is through knowledge of the sacrifice of Christ, and as it is offered on any altar now, the sacrifice of the Mass. What is sent (the *missa* of 'it has been sent', *Ite missa est*) effects what it signifies, exactly the theology of signification which we understand to be at work in sacramental theology.

The liturgy is even more basic than Scripture, since it is the means by which the Word of God is uttered, 'with respect to some which', i.e. the altar, which has the power to make available the hiddenness and knowledge of the unknown God. Symbolically the activity of the Sacred Liturgy as undertaken by the Apostles and their successors and their co-operators, the ranks of the clergy, is how the altar 'speaks' and how it enters human conversation. The conversation is double: it is the means by which the conversation between the First and Second Persons of the Divine Trinity is made available to the understanding of the baptized, and so how the baptized are inserted into the eternal conversation between the Father and the Son *through* the work of the Spirit, and it is the means by which mere human conversation is fully taken up into the divine life so that it can disclose, and so be, what it signifies. Speaking here does not just mean words: it means every symbolic or ritual gesture, every silence, that the liturgy employs in its divinely authorized activity.

The altar makes available a site or place, but a place with three specificities, not one. It allows several places to become visible and be seen all at once: it is itself *not* a place (hence again why nothing is *re-enacted* on it) in that it is precisely what *makes places*. It makes place with respect to its origin: it gives a place to the sacrifices of the pagans and to what St Thomas calls the sacraments of the old covenant – the sacrifices of Melchisedech and of the Aaronic priesthood and the means by which God (in his second person) manifested his hiddenness before the incarnation; it gives *us* a place, or rather we can now find a place with respect to the altar: as sinner; as baptized; and so as one made available to the means of salvation; and as ones receiving from the altar the means of our salvation. Finally the altar is the sign of the simultaneous altar of Calvary of the end-time: it indicates the place of the sacrifice and the heavenly altar (the only altar that has a proper, eternal, place) where the Lamb is worshipped in the New Jerusalem. As such the altar is the *centre* of the *Civitas Dei*, the New Jerusalem, the pole around which the redeemed become visible to one another in their entirety. It is – to paraphrase a philosophical text – the πόλο', the pole of the πόλι', the people, that God has redeemed through his Son. The altar *establishes* these relations and lets them be known, so that the Sacred Liturgy can be undertaken, both now and for all eternity. The altar therefore encompasses what was before us, what is to come, and the present (our present worship before it). The altar is a sign of how time, and so history, is to be understood. As such it represents fully the different ways in which God approaches man historically: both before, and now, and how God accomplishes the end of (human) time.

In this, the liturgy is even more basic than the sacraments, since it is the 'means by which', the conditioning *possibility* of the sacraments at all. Here the liturgy disappears in our consideration as some kind of a unified object (a 'thing'), and appears *only* as the form – *forma*, μορφέ – of Christ himself, since it is through the liturgy that the body of Christ becomes available to us. The form of Christ is unfolded through the liturgical cycle which makes available the form in its specificities, its specific moments: the pre- and post-resurrection life of our Lord on earth; and in his eternal identity and unity.

As more basic than the sacraments themselves, the Sacred Liturgy *as* the activity of Christ is – to steal the words of *Lumen Gentium* and to give them the ecclesiological significance that they really deserve – *veluti sacramentum* 'like a sacrament',[23] since the proper subject of the liturgy is Christ (who alone is the sacrament of the Father), and in so far as we insert ourselves into the what the liturgy inserts us into, we are inserted into the body of Christ. Only with respect to the liturgy and in its activity can the Church ever be genuinely said to be in the manner of a sacrament.[24]

If we are to understand the liturgy textually, we at the same time have to concede that there is so much we don't know about the origins of the Sacred Liturgy that we need to exercise far more caution than has been apt in what has been since 1911,[25] and especially since 1963, a period of

---

23 *Lumen Gentium* §1.

24 This is important, lest anyone read into my remarks too much the liturgy as some kind of 'realized eschatology' or, as some authors have suggested, that life 'in the Church' is tantamount to being already redeemed, already in heaven. From and with respect to the altar our present being and identity is referred to the being and identity we will receive at the end of time. Who we are now will from now on be referred to who we will be, but does not bring heaven to earth *now*, but refers everything we are now to the end of time and the new earth and new heaven we hope in faith to inhabit.

25 Cf. for a discussion of the liturgical reforms ushered in by St Pius X in 1911, L. Dobszay, *The Bugnini-Liturgy and the Reform of the Reform*, *Musicæ Sacræ Meletemata*,

dramatic, not to say revolutionary, liturgical reform. In particular, much that we have presumed was simply 'custom' can be argued to have an origin that was believed to have been divinely commanded, or a signification derived from a Dominical tradition.[26] In his 1917 *Preface* to Fr Adrian Fortescue's *Ceremonies of the Roman Rite Described*, Cardinal Bourne began by saying that

> the Catholic Church has surrounded all the acts of Divine Worship with a definite ceremonial to ensure on the one hand their due accomplishment, and on the other to safeguard the external reverence that should accompany them. She never employs ceremonial for the sake of ceremony itself. Each separate rite has grown out of the twofold object that we have enunciated, even though in the process of time the origin, and the history of the development, of such rite may long have been forgotten.[27]

There is here both a caution, an acknowledgement of provenance, and a *faith* in the historical record that many liturgists working (and making decisions about liturgical practice) more recently have disdained.

Too often the liturgy has been treated as a set of actions to be manipulated or controlled for specific outcomes or effects (outcomes and effects we believed ourselves exhaustively to understand – and here is the very 'boundless superiority of the subject' of which the Holy Father has spoken) with a degree of contempt for the deference to the sacredness of the liturgy that Cardinal Bourne evinces here. The meaning of the liturgy is not something at the disposal of the modern subject, rather is it something into which the Christian faithful have to grow as we advance in understanding and faith. The meaning of the liturgy is *primarily* for God, only *secondarily*, for us. With this understanding we return to the necessity that the liturgy is not underpinned by the *cogito*, or even the humanity of the Son, but the divinity of the Son and the hiddenness of the Father which the Son's humanity make manifest and is able, by no automatic or straightforward means, to exhibit. Above all this hiddenness is a gift of the Spirit, who constitutes us from out of the very future to which we are called. As we grow in perfection, and in understanding (through grace and the activity of the Spirit), we will *come* to understand what God already *knows to be true*. There is nothing wrong with

---

vol. 5 (Front Royal, VA: CMAA, 2003), esp. (for discussion of the 1911 reform of the Breviary) pp. 56–63.

26 The work of Margaret Barker points continually and tantalizingly in this direction. See especially M. Barker, *The Great High Priest: The Temple Roots of Christian Liturgy* (London: T & T Clark, 2003).

27 Cardinal F. Bourne, Preface in Fortescue, A., *The Ceremonies of the Roman Rite Described* (London: Burns & Oates, 1918), p. xi.

experiencing God as hidden and mysterious *through* the opacity of the rites that (we are confident, in faith) will make God manifest, because it is *we* who are to be made present to God, not *God* to us.

In the Sacred Liturgy *I* am recalled to the steps of Calvary, to the Sacrifice and the Sacred Banquet which atones for my sins and the sins of the entire world, and which unites me to the *Ecclesia* both extant and eternal through the sacrifice of Christ which ends my enmity with God. In that sense am I *em*bodied truly, in the body of Christ. I am included in the liturgical action by its very familiarity to me, to the central act of my redemption in its ritual form. I am assembled by action of the priest as one who is constituted through baptism (and my thereby having been sealed with the Spirit), through catechesis, through prayer and through penance. I thereby am (made – by the Spirit) worthy to be present (and through the merits of Christ alone) to take my part in participating in, and sharing in, the *singular* offering of the divine sacrifice of the Son to the Father, *through which* I share in the eternal conversation between the Father and the Son in the Spirit. Only *now* might I yet become the subject and site of divine revelation. Subject means here not the philosophical subject, the *cogito* in any of its forms, but a *ground* wherein the divine, salvific, Trinitarian, action is made manifest.

The form *lex orandi, lex credendi* is an abbreviation, a tag of the School-room. It originates in fact from Prosper of Aquitaine, where its proper order is quite unambiguously stated: *ut lex supplicandi legem statuat credendi*: let the law of prayer determine the law of belief.[28] This is *precisely* the opposite of Pius XII's formulation that I earlier quoted from *Mediator Dei* ('it is perfectly correct to say, *lex credendi legem statuat supplicandi*, let the rule of belief determine the rule of prayer').

Liturgical theology, and theology in general – precisely as St Thomas Aquinas himself held – can *never* be grounded in the practices or results of any of the human sciences, but *precisely and only* because the Sacred Liturgy is the continued means of God's continued self-disclosure of

---

28 Prosper of Aquitaine, Capitula Cœlestini, 8 in Patrologia Latina, vol. 51, 209–10. 'Præter beatissimæ et apostolicæ sedis inviolabiles sanctiones, quibus non piissimi patres, pestiferæ novitatis elatione dejecta, et bonæ voluntatis exordia, et incrementa probabilium studiorum, et in eis usque in finem perseverantium ad Christi gratiam referre docuerunt, obsecrationem quoque sacerdotalium sacramenta respiciamus, quæ ab apostolis tradita, in toto mundo atque in omni catholica Ecclesia uniformiter celebrantur, ut legem credendi lex statuat supplicandi.' ('In addition to these inviolable decisions of the blessed Apostolic See, by which our most holy fathers, rejecting the arrogance of this harmful novelty, have taught (us) to attribute to the grace of Christ both the first steps of a right will and the necessary progress to a praiseworthy ardour and even the perseverance in these efforts until the end, let us consider equally the rites of the priestly supplications which, transmitted by the apostles, are celebrated in the same manner in the entire world and in the whole catholic Church, in such a way that the order of supplication determines the rule of faith', translation by, T. M. Winger, *Studia Liturgica* vol. 24, 1994, p. 181.)

himself to the world through the sacrifice of his divine Son, every other science and branch of human wisdom is itself already grounded in the meaning of the Sacred Liturgy, by connections which, although trusted now in faith, will actually be revealed in their proper character not now but at the end of time. Theology is the queen of the sciences because the liturgy is the summit of human life as it is lived on earth: in death, when the subject of the liturgy in each of its aspects is completed and fulfilled, something greater will be given.

2

The Liturgical Self: An Exploration of Christian Anthropology in Light of the Liturgy

ROBERT BARRON

The nature of the self cannot really be determined abstractly, since no self finally exists apart from the practices and gestures that constitute it. In order to understand the human person, we must attend to what he does and how he moves, staying, as Wittgenstein said, 'close to the rough ground'.[1] To be sure, certain generic features of the human being across time and culture – rationality, the capacity for speech, sociability, etc. – can be identified easily enough, but these don't take us very far. People thickly display what they mean and who they are through their participation in certain distinctive games, movements, and activities. Thus the ancient Greek self came to light especially through the public discourse of the polis and the disciplined conversation of the philosophical community; and the contemporary Western self appears perhaps most clearly in the dynamics of the marketplace.[2] So where and how does the distinctively Christian self emerge? The Second Vatican Council famously asserted that the liturgy is the 'source and summit' of the Christian life, that is to say, the practice that most clearly defines the uniquely Christian way of being in the world.[3] Therefore, it is altogether reasonable to look precisely at the eucharistic liturgy to discover a thick description of who the Christian is, and this is the project that I will be pursuing in the course of this chapter.

---

[1] See Joseph Dunne, *Back to the Rough Ground: Practical Judgement and the Lure of Technique* (Notre Dame: University of Notre Dame Press, 1993), esp. pp. 64–5.

[2] See Alisdair MacIntyre, *After Virtue* (Notre Dame: University of Notre Dame Press, 1981).

[3] *Sacrosanctum Concilium*, para. 10, in Walter M. Abbot SJ *The Documents of Vatican II* (New York: Herder and Herder, 1966), p. 142.

The Sign of the Cross

Though it is preceded by the gathering of the people and by a procession of the ministers to the sanctuary, the liturgy proper commences with the sign of the cross and the words, 'in the name of the Father, and of the Son, and of the Holy Spirit'. Immediately we see something of great importance, namely, that the Christian self is claimed, positioned, named by another. From the first moment of the liturgy, the priest, ministers and people signal that they are not self-disposing, not in control of their lives. They stand, instead, within God, and what they are about to do will be done under the aegis of God. This de-centring of the self calls to mind Paul's salutation in his first letter to the Corinthians: 'Paul, called to be an apostle of Christ Jesus by the will of God . . .' (1 Cor. 1.1). The first thing that Paul says about himself is that his life has been placed in the passive voice: he is called, named, summoned by another. The second thing he specifies is that he is an Apostle of Christ Jesus, that is to say, someone sent and commissioned, a messenger of a higher power. Though Paul is writing a letter to the Corinthians, he himself is a letter sent by the author Christ. Emmanuel Lévinas argued throughout his career that the distinctive mark of the biblical self is just this radical passivity before God. Abraham heard a voice calling to him, and he responded, 'here I am', and all that Abraham came to be followed from that response.[4] Unlike the Greek heroes and philosophers who determined the course of their lives through action or creative thought, Abraham and his spiritual descendants were determined from the outside, placed in the passive voice.

This positioning by Another puts the Christian self at odds with the modern ego as well. Perhaps *the* characteristic of the Cartesian *cogito* is its sovereignty in regard to the whole of reality outside of itself. For Descartes, both the sensible universe and God are verified only in the measure that they conform to the epistemic demands of the *res cogitans*. And the Cartesian construal of the sovereign self can be found throughout modern philosophy: in Kant's aprioristic epistemology, in Hegel's virtual apotheosizing of the ego, in Nietzsche's will to power and in Sartre's granting of priority to existence over essence. And despite postmodern attempts to dismantle the modern ego, the Cartesian self has by no means disappeared from the contemporary scene. In its 1992 decision in the matter of Casey v. Planned Parenthood, the United States Supreme Court opined that it belongs to the very 'heart of liberty' to 'define one's own concept of existence, of meaning, of the universe, of the mystery of

---

4 Emmanuel Lévinas, *Otherwise than Being or Beyond Essence*, trans. Al Lingis (The Hague: Martinus Nijhoff, 1981), pp. 141–52.

human life'.⁵ That breathtaking statement takes us beyond the wildest fantasies of Nietzsche and Sartre, turning the free human subject into a godlike creator of value. This entire tradition of modern anthropology is repudiated when liturgical people gather as named and claimed by God.

But how is this passivity before God not tantamount to dehumanization? How is it not denigrating to human freedom, integrity and ontological independence? We must recall that the God invoked at the commencement of the liturgy is not a monolith, but rather a community of persons, whose coinherence constitutes the divine unity. The Father is Father only in relation to the Son, and the Son is Son only in the measure that he is generated by the Father, and the Holy Spirit is nothing other than the mutual love between the Father and the Son. These 'persons' are, in Aquinas's highly paradoxical language, 'subsistent relations', established as unique precisely in their being-toward the others. This means that, at the heart of ultimate reality, metaphysical integrity is not opposed to relationality; rather, the absolute and the relative coincide.⁶ The Son is fully divine, and yet, as Son, he stands in a relation of receptivity vis-à-vis the Father; and the Father is fully divine, and yet, as Father, *is* a relation to the Son; and the Holy Spirit is fully divine, and yet, *qua* Spirit, *is* a breathing forth from the Father and Son. In the simpler and more evocative language of the Scripture, God *is* love. All of this entails that ontological integrity and a total being-toward the other are not mutually exclusive, provided that the relationality is one of love and not domination. And thus, when the liturgical person says that he belongs utterly to the God who is love, he is affirming rather than denying his integrity.

The *Kyrie Eleison*

Just after the sign of the cross and the greeting of the people, the priest invites all the participants in the liturgy (including himself) to call to mind their sins and to beg for the divine mercy: *Kyrie eleison; Christe eleison; Kyrie eleison*. This is another practice that shapes the distinctively Christian self. In the tenth chapter of Mark's Gospel, we find the story of blind Bartimaeus, a beggar who sits outside the walls of Jericho and pleads for the mercy of Jesus. In Mark's Greek, he cries out, '*Uie David, eleison me, eleison me*' (Mark 10.47), anticipating the liturgical

---

5 *Casey v. Planned Parenthood of Southeastern Pennsylvania*, 112 Sup. Ct. 2791 at 2807.
6 See Joseph Cardinal Ratzinger, *Introduction to Christianity* (San Francisco: Ignatius Press, 1990), pp. 129–32.

cry. In the symbolic language of the Bible, blindness is evocative of sin, the inability to see the world aright, due to an alienation from God. And Jericho, the town whose walls were blown down in order to allow the Israelites to take possession of it, suggests the fallen city, the dysfunctional arena of sin – as in Jesus' famous parable in which we hear of a man who went *down* from Jerusalem to Jericho. More to it, Bartimaeus begs. It is a biblical commonplace that we are unable to save ourselves from sin, since the very powers that we would muster to do so – the mind, the will and the passions – are precisely what sin has compromised. Our only hope, therefore, is in the divine salvation offered as a gift. Thus blind Bartimaeus, crouching by the walls of Jericho and begging for help, is a *Jederman* figure, a symbol of sinful humanity.

It is precisely the attitude of Bartimaeus that the liturgical person is compelled to assume during the *Kyrie* prayer. An anthropology based upon schemas of perfectibility is thereby explicitly and operationally ruled out. This once more distinguishes the Christian conception of the self from either the classical or modern varieties. It goes without saying that neither the Nietzchean superman nor the Sartrean self-creating existentialist could honestly adopt the stance of Bartimaeus, but it is just as surely the case that the adepts of the classical philosophical schools would be hard pressed to pray the *Kyrie eleison* with any degree of conviction. Both Plato and Aristotle were aware of human weakness, but both felt that it could, through the proper discipline and education, be overcome. Plato's elite manage to escape from the realm of superficial perception through a carefully managed programme of physical and philosophical formation, culminating in the introduction to the realm of the forms and, finally, the form of the Good.[7] What blocks this ascent is essentially ignorance, an ordering of the mind toward the realm of the relatively unreal. And Aristotle's disciples endeavour to acquire virtue and hence happiness through education, habituation and the imitation of ethically upright models.[8] Though he clearly recognized the presence of vice – and even of beastlike forms of human behaviour – Aristotle felt that these could be mastered and that full human flourishing was a lively possibility.

Sin, in the biblical/Christian sense, is something far more radical and dangerous than either Platonic ignorance or Aristotelian vice, for it involves the unmooring of the self from its properly divine origin and telos. Because we are by nature supernaturally oriented toward intimacy with God, this disassociation results in the disordering and disintegration of

---

7 See Plato, *The Republic*, Bk. 7 in *The Collected Dialogues of Plato*, ed. Edith Hamilton (Princeton: Princeton University Press, 1961), pp. 747–50.

8 See Aristotle, *The Nichomachean Ethics*, Bk. 2 in *The Basic Works of Aristotle*, ed. Richard McKeon (New York: Random House, 1941), pp. 952–64.

the entire self: body, mind, spirit and passions. In rebellion against God – and not simply ignorant or vicious – the sinner finds himself powerless, incapable of realizing either his supernatural end or even those natural virtues identified by the classical tradition. There is a high paradox here. The Bible recognizes the supreme dysfunction of sin – beyond anything imagined by Plato or Aristotle – precisely in the measure that it recognizes simultaneously the supreme calling to friendship with God, which the human being has received. The great American Catholic writer Flannery O'Connor fully grasped this anthropology of the *Kyrie eleison* and set out, in story after story, to show it, in contrast to the illusory anthropology of complacency and perfectibility so characteristic of both antiquity and modernity. Very often, in her fiction, the moment of grace – the call to real divine friendship – coincides with the moment of judgement, that is to say, with the deep realization that one is incapable of achieving salvation.[9] The *Kyrie eleison* produces precisely this dynamic in the depth of the Christian self.

The *Gloria in Excelsis*

One of the most beautiful prayers in the liturgical tradition follows immediately after the *Kyrie*. In a sense, the whole of Christian theology is developed in the course of the *Gloria*, but I will focus only on the opening lines: 'Glory to God in the highest and peace to his people on earth.' This pithy formula effects a correlation between the praise of God and the building up of the human *communio*. It implies that when human beings honour God above all things – above pleasure, money, material goods, honour, country, political party, culture, etc. – then and only then will authentic peace obtain among them. The clear implication is that the deification of anything other than the true God produces, at best, a dysfunctional, ersatz communion and, at worst, outright conflict. Aristotle argued that a friendship will endure only in the measure that the friends push beyond a mere mutual love for one another and together fall in love with a transcendent third, be it beauty or truth or goodness. Only when they look together to a value greater than themselves will they escape a shared egotism that will, in time, devolve into animosity. The *Gloria* implies the same principle, but in radical form, for it speaks of the God who is, himself, nothing other than the fullness of truth, beauty and goodness. This notion was expressed in plastic form in the rose windows of the great medieval cathedrals. Invariably, the central feature of the rose is a depiction of Christ, and then around that

---

9 See esp. Flannery O'Connor, 'A Good Man is Hard to Find' in *O'Connor: Collected Works* (New York: Library of America, 1988), pp. 137–53.

anchoring point are arranged, in harmonious patterns, the remaining images and medallions. The window is, in a sense, a picture of the well-ordered soul and the properly functioning community.[10] When Christ is unambiguously the centre of one's life, then all the elements that constitute the self – mind, will, imagination, passion, sexuality – tend to fall into an ordered pattern around it. Similarly, when Christ is the transcendent third, loved in common by a variety of people, then that group becomes an authentic and beautiful *communio*.

We notice a striking contrast between this conception of *communio* and that proposed by the modern political tradition, with its roots in the speculation of Hobbes and Locke. Inheriting the breakdown of a participation metaphysics bequeathed to him by late-medieval nominalism, Hobbes held that the only real things are absolute individuals, particles in motion. This principle holds true in regard to both voluntary and involuntary movers. Thus, human beings are antagonistic, self-interested individuals, whose desires force them, almost invariably, to bounce into one another conflictually. What holds them together is the artificial expedient of the social contract, an agreement entered into on purely egotistic grounds, out of each participant's concern to avoid violent death. Though this programme is softened a bit by Locke, the essential Hobbesian framework remains in place in Locke's political philosophy, which in turn had such an influence on the formation of the modern liberal state both in Europe and America. What results from the social contract is at best a provisional and unstable peace, since it dissociates political *communio* from common praise and grounds it, instead, in some form of shared self-interest.

The analysis I've been offering is anticipated, of course, in Augustine's critique of Roman political society in the *City of God*. Augustine argued that, despite its claim to be the paragon of justice, the Roman Empire was, in fact, only a community of thieves, precisely because its common life was correlated to the wrong kind of praise.[11] Since the Roman gods and goddesses were nothing but deeply flawed human beings writ large and imagined as immortal, the worship of them simply confirmed the native egotism and self-absorption of the populace. The sheerest sign of this correlation, Augustine felt, was the centrality of violence in the maintenance and expansion of Roman power. From its earliest days, Rome had been continually at war, expressing relentlessly the *libido dominandi* in its relations to both its own citizens and neighbouring peoples. It thus stood as the paragon, not of right order, but of the *civitas*

---

10 See Robert Barron, *Bridging the Great Divide* (New York: Rowman and Littlefield Publishers, 2004), p. 80.

11 St Augustine, *The City of God Against the Pagans Bk. III*, ed. R.W. Dyson (Cambridge: Cambridge University Press, 1998), esp. pp. 94–120.

terrena, the earthly city of sin. The only solution, Augustine taught, was the adoption of the Christian way of life, at the centre of which stands the worship of the true God, the God of compassion made manifest in the cross and resurrection of Jesus.[12] The peaceful community, gathered together in giving glory to God in the highest, is the political vision implicit in the *Gloria* prayer.

Opening Up the Biblical World

After the *Gloria* and the opening collect of the Mass, the people sit in order to listen to the Word of God. Passages from the Old Testament, the epistles of Paul (usually) and the Gospels are read, and between the first and second readings, a psalm-based response is customarily sung. Following the proclamation of the Gospel, the deacon or priest preaches a homily. Though the entire liturgy is deeply biblical in inspiration, this section of the Mass constitutes a special immersion in the world of the Scripture, that is to say, the manner of thought, action, reaction and behaviour characteristic of the great characters of biblical revelation, including and especially that mysterious central figure of God. When he commenced his theological work in the second decade of the twentieth century, Karl Barth complained that the regnant liberalism of the period resulted in a bland, highly abstract and philosophical account of both God and the human being. One of Barth's principal sparring partners, Paul Tillich, proposed a description of God as *das Unbedingte*, the Unconditioned Reality, to which Barth responded: '*das Unbedingte*, that cold monster!' He meant that Tillich's name for God, largely derived from Kant's epistemology, had so little biblical resonance, and seemed only vaguely related to the dense narratives of the Scripture through which the character of God is delineated. To be fair, Barth had similar problems with the classically Catholic manner of naming God as 'necessary being' or 'unmoved mover', for he saw in this the same indifference to the particularity of the Bible.

What he proposed in answer to this blandness was a patient and thorough tour of the biblical world, that peculiar space through which move Adam, Noah, Abraham, Jacob, Jeremiah, Ezekiel, Esther, Daniel, Peter, Paul, Andrew and, most significantly, Jesus. Through our immersion in this environment, we discover who we are and who God is. The term 'immersion' is important here inasmuch as it suggests the only way that one can fully learn a foreign language. As any careful linguist knows, an attempt to learn an unfamiliar language through translation is doomed

---

12 See John Milbank, *Theology and Social Theory: Beyond Secular Reason* (Oxford: Blackwell, 1990), pp. 390–2.

to failure. On Barth's reading, so much of the liberal approach to theology and anthropology amounted to a translation project, a transposing of the biblical language into the categories and intellectual patterns of modernity. And this went a long way toward explaining just why, in his judgement, liberalism was a substantially flawed enterprise.

This Barthian approach informed the highly influential work of George Lindbeck and Hans Frei and the Yale school that grew up around them. In his *On the Nature of Doctrine: Theology in a Post-Liberal Age*, Lindbeck distinguished between an experiential-expressivist and a cultural-linguistic theory of doctrine.[13] According to the first construal, dogmas and doctrines are expressions of some undifferentiated, pre-verbal religious experience. The theologizing of Schleiermacher, Rahner and Tillich would be prime examples of this approach. According to the contrasting second interpretation, doctrines are cultural forms, rules of discourse and action, which serve to structure and make possible very particular types of experience. The theological methods of Barth himself and Hans Urs von Balthasar would aptly exemplify this cultural-linguistic model. On the more liberal reading, the biblical stories, poems, histories and myths are finally literary expressions of certain primordial religious experiences undergone by the heroes of Scripture and, in principle, accessible to present-day interpreters. Whereas on the second reading, the biblical material is a densely textured framework of meaning that serves to ground a distinctive kind of religious sensibility.

It seems to me that the liturgical presentation and exploration of the biblical texts makes much more sense on cultural-linguistic grounds than on experiential-expressivist. If the scriptural stories are only exemplifications of experiences that can be (and have been) thematized in other ways, then their prominence within the liturgy seems exaggerated, misplaced. From a purely experiential-expressivist perspective, it is not clear why the biblical texts would have a greater authority than, say, particularly evocative passages from Shakespeare, or Cervantes, or Dostoevsky, or even for that matter than sacred books from other religious traditions. In a word, the more liberal reading of the Bible assumes that the religious self is substantially in place, prior to and independent of the proclamation of the Scripture. But what the liturgy seems to take for granted, on the contrary, is the indispensability of the Bible in the formation of the self, that is to say, in the development of a distinctive manner of thinking, choosing, acting and reacting, especially in relation to God. The liturgical person discovers who he is in the context of a community that listens to and explains the Bible and acts in accord with it. In this, he stands opposed to those whose identity is shaped by the heroes, ideals

---

13 George Lindbeck, *The Nature of Doctrine: Theology in a Post-Liberal Age* (Philadelphia: The Westminster Press, 1984), pp. 31–41.

and norms of the environing secular culture and to those whose sense of self is formed by the texts and practices of other religions.

Before we quit this discussion of the scriptural world, I would like to say just a word about the liturgical act which follows immediately upon the conclusion of the homily: the proclamation of the Creed. Having been immersed in the biblical world, the people are then encouraged to declare their commitment in it. They do so by reciting the Nicene Creed, a tightly structured, doctrinal summary of the essentials of the scriptural narrative. I would like to focus only on the opening words of the Creed, the declaration that grounds and conditions everything that follows: *credo in unum Deum* (I believe in one God). The most elemental expression of Old Testament faith is the 'Shema' found in the book of Deuteronomy: 'Hear O Israel, the Lord your God is God alone' (Deut. 6.4). God's unity was, for the ancient Israelites, much more than one divine attribute among many; it was the defining feature of God's way of being. And monotheism was, consequently, much more than an intellectual conviction; it was an existential statement of the highest import. In saying that the God of Israel is the only God, the people were claiming, implicitly, that nothing other than God commands their final loyalty. No country, leader, political party, culture, civilization, moral ideal or rival god can compete with the one God. The *Shema*, in all of its radicality, is echoed in the opening line of the Creed, and this is why Joseph Cardinal Ratzinger, now Pope Benedict XVI, commented that *credo in unum Deum* is a properly subversive remark.[14] To hold that nothing in this world is one's ultimate concern is to be constituted as a biblically distinctive self.

The Offertory

After the liturgy of the Word draws to a close, the liturgy of the Eucharist commences. Though Vatican II placed a renewed stress on the liturgy of the Word, it would not be correct to say that the two principal sections of the Mass are coequal in importance. For at the heart of the liturgy of the Eucharist is the realization of the 'substantial' presence of Jesus Christ, a presence which is qualitatively different than those realized in the gathering of the people, the person of the priest or the proclamation of the Scriptures.[15] We might say that the liturgy of the Eucharist focuses and fully expresses what is inchoately present in the first part of the Mass. And thus, in accord with the central argument of this article, the Christian self will be most richly on display in this portion of the liturgy.

---

14 Ratzinger, *Introduction to Christianity*, pp. 73–6.
15 *Sacrosanctum Concilium*, para. 7.

Representatives from the congregation bring forth gifts of bread, wine and water, as well as, customarily, a financial offering. The bread is then presented to God accompanied by the words, 'Blessed are you, Lord God of all creation, for through your goodness, we have this bread to offer, which earth has given and human hands have made . . .' Then the wine, mixed with water, is offered with a similar prayer. These words and gestures are rooted in the 'Berakah' oration of the ancient Israelite tradition, by which the people thank God for the gift of the created universe. In the context of the Mass, the bread and wine speak beyond themselves and represent the whole of what God has given in making the world. The Berakah signals that biblical, liturgical people believe in the doctrine of creation, a belief that radicalizes and renders absolutely unique their sense of self.

Basic to the biblical revelation is the conviction that God is not a being in, above or alongside the world, precisely because God is the maker of the entire universe, both heaven and earth. God is properly called the Lord of creation, since he is not ingredient in creation and cannot be measured the way creatures are. He is not caught in the nexus of contingent relationality and hence cannot be, strictly speaking, compared or contrasted to created things.[16] Even as we say that God is *totaliter aliter* (completely other), we must maintain, simultaneously, that he is, in Nicholaus of Cusa's phrase, the *non aliud* (the non-other). In their attempt to express this biblical idea in more philosophical language, Christian theologians began to speak of *creatio ex nihilo* (creation from nothing). They implied thereby that the true God is not like the gods of ancient mythology or philosophy, who fashion the universe out of some pre-existing matter, or draw it forth from chaos. For the one who creates all of finitude, there can be nothing that stands over and against him, nothing that confronts him as independent. Therefore, he makes the universe '*ex nihilo*', which is to say, not from anything pre-existing. This crucially important doctrine tells us something about both how God exists and how we exist. Were God a mere fashioner of the world, he would be a being in it, a thing among things. But Aquinas tells us that the creator God is not so much the *ens summum* (the supreme being) as *ipsum esse subsistens* (the sheer act of to-be itself), that which grounds and conditions all creation even as it radically transcends it. And Anselm makes much the same point when he names God as 'that than which nothing greater can be thought'. Were God a being among beings, like one of the deities of mythology or philosophy, then he plus the rest of the universe would be greater than he alone. But the creator God must exist in such a way that the created world adds nothing to the perfection of

---

16 See Robert Sokolowski, *The God of Faith and Reason: Foundations of Christian Theology* (Notre Dame: University of Notre Dame Press, 1982), pp. 41–51.

his being: God plus the universe is not greater than God alone. And this very strangeness of the divine manner of being is the condition for the possibility of the real independence of the world. Precisely because he is not one being among many, God is not competitive with creation; since he is non-contrastively transcendent, he can let the other be, even as he remains absolutely immanent to it.

And what does this key doctrine tell us about the creaturely mode of being? It tells us that every creature, to the very core of its existence, is received. The 'positioning' of the self that we explored in connection with the sign of the cross is intensified here, for we see that it reaches to the roots of creaturely being. Thomas Aquinas comments that creation is not a change, since there is no independent substrate that takes in and perdures through the act of creation. Rather, he argues, every creature is a relationship to God: creation is *quaedam relatio ad creatorem cum novitate essendi* (a kind of relationship to the creator, with freshness of being).[17] This means that there is, quite literally, no place where a creature can stand apart from God; simply to be at all implies a connection of the most intimate sort to the creator. And now we can return to the Berakah prayer with greater perception. When the priest leads the people in rendering thanks to God for the bread and wine, which symbolize all of created reality, he is expressing and embodying that attitude which should rightly characterize a creature at his best. I am using the more neutral term 'creature' to signal the cosmological dimension of this liturgical act. In a certain sense, the Berakah gives voice to the ontological situation of all creation. Since the whole of a creature is received, the whole of his existence should be an act of thanksgiving.

The Law of the Gift

After the offering of the bread and wine, the priest moves into the eucharistic prayer, which involves the intonation of the preface, the singing of the *Sanctus* and the consecratory prayer proper. What becomes especially clear as the Mass comes to its highpoint is the relevance of the law of the gift, a principle centrally on display throughout the Bible and the tradition of the Church. The axiom can be stated simply enough: one's being increases and is enhanced in the measure that one gives it away. The Old Testament story of the encounter between the prophet Elijah and the widow of Zaraphath expresses the law poetically. When he comes upon her, the prophet asks the widow for something to eat. She informs him that she has precisely enough to make one more meal for

---

17 Thomas Aquinas, *Quaestiones disputatae de potentia Dei*, q. 3, art. 3, in *Quaestiones Disputatae*, Vol. II (Turin: Marietti, 1965), p. 43.

herself and her son before they die. At this point, Elijah, with extraordinary chutzpah, says, 'make me a little cake' (1 Kings 17.13). At the limit of her resources, against all reason, she does so – and her flour and oil are replenished, sustaining her throughout a time of famine.

We find the same law reaffirmed throughout the life and preaching of Jesus. In the parable of the Prodigal Son, the younger brother demands to have the share of his father's inheritance that is coming to him. Taking the money (significantly, the word *ousia* is used to designate it),[18] he moves into the *chora makra*, perhaps best translated as 'the great emptiness' There he quickly squanders what he had taken. Realizing his folly, he comes back home and is greeted with ring, and robe, and fatted calf. The point is clear: as long as he remains in a relationship of receptivity and gratitude vis-à-vis the giving of his father, he has enough; but when he severed that rapport and took for himself what he wanted, his *ousia* (substance) rapidly dissipated. And the older brother lives in his own version of the *chora makra*, isolated from his father in the measure that he attempts to buy his father's affection through a slavish moral effort. What he cannot take in is the father's assurance, 'everything I have is yours'. He too would have abundance of life if he could but enter into the loop of grace, accepting love as a gift and, with an answering abandon, return it as a gift. The principle is summed up in Jesus' pithy formula: 'the one who would cling to his life will lose it, while the one who gives his life away for my sake shall find it.' And it comes to richest expression when Jesus offers himself to the Father on the cross, returning totally what he had received: 'Father, into your hands I commend my spirit.'

This ethical and spiritual law is rooted in the distinctive metaphysics of creation that we sketched above. Because God is the non-competitive ground of created reality – and not a supreme being hovering threateningly over it – one's self-offering to God is tantamount to the flourishing of the one who so surrenders. Linked to the divine centre, a person can give and give and never find his being exhausted, just the contrary. Were God a being in or above the world, this total self-gift on the part of the creature would be debilitating, ontologically compromising. But given the way that God actually exists, the glory of God, as Irenaeus knew, dovetails with the human creature coming fully to life. It is upon this peculiar ethics and metaphysics that the spiritual efficacy of the liturgy hinges.

Thus in the liturgical setting, the bread and wine – symbolizing the whole of creation – are offered to God, and they come back to us infinitely enhanced, since they are transformed into the very body and blood of Christ. God takes what we have given him, and since he does not in

---

18 See Jean-Luc Marion, *God Without Being* (Chicago: University of Chicago Press, 1991), pp. 95–9.

any sense stand in need of it, he returns that offering to us, elevated in worth. It is as though our gift breaks against the rock of the divine self-sufficiency and redounds to our benefit. This idea of the loop of grace is elegantly expressed in one of the prefaces for weekday Mass: 'You have no need of our praise; yet our desire to thank you is itself your gift. Our prayer of thanksgiving adds nothing to your greatness, but makes us grow in grace.' It is in this context that we can best understand the sacrificial nature of the Mass. The Father has given his only Son to the world, and the Son has offered himself back to the Father, this mutual 'sacrificing' economically expressing the interior life of God, the love which *is* the Holy Spirit. In the liturgy, we join ourselves to the sacrifice of the Son, offering ourselves with him to the Father, and are thereby drawn into the dynamics of the Holy Spirit. There is a passage in eucharistic prayer number three which invokes the third person of the Trinity: 'May he make us an everlasting gift to you,' that is to say, may the Spirit draw us into the dynamics of the law of the gift, expressed utterly in the sacrifice of the Son to the Father. Now we see how the de-centring of the human self, hinted at in the sign of the cross and intensified in the Berakah prayer, comes to most radical expression. The properly Christian self is one which gives itself away in imitation of the God who is nothing but a community of self-surrendering persons. In regard to Christian identity, therefore, we must learn to speak, not so much the language of substance, but rather of sheer relationality and other-orientation, the coinherence of love.

Before closing this discussion of the eucharistic prayer, I would like to say a word about the *Sanctus*, in which the worshipping community joins its song to that of the angels and saints in heaven. It would be a great mistake to dismiss this prayer as a bit of pious decoration. In our discussion of the *Gloria*, we made it plain that the optimal human community is that which is constituted by a shared giving of glory to God in the highest. Just before the prayer of consecration, the Christian community here below – still too marked by sin, rivalry and violence – consciously joins itself to the *communio* of heaven, the angels and saints who have indeed found their connection through common praise of the true God. The blending of our voices with theirs is therefore a participation even now in the chorus of coinherence which is the heavenly life. We find an echo of *Sanctus* in the Our Father, the Lord's prayer which immediately follows the eucharistic prayer proper. When we pray that God's kingdom might come and his will be done on earth as in heaven, we are begging that the *ordo* of the angels and saints – the non-violent society – might set the tone for our struggling society here below.

The Sending

After the people receive the body and blood of the Lord, the priest prays the closing prayer of Mass, blesses the congregation and then dismisses them with the words, 'The Mass is ended; Go in peace to love and to serve the Lord.' It has been commented that, after the words of consecration themselves, these are the most sacred of the liturgy. Throughout the Bible, men and women are sent by God on mission. Abraham, at the age of 75, is told to leave the security of his life in Ur and to set out in search of a promised land; Moses sees the burning bush, hears the voice of Yahweh and then is sent back to Egypt to lead Israel to freedom; Isaiah experiences a vision of God in the Temple and then hears a summons to become God's spokesperson; Peter, James and John go up the mount of Transfiguration and then go down again to follow Jesus to Jerusalem; Saul sees the light and hears a voice and then receives a commission to preach the good news to the Gentiles. In point of fact, no one in the biblical tradition ever is granted an experience of God without being, subsequently, sent. Scriptural religion is a religion of mission.

Hans Urs von Balthasar has argued that, in a Christian context, the concepts of mission and person are tightly linked. The person of Jesus – in which divinity and humanity coinhere – is constituted by the mission that he has from his Father.[19] He is, at the deepest ground of his existence, the one who was sent by the Father into godforsakenness for the salvation of the world. Who is Jesus? The question cannot be adequately answered in an abstractly metaphysical or psychological manner, for he is, first and foremost, the One Sent. Now the personhood of the Christian is realized in the measure that he or she participates in this mission of the Son. This is why, Balthasar contends, the New Testament hero does not truly know who he is until he is properly commissioned.[20] This relationship is signalled by certain eloquent changes of name: Simon becomes 'Peter' when he realizes that his mission is to lead and defend the Church; Saul becomes 'Paul' when he knows that his task is to evangelize the Gentiles. These are not incidental reorientations of practical agendas; they are the moments when Peter and Paul become persons in the Person. Thus, the liturgical subject, sent by the priest out into the world to 'love and serve the Lord', is receiving much more than instructions for action. She is receiving her personhood.

Here we see, for the final time, the 'positioning' of the self that takes place throughout the Mass. The Christian subject is neither self-

---

19 Hans Urs von Balthasar, *Theo-Drama: Theological Dramatic Theory, Vol. III: Dramatis Personae: Persons in Christ*. (San Francisco: Ignatius Press, 1992), pp. 152–62.
20 von Balthasar, *Theo-Drama*, pp. 230–7.

grounding nor self-disposing, but utterly in the hands of the Other who makes him, claims him and sends him. And the nature of this mission, which is constitutive of the self, is always fundamentally the same, though it finds a myriad of variations. It is the task of carrying the dynamics of the liturgy out into the world. Like the dove sent forth from Noah's ark, the liturgical person is meant to convey to the wider society the form of life realized in the liturgical space. Commissioned by Christ, she now seeks to produce in others a deeper sense of belonging to God and of being a forgiven sinner, a richer participation in the Biblical world; a denser appreciation for the implications of the Creed, a fuller immersion into the rhythm of the gift, and a more complete sharing in the mystical body of Christ.

In this great act of giving to the other what one has received from the liturgy, the Christian self is both grounded and expressed.

3

Liturgical Polarity and Symbolic Hermeneutics

ÂNGELO MANUEL DOS SANTOS CARDITA

Before 'I think' must be posited 'I believe' in such a way that the I does not determine what is understood to be faith.[1]

Introduction

Thirty years ago, Vagaggini proposed for the first time a *liturgical aporia* which seems to be extant, and which comprises the comparison of 'ritual' with 'living faith', 'objectivity' with 'subjectivity', and 'reason' with 'emotion'. At stake in this juxtaposition is the relationship between the human immediacy of the liturgy and its divine origin. Contrary to what we might think, Vagaggini shows that the challenge, visible in the person of Christ himself, consists in affirming 'the established supremacy finally of the transcendent and divine pole (of the aporia), but [also] in the full survival of the human pole and in the continued dialectic tension between the two poles'.[2] On the other hand, the orthodox

---

1 E. Jüngel, *Dios como misterio del mundo* (Salamanca: Sígueme, 1984), p. 223.
2 C. Vagaggini, 'Riflessioni in prospettiva teologica sui dieci anni di riforma liturgica e sulla aporia del problema liturgico in questo momento', *Rivista Liturgica* 61 (1974), pp. 35–72, 69 (author's insertion). In this way, Vagaggini aligned himself with Guardini's thought. Cf. R. Guardini, *L'opposizione polare. Saggio per una filosofia del concreto vivente* (Brescia: Morcelliana, 1997). With respect to the 'liturgical polarity' in general, see also: J. M. Macquarrie, 'Subjectivity and objectivity in Theology and Worship', *Worship* 41 (1967), pp. 152–60. J. Séguy, 'Rationnel et émotionnel dans la pratique liturgique catholique. Un modèle théorique', *La Maison-Dieu* 129 (1977), pp. 73–92. E. Schillebeeckx, *Cristo y los cristianos. Gracia y liberación* (Madrid: Cristiandad, 1982), principally pp. 23–57. P. Buhle, 'A identidade cristã: entre a objectividade e a subjectividade', *Concilium* 216/2 (1988), pp. 25–36. P. Tena, 'La celebración del misterio: identidad interna y forma externa', *Phase* 172 (1989), pp. 271–86. G. Busani and R. Tagliaferri, 'Soggettività ed oggettività nella liturgia. Intuizioni di R. Guardini su una problematica attuale', *Rivista Liturgica* 77 (1990), pp. 659–72. G. Bonaccorso, 'Interiorità della mistica ed esteriorità del rito', in Bonaccorso (ed.), *Mistica e ritualità: mondi inconciliabili?* (Padua: Messaggero, 1999), pp. 143–63. L.-M. Chauvet, 'La liturgie demain: essai de prospective', in P. De Clerck (ed.), *La liturgie, lieu théologique* (Paris: Beauchesne, 1999), pp. 201–29.

theologian Constantin Andronikof states that liturgy – comprising the 'theanthropic essence'[3] of a true *methodological a priori* – makes it impossible to separate a subject from an object. Therefore it would not be possible to conjecture the liturgical polarity, since the action of the two subjects would converge into one and the same action (synergy) in such a way that ultimately, we could say, 'God prays to God'.[4]

The differences between these two perspectives are clear and, more than the distance of sensibilities between Western and Eastern theology, here at stake is both the affirmation of the human subject as independently self-aware and self-conscious, and the repercussions of that self-consciousness with respect to liturgy. While Vagaggini indicates a path to pursue for those who wish to take into account the modern concept of the individual, Andronikof thinks this aporia may simply be ignored. But the question is even more complex to the extent that in *looking from the outside* (at the ritual) and reason *separated* (from faith) we do not succeed in getting to the heart of the ritual phenomenon, lived and experienced intuitively *from within* as the confluence of an *earthly and mystic thought*. The *homo religiosus* finds himself at the centre of a tension that he is unable to perceive and so 'bring' to self-consciousness: in the ritual act, the human action seems to be intentionally addressed to a divine subject. This is to say that, in the ritual-religious sphere, the modern consciousness of the subject cannot be ignored, but is overcome so that the subject itself can be grasped! The subject is not exclusively the one who thinks, nor simply the one who believes, but the one who discovers himself determined in his 'I' through the 'I believe', which he pronounces and celebrates.

'The ritual act is a theophany and, at the same time, an anthropology'.[5] In this affirmation is implicit an undeniable aspect of the various epistemological methods that are possible in the study of liturgy: the *unity* between subject and object, in the sequence of its relation as *praxis* (dialectic) and *experience* (hermeneutics).[6] *Above all, phenomenologically*, the ritual act is enacted by having in view the *meeting* and the *experienced union* between God and man. Meeting implies 'distance' and

---

3 'En effet, si l'on considère celui qui prie comme le sujet, Celui qu'il prie n'est pas un object. . . . La nature même de la liturgie est faite de cette conjugaison opératoire (*synergisme*) des deux sujets: Dieu et l'homme. . . . C'est l'énergie divine qui mobilise l'énergie humaine du liturge et qui permet à celle-ci de lui devenir concomitante. . . . La liturgie est *théanthropique par essence*'. C. Andronikof, *Le sens de la liturgie. La relation entre Dieu et l'homme* (Paris: Cerf, 1988), pp. 35–7.

4 Andronikof, *Le sens de la liturgie*, p. 36.

5 J. A. Mourão, in A. L. Janeira, A. C. Carvalho, C. J. Correia and J. A. Mourão, *O regresso do sagrado* (Lisbon: Livros e Leituras, 1998), p. 46.

6 Cf. G. Bonaccorso, *Introduzione allo studio della liturgia* (Padua: Messaggero, 1990), p. 120.

union implies 'separation'. Thus, *logically* – in order to preserve these features – *polarity* is kept by the first aspect, while *conjugation* derives from the second one. The present study reverts constantly to this tension, illustrating it progressively in different forms not only by aiming to justify *symbolic* hermeneutics as the procedure which – in the present broad view of the subject – best expresses the liturgical *polarity*, but also by showing a logically developed interpretation and a hermeneutics to apply *dialectically*.

Turn in 'Anthropological Turn'

In the context of post-modernity, it is possible to glimpse a general tendency towards the transformation of these terms. In fact, if the term 'anthropology' aims at the *anthropos* it also comprises the 'positive' areas (biological, psychological, sociocultural) of the 'human sciences'. This has developed from out of the self-consciousness of the human subject, which originates in the philosophical-speculative field. This is not a relativization of the cosmocentric and theocentric vision of the human being, fully attained in theology, suggesting the need for an *anthropological turn*. In the context of post-modernity, the self-awareness (as self-consciousness) of the subject has pervaded all the traditional independent positive and human sciences that had previously regarded the human being as a theologically oriented being, a being 'for' God. Now, rather than self-oriented (because no longer oriented toward God), the subject appears as self-conscious. The need for an anthropological turn arises out of the reduction of each particular science to the self-consciousness of the subject who makes each particular (scientific) enquiry dependent on this discourse of self-consciousness. This transition from a religious discourse in the first person ('I believe') to a discourse about religion in the third person ('they believe') has found a point of support in the progressive *anthropological reduction* of religion, which has broken the bond between faith/religious belief and truth.[7]

Schleiermacher and Feuerbach are the two main figures to consider. The first set out to reconcile modern culture with the religious world, but at the cost of adapting religion to modern subjectivity. This meant the overcoming of any philosophical or theological investigation into religion because the essential matter was 'life' and not 'doctrine', 'emotion' or 'thought'. It is essential, though, to understand emotion in Schleiermacher over and above the purely psychological aspect as this determines

---

[7] Cf. A. N. Terrin, 'Scienza delle religioni o teologia? Le consegne del XX secolo e la sfida del futuro', in S. Ubbiali (ed.), *Teologia delle religioni e liturgia* (Padua: Messaggero, 2001), pp. 97–154, p. 135.

a comprehensive and existential mode of encounter – the immediacy of religious self-awareness, the discovery of the 'infinite in the finite', and 'sentiment and the propensity for the Infinite' (*Sinn und Geschmack für Unendliche*).[8] But if the flaw in Schleiermacher's hypothesis consists in his assimilating modern presuppositions, its worth resides precisely in the fact that it anticipates the possibility of a meeting between theology and anthropology.

In Schleiermacher, in fact, the theological enquiry takes shape and is joined inseparably with the anthropological enquiry. Having been the first to try to deduce the structure of historical and manifest religions out of an analysis of the religious experience, Schleiermacher appears as the precursor of 'The Science of Religions'. On the other hand, by placing the essence of religion 'above' (*über*) Christianity – inserted thus into the world of religions – Schleiermacher exposes Christianity to the very light of anthropology.[9] The train of thought to which we must adhere is of the utmost importance: the so-called anthropological reduction is due to the lack of a critical 'deconstructive' moment in relation to modern convictions, more than to the inherent capacity of theology to react to the anthropological challenge, and in so doing to the possibility of incorporating anthropology into itself.

With Feuerbach, the reduction is radicalized.[10] At root, we are faced with a play of projection of the human into the divine and of the divine into the human. His fundamental thesis consists precisely of considering the absolute as a simple projection or objectification of humanity.

> From his God, you know the man, and, inversely, from the man you know his God: the two are one. What God is for man: his spirit, his soul, and what is the human spirit itself, his heart: this is his God; God is what is within made manifest; religion is the solemn disclosure of the hidden treasures of man, the confession of his most intimate thoughts, the public confession of his secrets of love.[11]

But if God is nothing more than the self (*Selbst*) of man, are we not rather projecting – by diminishing – the divine into what is the human, than projecting – by exalting – what is human into the divine? As I have already said, probably Feuerbach's hypothesis consists of this paradox without resolution, but, in a way, confirms our perspective on

---

8 Cf. F. D. E. Schleiermacher, *Über die Religion. Reden an die Gebildeten unter ibren Verächtern*, 6th edition (Göttingen: Vandenhoeck & Ruprecht, 1967), p. 51.

9 Cf. Terrin, 'Scienza delle religioni o teologia?', p. 115.

10 Cf. M. Fraijó, 'Filosofía de la religión: una azarosa búsqueda de identidad', in Fraijó (ed.), *Filosofía de la religión. Estudios y textos*, 2nd edition (Madrid: Trotta, 2001), pp. 13–43, p. 26.

11 L. Feuerbach, *L'Essence du christianisme* (Paris: Maspero, 1968), p. 130.

anthropological reduction. From this perspective, the problem, with Feuerbach, is not the abandonment of theological enquiry but the dissolution of the anthropological enquiry into the theological enquiry to the point of inversion.[12] The short circuit lies in the attempt to maintain the metaphysical concept of God under the jurisdiction of thought based upon itself. By declaring the incompatibility between the essence and the existence of God, the finite nature of human existence has to be elevated to the level of divine essence.[13] But, rather than God, is it not man who gets lost while projected *into the divine*? *Sub contrario*, the capacity of theology to integrate anthropology into itself is confirmed; moreover, we are told that anthropology needs theology for its own self-delimitation. In the theological panorama, however, we will have to await the 'anthropological turn' of Karl Rahner in order to see this relationship accomplished in a positive manner.

The Anthropological [Re]-Turn in Theology

For Rahner, the anthropological enquiry *in the transcendental sense* involves theological consideration in its wholeness.[14] As we consider man a being of absolute transcendence in relation to God, we cannot say that 'theocentrism' conflicts with 'anthropocentrism'. Indeed, the discovery of the bonds between dogmatic content and anthropological experience constitutes the proper 'anthropological-transcendental turn' in theology. However, by necessity, this procedure results in the disappearance of the categorical mark of sacramental reality. Here arises a paradoxical situation: a theology, anthropologically interested, actually loses the human closeness of the sacraments. Briefly, according to this scheme, the manifestation of God coincides with the transcendental experience of the subject and then is translated through sacramental mediation.[15] The categorical closeness of the liturgy and of the Christian sacraments is only taken into account as an expression of something already offered, such as the eternal presence of grace in the world.[16] In spite of this difficulty, the question is not of renouncing the subjective dimension of the thought, but of assuming the aspect of its realization in the bond

---

12 Cf. Jüngel, *Dios como misterio del mundo*, p. 192 (body of text and note 140).

13 Cf. Jüngel, *Dios como misterio del mundo*, p. 201.

14 K. Rahner, 'Teologia e antropologia', in Rahner, *Nuovi saggi* III (Rome: Paoline, 1969), pp. 45–72. K. Rahner, 'Riflessioni sul metodo della teologia', in Rahner, *Nuovi saggi* IV (Rome: Paoline, 1973), pp. 99–159.

15 Cf. S. Ubbiali, 'Il sacramento cristiano e l'agire libero dell'uomo. Per una "Drammatica" dell'azione sacramentale', in N. Reali (ed.), *Il mondo del sacramento. Teologia e filosofia a confronto*, (Milan: Paoline, 2001), pp. 238–65, p. 252.

16 Cf. K. Rahner, 'Sulla teologia del culto divino', in Rahner, *Sollecitudine per la Chiesa. Nuovi saggi* VIII (Rome: Paoline, 1982), pp. 271–83, p. 279.

between man and divine truth to which the sacrament appeals: 'The form on the basis of which the sacrament is implied excludes the scission between divine truth and human activity and the role of the anthropological aspect of the sacrament must not be the mere occasion to set in motion the divine will to salvation for the benefit of man'.[17]

In the enunciation of historical reality (without renouncing totally the transcendental horizon, but 'situating it'), theology may meet with categorical anthropological reality, that is, with the reality of the human being. In a theological consideration of liturgy, this aspect is of crucial importance because liturgy and the sacraments assume ritual as their proper mode of existence; hence liturgy belongs in the categorical ambit of *liberty*. Thereby it is possible to correct the transcendental view that confines liberty to the mere expression of subjectivity, precluding any relationship with the object of worship. In ritual, in fact, liberty is constituted ideally out of its relationship with the world, history and men, and with the divine, recognising herein, in this typical form, its own existence. Therefore, 'ritual expresses the religious form of the free act'[18] coexisting in the structure of subjectivity. In this same sense, George Lindbeck recognizes that a religion 'is a common phenomenon that shapes the subjectivities of individuals rather than being primarily a manifestation of those subjectivities'.[19]

Both perspectives assume a concept of the subject that differs from the modern concept which grounds the subject on the principle of comprehension of the world from thought (*cogito*): a subject whose manifestation is referred back to a transcendental alterity as the basis and condition of possibility of all interpersonal relationship. Thus, the predicted movement of an anthropological leading back of theology may meet its justification and even its purpose in the post-modern form of reconsidering the subject.

'Post-modern' Reconsidering of the Subject

Understanding the subject is at the centre of what separates modernity from *post-modernity*. Summoned from its birth to expansion, the modern subject is still vulnerable to doubt. With the neologism of 'post-modernity' there may be an attempt to indicate, in fact, both the first movement and the recognition of a 'global subject', with a kind of attention to the subject that restores its lost confidence without exalting it.

---

17 Ubbiali, 'Il sacramento cristiano e l'agire libero', p. 254.
18 A. Caprioli, 'Sacramenti della fede o consuetudini sociali religiose? Un tentativo di chiarimento teologico', *Rivista Liturgica* 76 (1989), pp. 27–41, p. 40.
19 G. A. Lindbeck, *The Nature of Doctrine: Religion and Theology in a Post-Liberal Age* (London: SPCK, 1984), p. 33.

The difference among positions corresponds to the difference between the verbal infinite and the various functions assumed by the grammatical subject (which subordinates the verb to *conjugation*, while allowing it to *decline*) beyond the nominative. In fact, as the global subject acts in the present in a state of 'near immediacy' and of 'instantaneity', the 'flux' appears as a normal abyss that carries on its purpose according to the logic of the verbal infinite.[20] On the other hand, 'to deconstruct' subjectivity *makes the subject relative* in order to be able to *recover* it. Indeed, we are dealing here with *declining* the 'I'; in the accusative ('here I am' – ethical opening: Lévinas), in the dative ('I receive *myself*' – phenomenological opening: Marion), and even making the 'I' a *metaphor* (as other – ontological opening: Ricoeur).

Referring to the Platonic tradition and, principally, to Judaism, Lévinas proposes to surmount the ontology of Totality, centred on 'sameness' and 'identity' of the subject, to compose an ethic of the Infinite. In Lévinas, human subjectivity is considered *ethically*, from the other, in radical passivity; that is to say, as a *response* to the ethical appeal that springs from the other. In this sense, the autonomy of the subject is subjugated by exteriority, which opens the way to difference. The face of the other comprises not only that irrefutable reality of the 'same', but most of all a compelling invocation to an ethical response. Thus, the overcoming of Being will not yield by denying each other being, but 'displays' it in its difference and alterity. The subject ceases to have within itself its own justification, but is constituted through its relationship with the *other*. This is not 'I', nor 'you', but 'he', and it represents the transformation of transcendence, irreducible to the immanence of the 'same'. *Alterity* is, therefore, constitutive of personal identity. This can be interpreted as 'interpersonal' because it *associates* people among themselves without making them the same, respecting their unconditional character. So, the subject is not thought as a substrate of its acts but as *subject to others*, owing its responsibility to others. Personal identity comes from this: going out of oneself abandoning all 'self-seeking spontaneity' and self-centredness, in a movement without turning back. For Lévinas, *liberty* arises out of this call from the outward which decentralizes the subject. This form of understanding the subject declines it as an accusative which 'is not the modification of any nominative',[21] but where 'the word *I* means here I am, responding to everything and everyone'.[22]

If with Lévinas we have an ethical opening, Paul Ricoeur places his

---

20 Cf. L. Carmelo, *Órbitas da modernidade. Da era do sujeito à consciência global* (Lisbon: Mareantes, 2003), pp. 92, 107–8, 119.
21 E. Lévinas, *Autrement qu'être ou au-delà de l'essence* (The Hague: M. Nijhoff, 1974), p. 155.
22 Lévinas, *Autrement qu'être*, p. 145.

hermeneutical interpretation, explicitly opened to the ontological dimension, on a philosophical level situated (chrono-)logically between the exaltation of the *cogito* (Descartes) and its negation (Nietzsche). It is this peculiar situation of the subject which leads him to build up a dialectic of 'itself *as* other', conjugating *alterity* actively and passively, according to three forms: the body, the stranger and the consciousness. The moment of affirmation of the subject coincides with its reduction to the simplicity of the thought which thrives on doubt.[23] But if the permanency of certainty itself, which is always to conquer, is conferred by the existence of God, then only the *cogito* passes ontologically to the second plane,[24] as required by the following alternative: either the *subject* has intrinsic worth, or it is the idea of 'the perfect' which establishes it as finite. In the anti-*cogito* we do not have the inverse of *cogito* but the annihilation of the very question posited *by the cogito*.[25] In fact, Nietzsche does no more than to extend doubt to the 'internal experience' itself, that is, to thought itself and doubt itself.[26] In this situation, 'attestation defines in our eyes the type of certainty to which hermeneutics aspires'.[27] The reply of Paul Ricoeur, in face of Heidegger's 'aliency' and Lévinas's 'exteriority', obstinately opposes these with the original and derivative character of a third modality of alterity: the injunction that comes from the other in inner unity with the attestation of himself.[28]

Naturally both the ethical and ontological openings are grounded on the phenomenological. It is in this sense that the subject (let us call it so, for the time being) for Marion must not only be understood to be beyond

---

23 'La subjectivité qui se pose elle-même par réflexion sur son propre doute, doute radicalisé par le fable du grand trompeur, est une subjectivité désancrée, que Descartes, conservant le vocabulaire substancialiste des philosophies avec lesquelles il croit avoir rompu, peut encore appeler une âme. Mais c'est l'inverse qu'il veut dire: ce que la tradition appelle âme est en vérité *sujet*, et ce sujet se réduit à l'acte le plus simple et le plus dépouillé, celui de penser. Cet acte de penser, encore sans object déterminé, suffit à vaincre le doute, parce que le doute le contient déjà. Et, comme le doute est volontaire et libre, la pensée se pose en posant le doute. C'est dans ce sens que le "j'existe pensant" est une première vérité, c'est-à-dire une vérité que rien ne précède'. P. Ricoeur, *Soi-même comme un autre* (n.p.: Seuil, 1990), p. 18.

24 '... Livré à lui-même, le moi du *Cogito* est le Sisyphe condamné à remonter, d'instant en instant, le rocher de sa certitude à contre-pente du doute. En revanche, parce qu'il me conserve, Dieu confère à la certitude de moi-même la permanence que celle-ci ne tient pas d'elle-même'. Ricoeur, *Soi-même*, p. 20.

25 Cf. Ricoeur, *Soi-même*, p. 25.

26 '... il faut avoir présente à l'esprit l'attaque contre le positivisme; là où celui-ci dit: il n'y a que des *faits*, Nietzsche dit: les faits, c'est ce qu'il n'y a pas, seulement des interprétations. En étendant la critique à la soi-disant "expérience interne", Nietzsche ruine dans le principe le caractère d'exception du *Cogito* à l'égard du doute que Descartes dirigeait contre la distinction entre le monde du rêve et celui de la veille'. Ricoeur, *Soi-même*, p. 26.

27 Ricoeur, *Soi-même*, p. 33.

28 Cf. Ricoeur, *Soi-même*, p. 409.

all the caesura between 'thing' and 'feeling' which, in this way, is *opposed* to the perceived object, but must be grasped *by* the phenomenon, received *in* the movement of delivering [donation] of the phenomenon itself. This is so, for if the concept is incapable of *showing* the object it circumscribes, it also manifests itself through its *perceptible immediacy* by reaching the senses of the very recipient himself, who begins to define the 'I' implied in the act of receipt. More than a subject, the feeling is an 'attributable' which 'probes the very flesh of the phenomenon in a state of manifestation'.[29] In this way, rather than by overcoming the dichotomy, having received the attribute,[30] a path is cleared for the mediation between activity and passivity: because, in receiving what it is given, the 'attributable' allows it to be shown: gives it its *form*. But the 'attributable' *results* from what it forms according to its point of view, illuminating itself, so to speak, like a screen because 'only the impact of what it is given makes arise, from a single and self-same collision, the clarity which irradiates its first visibility and the screen itself on which it is projected'.[31] It is in this sense that the attributable appears *after* the subject, in the same form in which the 'self' (*soi*) of the phenomenon transmutes the *subject* into *witness*: the 'I' can no longer produce and possess the phenomenon, and instead comes to designate '*à qu[o]i*' ('to what [whom]') the phenomenon exhibits itself.[32]

The impotence of the metaphysical 'I' lies precisely in its incapacity to do justice to the signs of its own phenomenon. Hence by overcoming the *aporiae* which characterize it, it must be a new figure – the 'attributable' – that emerges. First, we ought to refute the *transcendental* 'I', according to Marion, for its *incapacity for individuation*: assuring its transcendentality at the cost of its qualities results in the loss of its own 'self'. Subsequently, the living *ego* gives way to *solipsism*, from which

---

29 '... Ce que la métaphysique disqualifie brutalement comme phénomène non-objectivé parvient seul à se donner en plénitude – à savoir à se donner au point de se montrer à partir de soi, de phénoménaliser sa donation jusqu'à rendre manifeste son ipséité insubstituable. Dès lors, le "moi" qui ressent par "sentiment" ne perd sa spontanéité constituante (*Je, ego*), que pour regagner la réceptivité envers la manifestation de ce qui se montre ("me", "à qu[o]i"). L'attributaire, tel que lui seul se met en situation de sentir et ressentir, épreuve la chair même du phénomène en état de manifestation'. J.-L. Marion, *Étant donné. Essai d'une phénomènologie de la donation*, 2nd edition (Paris: PUF, 1998), p. 363.

30 'Recevoir, pour l'attributaire, signifie donc rien de moins que d'accomplir la donation en la transmuant en manifestation, en accordant à ce qui se donne de se montrer à partir de soi'. Marion, *Étant donné*, p. 364.

31 Marion, *Étant donné*, p. 365.

32 Cf. Marion, *Étant donné*, p. 344. In this work, Marion overcomes two objections: the *metaphysical objection*, according to which the subject would be necessary for the representation of the object: and the *phenomenological objection*, which, from the possibility of perceiving the *gift* without the *giver*, would bring us to question its determination in respect of the *attributaire*.

it cannot free itself, so 'I think' ends as the same, radically, as 'I think myself'. Second, in respect of the *empirical* 'I', we must discuss its derivation from a synthesis of the diverse, on which it would depend, following its appearance in the intuition. Finally, the dichotomy itself of the subject, transcendental and empirical, must be overcome. The particularly phenomenological aporia arises and reaches resolution here. This has its roots in the paradox that when the subject aims to represent itself, it is placed firmly in the phenomenality of the object. Wishing to set itself up as the subject, it ends simply by *assimilating itself* with the object, without being able to ascertain its subjectivity.[33] In the radical reversal of position in which, according to Marion, the aporia disappears, the importance of the attribute posited as thing given is also overcome.

In this movement, the individualization (of the subject) does not represent its isolation, since the thing given is roused by a *call*.[34] Specifically, this invocation addresses the essence of the individual, in the sense that it inspires an original, unknown narrative: it proffers an *invitation;* contradicting intention, the invocation causes *surprise;* finally, it is possible to understand the subject in the dative (I receive *myself*) which even comprises the ablative (I open myself *to*), leading to *interlocution* and the *facticity* (or individuation): the invocation gives me to *myself* and gives me *as I am*, that is, it individualizes me. We are particularly interested in understanding the subject, so to speak, *pendant* and *dependant* on the invocation that is directed to it from outside. In this consists the phenomenological opening in post-modern understanding, declined in the dative: '. . . I receive *myself* the invocation which gives me to myself, before it gives me anything [else]. . . . Receiving itself from the call which invites it, the thing given opens itself therefore to an alterity, whose other may eventually fail, but which appears thus all the more.'[35]

The post-modern movement of reconstruction of the subject potentially includes a capacity of reference to liturgy, to the extent that liturgy shows us a 'decentred' subject.[36] But liturgical reflection risks turning

---

33 Appropriating the being (*Dasein*) from the 'I', Heidegger was the first to denounce its insufficiency, ending however in falling into the aporia of *solipsism* (*Dasein* discovers himself to be an empty identity) and of self-*sufficiency* (the reflexive character of *Dasein* reinstates the reflexive of the subject). Cf. Marion, *Étant donné*, pp. 355–61.

34 The *call* is proper to what Marion calls the 'saturated phenomena', which are characterized by excess of intuition. It is in the inversion of intentionality that the call becomes possible. Cf. Marion, *Étant donné*, pp. 366–9. For this reason, the *adonné* can briefly be described as the 'subjecti[vi]té entièrement conforme à la donation – qui se reçoit entièrement de ce qu'elle reçoit, donnée par le donné, donnée au donné'. Marion, *Étant donné*, p. 373.

35 Marion, *Étant donné*, p. 371.

36 For Lévinas, liturgy consisted of an explicit reference to his thought as the religious

nostalgically to the pre-modern subject. This being the case, only apparently are we offered a reconciliation, or rather: what a pre-modern vision (of the subject and liturgy itself) have in common with post-modern reconstruction is precisely what sets up the distance and the impossibility of conciliation between the two positions. The pre-modern understanding doesn't need to refer to the subject in order to elaborate its proper discourse. On the other hand, the modern and post-modern understanding can only derive its validity directly from an explicit reference to the subjectivity of the subject. Thus it is important to be aware of the possibility of an oscillation in a theological justification of liturgy between 'pre-modernity' and 'post-modernity'.

Naturally, the investigation into the subject is central. Round and about its (modern) comprehension one may delineate what one calls 'pre-modernity' and 'post-modernity'. Concerning the justification of worship in this context, this peculiar condition may be illustrated through the recent proposal of Samuel Rouvillois of a philosophy of the liturgy. The point of departure is the 'phenomenological' consideration of the *person*, 'once it discovers its being, affirming "I am" – not from the *cogito*, but from the experience of its concrete existence – it places itself beyond the objective-subjective, exteriority-interiority distinction'.[37] We are thus brought back to the theme of corporal mediation and of the mediatory function of the gesture and, more specifically, of the symbol. The body is the origin of the loving will and action *through* gesture. However, the gesture of love, more than manifestation or communication, seeks immediate communion. Thus, if the body is the *condition* of adoration, it is not, however, determinant for its fulfilment. Gesture is necessary so that interpersonal love may pass from affective union to effective union,[38] but, because (according to Rouvillois) in adoration it is impossible to conceive an effective union, the gesture must here be of pure gratitude, so that it transforms the act of the person (autonomy) into an act of the creature (heteronomy) which surrenders itself to the Creator.[39] The ethical act of adoration consists in this. Consequently, for Rouvillois, man opens himself for adoration as a creature, but not as a person; the *liturgical man* does not place himself before the Creator as a person

---

character of the invoking ethical exteriority. Cf. C. Beckert, 'A liturgia do próximo em Lévinas', *Communio* 18 (2001), pp. 67–77 (Portuguese edition). For Marion, it is the Eucharist which assumes eminence while the paradigmatic example of the 'phenomenology' of the phenomenon which, manifesting itself, yields 'until abandonment'. Cf. N. Reali, *Fino all'abandono. L'eucaristia nella fenomenalità de Jean-Luc Marion* (Rome: Città Nuova, 2001).

37 S. Rouvillois, *Corps et Sagesse. Philosophie de la liturgie* (n.p.: Fayard, 1995), p. 24.
38 Cf. Rouvillois, *Corps et sagesse*, p. 61.
39 Cf. Rouvillois, *Corps et sagesse*, p. 62.

before another person because 'the *I am a creature* present in adoration does not coincide with the experience of *I am* of the person'.[40]

This affirmation is astonishing in all it contains of the pre-modern. Wishing to overcome the difficulties that the modern concept of the subject brings to liturgy, Rouvillois avoids any confrontation with post-modernity, taking refuge in a pre-modern securing of the distance between finite and infinite or, to put it another way, of the *ontological difference*. We could posit a theological justification for liturgy so that it is understood as *cultus debitus* (in an ontological and moral way) upon this model of the relationship between God (Creator/Infinite) and the human being (creature/finite); but from the moment in which the human being sees himself as a free subject, the very notion of worship acquires a Promethean aspect, understood as the voluntary act of the man who aspires towards God. Bearing this in mind we can understand how a wider theological tradition – one might think of, for instance, of Saint Thomas Aquinas – had been able to use a notion now thought to be 'pre-theological'.[41] In this broader view, one of the merits of the discourse concerning the presence and action of Christ in the liturgy was that of having cleared the path to an intersubjective conception of the relationship between God and man, seen as a meeting of persons (the personalist way). In the light of this, we can recover the question of the symbol and its significance in the post-modern context (the symbolic way).

The Evolution of Liturgical Subject

In this first approach to the theme of the symbolic in this study, I wish to call attention to the fact that symbolic hermeneutics, in its theological use, must not end up by being simply a vague and imprecise application, expressing the most varied and even contrasting perspectives. By itself, the symbol may be as impotent in sacramental theology as any cultural use of other anachronistic categories of the past taken out of their proper context. Any resort to symbol must, then, correspond to the current (post-)modern awareness without succumbing to it, by providing for the something it lacks.

Between 'pre-modernity' and 'post-modernity' the danger appears that the truth of religion is eliminated by undue and unilateral emphasis (or attenuation) of one of its poles – immanent or transcendent – when, on the contrary, the religious phenomenon lives 'in constant mutual

---

40 Rouvillois, *Corps et sagesse*, p. 48.
41 See C. Braga, 'La natura della liturgia nella *Mediator Dei* e nella *Sacrosanctum Concilium*', in E. Carr (ed.), *Liturgia opus trinitatis. Epistemologia liturgica* (Rome: Centro Studi Sant'Anselmo, 2002), pp. 25–48, 31.

reference to both poles in a state of tension, so that one eliminates the exclusivism of the other'.[42] It is in this way that the absolutism of the rational, abstract, aspect in favour of the immanent autonomy of religion results paradoxically in relinquishing all its symbolic representation, both historical and temporal. For this reason it is important to recover the function of the symbol, and of embodiment, without succumbing to its rationalizing spiritualization, and thus to recover the value of ritual over and above the ethical-political. It is here that a question emerges about the relationship of the Christian faith to the category of religious experience: faith cannot be limited to spiritual adherence; it must be articulated in a concrete, or cultural, social or ritual form, or else fall into insignificance: 'therefore, it is important to embrace the opportunity which a given tendency of post-modernity offers us, to recover the cultural-symbolic dimension of the true Christian faith, and to overcome its spiritualising and, to some extent, Gnostic reduction'.[43]

Having illustrated the movement and oscillation which can occur between 'pre-modernity' and 'post-modernity', we can now appeal to the thesis developed by Samuel Rouvillois. For this author, the symbol allows the involvement of the person in a loving and effective will, but it is destined to 'withdraw' (*s'effacer*) because 'symbolic mediation involves the active lover and is prepared for him, but would not know how to be an *intermediary* within the bond of love.'[44] Transposing this to liturgical reality, it means that liturgy must be 'suffused with' adoration and that, in this movement of gratuitousness, the symbolic mediation must give way to the immediacy of the loving relationship. But were we to adopt this view, we would have lost the symbol itself and, with it, the anthropological (ritual, institutional and hierarchical) pole of liturgy. 'To consider mediations only with reference to God does not allow us to explain our necessity to accede to Him; on the contrary, in this light they [the mediations] could appear superfluous.'[45] In the light of this, we would have to put forward the view that praise can correct the tendency of worship to be self-preoccupied, and so idolatrous, without renouncing the polarity. This is because 'praise converts the rite into a symbol. But it continues to be a mediation which has its value and consistency at the level of being.'[46] The difference between the two solutions indicates the difference between pre-modernity and post-modernity in their manner of considering the symbol. On the other hand, as we shall see, in this opening of the symbolic to the ontological aspect there should

---

42 J. M. Duque, *Dizer Deus na pós-modernidade* (Lisbon: Alcalá, 2003), p. 198.
43 Duque, *Dizer Deus*, p. 203.
44 Rouvillois, *Corps et sagesse*, p. 122.
45 E. Vilanova, 'Un culto "en Espíritu y Verdad"', *Phase* 25 (1985), pp. 343–64, 358.
46 Vilanova, 'Un culto "en Espíritu y Verdad"', p. 359.

correspond a similar opening toward the epistemological. The condition and possibility of this movement is the way to encapsulate the liturgical subject and, consequently, the way to conceive participation in liturgy.

The liturgical subject is deeply implicated in the theme of participation. In fact, the liturgical subject is the 'real man' who *participates* in Church ritual. Participation allows the human subject – who appears here as *homo religiosus* – to recognize the act of God, the divine subject, within ritual, making effective with him an intentionally direct relationship, in an intersubjective and communitarian way. The commonest way of dealing with this theme is to differentiate between 'inward' and 'outward' participation: the presence and the act of Christ in liturgy as its only subject would belong to the inward order of participation, constituting its fundamental and permanent aspect, compared to the multiple possibilities of outwardness.

This model depends on the articulation of the two aspects which do not oppose them, ending up by neutralizing the outward dimension in order to safeguard the rights of inwardness, which, in itself, is not ascertainable. When this occurs and the two aspects are no longer *presupposed* and, consequently, *yield* to one another, the differentiation becomes a dichotomy. In the face of this situation, the recovery of the play between *outwardness which presupposes/yields to inwardness* changes to a reformulation of the set of problems which *makes explicit* the dynamism at work. Now, as we shall see, this may be achieved through *mediation*. To think of participation in terms of the dichotomy between inward and outward inevitably favours one or the other. In this case the prominence of the inward aspect relativizes any outward expression, confirming, at the same time, that in spite of the phenomenological priority of the outward aspect, it would be impossible to maintain its ontological dimension. To secure this aspect, perceived as 'fundamental', one actually loses the 'phenomenon' to be clarified.

In the use which the Liturgical Movement (from 1909, with Lambert Beauduin) made of the term, accentuating its ritual ('outward') character, its spiritual ('inward') foundation was in fact *presupposed*. The question takes on an ecclesiological character. Given the hierarchical society and nature of the Church, the faithful see themselves reduced to mere spectators of a rite executed exclusively by the clergy. This resulted in a call for 'outward' participation in the liturgy: heightening the dialogues, the song, gestures, etc., so as to surpass the mere mute and passive presence of the faithful. But could it be that in this appeal to the outwardness of the liturgy, those who represented the Liturgical Movement reduced the liturgy 'only'[47] to this dimension? *Spiritual reality* is

---

47 'Those who consider liturgy to be *only* an outward and perceptible part of divine service lack an exact perception of it [liturgy]'. *Mediator Dei*, no. 33 (my italics). The

presupposed from the *ritual evidence* of the Church with its call for participation. Therefore the contemporary difficulty is not resolved by affirming one or other aspect, but by *making explicit* what hitherto was simply *presupposed*.

Now according to my hypothesis, the problem increased *due* to the necessity of making it explicit but also because of the need – almost unheard of, but easily understood in a secularized context – of *ritual initiation*. That is to say, the religious ritual is incapable of leading towards the event of salvation which it celebrates because it still constitutes a 'linguistic game' with rules unknown to most of those who are called to participate in it. In its anthropological *evidence,* ritual *may* contain a theological basis. Once this evidence is ignored it is necessary to strengthen the strategy that upholds it: the strategy of *initiation*. But this returns us to the theme of participation: not only because participation encapsulates the goal of initiation, but chiefly because initiation precisely raises the question of the ritual aspect and the spiritual reality in a movement which shows their irreducible difference, making one yield to the other.

In short, the error is connected to the fact that the same term – participation – may indicate *diverse aspects* implied in the *same reality*. In fact, wanting to identify, without further qualification, 'outward' with 'inward' participation (as though by carrying out the former we might automatically accede to the latter) would be to collapse into magic. But to admit an 'inward' participation without any link to 'outward' participation, as though the latter was a religious residue or, at best, a means to express the former is to fall into idolatry. Yet, the expression is still relative to the possibility that by carrying out a religious rite we may come into contact with an event whose effect is salvation. In this sense, participation is equivalent to 'mediation'.

---

outstanding error is not to see liturgy as an 'outward' reality (or, if we wish, *ritual*) but 'only outward'. In the context of the Liturgical Movement, the question emerged strongly, at least on two occasions: in the discussion between the Benedictine Maurice Festugière and the Jesuit Navatel in 1913–14, and, later, with the book by the married couple Maritain about meditation and liturgy. It is obvious that Festugière, though defining liturgy as the *outward* worship of the Church, did not mean to reduce it to mere outwardness. It suffices to note that in the discussion with Navatel the controversial point is not this, but the relationship which outward liturgy may establish with the truth of faith: for Navatel, liturgy was only an occasion to express faith already won, while for Festugière access itself to faith was at stake in outwardness. Forty-five years later, with the book by the married couple Maritain about liturgy and meditation, the problem reappears. In attributing higher status to the 'inward' spiritual dimension of liturgy, to the point of dispensing with cultic outwardness, the Maritains showed, *sub contario*, that they had an 'outward only' perception of worship. Paradoxical, but revealing. On these episodes, see A. Grillo, *Introduzione alla teologia liturgica. Approccio teorico alla liturgia e ai sacramenti cristiani* (Padua: Messaggero, 1999), pp. 117–41 and 151–6.

The way of overcoming the differentiation between inwardness and outwardness is not by subordination of one term to the other. Under the paradigm of anthropological reduction, the accentuation of one of the aspects results in an annulment of the other. In the paradigm of the 'anthropological turn', the task is to construct a bridge that unites the poles in tension, that is to say (from the theological perspective) permitting a *mediatory immediacy*, the Holy Spirit arises as a condition of possibility of Christian mediation, central to liturgy, but also as the opening to its anthropological immediacy. From an anthropological viewpoint, focusing on the relationship between the act of performance and that which is *performed*,[48] participation corresponds to 'mediation' (anthropologically understood as immediacy) of the immediacy (theologically always needful of mediation). A mystical foundation of communion with God constitutes mediation, but when presenting itself, before all else, in its categorical and anthropological aspect, it cannot but appear as something immediate.

If in the description of this correlation between the theological foundation (pneumatological, Christological) and the anthropological dimension (ritual, communitarian) we have properly established the form of our thesis concerning symbolic hermeneutics/dialectics, then in its application we have the possibility of adequately relating 'action' to 'contemplation'. Effectively, participation vindicates in itself the synthesis of the two aspects, and may be described as the blossoming of God's 'contemplation' in human 'action'. To read participation as mediation means that, in its communitarian dimension (that is, participation as necessary in the ritual 'performance', *immediately 'active'*), participation must function as *'contemplative' mediation*; in the same way, in the spiritual dimension (or in participation as access to the grace of God, *immediately 'contemplative'*), it must yield to the first aspect as *'active' mediation*.

In short, we are concerned with avoiding idolatry, whether it consists in confusing rite with the adored God, or, by wishing to safeguard divine transcendence, in betraying it, renouncing each and every mediation. To

---

48 'Without performance there is no ritual, no liturgical order.... Performance is not merely one way to present or express liturgical orders but is itself a crucial aspect or component of the messages those orders carry.... A liturgical order is a sequence of formal acts and utterances, and as such it is realized – made real, made into a *res* – only when those acts are performed and those utterances voiced. This relationship of the act of performance to that which is being performed – that it brings it into being – cannot help but specify as well the relationship of the performer to that which he is performing. He is not merely transmitting messages he finds encoded in the liturgy. He is participating in – that is, *becoming part of* – the order to which his own body and breath give life'. R. A. Rappaport, *Ritual and Religion in the Making of Humanity* (Cambridge and New York: Cambridge University Press, 1999), p. 118.

claim that, by participating *in* ritual, one participates *in* the mystery of God that the ritual celebrates is to claim that one or more 'realities' are involved and converge at a given 'moment' or 'point of encounter'. *Participation* is the term which designates such a moment. Anyone who performs a rite without intending thereby to *surpass* the rite itself, and likewise anyone who thinks that this superiority can *eliminate the* ritual, would fall into the falseness and error constantly denounced by prophecy. *To participate in* ritual, understood under the dialectic of mediation, is to place oneself at that 'point' at which one may *participate in* the mystery of God.

The elements at stake so far are also linked with the way the liturgy is studied. The two overall lines of thought proposed here, namely, 'anthropological appropriation' and 'theological radicalization', do not fully illustrate the relationship between theology and anthropology as a dichotomy, but present them instead in the form of an 'inverted proportion', to the extent that the anthropological perspective does not refuse to reach the theological dimension, while the latter thinks it may get away with only the former. In this sense the liturgical polarity is annulled, leading to a transcendentalizing spiritualization; this renders difficult any hermeneutics of union. On the other hand, the nature of the phenomenon is prevented from indicating its transcendental depth. In these terms, anthropology risks remaining separated from theology, a theology which is then projected onto the ritual as explanatory of its real meaning. In dialogue, theology and anthropology will increasingly become what they really are. The anthropological aim is to indicate man's forgetting his intrinsic relationship to the divine; and the corresponding theological fear is that of 'incarnating' the transcendent – in this consists the epistemological division. Union will come about, and the violence which drove them apart will be calmed. The sign of healing will be, clearly, the permanence of theology and of anthropology as two autonomous, though complementary, spheres of knowledge. Thus in understanding liturgy 'only' as a rite, theology must recapitulate its inner wisdom; forgetting its empirical presuppositions, anthropology must recover its properly anthropological dimension. The path of anthropological appropriation to which theology is invited must be completed in order to free anthropology from its immanent prison, and so provide a phenomenal indication of the immediacy of the theological element at issue in ritual itself.

It is important both to be aware of the presence and action of God in the world and in all life that is postulated by any transcendental method and of the requirement for an immanent method to explain his presence in the liturgy.[49] Therefore, beside a religious phenomenology of ritual,

---

49 See G. Guiver, *Pursuing the Mystery. Worship and Daily Life as Presences of God* (London: SPCK, 1996), p. 49.

one would place the transcendental perusal of the presence of God in daily life, in a mutual 'inter-illumination', highlighting the difference of ritual in relation to daily life and the succeeding difference of the sacred in relation to the profane. In this play of complementarity between the immanent perspective imposed by the category of ritual and the hermeneutics of the transcendental dimension of existence, it is possible to renew the meaning of the anthropological density of ritual in relation to theology and the weight of its believing (and so theological) interpretation to the discipline of anthropology.

From the 'Ontological Symbol' to the 'Symbolic Ontology'

If the authors who develop their thinking from an anthropological perspective succumb to the fear of weakening the theological aspect of liturgy, those who adopt an attitude derived from theological radicalization show no fear of losing the anthropological density of liturgy. The second position is centred exclusively in the *semantic* and *referential* aspect of liturgy, while the first reaction arises from the prevailingly *syntactic* and *structural* character of anthropology in ritual.

The unexplored hypothesis is of a symbolic vision of conjunction, which is precisely what the symbol offers us. The symbol fascinates and, for this reason, the temptation is always to subdue its abundance. If we discover the sense which it conveys, we will easily lose the materiality which weighs it down; and, knowing the symbolic strength of the corporeal, we will with the same ease forget the transcendence that it manifests.[50] But, in the symbol, the 'symbolic reality' and the 'symbolism of reality' are offered to us as a whole, simultaneously. It is here that hermeneutic thought intervenes, open to *symbolic sense*. But if we fail to determine the correlation between the 'significant inwardness' (semantic) and 'significant outwardness' (syntactic) of the symbol, it can be seen that, assuming a perspective in which materiality (categorical) is forgotten, the (transcendental) sense sought is lost, because it loses sight of what it indicates. It is urgent that we propose, therefore, a symbolic hermeneutics where the two aspects can reunite, but this assumes the healing of the epistemological division concealed in the distinction between anthropology and theology, and driving it in the direction of a dialectic where the active and the contemplative complement one another. The symbol is itself characterized by a dynamism that, (not to degrade it in one's imagination) makes us see a phenomenal continuity where an

---

50 At the level of the history of thought, the two tendencies appear linked respectively to *illuminism* and *romanticism*. Cf. S. Maggiani, 'Nella foresta dei simboli. Significato e prospettiva di una ricerca', *Rivista Liturgica* 68 (1980), pp. 291–316.

epistemological division had once existed.[51] In its objectivity the symbol represents, at the same time, a particular subjective prominence: objectively, the symbol tends towards the essence of reality to which it yields; subjectively, in this same movement, personal expectations, attitudes, and vital interests, are involved. Therefore, the objective dimension and subjective resonance join in the same *intentionality*.

Still we must recognize that, in its fragility, the symbol is exposed to two 'religious errors': patent *objectivism* in its supernatural rationalisation and *subjectivism* that arises out of the ingenuity of believing that 'our imagination represents the reality which thought does not reach'.[52] Closely linked with the aim of seizing upon God, both positions converge in the temptation of objectivism: in the guise of 'understanding' (the temptation of 'transparency') which removes the theological pertinence of the symbolic; and in the guise of 'emotion' (the temptation of 'ownership') which exalts the mystical nearness of our heart towards God. The 'direct' experience of the Mystery is invoked, according to Mardones, as a strategy in the face of post-modern uncertainties about the renewal of Christianity. The positive aspect lies in the possibility of relativization of the rational mediations which, made absolute, turn faith into mere belief. The central question for Mardones is whether 'there exists such a direct experience of the Mystery without mediation.'[53] But 'there is no way to escape mediation'[54] without falling into errors that have been denounced. Only by taking the encounter with God as a symbol and, therefore, as something which resists any endeavour to objectify it, may we maintain 'intimate closeness' in the distance of his transcendence.

We must then return to the symbol with a '"second innocence": we must return to the symbol with the spontaneity and innocence of the discovery of the immediacy of the Mystery and with the untrammelled freedom of those who have ignored the critic'.[55] This is not a simple return to the pre-rational, but a flight over reason. Armido Rizzi affirms that 'On one hand, if the symbol leaves causality and Reason behind, on the other, it attains to the order of finality and sense, that is to the identity of the phenomenon and noumenon (of the 'something for us' and the 'something in itself') which we are.[56] In this way the human being has in the symbol the opportunity to uncover himself as a synthe-

---

51 See A. Rizzi, 'Approccio al simbolo. Definizione, competenza, potenza', *Rivista Liturgica* 73 (1986), pp. 11-26, 12.
52 J. M. Mardones, 'La vida del símbolo. La dimensión simbólica de la religión' (Santander: Sal Terrae, 2003), p. 156.
53 Mardones, 'La vida del símbolo', p. 153.
54 Mardones, 'La vida del símbolo', p. 154.
55 Mardones, 'La vida del símbolo', p. 160.
56 Rizzi, 'Approccio al simbolo', p. 23.

sis of subjective–objective convergence in a single intention, from which (according to Rizzi) the following also find themselves:

- the gnoseologic aspect and the existential moment: the symbol appears as the origin of *knowledge,* and its superation in the *sense*;
- language and corporality, coming into harmony, in what touches the symbolic sphere, the ontological perspective and the anthropological one;
- the originating abundance of the sense of the symbol and its unabating flow through hermeneutics, which describe symbolic power.

Rizzi's suggestion may be illustrated by the various discussions that (1) depart from a vision of the symbol in the ontological perspective (Rahner), (2) proceed through the moment of surpassing onto-theology precisely through the symbol united with corporeality and language (Chauvet), on (3) to the recent challenge to recover the 'ontological difference' (Sequeri).

Ontological Foundation and the Linguistic-Symbolic Surpass of Onto-theology

To summarize the whole of the Rahnerian proposal at a single glance, I begin by transcribing six propositions on the symbolic, and I will give an explanation of them afterwards.

1st proposition: 'being is necessarily symbolic to itself, because it necessarily "expresses" itself in order to find its own essence'.[57]

2nd proposition: 'the true and particular symbol (real symbol) is a self-realization, comprising part of its substantial constitution, that of one being in another'.[58]

3rd proposition: the concept of the real symbol is essential for all theological theses, permitting each its proper connotation and its relationship with its fellows.[59]

4th proposition: the act bringing salvation is always God himself (who offers himself to man) accepted by man in the symbol which does not replace this reality but renders it present in a 'manifest' form.[60]

---

57 K. Rahner, 'Sulla teologia del simbolo', in Rahner, *Saggi sui sacramenti e sull'escatologia,* 2nd edition (Rome: Paoline, 1969), pp. 51–107, 57.
58 Rahner, 'Sulla teologia del simbolo', p. 74.
59 See Rahner, 'Sulla teologia del simbolo', p. 94.
60 See Rahner, 'Sulla teologia del simbolo', pp. 94–95.

5th proposition: 'the body is the symbol of the soul while it is formed by the soul as its self-realization (though inadequate); in the body, as in another separate from itself, the soul becomes present and "manifests"'.[61]

6th proposition: in this symbolic union (symbol and thing symbolised), the various parts of the body are not only parts of a quantitative sum, but parts which always comprise the whole.[62]

The first two propositions refer explicitly to the ontology of the symbol in general (thus constituting the point of departure of meditation on symbolic *reality*); the third and fourth propositions are directly concerned with the theological use of the perspective, making evident its Christological root in the reality of incarnation, extended through the Church and the sacraments; the two last propositions constitute an ontological counter-proof, open to the corporality of man as its self-realization.[63] Rahner departs from the principle that, in its plurality, one being may appear as a substantial expression of another. But the plural factors must have among themselves a profound [unity]. A plurality in an originating unity may only be conceived as a 'detachment' within the one, manifesting itself through a plurality in order to find itself.[64] We come to the first proposition whose formal meaning is that the being is

'symbolic' *in itself*. It expresses and owns itself. It manifests itself in the other and by knowing and loving the other, encounters itself, since by adopting the 'other's' immanence it arrives at (or through) its self-realization, which is the assumption (or the act) of the conscious and loving possession of itself.[65]

In this way, too, we understand the value of the second proposition against the background of the *analogia entis*. The concept of being is 'analogous': it indicates the always diverse accomplishment of each being; whereas the being in itself (and therefore the concept and the reality of the symbol) is not univocal, sharing *the Being* with symbolized reality.

---

61 Rahner, 'Sulla teologia del simbolo', p. 99.
62 See Rahner, 'Sulla teologia del simbolo', p. 99.
63 In the economy of the text and the reflection of Rahner, these propositions aim to clarify his point of departure and what also was his opportunity: a theology of the Heart of Jesus.
64 See Rahner, 'Sulla teologia del simbolo', pp. 62–3. Rahner already catches a glimpse here of the Trinity, which constitutes the supreme form of a unity which manifests itself in a plurality.
65 Rahner, 'Sulla teologia del simbolo', p. 66.

In respect of explicit theological interest in the second group of propositions, we must emphasize the *Christological centrality,* from which the analogic succession (Church–sacraments) is detached. In effect, the fundamental affirmation which results from the application of the symbolic perspective in the theological sense (concretely to incarnation) is that Son/Logos is the symbol of the Father, in his own humanity. This means that any created reality speaks for *all* reality, speaking also of God and belonging to him, in Christ, with his substantial determination (as in the incarnation to flesh, which is not only an instrument of divinity). The Church continues in the world this symbolic function of the Logos. Of its essence it participates in the grace of salvation: the Church is then a symbol that contains what it means; it is a primordial sacrament.[66] In the same way, the sacraments make real and bring up to date the symbolic reality of the Church. Concretely, the sacraments cause grace because grace is the cause of the sacraments. The two last propositions develop in the sequence of the Thomist perspective of the soul as a substantial form of *materia prima*. In this sense, the body is seen as the presence of the soul in another, that is, as the self-realization of the soul in *materia prima*. In this way, in each expression of man there is expressed and is present the whole man, though the expressive form owes itself to only one part of the body. The scholastic doctrine of the presence of the soul in each part of the body acquires a new aspect, coming to mean that the soul 'forms part *as* part of the *whole*'.[67]

From a [strictly] ontological perspective, the symbol – as Karl Rahner thinks it – presented itself as common philosophical ground of both the anthropological-transcendental reflection and the Christological, such that it constitutes what we might call a 'third dimension' of his theology.[68] The proposal won approval in recent sacramental theology, opening various further paths of development and enriching the notion of 'analogical succession'. This suggests that the sacraments originate primordially (*Ur*) from Christ the primordial sacrament (*Ursakrament*), and are given fundamentally (*Grundlich*) through the Church (as 'fundamental sacrament' (*Grundsakrament*)), in the specificity of the seven sacraments, themselves expressions of the essence of the Church in relation to Christ – with an anthropological base in harmony with the

---

66 Cf. Rahner, 'Sulla teologia del simbolo', pp. 87–8 (in note 14, page 87, it is explained that the Church is 'a primordial sacrament' in relation to the sacraments and not in relation to Christ, 'fundamental sacrament').

67 Rahner, 'Sulla teologia del simbolo', p. 100. In this way the symbolic designation of one part of the body (the heart) may refer to the whole body (Jesus).

68 Cf. G. Pasquale, *La teologia della Storia della Salvezza nel secolo XX* (Bologna: Dehoniane, 2001), p. 236 (body of text and note 72).

theological perspective.⁶⁹ Grace contains everything and, for this reason, everything may become an expression of grace. This is the result of the synthesis between the theses on the real symbol and the need for a new, non-material concept of the act of grace of God in the world. Yet for Patrick Bosson, in a reading which adequately discerns the ontological dimension of the *Realsymbol,* Rahner does not leap over the categorical, that is, the materiality of grace, but remains there, in a radical way.⁷⁰ Yet one of the most promising ways was what developed as the principle of mediation. The symbol mediates, and reality creates connections which link the subjects as members of social groups and within themselves, giving sense to the world and revealing its identity. Here the symbol endures, as part of the subject which is constituted in the movement of the construction of symbols. This is the perspective in which we place the project of surpassing onto-theology through linguistic and symbolic mediation.

It is in this sense that Chauvet develops a linguistic and symbolic approach to the sacraments. His viewpoint does not gainsay metaphysics, but is set in another epistemological area,⁷¹ where being is not found 'ideologically enclosed in the role of ground as such'.⁷² Chauvet follows Heidegger's discussion of onto-theology and denounces the 'visceral anthropocentrism' which makes 'presence to itself' the measure of the world, according to a utilitarian 'logic of self' which reduces being to reason.⁷³ This kind of philosophy tends to make of language an instrument, so that it appears as a 'translation' of thought; correlatively, sacramental theology can only refer to sacraments in terms of causality and efficacy. Metaphysics must therefore be surpassed, concretely, in Christian theology, as it is faced with the folly of the cross.⁷⁴ Recalling that it is impossible to understand reality in an immediate way, 'reality is never present to us unless it is mediated, that is to say *constructed* through the symbolic network of the culture which shapes us'.⁷⁵ It concerns us therefore to understand language, not as an instrument, but as mediation. From here emerges the paradigm of 'symbolic exchange' (a gift for a gift), where 'the true objects of exchange are the subjects

---

69 Cf. A. Bozzolo, *La teologia sacramentaria dopo Rahner. Il dibattito e i problemi* (Rome: LAS, 1999), pp. 19–70.

70 Cf. P. Bosson, 'La matérialité sacramentelle. Le rapport grâce-sacrement selon une perspective rahnérienne "revisitée"', *Ecclesia Orans* 19 (2002), pp. 111–38.

71 Cf. L.-M. Chauvet, *Symbole et sacrement. Une relecture sacramentelle de l'existence chrétienne* (Paris: Cerf, 1987), p. 15.

72 Chauvet, *Symbole et sacrement*, p. 48.

73 Cf. Chauvet, *Symbole et sacrement*, pp. 32–3.

74 Cf. Chauvet, *Symbole et sacrement*, p. 86.

75 Chauvet, *Symbole et sacrement*, p. 89.

themselves' (alliance).⁷⁶ Hence the theology of grace may converge with symbolic hermeneutics.

The perspective from which the Italian theologian Pierangelo Sequeri develops the theme of the symbolic is multifaceted, lending itself to various possibilities of approach.⁷⁷ In effect, in this operation Sequeri recovers a theory of affects, but also reintegrates ritual in the body of fundamental theology precisely as a modality typical of the exercise of the symbol; concerning the symbol, the author develops a peculiar phenomenology of faith, attending to its 'effectivity' and 'intentionality', directly linked to the 'presence' and to the 'action' of the Lord Jesus in relation to the 'believing conscience'. The confluence of various trajectories of the symbolic demands that the analysis of the perspective defines within it the problem with which Sequeri struggles. It is at this point that the proposal encounters the context of the present study: the interest in the symbolic in Sequeri is 'ancillary' in relation to an ontology discussed from the viewpoint of faith. But it is precisely for this reason that the interest in the symbolic assumes a unique pertinence, without being shaped by a previous ontological view. On the contrary: the symbol leads to beings, whose form of existence is before all else . . . symbolic.

Conclusion

The theoretical elaboration and successive assessment of the pertinence of symbolic hermeneutics outlined here is still to be realized. Meanwhile it already lives in the place where it blossomed, that is, in the symbol itself. The 'form' and 'dynamism' of Christian ritual symbols, in their mediatory and structural capacity for faith may be illustrated by the apparition of the Risen Christ to Thomas (John 20.24–29). The evangelical text does not aim to censure the incredulity of the Apostle, but to explain the form and dynamism of the inscription of faith in our bodies and in our hearts. The text does not aim to say that, unlike the Apostles, Christians of future generations must content themselves by believing without seeing. On the contrary, this episode tells us that with no personal relationship with the Risen One, to the point of 'seeing' and 'touching', it is impossible to be honoured with the joy of faith.

The birth of faith cannot be achieved through the intellect or even through ethics, but only through religion and ritual, in an act that is both

---

76 Chauvet, *Symbole et sacrement*, p. 111.
77 See P. Sequeri, *Il Dio affidabile. Saggio di teologia fondamentale*, 3rd edition (Brescia: Queriniana, 2000), pp. 465–86. 'La presenza e il fare. Ritrattazioni filosofico-teologiche sul modello liturgico della coscienza credente', in *L'arte del celebrare* (Rome: Centro Liturgico Vicenziano, 1999), pp. 21–40. 'Affidabilità di Dio e inaffidabilità del linguaggio?', *Teologia* 25 (2000), pp. 241–56.

inclusive and bonding. Here is the form. In ritual we see the Invisible and touch the Absent, or rather, he appears and manifests himself, allowing himself to be touched by us. It is in this moment that faith is born. Here is the dynamism. If the text supports this kind of understanding, then it also describes to us the peculiar condition of the liturgical subject, as an 'I' determined by the religious form and by the ritual energy of faith, an 'I' who can say with truth: my Lord and my God (cf. John 20.28).

4

What does the 'Roman Rite' Denominate?

LÁSZLÓ DOBSZAY

At first glance an answer to this question seems straightforward enough; however, upon further reflection, it appears almost impossible to answer. One initial response might be that 'the Roman Rite is the official worship of the Roman Church'. But 'official' is that which has been defined as such by the Holy See and is by its very nature a legalistic term. We speak in laudatory tones of the Roman Rite and revere it not simply because it has been granted 'Roman' approval but because there is something real and active which the name 'Roman' endeavours to bring to disclosure and, in so-doing, to preserve.

The essence of the Roman Rite is not to be found in its approbation but in the *material content* of the rite itself. It is this, the content of the rite, which claims a compulsory obedience from us. Individuals, priest or lay, have no authority to interfere with this; if they do, the result is that the name no longer denominates the material content, and an almost irresolvable inner conflict is introduced as, for example, when an erroneous liturgical translation is formally approved. The legalistic approach is inadequate; even if a person obediently follows the regulations in his everyday observances and is well versed in matters of religion and liturgy, he is not thereby exonerated from the duty of pondering the material content of things.

History, Identity, Communication

The history of the Roman Rite is one possible point of departure in any study of the Rite's content. This is not because the Church is a 'museum' (a charge frequently levelled against it) but rather because certain elements of the liturgy find their provenance in Christ's direct commands in whose ordinances something ineffaceable is to be found. But this alone is not sufficient to regulate, nor does it provide a measure for, the liturgy as a whole. While the sacred tradition may witness to revelation and have equal rank with Scripture, it is from the liturgy, nevertheless, that tradition (with the exception of doctrinal decrees) pre-eminently springs. This function of the liturgy is not confined to doctrinal orthodoxy for it is much more than a *lex supplicandi* through which the *lex credendi* manifests itself. Such an interpretation of the relationship between tradition and liturgy is too narrow, if not altogether speculative. The liturgy is not merely the sum of a random collection of liturgical texts, but is, rather, a living organism. It speaks as a totality, like our bodies and other living organisms, being carefully constructed from texts, customs, gestures and rubrics. Such an organism is individual and a kind of singularity or whole. It enables us to speak of the Syrian, Milanese, Coptic or simply Roman liturgies.

Of course, the totality of the liturgy's content is multilayered. Its roots are to be found in the spiritual instincts of mankind, a primordial and ancient human layer inherited from classical antiquity, from the time of Christ and by long convention arising at the most fitting time. This deepest layer originates from and was founded by Christ himself. Another stratum is what we might call our common Christian heritage. For instance, the sequence of the liturgy of the Word, followed by the liturgy of the Eucharist, was not the result of a specific command from Christ. Instead it is a common and basic Christian structure that is to be preserved, less because of a preoccupation with antiquity and more because of its essential theological, cultic and spiritual implications. Historians might detect a 'Latin' stratum, for example, in the genre of liturgical sequences (antiphons, various responsories, etc.) or in the custom of singing the Magnificat at Vespers, a peculiarly Roman feature characteristic of ancient Latin rites and those found, inter alia, in Milan, Iberia, Central Italy (perhaps), North Africa and Gaul.

These common layers are merely abstractions, however, in the absence of an individual liturgical subject, from say Milan or Rome, who is required to breathe life into the rite through the performance of its detail. This is the moment of the liturgy's individuation, the point at which it obtains a distinct identity. It is from this perspective that liturgical detail should be considered, whether it be liturgical terminology, its linguistic background or the configuration of various elements in liturgical celebrations and in time, for example the vestments, the style of gestures, the organization of liturgical space and many other features. In short, it is an ethos or a style that manifests in a physical reality or, in scholastic terms, an essential *form* impressed within the *matter* of the liturgy.

These elements when structured into a totality are constitutive of more than merely external ceremony, first because the elements taken *together* represent sacred tradition in a living and dynamic way. They do not enunciate individual dogmas but rather manifest the interrelation of essential aspects of our faith, the proportions and accents of the spiritual life and an approach to appropriate mental and moral behaviour. A most exquisite explanation of the doctrine of grace is to be found, not in papal decrees, nor in theological monographs, but instead in the post-Pentecostal collects.

Second, the liturgy has the capacity, through its transcending intellectual communication, to transmit the faith in its entirety and in all its human complexity. Its power is not restrained by words and commentaries on the faith but rather does it inspire reverence to God, Church, sacraments and the spiritual life. It educates men to *devotion* (full adherence), *piety* (calm self-surrender) and Christian *humility*, through its ethos and organic life. To reduce the liturgy therefore to a noisy public forum for discussing social problems, to a place for self-realization, is to attack its most essential core.

To the best of my knowledge, *Liturgicam Authenticam* is the first document in recent liturgical legislation that has dared speak of the 'identity and unitary expression', or the ethos, of the Roman Rite. By so doing it has elevated the issue above simply legal considerations and set a new standard. It has shown that the complexity of the Roman Rite (detailed above) has an ineffable quality and ethos that must be defended as much as the elements singled out from the whole. If we had more time it would not be difficult to document the rich religious and spiritual value of the Roman Rite, or dare we say, its cultic and cultural value, which is pre-eminent among associated rites.

Identity and Continuity

With this in mind, our question 'What does the 'Roman Rite' denominate?' becomes more engaging. What ought we to think of when we speak of it . . . the Tridentine Rite? . . . the *Novus Ordo*? . . . both, since both have been approved? And more specifically: is there *anything* with any degree of stasis that can be named 'Roman'? What is the significance of this historical change in the life of the Roman Rite? This problem, now so clearly articulated, was unknown prior to Vatican II. The Council spoke of 'legitimate progress' and 'careful' revision, adding, however, that 'there must be no innovations unless the good of the Church genuinely and certainly requires them' and that 'care must be taken that any new forms adopted should in some way grow organically from forms already existing' (*Sacrosanctum Concilium*, para 23).

It is often said that the liturgy must be adapted to our times. This notion carries with it the implication that in centuries gone by the liturgy was adapted to accommodate the demands of different ages in different regions and that it was only with the Tridentine reforms that this dynamic process started to calcify. The situation remained until Vatican II, which liberated the liturgy once again so that it could respond freely and without reservation to these pastoral pressures.

On the other hand, traditional groups regarded any change as a desecration of the Roman liturgy and were suspicious that an undisclosed theological agenda was at work which posed a dangerous threat to the faith. The Roman Rite lost its unique identity when, for instance, the prayer *'Suscipe sancte Pater'* was excised from the Offertory so that the sacrificial quality of the Mass was compromised if not altogether denied. So much more is at stake here than, let's say, just the omission of Psalm 42 at the beginning of the Mass.

At this juncture we must not neglect the testimony of liturgical history. Quite apart from theological truth, the liturgy has its own *liturgical truth*. Perhaps it is not possible to harm the liturgy as such, only to offend against its truth, the truth of the Roman liturgy. Without doubt, it is more difficult to bring to disclosure these offences, although historical facts may assist with this undertaking.

It is incorrect to assert that Vatican II restored the 'ancient' Christian liturgy. We know very little about what this liturgy might have looked like, although one thing is certain: we can tell from the sermons of the Church Fathers and other sources that the developments following the decrees of the Council were contrary to its spirit. The one outstanding mark of Christian antiquity was its deep reverence for the sacred, so that to desacralize is to profane. The earliest books of the Roman liturgy date back to the eighth or ninth century. With very careful analysis it is possible to draw conclusions, at least in some areas, concerning this earlier period.

It may perhaps come as something of a surprise, but the most stable part of the liturgy of the Mass was the *Antiphonarium Missae*, the order of Proper Chants. The earliest choir-books and the Old Roman graduals, which reflect the seventh-century rite, are almost identical to the *Missale Romanum* which was valid until 1970. After this early period, the repertoire of chants was augmented, to take account of new feasts, with new alleluias and, in exceptional cases, with regional pieces in different genres (e.g. Tracts). Variations start to appear principally with the assignment of communal chants on particular saints' days. The most significant change during the Middle Ages was the emergence of paraliturgical or semi-liturgical genres like tropes and sequences. In many parts these formed valuable repertories which unfortunately were abolished by the Council of Trent.

The *Sacramentaries*, going back to old Roman usage (Gelasianum, Leonianum, Gregorianum) record many more prayers than do the medieval and more recent missals (although everything found in later editions was to be found in earlier ones). These additional prayers are in full harmony with the Roman tradition in both style and in theology. What Rome did in the seventh century was possibly no more than to establish an equilibrium: a rich traditional repertory was properly selected and individual texts were ascribed to given liturgical days. The local and historical variations of the Middle Ages are exceptional but apply only to certain new feasts.

From early times, the sequence of readings was recorded in registers for the forthcoming year. There is a remarkable consistency in the assignation of pericopes to particular days in these early texts. These allocations were regularized in the eighth and ninth centuries from which time regional and historical variations were negligible.

The Roman Rite, as reflected in written documents from this period, is a singular and unchanged *Ordo Missae*; there is no evidence to be found in them of alternating the canons of the Mass. One can, however, distinguish the strictly liturgical parts of the *Ordo* from the silent prayers (*apologiae*) of the priest. For these 'private' prayers a broader repertoire was available than in the late medieval missals or Tridentine texts. They witness in a moving way to the influence the liturgy had on priestly spirituality but can not be taken as integral parts of the Roman liturgy in the same way as, say, can the Canon of the Mass.

Although liturgical documents for the *Divine Office* appear only late in the ninth century, there is nevertheless one text which, though lacking in detail, furnishes information about the Roman Office dating back to a much earlier time. This is the Rule of Saint Benedict of Nursia who describes the Office of the monks living near Rome at the beginning of the sixth century. The frequently cited sentence from Benedict, *'sicut psallit Romana ecclesia'*, (as the Roman Church sings and prays) hints only at the Old Testament weekday canticles. A careful analysis of the Rule, however, comparing it with more ancient sources, clearly reveals that Benedict did *not* create a new Office but merely adapted the rite of Rome to the life of his monks. This rite was in use from the fifth century at the very latest (though possibly, in my opinion, from as early as the late fourth century). This kind of analysis reveals what the Roman Office of some sixteen centuries ago was like. Its essence is constituted of three elements:

1. *The character and structure of the individual Hours.* In this respect there is no difference whatsoever between the early Roman Office and the *Breviarium Romanum* which was in use until 1970.
    a. Lauds and Vespers are ordered as follows:
    Old Testament psalms
    Biblical extracts (the *'capitulum'* often with a responsory) with hymn and versicle.

New Testament Canticle
Closing prayers (according to Benedict's Rule, only the *Kyrie* and the Lord's Prayer).
b. Vigils, or Matins was structured thus:
An invitatory psalm and two or three nocturnes (each with a longer psalmody and readings).
c. The five short daytime Hours
A hymn, three short psalms, a *capitulum* with response and closing prayers, each six to eight minutes long.
These are almost the same each day so that they could be recited by heart.

2. *The distribution of psalms in accordance with the sequence of Hours.* This was a Roman adaptation of a very ancient and commonplace principle. Being a remnant of the old 'Cathedral-Parish Office', fixed psalms were selected for every day in most of the Hours (for the Little Hours, in particular, three of the five morning psalms) or the same psalms for any given day of the week (two psalms from the five daily morning psalms). All other psalms were prayed in the Vigils and Vespers although in a continually running order, namely, in the order divine inspiration gave us in the very form of the Psalter itself. These two principles were blended together perfectly in Rome, and St Benedict changed very little.

3. *The Antiphonale Officii . . . The repertoire of antiphons and responsories with their assignment to days and hours.* Although St Benedict, naturally enough, did not list each and every item nevertheless he hinted at the full range and their assignments. The Antiphonal at this time might have contained, to my reckoning, no more than about 400 antiphons (about 120 in the weekly psalmody, 150 for the solemnities and 100 for Saints' feast days) and about 200 responsories. This remained the basic structure of the Antiphonal until 1970.

In early times the head of the community was more or less free to choose the Office readings. Within a short while, however, the order of biblical readings was fixed: Moses from March onwards; Jeremiah in Passiontide; Acts, Revelation and Catholic letters at Eastertide; the Book of Kings from the end of June; the Books of Wisdom in August; Job, Tobias, Judith and Esther in September; Maccabees in October; the Prophets in November; Isaiah in December and, lastly, St Paul's letters in January. For several centuries no hymn was chanted in the Roman Church, although where it was accepted it was positioned in the same place as given in St Benedict's Rule: before the New Testament canticle in Lauds, Vespers and Compline, and at the other Hours, at the beginning.

WHAT DOES THE 'ROMAN RITE' DENOMINATE?

It is not unreasonable to speculate that, if the sequence of the Office was fixed in the fifth century and remained in use uninterruptedly thereafter, perhaps the Mass in the Roman rite remained unchanged as well over the same long period of time.

Additions, not Modifications

The rite – as defined above – was not modified, but only added to, during the centuries of the Middle Ages. New texts and musical sequences emerged from the Carolingian era and initially were added to the Divine Office. A great part of the Alleluia repertoire and priestly private prayers were composed in this period in addition to the services added to the Mass, such as the liturgy, blessings and procession of the Feast of the Purification and the ceremonies of Ash Wednesday.

The Office antiphonary was added to in a dignified way, with new compositions for Advent, Lent and for individual feasts, in the centuries following the reign of Benedict of Nursia. The process was completed in the Carolingian period with antiphons being added to the *Benedictus* and *Magnificat* and chants to new feasts. This incremental process continued after 1000 at a regional or local level with the veneration of relics, local patron saints etc. The average medieval antiphonary listed between 2,000 and 2,500 antiphons and 1,000 responsories.

Once the Iberian, Galician, Beneventian, etc. rites had ceased to exist, the essential *matter* of the liturgy, including a common liturgical calendar, became uniform everywhere in the Latin church. Local churches, dioceses and religious orders however were affected in a different way by this incremental process and developed stable rites, variants of this Roman Rite, for themselves. This was an extremely important development about which we should say something further.

It was not simply that in the beginning there was a detailed and strictly defined rite which was subsequently varied in response to regional and geographical differences. The truth lies rather in the fact that, in the medieval period, the Roman Rite always implied a combination of a common, universal, essence with local variants.

What constituted its unchanging essence and regional variation was not decided arbitrarily. Rather, it came about as a result of prioritizing certain elements: in the Mass uniformity prevailed; in the Office, however, there was greater opportunity for regional variation. Uniformity characterized the temporal rather than the spiritual. Ancient genres and repertoires, for example, the Introit, were not uncommon. Where regional variations were permitted new genres and repertoires were developed, for example, the Alleluia, the Sequence and new antiphons. Through balancing unchanging essence with regional variation, the unity of the rite was not endangered. Rather each component was endowed with a certain dignity.

In the same way that the Roman Rite was not imposed on local churches by direct pressure from Rome, so regional diversity was not orchestrated as a defiant expression of local independence. Historically, missionaries implanted the Roman Rite within the new churches and conveyed the way of faith. As time passed, however, local churches transmitted their Roman heritage to future generations as if it were their own tradition. 'Rome does things this way' was a formula invoked only in exceptional cases when particular historical events occasioned an application to Rome for guidance. More often diocesan chapters presented the liturgy of Rome to secular clergy as the liturgy of the diocese. 'Local tradition', in this complex sense, with its regional and local devices (*mos patriae*) blended unobtrusively with the more universal and timeless elements. Clear guidelines were established for occasional local decisions, for example, the proper chant of a particular saint could be used if this was contained in a prayer book. Local variations were not unconstrained. The local custom was set by the chapter or, in many cases, the provincial archbishop.

Variations in the medieval liturgy were not random historical developments. Rather, were they the outcomes of slow processes which consequently possessed peculiar liturgical and pastoral value. It is something of a paradox that such variability underlined the importance of a shared and common heritage. When someone visited another diocese the main texts, customs and structures would have been identical with their home diocese. They would have experienced the universality and catholicity of the Roman Rite, and would have been spiritually nourished by these hidden and inner constancies. On the other hand, regional variations coloured local liturgies. The consistency manifested in them though would have been carefully chosen with the exercise of both taste and discernment, so that a visitor might nevertheless feel at home. This feeling would have been expressed and articulated in formulas like '*secundum consuetudinem almae ecclesiae X*', '*secundum chorum nostrum*' and so on.

All that has been said so far can be summarized as follows: once the rite was raised up from being an urban liturgy to manifesting itself as a continental one, it preserved in all its essentials a continuity and self-identity that helped to spawn many daughter rites. '*Astitit regina in dexteris tuis in vestitu deaurato circumdata varietate.*' The Second Vatican Council appreciated this traditional diversity and spoke of it with applause. At least, I suppose, paragraph 37 of *Sacrosanctum Concilium* refers not simply to the pagan rites of exotic peoples, but also to Catholic liturgical traditions:

> The Church ... respects and fosters the genius and talents of the various races and peoples. Provisions shall be made ... for legitimate variations and adaptations to different groups, regions and peoples ... provided that the substantial unity of the Roman Rite is preserved.

The Roman Rite during the Middle Ages represented rich cultural material, though not in the sense of a raw material. It was an ordered complexity, perfected by regional and local best practice, that was repeatedly integrated by prestigious churches into the juridical structures of the liturgy. Temporal and spatial changes were barely perceptible and were no more noticeable than the modifications every 40 or 50 years following the Council of Trent.

The Middle Ages introduced two important innovations in the history of the Roman Rite. On the one hand, the proliferation of 'private' Masses and the private recitation of the Office. Strange as it may sound this has influenced the liturgy up to the present day, for example, in the case of the 'Breviary'.

On the other hand, there have been additions to the liturgy, or rather the composition of para-liturgical practices like the 'Little Offices', various devotional practices, liturgical insertions, local variations of rubrics, etc. With the arrival of the sixteenth century people began to believe that these shows of exuberance were corrosive of the Roman Rite and decided they should be proscribed. In the main, the sixteenth century was characterized by reform: renovation rather than innovation. Restoration and consolidation became urgent concerns not simply because of medieval preoccupations, but because of the liturgical and doctrinal challenges represented by Protestantism. Their purpose was not the transformation of the Roman liturgy, but rather its preservation (though not in an excessively puritanical sense). Although the Council of Trent did not condemn particular branches of the great tradition, these nevertheless disappeared in certain decades, being replaced by new texts edited after the Council. These presented the Roman liturgy not in the hallowed tradition of the great Roman basilicas but in accordance with a variation designed for the Roman Curia, that is, for priests in the Papal administration.

The liturgy of the Curia was based on a format from central Italy, an archaic branch of tradition that excellently represented the Roman Rite although it omitted valuable parts from the liturgical and pastoral tradition. It is not correct to assert an equality between the Tridentine and the Roman Rite nor to think (not entirely innocently) of the former as a liturgy conditioned by the spirit of its times, like a Renaissance or baroque building. The Tridentine Rite, though not unique nor a perfect representation, is nevertheless an excellent form of the Roman Rite. From the seventeenth century the Tridentine Rite prevailed in the Church (except in some Orders) and became *the* Roman Rite in the eyes of many generations. It is the only form today (outside the forms pertaining to the Religious Orders) that has grown organically from the traditional Roman liturgy and which can lawfully be celebrated.

Identity and Discontinuity

Does this mean that every rite denominated 'Roman' is the 'Roman Rite'? No doubt documents pre-dating the sixteenth century describe the rite as essentially identical and continuous with its predecessor, with only minor and barely perceptible variations or developments. The rite before the ninth century should be excluded from these considerations since we have no reliable information or documentation about it. It may even be the unacknowledged precedent to the Roman Rite, the form which gave rise to what followed.

After the sixteenth century the situation is quite different. At the start of that century strange ideas had started to emerge concerning liturgical reform. Although most proposals were presented as motivated by entirely rational concerns, they were nevertheless absurd. (This serves to demonstrate that in spite of the fact the liturgy cannot be contrary to human reason, it draws on deep motivations that are beyond rational argumentation). Some of the 'reformed' liturgies were published privately; others were introduced officially. For example, the Breviary published in the name of Cardinal Quiñones and approved by Rome was fundamentally rationalistically organized and entirely opposed to what we find in liturgical tradition. All its Hours followed the same schema, each with three psalms. Psalms were allocated according to speculative principles far removed from ancient tradition. Non-biblical texts were abolished. It became normative to read the Office in private rather than in community.

If 'Roman' is an adjective used to indicate official approval then this can, in good faith, be called a Roman Office. However, if we focus on its content, its claim to be derived from the Roman rite must seriously be contested. It is merely the outcome of an abrupt and radical transformation, a wilful incursion prompted by speculative reason, rather than an organic and gradual development that is part of the normal rhythm of life and a natural evolution of tradition.

Within 30 years the Quiñones Breviary was prohibited by Rome and had disappeared. In parallel with the use of the Tridentine rite, reforms involving similar experiments were repeatedly attempted. It was principally the French dioceses that promoted these reformed liturgies. Each diocese had its own liturgical proposal which received approval, at least from the bishop. This tendency is well illustrated by the *Breviarium Maurinum* (printed French choir-books). In spite of superficial differences, there were certain common main features in the Neo-Gallican reform liturgies: abrupt changes that disturbed the process of gradual evolution; individual innovations interrupting otherwise integrated Church life and voluntary interventions disrupting organic liturgical developments. The real liturgical renewal of the nineteenth century began as a reaction against these reform liturgies.

Rome herself inflicted bloody wounds upon the liturgy. At the start of the twentieth century the psalms of the Office had been rearranged entirely against the traditional arrangement, and therefore the tradition itself; any sense of the harmony implicit in the ancient structures has now been expunged from the hearts of at least four generations of priests. Four decades later the text of the entire Psalter was (optionally) replaced by the *Psalterium Pianum*, written by a bureau (this regrettable experiment lapsed appropriately into oblivion, though not until after the first edition of the post–70 Breviary). Both experiments affected isolated parts of the Offices, and did no harm to the rite as a whole. They demonstrate the truth that even though no theological error is involved, the rite can nevertheless be damaged.

We are now well positioned to answer the question directing our discussion, namely, what does the 'Roman Rite' denominate? – We would say that it is that common and 1200-year-old heritage continuously evolving and organically developing throughout history. That which disturbs this progression is not Roman, in spite of the fact that juridically it can be denominated as such. With this definition in mind, let us turn our attention now to the relationship between the *Novus Ordo* and the Roman Rite. Disregarding the adoption of the vernacular and the orientation of the altar, the main differences are as follows:

- Although in the *Ordo Missae* the changes were not so radical, in so far as the Ordinary texts remained essentially unchanged, nevertheless, in addition to the Roman Canon, three (if not more) new Canons appeared; private apologies were omitted or replaced and the tradition of gestures, movements, rubrics and ways of assisting largely disappeared.
- Alterations to the Proper of the Mass were more pronounced: the old sequence of readings, the system for assigning texts and the principle for determining the allocation of pericopes to particular liturgical days were all abolished. A three-year cycle, which bore little resemblance to its Roman equivalent (still observed by Lutherans), was introduced.
- The Sacramentary was fundamentally altered. Many new texts were

added, some from old liturgical books (often transcriptions) and others, new compositions with a 'modern' message. What remained was rearranged: in any given year, for example, of the 34 *per annum* Sundays, only five had the same collects as before.
- The Proper Chant – perhaps the most ancient component of the Roman Rite – practically disappeared from the Mass. (By way of background, the 1970 *Missal* is not a copy of chant texts from the *Graduale* (choirbook) but has a different provenance: it often contains new texts in the places where ordinarily the Propers would be sung without any accompanying musical sequences). The new *Graduale Romanum* (which can be replaced by the *Graduale Simplex*) is a rearrangement of the old one, though often with certain passages switched between days. The main problem however is that the *General Instruction* that regulates the rubrics of the Missal allowed the chants of the *Graduale* to be substituted by 'any appropriate song'. The result is that, in 99% of Masses, the liturgical chant texts are no longer chanted. This means the Mass has no set chant texts (except the – newly composed – psalms and responsorial antiphons of the Lectionary); the liturgical message of the daily Mass is no longer borne and conveyed by chant. Chant has become quite independent from the celebration of the liturgy.
- Like the Mass proper, so too the rites of Holy Week have been radically altered (I have discussed this in some detail in my book *The Bugnini-Liturgy*).
- The *Liturgy of the Hours* (the name of the reformed books of the Breviary), although it has preserved some fragments of the *Roman Breviary*, or Offices, is nevertheless a new composition with a different structure and content.
- The liturgy of the Sacraments has likewise been radically altered, although some texts are cited directly from the old text. The changes here have theological repercussions.

Analysing the Intentions

What is the background to these momentous changes? It is not easy to put this into words. The arguments of the Liturgical Constitution are open to various different interpretations: although it can be claimed that they represent the changes intended by the Council, this cannot adequately account for all that happened in the period of reform after the Council took place. Other arguments, in quite different registers and with different accents, are based more on popular opinion than systematically articulated principles. Furthermore, the changes are frequently associated with ideas and ideals that are more psychological than logical. As ideas changed so did the liturgy; the intrusive primacy of rational argument determined liturgical reform.

'Pastoral interest' was the argument frequently put forwards: the liturgy is for the people (and not the people for the liturgy). It must therefore adapt to the changing needs of different generations. It cannot remain rooted in medieval or baroque forms, which perhaps were relevant for their times but which carry little significance for contemporary man.

Advocates of this relativism, however, forget one fact: although we may concede that the liturgy of Trent reflects the mentality of the sixteenth century and was out of date within four centuries, nevertheless, the Tridentine rite is more or less identical with the medieval liturgy and so adequately answered the needs of medieval man. But the medieval liturgy itself is essentially the same as the Carolingian liturgy which in turn is the same as the liturgy of ancient Christian Rome. If this is the case, then to whose needs did the liturgy adequately respond? Was the mentality of sixth-century Christians identical to those who followed in the ninth century? Were the spiritual demands of medieval man the same as those from the sixteenth century? How is it possible for the same liturgy to serve the needs of the seventh-, nineteenth- or twentieth-century Church? Has the mind of late twentieth-century Christians changed so radically that the Roman liturgy, adequate for twelve or fourteen centuries, no longer addresses our contemporary situation? Were the changes between the seventh and tenth centuries any less influential than those between the seventeenth and twentieth?

The chronology concealed in any argument derived from relativism is grounded on false principles for theological, liturgical and anthropological reasons.

While the conditions of our life are closely bound up with everyday events, with social systems and the products of civilization, our salvation (the object of the liturgy) is independent or very loosely associated with these. The things which concern salvation – the Trinity, Heaven, sin, redemption, grace, virtue – are (if we accept them to be really true) beyond the realm of transience. When the liturgy addresses man and his actions, it does not offer concrete advice but speaks *sub specie aeternitatis*. The particulars of any given age merely provide a context for eternal expectations. If 100 years ago somebody gained access to his neighbour's dwelling and stole his personal effects, or if today a hacker gains access to a computer, these two scenarios are indeed very different and rely on different contexts. There were no hackers in the sixth century. From the perspective of the liturgy however there is little difference between the two: both represent infringements of the Seventh Commandment.

The horizon of the liturgy is universal in yet a further sense: sin, grace, God's will, and our response to it. The liturgy is a summary of everything that might happen in our lives irrespective of *how* it happens. If this were not the case then only private liturgies would be valid. Whoever thinks they can draw close to the people by bringing their 'life problems' into the liturgy, falls prey to an illusion. The liturgy speaks to the human soul, not when it addresses the superficialities of everyday existence, but rather when (in a symbolic-abstract way) it touches our deepest reality. It is sufficient to understand that the liturgy touches the primordial realities of human existence and brings relief to everyday suffering. The ebbs and flows of ordinary life thereby find a place in the liturgy.

In respect of the liturgy's content, there is therefore no need for major changes. If the Church authentically presents these basic realities in a traditional liturgy, abstract symbolism allows everyone to immerse their lives within its universality. Tireless efforts to draw close to 'modern man' result in religious kitsch and endanger the liturgy's greatest virtue: reverence for the human soul.

Behind every effort to enshrine everyday life in the texts and actions of the liturgy lurks a crisis in faith. Since our belief in such phenomena as reconciliation and redemption is now lacking, we look to give these words a seemingly 'user-friendly' meaning.

Mediation

The next consideration is liturgical in nature, although it also touches on the strength of faith. A widespread liturgical heresy – which opposes the Council's liturgical constitution *Sacrosanctum Concilium* – reduces the liturgy to a pastoral tool: the liturgy articulates the mind of the congregation and speaks directly to the congregation (here the orientation of celebrant becomes a theological question) and so not directly to God.

The texts of liturgical prayers however address the Lord and speak directly to him. Many priests today refuse to acknowledge this and prefer instead to communicate with the assembly. The truth is that in the liturgy the Church, through Christ, the High Priest, deals, before God himself, with the most important issue confronting human existence, namely, its salvation. Although the following metaphor may appear trivial it does help nevertheless to accentuate one aspect of the matter: the success of a medical operation is not dependent on whether the sick person knows and follows in detail what is happening during surgery. Although he may be anaesthetized the operation is performed for the sake of his health.

Do we really believe that the priest stands before God for our sake, advocating our case before him, offering the one eternal sacrifice for our sins and imploring his grace for us? Or instead do we rather think that, at best, God knows our needs so completely that there is no need to ask anything from him. Even if we concede that the Lord should be petitioned, the ordinary believing individual is quite competent for this on his own and so has no need for a representative before the throne of God. On the contrary, to accept the truth of the liturgy, a profound and supernatural faith is required! Did Christ really have to die to save us from our sins? Can the Mass function as a sacrifice of reconciliation? Or is the whole liturgy merely a theatrical performance? Otherwise we appear to be speaking to God in the name of the Church, whereas really our purpose is to manipulate people in an expression of pastoral efficiency.

The problem may look as though it has been exaggerated. However, the texts of the *Novus Ordo* address the Lord, beseech him for the forgiveness of sins and implore his grace. This approach became common in everyday practice and intruded to some extent into the liturgy itself. For example, the new rite of baptism highlights the responsibility of parents and godparents at the expense of the sacrament's objective function, encapsulated by the formula of the Council of Trent, *'ex opere operato'*.

The liturgy should, however, influence the Christian community, though not in such obvious and direct ways. The 'target' of the liturgy is not only (or even mainly) the faithful assembled here and now. Rather, it nourishes the whole life of the Church: theology, mystical experience, gracious living, spirituality, priestly formation and so on. Everything sustains the religious life of the faithful, in groups or individually. To allow the liturgy direct influence over the immediately present assembly is like having an isolated power supply for each and every item of household electrical equipment. The liturgy works instead like a communal generator which accumulates and then distributes power throughout the Church.

Of course, I do not want to deny the importance of the liturgy's power to educate directly. As we know, it does this both for the praise of the Lord and for the sanctification of man. We might also add that, in a very special way, it forms the Christian mind. But this happens not because of aggressive and militant pastoral activity but because of a deep reverence for the sanctuary of the soul. The liturgy recommends itself to souls, gently persuading me to forget myself so that, with a godlier mind, I might return to everyday life transformed. It is not about the place for *learning* the practices of religious life, but *is* the performance of that life. The warmth of God's love emanates from the liturgy pervading the human soul with the spirit of humility, obedience, mild gladness, serenity and discipline. It is a travesty if violence, arbitrary innovation, creativity, manipulation and technology deprive the faithful of the inestimable blessings of the liturgy.

Salvation and Sanctification

At last we arrive at the anthropological and psychological characteristics of the liturgy. Nobody denies in principle that the content of the liturgy is the matter of salvation, the praise of God and the sanctification of souls. We have seen, however, that the signs, texts, terminology and language which convey this content often appear to be, or are claimed to be, incomprehensible to the contemporary person. Following the Council, we read the counsel of the liturgical reformers that, roughly speaking, vernacular translations revealed obsolete meanings previously hidden by their being in Latin. The demand arose for a new liturgy comprehensible to everyone on first hearing.

The weight of Church history however cautions against this. The substance of the liturgy had always been presented as a hidden wisdom, something given to us that can only be attained through an inward ascent of the soul. The *mystagogia*, through insertion into the mystery, is, generally speaking, more than moral admonition, enthusiastic exhortation or meditation. The *mystagogue* is someone initiated into the mystery. Initiation is performed through the words and action of the mystery. More than anything else, initiation is an ontological process. The mystery is received into one's being, not simply one's intellect. The intellect ascends because of what being already possesses. Intellectual elevation does not rely on sophisticated theological speculation or scientific biblical exegesis. Rather, in a child-like way, we must first utter the holy words and perform the external gestures. If we do this with full devotion, mind and heart engaged with the words and signs, we will learn, through this engagement, what they mean both in an objective sense and to us specifically. This is not the case when words and signs are fabricated for worship and evaluated in accordance with imaginary demands.

First, as we imitate the sign, repeating the word, both sign and word reveal their meaning to the humble soul. This truth has been articulated axiomatically in the Rule of St Benedict: instead of *'a voice concordant with the mind'* (the contemporary ideal) the traditional understanding is that *'the mind is made to concord with the voice'*. A harmony between soul and voice establishes itself not when the soul expresses itself vocally but when it conforms to the sounds placed upon its lips by the Church and the Holy Spirit.

If the content of the liturgy is determined by the demands of a particular group, a given age, a gender or a profession, people remain enclosed within the finitude of their limited worlds. The liturgy is incapable, in these circumstances, of raising up the individual or the community; in expressing themselves they remain what they are. If, however, an individual or community encounters a reality which transcends their particular world, they will grow towards it. This is a general principle of growth. An anthropocentric vision of liturgy encourages fatalism whereas a liturgy-centric vision offers optimistic hope for the future.

One can tread this path from the objectivity of words and signs to the assimilation of their content by entertaining an unshakeable confidence in the efficaciousness of liturgical forms. It is no longer possible to conceive today's liturgy in terms of this group or that priest or a historical committee that happened to obtain official approval.

A liturgy worthy of our reverence has been bequeathed to us from the depths of history, its provenance shrouded in anonymity. Our daily liturgy, in discovering this, recovers its ancient genealogy. Even if we are not wholly immune to the human aspect of the liturgy's development, the feeling of divine origin embedded in tradition is no longer elusive. The books of Moses derived the minutiae of ritual from God's direct utterance.

I remember an occasion when a priest improvised the entire liturgy. When he was asked 'why?', he responded 'the new liturgy was created by people in Rome. Why should I not do the same?' This aberration cannot successfully be challenged through appeal to obedience, liturgical discipline or the provisions of legislation. This would be an affront to the deep and eternal desires of man. The right celebration of the liturgy can be measured only from the perspective of sacred tradition and continuity.

We have seen that the law of continuity does not preclude change, nor should it have done in 1960. Similarly, the universality of the rite does not disallow local variation. Only if the changes are so small that they actively preserve sacred tradition rather than demolish it, can people be raised up to a realm where the Holy Other can be encountered. Likewise, the universality of the liturgy that transcends individual concerns and partisan interests can only be experienced if the relationship between unity and diversity is well ordered. It is not impossible to rediscover the balance between stability and change, between unity and local variation. Only when we recover this delicate equilibrium can the Roman rite be said to be alive again. This is my understanding of the Reform of the Reform.

5

Eucharistic Personalism

EDUARDO J. ECHEVERRIA

In this chapter, I reflect on the relationship between the Church's liturgy and Christian anthropology – its philosophical and theological aspects – in the thought of the Pope John Paul II and the former Joseph Cardinal Ratzinger, now Pope Benedict XVI.

In the first section, I begin by exploring the thesis of Benedict XVI in his study, *A New Song for the Lord*, that the Church's liturgy is in crisis. In particular, he says, there is a loss of focus on the liturgical subject, as a result of a crisis of Christian faith.[1] I follow this with an account of the theology of the liturgy of Benedict XVI and of John Paul II. Especially central to this account is Joseph Cardinal Ratzinger's *The Spirit of the Liturgy*, John Paul II's 2003 encyclical letter, *Ecclesia de Eucharistia* and the 'high doctrine' of the liturgy expressed in the *Catechism of the Catholic Church*.[2]

In my third section, I turn to the philosophical anthropology of John Paul II – Christian personalism as it is found in several papers prior to his election to the papacy.[3] The cosmic meaning of the liturgy has implications for our understanding of the meaning of the Christian life

---

1 Joseph Cardinal Ratzinger, *A New Song for the Lord: Faith in Christ and Liturgy Today*, translated from the German by Martha M. Matesich (New York: Crossroad, 1996), p. 148. Subsequent references to this work (hereafter *NSL*) will be made parenthetically in the text.

2 Joseph Cardinal Ratzinger, *The Spirit of the Liturgy*, translated by John Saward (San Francisco: Ignatius Press, 2000). Subsequent references to this work (hereafter *SL*) will be made parenthetically in the text. In referring to the doctrine of the liturgy in the *Catechism* as 'high doctrine', I am following Aidan Nichols OP, *The Service of Glory: The Catechism of the Catholic Church on Worship, Ethics, Spirituality* (Steubenville, Ohio: Franciscan University Press, 1997), p. 3.

3 My chief source in this essay for Karol Wojtyla's philosophical anthropology is in the collection entitled, *Person and Community: Selected Essays*, translated by Theresa Sandok OSM (New York: Peter Lang, 1993), pp. 197–261, 'Participation or Alienation?' (1975), 'Subjectivity and the Irreducible in the Human Being' (1975), 'The Person: Subject and Community' (1976); pp. 315–61, 'The Family as a Community of Persons' (1974), 'Parenthood as a Community of Persons' (1975), and 'Pastoral Reflections on the Family' (1975). Subsequent references to this work (hereafter *PC*) will be made parenthetically in the text.

and of human existence itself, and vice versa: that understanding also shapes our theology of the liturgy. I propose that Christian personalism, as John Paul II understands its bearing particularly on the relationship of person and community, and of self-transcendence and self-fulfilment, can contribute to the rediscovery of the Church as *communio* and hence to the renewal of the Church's liturgy.[4]

'Alienation', philosopher Roger Scruton tells us, is about 'the isolated individual, his quest for home and community or his lapse into solitude and estrangement'.[5] Against this background, I will also explore John Paul II's account of human alienation and also of participation in community, both interpersonal community and social community, and which, as the antithesis of alienation, is 'a necessary condition for an authentic *communio personarum*' (*PC*, p. 255). Of course, for John Paul II, the concept of *communio* is an analogical concept. The primary analogate is Trinitarian communion from whence is derived the Christian theological meaning that is inherently connected with eucharistic communion: 'a *sacramentum communionis*', says John Paul II, 'between Christ and his disciples – between God and human beings' (*PC*, p. 320). In this light, we can understand why John Paul II, writing as Karol Wojtyła shortly after the Second Vatican Council, affirms the overcoming of human alienation in Jesus Christ. Christ not only reveals to us the living God himself, but also reveals man to himself by singling him out and calling him into communion with the Father, in Christ and through the Holy Spirit. Put differently, there is no true self-knowledge apart from Jesus Christ because in him alone we have the answer to the question that is every human life.[6]

Finally, I conclude with Benedict XVI's view regarding what he calls 'Eucharistic Personalism' (*SL*, p. 87) and the concomitant notion of 'Eucharistic communion', which is the mystery of the communion of believers in Christ, in the Church that is his Body. This view enriches John Paul II's account of alienation and its overcoming in Christ. Our society is full of people who live as 'strangers in a society of strangers'.[7] They long for community, to come home to their true community, 'the homeland of the heart'.[8] The longing of these strangers will be fulfilled

---

4 On this, see the late Msgr Luigi Giussani, *Why the Church?* translated by Viviane Hewitt (Montreal & Kingston: McGill-Queen's University Press, 2001). Especially helpful was Romano Guardini, *The Church and The Catholic and The Spirit of the Liturgy*, translated by Ada Lane (New York: Sheed & Ward, 1935).

5 Roger Scruton, *Modern Culture* (New York: Continuum, 1998), p. 18.

6 This is Wojtyła's gloss on *Gaudium et Spes*, no. 22, 'The truth is that only in the mystery of the Incarnate Word does the mystery of man take on light,' which is later to be the *leitmotif* of John Paul II's pontificate of almost 27 years.

7 Scruton, *Modern Culture*, p. 28.

8 Joseph Cardinal Ratzinger, 'Theology of the Liturgy', http://www.oriensjournal.com/11librat.html, p. 8.

by rediscovering the centrality of God, revealed in Jesus Christ as a Trinitarian communion of persons, in the Church and in their lives. This divine community, which is the ultimate relationship, is the new and reborn humanity in Christ, namely, the eucharistic communion, the Church, called into existence by God, who not only called me into existence but also continues to call me to give myself completely to him by 'becoming one with the self-giving of Jesus Christ, with his great act of love, which is as such the true worship of God', in the words of the future Pope Benedict XVI.[9]

The Crisis of the Liturgy: The Liturgical Subject

In *The Spirit of the Liturgy*, Joseph Cardinal Ratzinger develops a foundational theology of the liturgy in which the subject of the liturgy is God's saving deeds in and through the economy of redemptive history. The liturgy, in his account, is also cosmic in scope. It has a Christ-centred meaning: Christ restoring all of fallen creation into communion with God. It is also ultimately grounded in a Trinitarian way as the work of God, of the Holy Trinity, Father, Son and Holy Spirit.

Especially important in Ratzinger's theology of the liturgy is that liturgical acts of worship, being acts of adoration, are a *response* of gratitude and thanksgiving,[10] in faith, to God inasmuch as these acts sacramentally *participate* in Jesus Christ's historical, redemptive actions, that is, God's special revelation of himself in and through the finished saving work of Christ – the paschal mystery of his blessed passion, death, resurrection from the dead, and glorious ascension. Without the revelation of God in Jesus Christ on Calvary as the saving event in which the liturgy is anchored, the liturgy threatens to become a work of man, indeed a mere ritual, rather than 'the feast in which the great reality comes to us that we ourselves do not manufacture but receive as a gift.' Liturgy as mere ritual 'is a house built on sand', Ratzinger adds, 'and remains totally empty, however much human artistry may adorn it' (*SL*, pp. 167–8). Ratzinger explains:

> Man himself cannot simply 'make' worship. If God does not reveal himself, man is clutching empty space. Moses says to Pharaoh: '[W]e do not know with what we must serve the Lord' (Exodus 10:26).

---

9 Joseph Cardinal Ratzinger, *Pilgrim Fellowship of Faith: The Church as Communion*, edited by Stephan Otto Horn and Vinzenz Pfnür, translated by Henry Taylor (San Francisco: Ignatius Press, 2005), p. 112. Subsequent references to this work (hereafter *PFF*) will be made parenthetically in the text.

10 *Catechism of the Catholic Church* (hereafter CCC in text), no. 2367: 'Eucharist means first of all "thanksgiving".'

These words display a fundamental law of all liturgy. When God does not reveal himself, man can, of course, from the sense of God within him, build altars 'to the unknown god' (cf. Acts 17:23). He can reach out toward God in his thinking and try to feel his way towards him. But real liturgy implies that God responds and reveals how we can worship him. In any form, liturgy includes some kind of 'institution.' It cannot spring from imagination, our own creativity – then it would remain just a cry in the dark or mere self-affirmation. Liturgy implies a real relationship with Another, who reveals himself to us and gives our existence a new direction. (*SL*, pp. 21–2)

Expressed here in this passage is a key theme of Ratzinger's writings on the liturgy: the liturgy is *not* the work of man, but rather the 'work of God' (CCC, no. 1069). This emphasis on the liturgy as the work of God does not preclude human mediation and development of liturgical life. He writes: 'Christians know that God has spoken through man and that the human and historical factor is, therefore, part of the way God acts.... That is why there can be development in the "Divine Liturgy," a development, though, that takes place without haste or aggressive intervention, like the grain that grows "of itself" in the earth [cf. Mark 4.28]' (*SL*, p. 169). Ratzinger's proposal here encourages us to think of the liturgy's development as a living organism, so to speak, which in its origin already contains its essential identity. As the Fathers of the Second Vatican Council wrote in *Sacrosanctum Concilium*: 'For the liturgy is made up of unchangeable elements divinely instituted, and of elements subject to change. These latter not only may be changed but ought to be changed with the passage of time, if they have suffered from the intrusion of anything out of harmony with the inner nature of the liturgy.'[11]

Also, Ratzinger's emphasis on the sacred liturgy as the work of God does not overlook one of the main ideas of the Second Vatican Council regarding the renewal of the liturgy, namely, the concept of 'active participation'. 'Mother Church earnestly desires that all the faithful should be led to that full, conscious, and active participation in liturgical celebrations that is demanded by the very nature of the liturgy, and to which the Christian people, "a chosen race, a royal priesthood, a holy nation, a redeemed people" (1 Pet. 2.9, 4–5) have a right and obligation by reason of their baptism.'[12] Although the council quite rightly stressed the 'active participation' of the whole holy people of God, says Ratzinger, questions remain regarding the meaning of this participation.

For one thing, Ratzinger judges, 'Unfortunately, the word [participation] was very quickly misunderstood to mean something external,

---

11 Vatican II, *Sacrosanctum Concilium*, 4 December 1963, no. 21.
12 *Sacrosanctum Concilium*, no. 14.

entailing a need for general activity, as if as many people as possible, as often as possible, should be visibly engaged in action' (*SL*, p. 171). Yes, the whole people of God are called to participate in the liturgy, with participating referring to 'principal action in which everyone has a "part."' But to understand precisely what active participation involves, says Ratzinger, 'we need, first of all, to determine what this central *actio* is in which all the members of the community are supposed to participate' (*SL*, p. 171). What, then, is the central action of the sacred liturgy?

> The real 'action' in the liturgy in which we are all supposed to participate is the action of God himself. This is what is new and distinctive about the Christian liturgy: God himself acts and does what is essential. He inaugurates the new creation, makes himself accessible to us, so that, through the things of the earth, through our gifts, we can communicate with him in a personal way. But how can we participate, have a part, in this action? Are not God and man completely incommensurable? Can man, the finite and sinful one, cooperate with God, the Infinite and Holy One? Yes, he can, precisely because God himself has become man, become his body to us who live in the body. The whole event of the Incarnation, Cross, Resurrection, and Second Coming is present as the way by which God draws man into co-operation with himself (*SL*, p. 173).

Now, given Ratzinger's understanding of liturgical participation, namely, that it consists in the 'full, active participation of all God's holy people' in the work of God, we can easily understand why he stresses that the true liturgical action is the *actio Christi*. 'The decisive factor, therefore, is the primacy of Christology,' that is, it is Christ himself, the Word made flesh, Christ crucified and glorified, who acts in and through the Church's liturgy.[13] 'Liturgy is', he adds, 'God's work or it does not exist at all.' 'Liturgy', in other words, 'presupposes ... that the heavens have been opened; only if this is the case is there liturgy at all. If the heavens are not open, then whatever liturgy was is reduced to role-playing and, in the end, to a trivial pursuit of congregational self-fulfilment in which nothing really happens' (*NSL*, p. 170). Liturgical actions, therefore, have meaning only in relation to Christ's historical redeeming acts, to saving events that really happened. Otherwise: 'Without the Cross and Resurrection, Christian worship is null and void, and a theology of liturgy that omitted any reference to them would really just be talking about an empty game' (*SL*, p. 55).

Precisely the priority of the *divine initiative*, the *givenness* of the

---

13 On this, see Msgr Luigi Giussani, *Why the Church?*, pp. 193–4.

liturgy in divine revelation, Ratzinger insists (*SL*, p. 165), threatens to recede behind the emphasis that *human beings are the main actors of the liturgy.* Rather than '[T]he liturgy [being] *opus Dei* in which God himself first acts and we become redeemed people precisely through [and in response to] his [prior] action' (*NSL*, p. 148), liturgical actions appear to be sociologically regarded almost exclusively as merely group rituals concerned chiefly with the upbuilding of a community. Furthermore, the dimension of divine mystery in the reality of the Church as the convocation (from the Latin for 'being called') of men in Christ threatens to disappear behind the emphasis that each assembly, or parish community, is an autonomous and self-constituting group, which is congregationalism. The Church herself is '*convocatio* before being *congregatio.*'[14] She is first a convocation of people elected and called by God, the reborn humanity in Christ, brought together by His divine election and covenant to share in his divine life revealed in Jesus Christ as a Trinitarian communion of persons, prior to being an assembly or congregation of people who have accepted the gospel.[15]

Ratzinger argues that driving this conception of the 'liturgy of the group', as he calls it, is an anti-institutional motive: an idea of freedom and its logical corollary of human rational mastery over the liturgy, making such a liturgy an opponent of the Church that, on this conception, 'appears only as an institution, as a bearer of power and thus as an opponent of freedom and a hindrance to redemption' (*NSL*, p. 147). In sum: 'Where all act so that all may themselves be subjects [read: so that each person may come into his own as an active participant in the liturgy], *the One who truly acts in the liturgy also disappears with the collective subject, the Church*' (*NSL*, p. 148; italics added).

Moreover, the liturgy of the group seems to have lost sight of the liturgy's cosmic dimension – 'the liturgy embraces everything in existence', as Fr Romano Guardini once famously put it,[16] in so far as Christ's one single sacrifice, offered on Calvary and in the Eucharist, reconciles the entire fallen created world in a return to the Father. (CCC, no. 1367). As John Paul II wrote in *Ecclesia de Eucharistia,*

> The Eucharist is always in some way celebrated *on the altar of the world.* It unites heaven and earth. It embraces and permeates all

---

14 So rightly says Fr Henri de Lubac SJ, *Catholicism: Christ and the Common Destiny of Man*, translated by L. C. Sheppard and E. Englund (San Francisco: Ignatius Press, 1988), p. 64. On the Church as 'convocation,' see also CCC, nos. 751-2, 760.

15 On the important difference between 'convocatio' and 'congregatio', see Msgr Luigi Giussani, *Why the Church?*, p. 84. See also, Vatican II, *Lumen Gentium*, 21 November 1964, no. 9.

16 Romano Guardini, *The Church and The Catholic and The Spirit of the Liturgy*, p. 29.

creation. The Son of God became man in order to restore all creation, in one supreme act of praise to the One who made it from nothing. He, the Eternal High Priest who by the blood of his cross entered the eternal sanctuary, thus gives back to the Creator and Father all [fallen] creation redeemed.[17]

Thus, the 'Theodrama' described here by John Paul II involves the reciprocity between the cosmos and history, between creation and redemption as ordered to one another, such that, as Ratzinger puts it, 'Creation looks toward the covenant, but the covenant completes [fulfils] creation and does not simply exist along with it', with grace restoring nature, indeed 'the whole of reality into communion with God' (SL, p. 27). Guardini, to whom John Paul II and Benedict XVI are indebted, elaborates:

The liturgy is throughout reality. ... In it man is confronted with physical realities – men, things, ceremonies, ornaments – and with metaphysical realities – a real Christ, real grace. ... [T]he liturgy embraces everything in existence, ... all the contents and events of life; in short, the whole of reality. Creation as a whole embraced in the relation with God established by prayer; the fullness of nature, evoked and transfigured by the fullness of grace, organized by the organic law of the Triune God, and steadily growing to a rhythm perfectly simple yet infinitely rich; the vessel and expression of the life of Christ and the Christian – this is the liturgy. The liturgy is creation, redeemed and at prayer, because it is the Church at prayer.[18]

In addition, with its emphasis on human beings as the main actors of the liturgy, the liturgy of the group threatens to collapse into an *anthropological reduction*: 'the primary subject of the liturgy is neither God nor Christ, but the "we" of the ones celebrating' (NSL, p. 39). But, Ratzinger urges, 'The beginning of the liturgical event never lies in us' (NSL, p. 150). That is, it is not a 'self-initiated and self-seeking worship' ... or 'a festival of self-affirmation' (SL, p. 23). Rather, 'it is a response to an initiative coming from above, to a call and an act of love which is [the paschal] mystery' (NSL, p. 150). Thus, this conception of the liturgy of the group, says Ratzinger elsewhere, has 'apparently lost sight of the fact that the liturgy is actually "done" for God and not for ourselves.' Ironically, he adds, '[t]he more we do it for ourselves, however, the less it attracts people, because everyone can clearly sense that what is essential

---

17 John Paul II, 2003 Encyclical Letter, *Ecclesia de Eucharistia*, no. 8.
18 Romano Guardini, *The Church and The Catholic and The Spirit of the Liturgy*, pp. 29–31.

is increasingly eluding us' (*PFF*, p. 126). What is essential in the liturgy is 'participation in the Trinitarian dialogue of Father, Son, and Holy Spirit; only in this way is it not our "doing," but *opus Dei* – God's action in us and with us' (*NSL*, p. 149). In addition, the threat of anthropological reduction is exacerbated by Deism: the image of God as an absentee landlord who neither takes care of the individual nor really acts in the world.[19] Conversely, the concept of sin altogether disappears because human acts could not offend a God who no longer has anything to do with us. Consequently, 'there is really no further need for redemption in the classical sense [expiatory sacrifice, vicarious substitutionary satisfaction] of Christian faith since it hardly occurs to anyone to see sin as the cause of the misery in the world and in one's own life.' Furthermore, in this light, 'there can naturally be no Son of God either who comes into the world to redeem us from sin and who for this [sin] dies on the cross' (*NSL*, p. 38–9).

Thus, given the crisis of faith, the liturgy degenerates into what theologian Aidan Nichols, following Ratzinger, has called 'liturgical horizontalism'[20] or 'cultic immanentism'.[21] These terms refer to reductionist views of the liturgy. Liturgical horizontalism is the fruit of a non-doctrinal Catholicism, a this-worldly mentality, and a social gospel of justice and peace, which is chiefly concerned with the transformation of society itself as the purpose of the liturgy. Cultic immanentism refers to the idea of liturgical participation that focuses on turning 'towards the assembly [so] that we often forget to turn ourselves, together, people and priests, towards God! Yet, without this essential orientation [toward God], the celebration no longer has any Christian meaning.'[22] In short, the latter, in particular, means to describe the gospel as a this-worldly self-liberation, either political/collective or psychological/individual, based on a non-doctrinal Christianity. Central doctrines such as Christ's atoning death, justification, repentance, conversion, along with holiness of life and bearing witness to the saving events of Christ's life, death, resurrection and ascension are either watered-down or, implicitly or explicitly,

---

19 Regarding the deistic notion of God's remoteness from the world and hence a loss of his presence, see Ratzinger's Preface to the 2000 edition of *Introduction to Christianity*, translated by J. R. Foster, published with a new preface [2000] (San Francisco: Ignatius Press, [1968] 2004), p. 28.

20 Aidan Nichols OP, *Christendom Awake: On Reenergizing the Church in Culture* (Grand Rapids, MI: Eerdmans, 1999), 'Re-enchanting the Liturgy,' pp, 21–39, and for this phrase, p. 26.

21 Aidan Nichols OP, *Looking at the Liturgy: A Critical View of its Contemporary Form* (San Francisco: Ignatius, 1996), p. 97.

22 Cardinal Albert Decourtray, 'Mystère et morale', in *Documentation Catholique* for 21 June 1992, p. 613, as cited in Aidan Nichols OP, *Christendom Awake*, 'Re-enchanting the Liturgy', p. 37.

called into question. Cultic immanentism is chiefly concerned either with the social good of making a better world (by promoting the so-called gospel values of inclusion, tolerance and diversity) or the personal peace of positive thinking and self-affirmation ('I'm okay; you're okay').[23] 'In both schemes', says Nichols, 'the one collective, the other individual, redemption becomes auto-liberation by reference to Jesus as human model, and the Church and her worship loses their salvific meaning.'[24]

Ratzinger, whom Nichols follows closely here, adds: 'This Jesus *has* not redeemed us, but he can be a role model for the way redemption or liberation comes about. If, however, there is no already bestowed gift of redemption to convey, but only instructions for our self-redemption, then the Church as commonly understood is an absurdity, indeed an outrage. She then has no authority in and of herself; under these circumstances the authority she does claim is merely assumed power. She should become a place of "freedom" in the psychological or political sense instead' (*NSL*, p. 38).

On this view of the gospel and hence the liturgy, Nichols explains,

> there is inadequate advertence to that supreme act whereby the divine transcendence engaged itself in Trinitarian fashion for our definitive salvation on Calvary, when the Son offered himself to the Father in the Spirit so that his Sacrifice could be fruitful in the renewed pouring out of himself in the propitiatory intercession of the Eucharist and its foundation in his High Priestly prayer in the heavens.[25]

This 'inadequate advertence', which results in 'the truncation of liturgical consciousness', derives, partly, from attempts to separate the Jesus of history and the Christ of faith – the humanity of Jesus apart from the incarnational narrative, a Jesus of history apart from the full

---

23 Joseph Cardinal Ratzinger, *PFF*, p. 111, 'Anyone who wants Christianity to be just a joyful message in which there can be no threat of the judgement is distorting it. Faith does not reinforce the pride of a sleeping conscience, the vainglory of people who make their own wishes the norm for their life, and who thus refashion grace so as to devalue both God and man, because God can then in any case only approve, and is only allowed to approve, everything.' The good news of the gospel of Jesus Christ is, however, adds Ratzinger: 'Yet any one of us who is suffering and struggling can be certain that "God is greater than our hearts" (1 John 3.20) and that whatever my failures, I may be full of confident trust, *because Christ suffered for me, too, and has already paid the price [of my sins] for me*' (italics added). Ratzinger distinguishes here, clearly, between a theology of divine acceptance and a theology of divine redemption. On the practical difference between these two theologies, see Philip Turner, 'An Unworkable Theology', *First Things* 154 (June/July 2005), pp. 10–12.
24 Aidan Nichols OP, *Christendom Awake*, p. 27.
25 Aidan Nichols OP, *Looking at the Liturgy*, p. 68.

biblical portrait of Christ in the Old and New Testaments. And this, in turn, derives from the huge failure to understand the Christian doctrine of redemption. 'The ideas of expiation, supplication and reparatory satisfaction central to the Atonement and so to the sacrifice of the altar, the midpoint of the entire Liturgy, say nothing to the modern West.'[26] As Ratzinger adds, 'What the word Christ or Messiah denotes is not part of their lives and this remains an empty formula. In this way the profession that Jesus is Christ falls by the wayside all by itself' (*NSL*, p. 37).

Against the background of these reductionist views of the liturgy, we can easily understand Ratzinger's criticism of the misguided 'attempt to replace "orthodoxy" by "orthopraxy" – there is no common [Christian] faith any more (*because truth is unattainable*), only common praxis' (*SL*, p. 155; italics added). This shift from 'orthodoxy' to 'orthopraxis' is motivated, suggests Ratzinger, by scepticism in the truth-attaining capacities of human reason, by an anti-metaphysical and anti-doctrinal mentality. This scepticism not only totally opposes faith and reason, but also implies that faith does not involve holding certain propositions to be true; an implication that leaves faith's belief content devoid of reality, as a consequence of being divorced from the truth. Thus, what ultimately concerns us in matters of faith is what we do, *not* what we affirm to be true. But if what we do (common liturgical, moral, social practices, however defined), takes precedence, irrespective of metaphysical or doctrinal commitments, then the objective reality that gives them their point becomes secondary, and thus we begin to lose our grounding in truth and, in consequence, these common practices become anthropocentric. This is why Ratzinger writes critically of the shift from orthodoxy to orthopraxis. 'For if the word "orthopraxis" is pushed to its most radical meaning, it presumes that no truth exists that is antecedent to praxis but rather that truth can be established only on the basis of correct praxis.' 'Theology becomes then no more than a guide to action', Ratzinger adds, 'which, by reflecting on praxis, continually develops new modes of praxis. If not only redemption but truth as well is regarded as "*post hoc*," then truth becomes the product of man.'[27] In other words, what we hold to be true as Christians becomes a creation out of common practices, rather than, as avowed metaphysical realist Ratzinger says, a reflection of the way things are. Put differently, says Ratzinger elsewhere, *ethos* has taken precedence over *logos*, which

---

26 Aidan Nichols OP, *Christendom Awake*, p. 27.
27 Joseph Cardinal Ratzinger, *Principles of Catholic Theology*, translated by Sister Mary Francis McCarthy SND (San Francisco: Ignatius Press, 1987[1982]), pp. 315–22, and for this quote, p. 318.

also brings about an anthropocentric shift in the understanding of theology.[28] He explains:

> In the early 1920s, Romano Guardini spoke of the primacy of *logos* over *ethos*, intending thereby to defend the Thomistic position of *scientia speculativa*: a view of theology in which the meaning of Christocentrism consists in transcending oneself and, through the *history* of God's dealings with mankind, making possible the encounter with the *being* [and truth] of God himself.... Such a metaphysical (ontological) alignment of theology is not, as we have long feared, a betrayal of salvation history. On the contrary, if theology will remain true to its historical beginning, to the salvation even in Christ to which the Bible bears witness, it must transcend history and speak ultimately of God himself. If it will remain true to the *practical* content of the gospel, which is the salvation of mankind, it must first be a *scientia speculativa*; it cannot start by being a *scientia practica*. It must preserve the primacy of the truth that is self-subsistent and that must be discovered [as it is in itself] before it can be measured in terms of its usefulness to mankind.[29]

What, then, does the replacement of orthodoxy with orthopraxis mean in relation to Ratzinger's theology of the liturgy? For one thing, it means that the human person is no longer bound to the truth that transcends him: the selfsame Logos through whom all things were made also became flesh in history so that all things in redemption were accomplished through him (cf. *NSL*, p. 173). 'The confession of Jesus Christ as Logos (Word) means that in him God himself is revealed, the truth of all things.'[30]

For another, it implies that there is no cosmic meaning: 'The Word incarnate in Christ, the Logos, is not just the power that gives meaning to the individual, not even just the power that gives meaning to history. No, he is the creative Meaning from which the universe comes and which the universe, the cosmos, reflects' (*SL*, p. 151). If there is no Christ, the Word, the Logos, the great Meaning that creates and sustains all life,

---

28 On this, see Fr Romano Guardini, whom Ratzinger closely follows, *The Church and The Catholic and The Spirit of the Liturgy*, 'The Primacy of the Logos over the Ethos,' pp. 199–211. For Ratzinger's extended reflections on the epistemological issues arising here, see *Introduction to Christianity*, pp. 39–81. See also, *Principles of Catholic Theology*, pp. 315–64; and, most recently, *Truth and Tolerance: Christian Belief and World Religions*, translated by Henry Taylor (San Francisco: Ignatius Press, 2004).

29 Joseph Cardinal Ratzinger, *Principles of Catholic Theology*, pp. 319–20, and for a more extensive and instructive discussion on the relation between metaphysics and salvation history, see pp. 153–90.

30 Joseph Cardinal Ratzinger, *Principles of Catholic Theology*, p. 338.

then 'nothing meaningful at all precedes human existence' (NSL, p. 133), according to Ratzinger. In particular, absent the Logos we are left with 'the dissolution of reason into an irrationally understood cosmos' (NSL, p. 173). Man swings back and becomes self-centred, says Ratzinger, disintegrating into the 'intoxication of the senses' that 'crushes rationality' (SL, p. 150).

Furthermore, since the human person is no longer 'primarily receptive – it does not receive, but is only productive' (NSL, p. 133), his creative freedom becomes meaningless, absurd and untrue. 'The dissolution of the [rational] subject, which coincides for us today with radical forms of subjectivism, has led to "deconstructionism" – the anarchistic theory of art' (SL, p. 155).[31] 'In this way', Ratzinger explains, 'it becomes apparent that human creativity that does not want to be receptivity and participation [being bound to a truth that transcends man] is by its very nature absurd and untrue since humans can only be themselves through receptivity and participation. Such creativity is a flight from the *conditio humana* and therefore untruth. This is the reason why cultural disintegration begins wherever faith in God disappears and a professed ratio of being [*Vernunft des Seins*] is automatically called into question' (NSL, p. 151).

Is it any wonder that Ratzinger calls for the reversal of the course of contemporary Christianity: the primacy of the *Logos* over the *Ethos*. The cosmic character of the liturgy that always has God as its ultimate end is grounded in the ordering of all Christian worship to the *Logos*. 'Perhaps this will help us to overcome the unbounded inflation of subjectivity and to recognize once more that a relationship with the Logos, who was at the beginning, brings salvation to the subject, that is, to the person. At the same time it puts us into a true relationship of communion that is ultimately grounded in Trinitarian love' (SL, p. 155).

---

[31] What is 'deconstructionism,' according to Ratzinger? He doesn't actually say, but I surmise that he would agree that 'deconstructionist theology' (to use Roger Scruton's phrase) includes the following claims: '(1) There is no legitimacy or authority in the world, but only human constructs, whose foundation is power. (2) There is no truth, but only "truth" in inverted commas . . . (3) There is no "transcendental creator", nothing that produces what we perceive (the "text") apart from those who read it. . . (4) In particular, there is no meaning . . . The world is haunted by absence, by the Nothingness of Sartre and Heidegger . . . (5) Thus is inverted the central idea of our religious tradition: the idea of a sacred utterance, the Word of God, enshrined in a text. The text remains sacred, but is no longer the word (the *logos*). It is the absence of the word, the "taking back" of God's primeval utterance. . . (6) However, while truth, legitimacy, authority, objectivity, meaning and reality all slip into the void, one thing remains: the skeleton on which these masks were hung, which is power . . .' (*Modern Culture*, pp. 145–6). Most relevant for a theology of liturgy, Scruton writes: 'The god of deconstruction is not a "real presence", in the Christian sense, but an absence: a negativity. The revelation of the god is a revelation, so to speak, of a transcendental emptiness, an unmeaning, where meaning should have been' (p. 144).

The Cosmic Drama of the Church's Liturgy: Creator and Redeemer, Nature and Grace

A proper theological understanding of the cosmic drama of the Church's sacred liturgy requires us to grasp this essential point, 'The creator and redeemer is one and the same God.' 'In redemption', adds Ratzinger, 'he [God] does not take creation back but rather makes it whole and raises it up.'[32] Utilizing the conceptual framework of the going out and return, of *exitus* and *reditus*, of being, common in Christian antiquity and the Middle Ages, Ratzinger interprets the *exitus* as thoroughly positive. 'It is the Creator's free act of creation. It is his positive will that the created order should exist as something good in relation to himself, from which a response of freedom and love can be given back to him' (*SL*, p. 32). 'The *exitus*, or rather God's free act of creation', adds Ratzinger, 'is indeed ordered toward the *reditus*. This *reditus* is a "return," but it does not abolish creation; rather, it bestows its full and final perfection.' Man has the freedom, however, 'to turn the positive *exitus* of its creation around, as it were, to rupture it in the Fall: this is the refusal to be dependent, saying No to the *reditus*. Love is seen as dependence and is rejected. In its place come autonomy and autarchy: existing from oneself and in oneself, being a god of one's own making. *The arch from exitus to reditus is broken*' (*SL*, p. 32–3; italics added to last sentence). In consequence, man now needs the Redeemer to make possible the *reditus*.

Ratzinger regards the parable of the Lost Sheep as a metaphor for the human condition.

> He cannot get out of the thicket and find his way back to God. The shepherd who rescues him and takes him home is the Logos himself, the eternal Word, the eternal Meaning of the universe dwelling in the Son. He it is who makes his way to us and takes the sheep onto his shoulders, that is, he assumes human nature, and as the God-Man he carries man the creature home to God. And so the *reditus* becomes possible (*SL*, p. 33–4).

The process of returning creation through the historical 'Pasch' of Christ, his sacrifice on the cross and resurrection from the dead, is not seen as a rescue from 'fall into finitude'; rather, it is the recapitulation of the whole fallen creation. In the words of John Paul II, 'the world which came forth from the hands of God the Creator now returns to

---

32 Joseph Cardinal Ratzinger, *The Yes of Jesus Christ: Spiritual Exercises in Faith, Hope, and Love*, translated by Robert Nowell (New York: Crossroad Publishing Co., 1991), p. 89.

him redeemed by Christ'.[33] And as St Paul teaches: 'It was his [God's] loving design, centred in Christ, to give history its fulfilment by resuming everything in him, all that is in heaven, all that is on earth, summed up in him' (Eph. 1.10). Again: 'It was God's good pleasure to let all completeness dwell in him, and through him to win back all things, whether on earth or in heaven, into union with himself, making peace with them through his blood, shed on the cross' (Col. 1.19–20).

Put differently: on the one hand, grace doesn't replace nature, with nature being so corrupted that grace, no longer able to transform it, merely replaces it altogether by adding the spiritual realm over and above creation, a *donum superadditum*. Nor does grace leave nature untouched, on the other hand, merely completing or supplementing it, with nature taken to be unaffected by fall or redemption internally, which effectively limits the scope of sin and redemption to the supernatural realm and results in naturalism on the level of nature.[34] In the early twentieth century, the great French Catholic thinker, Jacques Maritain, wisely noted that it is erroneous to ignore both the distinction between nature and grace as well as their union.[35] How then does Ratzinger understand the union-in-distinctness of nature and grace? In particular, how does he understand the Thomistic dictum that grace does not abolish nature but presupposes it? The brief answer to this question must be that *grace restores or renews nature*, meaning thereby that God's grace in Christ *restores all life to its fullness, penetrating and perfecting and transforming the fallen creation from within its own order,* bringing creation into conformity with his will and purpose. In the words of Henri Cardinal De Lubac, 'The supernatural does not merely *elevate* (this traditional term is correct, but it is inadequate by itself) . . . [Rather] it *transforms it* . . . "Behold, I make all things new!" (Rev. 21.5). Christianity is "a doctrine of transformation" because the Spirit of Christ comes to permeate the first creation and make of it a "new creature". What is true of the final great transformation, on the occasion of the "Parousia" at which there will arise "new heavens and a new earth" (Revelation 21), is already

---

33 John Paul II, 2003 Encyclical Letter, *Ecclesia de Eucharistia*, no. 8.

34 On this point, see Henri de Lubac SJ, *Catholicism: Christ and the Common Destiny of Man*, pp. 313–14. My thinking on the relation between nature and grace is heavily indebted to Dutch neo-Calvinist philosopher Herman Dooyeweerd (1894–1977). For a brief introduction to his thought, see *In the Twilight of Western Thought: Studies in the Pretended Autonomy of Philosophical Thought* (Nutley, NJ: Craig Press, 1968).

35 Jacques Maritain, *Clairvoyance de Rome* (Paris, 1929), p. 222 (italics added), 'There is one error that consists in ignoring the distinction between nature and grace. There is another that consists in ignoring their union,' as cited in Henri De Lubac, 'Apologetics and Theology', *Theological Fragments* (San Francisco: Ignatius Press, 1989), pp. 91–104, and this citation at p. 103, note 28.

true now, according to St Paul, of each one of us.'[36] Thus, the key idea in Ratzinger's theology of the liturgy is that *grace restores nature*. 'Faith in redemption cannot be separated from faith in the Creator.' Redemption, adds Ratzinger, 'is an act of new creation, the restoration of creation to its true identity' (*SL*, pp. 24, 34).

Creation, Fall into Sin, Redemption in Jesus Christ and Consummation

Shortly before his death, John Paul II published his last book, leaving the Church, indeed the whole of humanity, the beautiful gift of his reflections, entitled *Memory and Identity*. Relevant to the question of the indivisible unity of creation and redemption, of nature and grace, is the following passage from this work:

> The resurrection of Christ clearly illustrated that only the measure of good introduced by God into history through the mystery of Redemption is sufficient to correspond fully to the truth of the human being. The Paschal Mystery thus becomes the definitive measure of man's existence in the world created by God. In this mystery, not only is eschatological truth revealed to us, that is to say the fullness of the Gospel, or Good News. There also shines forth a light to enlighten the whole of human existence in its temporal dimension and this light is then reflected onto the created world. Christ, through his Resurrection, has so to speak 'justified' the work of creation, and especially the creation of man. He has 'justified' it in the sense that he revealed the 'just measure' of good intended by God at the beginning of human existence. This measure is not merely what was provided by him in creation and then compromised by man through sin; it is a superabundant measure, in which the original plan finds a higher realization (cf. Genesis 3.14–15). In Christ, man is called to a new life, as son in the Son, the perfect expression of God's glory.[37]

At the core of the Christian worldview is an interlocking set of life-orienting beliefs regarding the creation, the fall into sin and redemption (i.e. incarnation, passion, resurrection and ascension). First, God created the world good. Given the cultural mandate to subdue and have dominion over created reality, this 'goodness' extends to the work of man's hands when accomplished in the light of 'the truth about ourselves

---

36 Henri de Lubac, *A Brief Catechesis on Nature & Grace* (San Francisco: Ignatius Press, 1984), pp. 81–2.
37 John Paul II, *Memory & Identity, Conversations at the Dawn of a Millennium* (New York: Rizzoli, 2005), p. 25.

and about the world'.³⁸ Indeed, the totality of creation, especially man who is its crown, actually manifests God's goodness, being created in the image and likeness of God. This manifestation of goodness is God's thesis, his affirmation, his *Yes* to the creation (Gen. 1.31).

Second, all creation (i.e. nature, culture, history, society) is fallen through original sin. Human nature as a whole has lost its original harmony, and man is wounded at the very root of his being, estranged from God, from himself, and from his fellow man. His humanity exhibits the marks of being sinful, prone to sin, with sin being a violation of God's will and purpose. This sinfulness denies God's thesis and has its beginnings in Genesis 3. God's response to man's sin is *Yes*, but also *No*. *Yes*, because God, full of love, mercy and grace, does not abandon the fallen creation. Indeed, Genesis 3.15 contains the first proclamation of the Messiah, the *proto-evangelium*. Says Ratzinger, 'God's second "yes" that was made manifest on the cross is our rebirth and that it is only this rebirth that finally and definitively makes us alive.' He adds more fully: 'It is the irruption of God's "yes" into my life through Jesus Christ's "yes" to us who had distanced ourselves from God's "yes," a "yes" upheld in the incarnation, the cross, and the resurrection.'³⁹ But also *No*, because God, judging man in the light of his perfect justice and holiness is the author of the antithesis, of the sign of contradiction between good and evil, between the seed of the woman and the seed of the serpent.

Third, the redemption accomplished through the mystery of the incarnation and Christ's finished work – his life, passion, death, resurrection and ascension – abrogates the antithesis between sin and creation. Put differently, the incarnation, passion, and resurrection in Jesus Christ means that his grace restores an original good creation. God's original thesis is reasserted and re-established, but also, as John Paul II asserts in the above quote, enriched, fulfilled and perfected. This redemption restores the very heart of human nature, causing the rebirth of the human self in Christ (Colossians 2.13; 2 Corinthians 5.17). 'Christ alone, through his humanity, reveals the totality of the mystery of man ... The key to his self-understanding lies in contemplating the divine Prototype, the Word made flesh, the eternal Son of the Father.' 'Without the Gospel', John Paul II adds, 'man remains a dramatic question with no adequate answer. The correct response to the question about man is Christ, *Redemptor Hominis*.'⁴⁰ This rebirth manifests itself in the integral redemption of the whole man in Christ through the fellowship of the Father, Son and Holy Spirit, and with one another in them, which has been given to us in grace (Rom. 5.5). Indeed, this redemption in Christ becomes a vision of cosmic

---

38 John Paul II, *Memory & Identity*, p. 81.
39 Joseph Cardinal Ratzinger, *The Yes of Jesus Christ*, pp. 91, 101, respectively.
40 John Paul II, *Memory & Identity*, pp. 110, 114.

redemption for the whole creation, including the life of culture. Indeed, God's grace in Christ *restores all life to its fullness, penetrating and perfecting and transforming the fallen creation from within its own order,* bringing creation into conformity with his will and purpose.[41]

Fourth and last, 'The great gesture of embrace emanating from the Crucified has not yet reached its goal; it has only just begun.' In Jesus Christ's preaching of the coming of the kingdom and his self-revelation, there is not only fulfilment, even now, but also expectation of what is to come – the *eschaton*, the Second Coming of Christ. There is an eschatological dynamism to the Christian life, indeed to the liturgy itself: 'Christian liturgy is liturgy on the way, a liturgy of pilgrimage toward the transfiguration of the world, which will only take place when God is "all in all" [1 Corinthians 15.28]' (*SL*, p. 50; see also pp. 57, 59). Still, this eschatological dynamic is at work historically, even now, in the renewal of the whole reality of creation.

Sacramental Realism, Eucharistic Presence and Transformation

Against the background of this cosmic drama, I can now focus my attention on the relationship of the sacred liturgy to the historical, redeeming acts of the economy of salvation, the saving event of the death and resurrection of Christ, that are re-enacted in the sacrament of the Eucharist.[42] In that sacrament, the indivisibility of creation, fall and redemption are expressed. 'The Eucharist, the sacrament of our salvation accomplished by Christ on the cross, is also a sacrifice of praise in thanksgiving for the work of creation. In the Eucharistic sacrifice the whole of [fallen] creation loved by God is presented to the Father through the death and the Resurrection of Christ.' In addition, 'Through Christ the Church can offer the sacrifice of praise in thanksgiving for all that God has made good, beautiful, and just in creation and in humanity' (*CCC*, no. 1359; see also nos. 1360–61). In exploring this relationship between the sacramental economy and the economy of salvation, Ratzinger identifies three dimensions in the Church's theology of the liturgy.

First, there is the dimension of the historical Pasch of Christ, his sacrifice on the cross and resurrection, which is the foundation of the

---

41 Portions of these three paragraphs were originally published in my article, 'Living Truth for a Post-Christian World: The Message of Francis Schaeffer and Karol Wojtyła', *Religion & Liberty* 12(6) (November/December 2002).

42 Especially helpful in this part of my essay has been Robert Sokolowski, *Eucharistic Presence* (Washington, DC: Catholic University of America Press, 1993), pp. 13–21, 27–81, and 101–8. See also, 'Phenomenology and the Eucharist' and 'The Eucharist and Transubstantiation,' in Sokolowski's collection, *Christian Faith & Human Understanding: Studies on the Eucharist, Trinity, and the Human Person* (Washington, DC: Catholic University of America Press, 2006), pp. 69–85, and 95–112, respectively.

liturgy's objective reality. 'This once-for-all event has become the ever-abiding form of the liturgy' (*SL*, p. 60). Elsewhere Ratzinger writes, 'the interpretation of Christ's death on the Cross . . . represents the inner presupposition of all eucharistic theology' (*PFF*, p. 94). 'Without the Cross,' he adds, 'the Eucharist would remain mere ritual; without the Eucharist, the Cross would be merely a horrible profane event' (*PFF*, p. 98). Now, if I understand Ratzinger correctly, these events are the foundation of the liturgy's sacramental realism, meaning thereby that the sacramental economy derives its efficacy from the Paschal mystery by which Christ accomplished once for all the work of our salvation (cf. CCC, nos. 1066–8, 1076). That is, sacramental actions, such as the Eucharistic sacrifice of the Mass, do not stand on their own. Rather, such acts have 'meaning only in relation to something that really happens, to a reality that is substantially present [namely, the saving work of Christ, accomplished once for all]. Otherwise it would lack real content, like bank notes without funds to cover them. The Lord could say that his Body was "given" only because he *had* in fact given it; he could present his Blood in the new chalice as shed for many only because he really *had* shed it' (*SL*, p. 55). The efficacy of the sacraments is subordinate to the efficacy of Christ's saving work. The sacraments are acts of Christ – he himself is at work through the power of the Holy Spirit to make present efficaciously the grace signified by the sacraments (cf. CCC, nos. 1084, 1127–8). This last point brings us to the second dimension in Ratzinger's theology of the liturgy.

Second, this theology of the liturgy stresses that, in the eucharistic sacrifice of the Mass, we not only recollect the saving works of Christ, but also we become 'contemporaries with what lies at the foundation of that liturgy' – the paschal mystery of Christ (*SL*, p. 57). This raises the all-important question: how is the redemptive sacrifice of Christ, a historically real event, unique, belonging to the past, which accomplished our salvation once for all, made present, here and now, in the eucharistic sacrifice of the Mass. In other words, how can the eucharistic sacrifice, here and now, re-enact the same redemptive sacrifice offered on the cross of Calvary in the past? As Catholic philosopher Robert Sokolowski pointedly asks, 'How can the same redemptive action ["one single sacrifice"[43]] be achieved at different times and places?'[44]

The biblical key to answering this question, if I understand Ratzinger correctly, is given in the understanding that in the sacred liturgy we participate, are caught up and made contemporary, even now, in 'the offering

---

43 CCC, no. 1367: 'The sacrifice of Christ and the sacrifice of the Eucharist are *one single sacrifice*.' The *Catechism* is summarizing the teaching of the Council of Trent (1562), Session XXII, chapters 1 and 2.

44 Sokolowski, *Eucharistic Presence*, p. 13.

of the Son to the Father, an action that was once achieved in the past but endures as an eternal offering in heaven (Heb. 8.1–2, 9.23–26).'[45] 'The eternal is embodied in what is once-for-all' (*SL*, p. 60), according to Ratzinger, because what Christ accomplished, once for all, through his redemptive action was not just a worldly event; rather, it was, at its core, 'an action in time that was related to the eternal Father. Although in time, it touched eternity. It changed the relationship between creation and the Father.'[46] Sokolowski explains,

> It was a transaction, an exchange, between Christ and the Father. Although it took place in time, it touched eternity as did no other event in history. It did so because of the person who achieved it and also because of what was done. It was the perfect sacrifice offered to the Father, the perfect act of obedience of the Son, different from all the other actions he performed in his life on earth. Because the sacrifice of Christ touched eternity in this way, it was not just a historical event: it took on the kind of presence that marks the eternal moment, the moment out of time: 'For Christ did not enter into a sanctuary made by hands . . . but heaven itself, that he might now appear before God on our behalf' (Hebrews 9.24). The sacrifice of Christ is eternally present to the Father; the Lamb in the Apocalypse appears as having been slain (Revelation 5.6–12), and the wounds of the passion remain in the Risen Lord.[47]

So then, how does the eucharistic sacrifice, here and now, re-enact an event from the past, the redeeming death and resurrection of Christ? Alternatively put, how does the eternal enter into the present moment of our liturgical action (*SL*, p. 60)? The brief answer to this question must be: 'The Eucharist can reenact an event from the past because it joins with that event in the eternal present of God,'[48] namely in the action of the incarnate Son before the Eternal Father who is directly involved and invoked in the Eucharist.[49] As Ratzinger puts it,

---

45 Sokolowski, *Eucharistic Presence*, p. 20.
46 Sokolowski, 'The Eucharist and Transubstantiation', p. 98. See also, CCC, no. 1085: 'His Paschal mystery is a real event that occurred in our history, but it is unique: all other historical events happen once, and then they pass away, swallowed up in the past. The Paschal mystery of Christ, by contrast, cannot remain only in the past, because by his death he destroyed death, and all that Christ is – all that he did and suffered for all men – *participates in the divine eternity, and so transcends all times while being made present in them all* [italics added]. The event of the Cross and Resurrection abides and draws everything toward life.'
47 Sokolowski, 'Phenomenology and the Eucharist', pp. 80–1.
48 Sokolowski, 'Phenomenology and the Eucharist', p. 81.
49 On this, see Sokolowski, *Eucharistic Presence*, p. 106f.

The words of institution [of the Mass] are a theology of the Cross and a theology of the Resurrection – they reach right down into the heart of the historical event, and in the inwardness of Jesus that transcends time they rise up so that *this essential core of the event now reaches into every age: this inner core now becomes the point at which time opens up to God's eternity.* That is why the 'memorial' constituted by the Eucharist is more than a remembrance of something in the past: is the act of entering into that inner core which can no longer pass away. (*PFF*, p. 110)[50]

Third and lastly, Ratzinger underlines the intrinsic connection between the cosmic liturgy and a transformed existence, which entails a commitment to transforming the world for Christ's sake. In conclusion of this section and in preparation for the next, I quote Ratzinger on the nature of that transformation: 'The Blessed Sacrament contains a dynamism, which has the goal of transforming mankind and the world into the New Heaven and the New Earth, into the unity of the risen Body . . . The Eucharist is not aimed primarily at the individual. *Eucharistic personalism is a drive toward union, the overcoming of the barriers between God and man, between "I" and "thou" in the new "we" of the communion of saints*' (*SL*, p. 87; italics added). Ratzinger speaks in this passage of 'Eucharistic personalism' as the fruit of eucharistic communion so that 'the goal of the Eucharist is our own transformation, so that we become "one body and spirit" with Christ' (cf. 1 Cor. 6.17). In short, 'the Eucharist is meant to transform *us*, to change humanity itself into the living temple of God, into the Body of Christ' (*SL*, p. 86).

Now, in the next section, I present John Paul II's philosophical account of personalism, especially as it bears on the relation between person and community, as the foundation of his Christian anthropology. In the concluding section of this essay, I then enrich his account with Ratzinger's theological anthropology of 'Eucharistic personalism' and its concomitant ecclesiology of 'Eucharistic Communion', which is at the centre of the Church's mission to the world.

---

50 On this, see also Aidan Nichols OP, 'The Holy Oblation: On the Primacy of Eucharistic Sacrifice', *The Downside Review* 122 (October 2004), pp. 259–72, 'From a Catholic perspective, the Evangelical [Protestant] emphasis on the "once-for-all-ness" of Calvary is skewed by a failure to grasp that Atonement is also a meta-historical action, in which the only-begotten Son made man still stands before the Father as the Lamb bearing the marks of its wounds, pleading for sinners here and now in a sacrificial intercession to which the Church becomes privy in her mysteries – in, precisely, the sacrifice of the altar' (p. 264).

Christian Personalism: Communio, *Person, and Community Man: The Image of God*

The Second Vatican Council's teaching on the human person in *Gaudium et Spes* (no. 24) is the starting point for John Paul II's reflections on the relationship between person and community, between self-transcendence and self-fulfilment. The Council teaches, 'Man, who is the only creature on earth that God willed for itself [for its own sake], [nevertheless] can fully discover his true self only in a sincere giving of himself.' The human person is, summarily stated, a fundamental polarity of self-possession and self-donation.[51] On the one hand, the human person is an end in himself, existing as a being of his own, for his own sake, unique and unrepeatable, a whole of his own and never a mere part of any totality (cf. *PC*, p. 199). Little wonder that John Paul II rejects socialism, regarding its fundamental error, he says, to be anthropological in nature, depersonalizing and self-alienating human beings.

> Socialism considers the individual person simply as an element, a molecule within the social organism, so that the good of the individual is completely subordinated to the functioning of the socio-economic mechanism. Socialism likewise maintains that the good of the individual can be realized without reference to his free choice, to the unique and exclusive responsibility that he exercises in the face of good or evil. Man is thus reduced to a series of social relationships, and the concept of the person as the autonomous subject of moral decision disappears, the very subject whose decisions build the social order.[52]

On the other hand, *Gaudium et Spes* also emphasizes that persons are made for communion with other persons and that in this way man's likeness to God is implied in the truth that humans are relational, that is, by reason of their capacity for community with other persons. In short, for man to be in the image of God implies relationality, which is to say 'that no one can live of or for himself alone'.[53] This is why man

---

51 In my exposition of John Paul II's anthropology, I have profited from John F. Crosby, 'John Paul II's Vision of Sexuality and Marriage', in *The Legacy of Pope John Paul II: His Contribution to Catholic Thought*, edited by Geoffrey Gneuhs (New York: Crossroad, 2000), pp. 52–70; and especially his entry on the 'Human Person' in the *Encyclopedia of Catholic Doctrine*, edited by Russell Shaw (Huntington, Indiana: Our Sunday Visitor, 1997), pp. 307–11. See also his magisterial study, *The Selfhood of the Human Person* (Washington, DC: Catholic University of America Press, 1996).

52 John Paul II, Encyclical Letter, *Centesimus Annus* ['On the 100th Anniversary of *Rerum Novarum*'], 1 May 1991, no. 13.

53 On this point, see Joseph Cardinal Ratzinger's sermons on Genesis 1—3, *In the Beginning*, translated by Boniface Ramsey OP (Huntington, Indiana: Our Sunday Visitor, 1990), esp. pp. 62–3, 90.

can only find himself, that is, be self-fulfilled, by making a sincere gift of himself, which John Paul II has called the 'law of the gift'. And this striving for self-fulfilment in communion with others is evidence of the self-transcendence that is proper to man as a person. 'Each of us is capable of such a gift because each of us is a person, and the structure proper to a person is the structure of self-possession and self-governance.' 'Hence', adds John Paul II, 'we are capable of giving ourselves because we possess ourselves and also because we are our own masters in the dimension of ourselves as subjects' (*PC*, pp. 319, 322). Self-possession, belonging to oneself, quite clearly, has nothing in common with the isolated unity of the Leibnizian monad, as if the human person is completely closed in upon himself (*PC*, p. 254). Indeed, God did not create man a solitary being. He created us in his image, and since God is an internal community of three divine Persons in which relationship is constitutive, with real love and real communication, it stands to reason that He would create persons who flourish living in the communion of truth and charity with one another. As Catholic philosopher John Crosby puts it,

> A world in which there could be only one person would make no sense. Such a solitary person would suffer a devastating deprivation by being unable either to utter a word to another person or hear the word uttered by the other. This is why we were created as man and woman. This is why God exists as a community of Persons and not as a solitary Person. . . . We resemble the Trinitarian God through our interpersonal communion.[54]

In sum, man is at once a self-determining and self-possessing agent, existing and choosing for himself, and also a being who is not closed in upon himself but rather is relational. So looked at in one way man is the image of God's own supreme self-possession. To quote Crosby again, God 'possesses Himself by existing through himself and on his own; and we, who do not exist through ourselves, show forth something of God's being insofar as each of us is one's own end, a kind of whole of one's own, an unrepeatable being.'[55] But in another way, relationality (as distinct from mere social coexistence) is expressive of the image of

---

54 Crosby, 'Human Person', pp. 309–10.
55 Crosby, 'Human Person', p. 310. In an insightful study of the *Catechism of the Catholic Church*, a crucial point is made that we should keep in mind when speaking of God's self-possession, namely, 'God is one but not solitary' (CCC, no. 254). 'The One who created and sustains the universe dwells not in splendid isolation or in static self-possession but in the glory of interpersonal communion.' This is the 'uncreated interpersonal life' of Trinitarian communion 'shared by the Father, Son, and Holy Spirit' (*The Love that Never Ends: A Key to the Catechism of the Catholic Church*, J. Augustine Di Noia OP et al. [Huntington, Indiana: Our Sunday Visitor, 1996], p. 24).

God, say the Council Fathers in the same paragraph: 'Indeed, the Lord Jesus, when He prayed to the Father, "that all may be one . . . as we are one" (John 17.21–22) opened up vistas closed to human reason. For He implied a certain likeness between the union of the divine Persons and the union of God's sons in truth and charity.' This, too, is the truth concerning man's likeness to God. It expresses the truth that God himself as Trinity, as a communion of Persons who totally share one single being, life, knowledge and love, is the model for understanding the human person.

Communio: 'I and thou' and 'We' Relationships

Against this background, we can easily appreciate the fundamental question that Karol Wojtyła posed in a number of seminal studies during the period 1961–76: how to actualize *communio personarum* – that is, a community of persons, fulfilling themselves as persons by mutually interacting with others, in different inter-individual and social relations, giving and, in turn, receiving acceptance, respect, trust, love, indeed, the gift of self (cf. *PC*, pp. 197–207, 236–61).[56] As Wojtyła puts it, *communio* 'refers to community as a mode of being and acting (in common, of course) through which the persons involved mutually confirm and affirm one another, a mode of being and acting that promotes the personal fulfilment of each of them by virtue of their mutual relationship' (*PC*, p. 321). In his account of *communio*, he speaks of the different 'dimensions' of community distinguishing the 'inter-individual or inter-personal dimension of community' from the 'social dimension of community.' Wojtyła calls the former the *I-Thou* relationship; the latter is called the *we* relationship. Importantly, these relationships, as instances of *communio personarum*, are authentic achievements of self-transcendence.

An essential condition for realizing *communio* is that, in existing and acting together with other persons *qua* persons, we *participate* in actions that fulfil us by bringing about the realization of our ends as persons. Wojtyła calls the 'personalistic' value of an action that feature of the action *qua* action that fulfils us. But this 'personalistic' value is not unacceptably self-regarding, in opposition to the claim of the *other* upon me, because Wojtyła affirms 'that the *other* is also an *I*.' 'An understanding of this truth defines to some extent the relation of my own

---

56 See also, Karol Wojtyła, *The Acting Person*, trans. A. Potocki, rev. Anna-Teresa Tymieniecka (Boston: Reidel, 1979; originally published in Polish, 1969), pp. 261–300. Subsequent references to this work (hereafter *AP*) will be made parenthetically in the text. On *communio*, especially, but not only, regarding the reality of the Church (pp. 135–54), see also Karol Wojtyła, *Sources of Renewal: The Implementation of the Second Vatican Council*, translated by P. S. Falla (London: Collins, 1980), p. 61.

concrete *I* to all other human beings. They are not just *others* in relation to my *I*; each of them is also another *I*' (PC, p. 200).

Yes, Wojtyła does insist on the primacy of others to the self, that is, on the 'irrevocable primacy of the personal subject in relation to community' (PC, p. 237). But this self-fulfilment can only take place when, in acting together with others, we participate, as self-transcending subjects, in a relationship where we reciprocally recognize each other's very humanity (fully constituted, independent, personal subjects, which in each instance is unique, unrepeatable, incommunicable). 'The concept of participation basically serves to express the property by virtue of which we as persons exist and act together with others, while not ceasing to be ourselves or to fulfil ourselves in action, in our own acts ... which means our own *I*'s' (PC, p. 200). Again, says Wojtyła,

> The actualization of the *I-other* relationship starts by my becoming aware of the ... humanity of a specific human being apart from myself, one of the others, but it takes place by experiencing that other *I* as a person. *Participation signifies a basic personalization of the relationship of one human being to another* [italics added]. I cannot experience another as I experience myself, because my own *I* as such is nontransferable. When I experience another as a person, [however] I come as close as I can to what determines the other's *I* as the unique and unrepeatable reality of the human being. (PC, p. 202)

Most important, the personalistic value of human acts is not unacceptably self-regarding, on Wojtyła's view, because self-fulfilment requires self-transcendence, that is, a self-giving – a gift of self through which we are able to participate in the life of other personal subjects in community.

Now, the reality of *communio*, which at its most elemental is an *I-other* relationship, unfolds into an interpersonal *I-thou* relationship and, thereafter, into the social dimension of community – as a *we*. What makes *communio* possible in an *I-other* relationship? To this question, Wojtyła answers that another person is an *other* to me not merely because we share a common humanity as human beings, however necessary that commonality may be, 'but chiefly because the other is another *I*' (PC, p. 201). In other words, sharing a common humanity as human beings is a necessary but not a sufficient condition to give rise to an *I-other* relationship. This commonality is by nature general, signifying that the other person is the same kind of being as I am, but it fails to bring us close enough to the human being as a concrete person – the *other*, another *I*, in short, my *neighbour*. 'The [*I-other*] relationship does not emerge from having a universal concept of the human being, a concept that embraces all people without exception.' 'The *I-other* relationship is not universal', adds John Paul II, 'but always interhuman, unique and unrepeatable in each and every instance' (PC, p. 201). This *I-other* relationship unfolds into an interpersonal *I-thou* relationship and into social relations John Paul II calls *we* relationships. And each of these relationships presents us with a different dimension of community.

In the interpersonal *I-thou* relationship of *communio*, we find the main kinds of interpersonal love, including the love of a man and woman, of a mother and child, and of friendship. We also find the elementary interpersonal relation of treating and experiencing 'the other as oneself', which is the meaning of neighbour. Looking more closely at the distinguishing feature of *I-thou* relationships, they involve persons 'mutually revealing themselves to one another in their personal human subjectivity and in all that goes to make up this subjectivity' (PC, p. 245). This make-up is described by Wojtyła as follows:

> The *thou* stands before my self as a true and complete 'other self', which, like my own self, is characterized not only by self-determination, but also and above all by self-possession and self-governance. . . . This whole structure of personal subjectivity proper to the *I* as a self and to the *thou* as another self is mutually revealed through the community proper to the *I-thou* relationship, since, by virtue of the mutuality of the *I-thou* relationship, *I* am simultaneously a *thou* for the *I* that is a *thou* for me. In this way, the *I-thou* relationship as a mutual relation of two subjects . . . not only takes on meaning but also truly becomes an authentic subjective community. (PC, p. 245)

This interpersonal relationship of *communio* may unfold into a more profound, integral and intense bond and, in doing so, it will involve trust, self-giving and a sense of belonging. This unfolding requires approaching each other in mutual acceptance and affirmation of the transcendent value of the human person, and hence its dignity, and in this way we become mutually responsible for one another (cf. PC, p. 245–6). What occurs here is the reality of *communio*, says Wojtyła, an authentic interpersonal community 'which is *a mode of being and acting in mutual relation to one another* (not just "in common" with one another) *such that through this being and acting they mutually confirm one another as persons*' (PC, p. 321). 'Only such a relationship', adds Wojtyła, 'seems to deserve the name *communio personarum*' (PC, p. 246).

But there is also the *we* form of authentic community, namely, the social dimension of community, which occurs when human beings exist and act together, as self-transcending subjects, in reference to the *common good*. As John Paul II says,

> The relation of many *I*'s to a common good seems to be the very core of social community. By virtue of this relation, the people involved in it, while experiencing their personal subjectivity – the factual multiplicity of human *I*'s – are aware that they form a specific *we*, and they experience themselves in this new dimension. This is the social dimension, different from the *I-thou* dimension, although in it the persons remain themselves (they remain an *I* and a *thou*), but the direction of the relation is fundamentally changed. This direction is determined by the common good. In this relation the *I* and the *thou* also find their mutual relationship in a new dimension: they find their *I-thou* through the common good, which establishes a new union between them. (PC, p. 247)

What is this new dimension of their mutual relationship, establishing a new kind of union between persons? The answer must be that their relation to the common good adds the experienced reality of 'we' to the interpersonal reality of 'I' and 'thou' and therefore many human *I*'s are integrated, indeed, transformed into a *we*, which is the unique 'subjectivity' of this union in its existence and activity. 'Subjectivity' here is an analogical concept reflecting the different but analogous *we* relationships such as marriage or family, a particular group of friends, a professional association, a nation, a country, or even, the human family (cf. PC, p. 251).

There is a correlation between the *we* form of *communio* and the aforementioned notion of the *common good*, meaning thereby the teleology of social wholes, such as marriage and family, and so forth. It is the 'common relation of many *I*'s to a common good,' says Wojtyła, 'that unites the multiplicity of subjects into one *we*' (PC, p. 249). To understand the notion of the common good properly, we need to see its correlation to the notion of authentic self-transcendence, on the one hand, and to certain normative demands or obligations, on the other. Such demands emanating beyond the 'we' are grounded in the order of truth and are the conditions for realizing authentic self-transcendence. In this light, we can understand Wojtyła's point that the 'we' relation to the common good properly actualizes the self-transcendence of the human being, given that the common good of a specific 'we' relationship is the good of each person in that relationship, bringing about authentic self-fulfilment when the normative demands of the 'we' relationship are heeded. 'Through this [*we*] relationship, a human being, a concrete *I*, discovers different confirmations of his ... personal subjectivity from those that occur in interpersonal relationships. And yet, this confirmation of the subject *I* in the community *we* agrees profoundly with the nature of this subject. Perhaps it is just such verification that lies at the basis of all that has ever been said concerning the social nature of the human being' (*PC*, pp. 249–50).

Self-fulfilment does not shut out our ties to others expressed in the 'we' relationship or, as I will argue below, the bonds of solidarity. 'In a particular way', adds Wojtyła, 'the relation to the common good actualizes this transcendence because of the essential correlation between the social dimension of community, the "we" relationship, and the tendency toward self-fulfilment proper to human subjectivity' (*PC*, pp. 249–50). 'We fulfil ourselves as persons through interpersonal *I-thou* relationships, as well as through a relation to the common good, which allows us to exist and act together with others as a *we*' (*PC*, p. 253). The concept of the common good is also an analogical concept, because the reality of this good is proportional to the different *we*s and in accord with the unique ends proper to communities such as a fraternal community, marital community, family community, political community, school community and, in the widest scope, the human community. 'The common good is essentially the good of many, and in its fullest dimension the good of all. This multiplicity can be quantitatively diverse: two in the case of marriage (no longer just one + one, but a couple), several in the case of a family, millions in the case of a particular nation, billions in the case of all humanity' (*PC*, p. 249). That is, 'The human *we* is also realized in [the different forms and varieties of social community] in an analogous way. In all of these realizations, however, the common good corresponds to the transcendence of the person and forms the objective basis for their constitution as a social community – as a *we*' (*PC*, p. 249).

Similarly, we can also understand the importance of the transcendence of the human person and his concomitant relation to the common good, a relation that Wojtyła grounds in the objective order of truth, in particular, the truth about the common good of marriage and family, of the human family and so forth. Wojtyła is not oblivious to the various obstacles currently afoot, such as utilitarianism, totalitarianism, social egoism, relativism, that hinder our ability to 'attain the "true" common good that corresponds to the essence of both the social community proper to the human *we* and the personal transcendence proper to the human *I*' (*PC*, p. 250). Nonetheless, these obstacles and others such as, in general, our fallen human condition, do not completely distort the human person's place within, and relation to, the order of truth. 'Objectively,' insists Wojtyła, 'transcendence is realized in a relation to truth and to the good as "true." The relation to the common good, a relation that unites the multiplicity of subjects into one *we*, should likewise be grounded in a relation to truth and to a "true" good' (*PC*, p. 249). The objective truth about the common good is proportionate to the social community and its particular nature. 'In behalf of this truth, human beings as members of a community embrace the hardships connected with the realization of the common good ... In behalf of the same truth of the common good, however, they also achieve all those values that go to make up the true and inviolable good of the person' (PC, p. 251).

Participation, Individualism and Totalism

Wojtyła does not develop a theory of institutional communities such as the state, family, marriage and so forth.[57] His main concern is 'only with elementary condition under which existence and activity "together with others" promotes the self-fulfilment of the human being as a person' (PC, p. 236). Significantly, the concept of *communio* does not refer merely to the social nature of man, meaning thereby 'the experience that man exists, lives, and acts together with other men' (AP, p. 268). To make his point clear, Wojtyła distinguishes the complementary claims that the human person not only has a social nature but also 'has the capacity for rational community as *communio*' (PC, p. 319). Although these claims are complementary, says Wojtyła, '*Communio* is far more indicative of the personal and interpersonal dimension of all social systems' (PC, p. 319). That is, only *communio* and the concomitant notion of *participation* 'allows man, when he acts together with other men, to realize thereby and at once the *authentically personalistic value* [of human actions] – the performance of the action and the fulfilment of himself in the action' (AP, p. 270). Furthermore, the concepts of *communio* and *participation* pertain as such to the '*genuinely personalistic structure of human existence in a community*, that is, *in every community to which that man belongs* – for instance, a family, a national group, a religious community, or the citizens of a state' (AP, p. 282). In other words, the concept of *communio* 'may be applied analogously to different kinds of interpersonal structures and relationships, both those between God and human beings and those between human beings themselves' (PC, p. 320).

Indeed, Wojtyła insists on the primacy of *communio* over the category of society, or institutional communities such as the state, business, universities and so forth. '*Membership in any of these communities is not to be identified with participation.*' A person's membership in any

---

57 For a fully developed account of the distinction between institutional communities such as the state, family, marriage and so forth, and inter-individual relationships, see Herman Dooyeweerd's magisterial work, *A New Critique of Theoretical Thought*, Vol. III, *The Structures of Individuality of Temporal Reality*, translated by David H. Freeman and H. De Jongste (Philadelphia: Presbyterian and Reformed Publishing Co., 1969 [1936]), pp. 177–84.

objective community is defined according to the ends and purposes that brought him to act together with others in this community, for instance, labourers digging ditches, students attending lectures, etc. Yet, 'From the point of view of the person and the action, it is not only the objective community of acting but also its subjective moment, which we have here called "participation," that is important.' 'The question', adds Wojtyła, 'is whether a man belonging to a community of acting ... is in a position in his communal acting to perform real actions and fulfil himself in them; the possibility of this performance and the fulfilment it brings about are determined by participation. Nevertheless, even when acting "together with others" man can remain outside the community that is constituted by participation' (*AP*, pp. 279–80). For mere social coexistence is different from *participation* and hence *communio*.

Furthermore, the concept of *communio* is not used by Wojtyła merely to counteract individualism, in other words, social *atomism*, which is the 'belief that the individual has a primary reality whereas society is a second-order, derived or artificial construct.'[58] In Wojtyła's own words, 'Individualism sees in the individual the supreme and fundamental good, to which all interests of the community or the society have to be subordinated' (*AP*, p. 273). 'Individualism carries with it an implied denial and rejection of participation. . . . From the individualistic point of view', adds Wojtyła, 'an essentially constituent human property that allows the person to fulfil himself in acting "together with others" simply does not exist' (*AP*, p. 274).

Of course, Wojtyła is a social realist rather than an individualistic nominalist. The latter construes 'society from its supposed "elements," that is, from elementary interrelations between individuals',[59] and also holds that only individual things exist. Accordingly, there are no such things as universals, forms or kinds of things. Wojtyła, by contrast, regards communities to be as real as individuals. Thus, to be a social realist means you hold that organized institutional communities such as the state, and natural communities such as marriage and family, are real social wholes having their own nature and ends, and not just 'fictitious entities' constructed by a contract between individuals.[60] Yet, Wojtyła also rejects anti-individualism, or what he calls, 'objective totalism', which alludes to his aforementioned rejection of socialism, meaning thereby the view

---

58 I am following here the definitions of individualism and social realism found in the celebrated study by Robert N. Bellah, et al., *Habits of the Heart: Individualism and Commitment in American Life* (New York: Harper & Row, 1985), Glossary, entry on 'Individualism,' p. 334. I am also indebted to Herman Dooyeweerd, *A New Critique of Theoretical Thought*, Vol. III, pp. 157–261.

59 Herman Dooyeweerd, *A New Critique of Theoretical Thought*, Vol. III, p. 182.

60 On this, see Herman Dooyeweerd, *A New Critique of Theoretical Thought*, Vol. III, pp. 182–3.

that sees the individual as the chief enemy of society and of the common good. 'Since totalism assumes that inherent in the individual there is only the striving for individual good, that any tendency toward participation or fulfilment in acting and living together with others is totally alien to him, it follows that the "common good" can be attained only by limiting the individual. . . . Consequently, the realization of the common good frequently presupposes the use of coercion' (*AP*, p. 274). Wojtyła rejects both individualism and totalism (anti-individualism) because both views have a faulty anthropology – the essentially constituent human property of participation is denied and thus there seems to be 'no sufficient foundation for any authentic human community' (*AP*, p. 276).

Alienation, Christian Anthropology and Communione Sanctissimae Trinitatis

Given the importance of *communio* for Wojtyła, we can easily appreciate why he claims that 'the central problem of life for humanity in our times, perhaps in all times, is this: *participation or alienation?*' (*PC*, p. 206). From this point of view, interpersonal and social relations such as marriage and family in a given society can become a source of alienation in proportion to the erosion of participation. As a result, there is a dehumanization of the relations experienced by the individual subjects because they are deprived of 'the possibility of fulfilling themselves in community, either in the social community of a *we* or in the interpersonal community of an *I-thou*' (*PC*, p. 256). Thus, alienation is the antithesis of participation because it inhibits the transcendence proper to the person, which is an openness of one human being to an other, who is another *I* – 'this subverts the lived experience of the truth of humanity, the truth of the essential worth of the person, in the human *thou*.' Alienation also occurs 'when the multiplicity of human subjects, each of whom is a particular *I*, is unable to develop appropriately in the direction of an authentic *we*' (*PC*, p. 256). What is needed to overcome alienation is a Christian anthropology seen in a Trinitarian light – the *communio personarum* of God himself in the Trinity of Persons.[61]

At its most profound level, the truth and inviolable good of man is grounded in his being created in God's image and likeness (Gen. 1.27; 5.1–2). In one sense, this divine image in man consists not only in our imaging the intelligence and freedom of God, a creating Intelligence, but also in being capable of self-determination, self-possession and of being an end-in-himself (cf. *PC*, pp. 316–17). In another sense, however, the divine image in man is reflected in his likeness to God '*by reason of*

---

61 Karol Wojtyła, *Sources of Renewal*, p. 121.

a relation that unites persons'. The Council Fathers 'speak of a "certain likeness between the union of the divine persons and the union of God's sons in truth and charity."' 'Humans beings are like unto God not only by reason of their spiritual nature [being rational and free],' adds Wojtyła, 'which accounts for their existence as persons, but also by reason of their *capacity for community with other persons*' (PC, p. 318). Most important in this connection is that the interpersonal and social relation that occurs between persons and in which they fulfil themselves 'is realized through the mutual gift of self, a gift that has a disinterested character'. This gift is not given out of self-interest, for then it would no longer be a gift. 'The whole tradition of Christian thought defends the *trans-utilitarian* dimension of human activity and existence – this dimension of the divine image in man means that man is called to exist "for" others, to become a gift,' as Wojtyła puts it (PC, p. 322). For, he adds in characteristic fashion, 'man can fully discover his true self only in a sincere giving of himself', and this gift *qua* gift, in light of the reality of *communio*, demands that it be '*given* but also *received in the whole of its truth and authenticity*' (PC, p. 322).

In this way, the human 'we' resembles the Trinitarian communion, the divine 'we' that is an interpersonal community of real love and real communication in himself, and living the mystery of the eternal exchange of love as total self-giving to each other. As Catholic theologian Joyce Little puts it, 'The Father gives all He has to the Son, and the two of them in turn give all they have to the Holy Spirit.'[62] But God is not only eternal love in himself, he is also love in relationship to us: the love of the Father manifested in the gift of the Son and communicated through the Holy Spirit. 'In this the love of God was manifested toward us, that God has sent His only begotten Son into the world, that we might live through Him. In this is love, not that we loved God, but that He loved us and sent His Son to be the atoning sacrifice for our sins. Beloved, if God so loved us, we also ought to love one another' (1 John 4.9–11). Love, then, at its most profound level, is the gift of God to man. God calls us to love one another with the very same love that he loved us in Christ. 'Love one another as I have loved you' (John 13.34).

This great truth of the outpouring gift of the Father's love manifested in the Son and communicated through the agency of the Holy Spirit (cf. Rom. 5.5) is shared by those transformed in their encounter with the triune God. We are born again from the Father, in Christ, through the Holy Spirit. This transformation enables us to participate, by his grace, in the divine life by being in communion with the Father, Son and Holy Spirit, but it also enables us to love others with God's own love. In short,

---

62 Joyce Little, 'Trinity', in the *Encyclopedia of Catholic Doctrine*, pp. 682–5, and for this quote see p. 684.

in the mystery of the incarnation God teaches us to love as he loved us. In this light, we can understand that the deep inner dynamism of love is self-giving to others. 'In interhuman relationships, therefore, the disinterested gift of self (of the person) stands at the basis of the whole order of love and the whole authenticity of love' (PC, p. 322).

The mutual gift of self – *communio* – is the fruit of a personal encounter with the triune God. No less important, however, is *solidarity*. In *Ecclesia in America*, John Paul II affirms, 'solidarity is the fruit of the communion that is grounded in the mystery of triune God, and in the Son of God who took flesh and died for all. It is expressed in Christian love that seeks the good of others, especially of those most in need.' 'Conversion', he adds, 'urges solidarity, because it makes us aware that whatever we do for others, especially for the poorest, we do for Christ Himself.'[63]

Yet, there is more to the notion of solidarity. As Catholic philosopher Russell Hittinger comments, 'solidarity is an inherently complex notion'. 'Solidarity means', he explains, '(1) common material things, which are subject to distributive justice; (2) sociological or economic states of affairs, such as technological and economic interdependence; (3) personal attitudes, dispositions, or virtues with regard to what is, or should be, common; (4) activities, in the sense of teamwork and collaboration toward common ends; (5) loving communion between persons, where communion is the very goal of action.'[64] In his 1987 encyclical letter *Sollicitudo Rei Socialis*, John Paul II initially describes solidarity as involving an awareness of interdependence among individuals and nations. Yet, he says the virtue of solidarity is above all a certain moral attitude taken toward interdependence (numbers 2 and 3 above). This point is developed further: 'It is above all a question of *interdependence*, sensed as a *system determining* relationships in the contemporary world, in its economic, cultural, political, and religious elements, and accepted as a *moral category*.' 'When interdependence becomes recognized in this way', John Paul II adds, 'the correlative response as a moral and social attitude, as a "virtue," is *solidarity*.' A key ingredient in this notion of solidarity is a proper understanding of the relationship between solidarity and the common good. '[Solidarity] is a *firm and persevering determination* to commit oneself to the *common good*; that

---

63 John Paul II, Post-Synodal Apostolic Exhortation, *Ecclesia in America*, 22 January 1999, nos. 52 and 26, respectively. For a marvellous study of this text, see Peter Casarella, 'Solidarity as the Fruit of Communion: *Ecclesia in America*, 'Post-Liberation' Theology, and the Earth', in *Communio: International Catholic Review* Spring 2000, 98–123.

64 Russell Hittinger, 'Making Sense of the Civilization of Love: John Paul II's Contribution to Social Thought', in *The Legacy of John Paul II: His Contribution to Catholic Thought*, edited by Geoffrey Gneuhs (New York: Crossroad, 2000), pp. 71–93, and this quote at p. 86.

is to say the good of all and of each individual, because we are *all* really responsible *for all.*'65

John Paul II brings out the implications of this perspective regarding solidarity. He writes:

> The exercise of solidarity *within each society* is valid when its members recognize one another as persons. Those who are more influential, because they have a greater share of goods and common services, should feel *responsible* for the weaker and be ready to share with them all they possess. Those who are weaker, for their part, in the same spirit of *solidarity*, should not adopt a purely *passive* attitude or one that is *destructive* of the social fabric, but while claiming their legitimate rights, should do all they can for the good of all. The intermediate groups for their part, should not selfishly insist on their particular interests, but respect the interests of others. (SS, no. 39)

Moreover, consistent with the Thomistic principle that grace perfects nature, the infusion of supernatural charity into the moral virtue of solidarity transforms this virtue into a distinctly Christian virtue (number 5 above).

> In the light of faith, solidarity seeks to go beyond itself, to take on the *specifically Christian* dimensions of total gratuity, forgiveness and reconciliation. One's neighbour is then not only a human being with his or her own rights and a fundamental equality with everyone else, but becomes the *living image* of God the Father, redeemed by the blood of Jesus Christ and placed under the permanent action of the Holy Spirit. One's neighbour must therefore be loved, even if an enemy, with the same love with which the Lord loves him or her; and for that person's sake one must be ready for sacrifice, even the ultimate one: to lay down one's life for the brethren (cf. 1 John 3.16). (SS, no. 40)

A further deepening of solidarity draws out the Trinitarian dimensions of this Christian virtue:

> Awareness of the common fatherhood of God, of the brotherhood of all in Christ – 'sons in the Son' – and of the presence and life-giving action of the Holy Spirit will bring to our vision of the world *a new criterion* for interpreting it. Beyond human and natural bonds, already so close and strong, there is discerned in the light of faith a new

---

65 John Paul II, Encyclical Letter, *Sollicitudo Rei Socialis* ['On Social Concern'], 30 December 1987, no. 38. Subsequent references to this work (hereafter SS) will be made parenthetically in the text.

model of the *unity* of the human race, which must ultimately inspire our *solidarity*. This supreme *model of unity*, which is a reflection of the intimate life of God, one God in three Persons, is what we Christians mean by the word *'communion'*. (SS, no. 40)

The *Catechism of the Catholic Church* teaches us that there is no solution to the social question of solidarity apart from the gospel. 'Where sin has perverted the social climate, it is necessary to call for the conversion of hearts and appeal to the grace of God. Charity urges just reforms . . . This is the path of charity, that is, of the love of God and of neighbour. Charity is the greatest social commandment. It respects others and their rights. It requires the practice of justice, and alone makes us capable of it. *Charity inspires a life of self-giving*: "Whoever seeks to gain his life will lose it, but whoever loses his life will preserve it" [Luke 17.33]'. (CCC, no. 1896)

Notice that all the meanings of charity in this citation are ordered to charity as a life of self-giving. This brings us back to the concept of *communio*, namely, discovery and self-fulfilment through the free gift of self to others. In that self-giving, man not only truly fulfils himself but he also actualizes an authentic community. This life of self-giving finds its ultimate reality and model in the *communio personarum* of God himself, the Trinity of Persons, which is an interpersonal community of love and who, in himself, lives a mystery of love as total self-giving to another, with the Father giving all he has to the Son, and they in turn giving all they have to the Holy Spirit. Here we meet again the central motif in John Paul II's Trinitarian view of the person: 'There is a certain resemblance between the unity of the divine persons and the fraternity that men are to establish among themselves in truth and love. Love of neighbour is inseparable from love for God' (CCC, no. 1889). What then is the path to conversion, communion and solidarity?

In *Ecclesia in America*, John Paul II proclaims, 'the encounter with the living Jesus Christ is the path to conversion, communion and solidarity.' Where, then, do we encounter the living Christ? The answer must be, John Paul II adds,

The Church is the place where men and women by encountering Jesus, can come to know the love of the Father, for whoever has seen Jesus has seen the Father (cf. John 14.9). After his ascension into heaven, Jesus acts through the powerful agency of the Holy Spirit, the Paraclete (cf. John 16.17), who transforms believers by giving them new life. Thus they become capable of loving with God's own love, which 'has been poured into our hearts through the Holy Spirit that has been given to us' (Rom. 5.5). God's grace also enables Christians to work for the transformation of the world, in order to bring about a new civilization, which my Predecessor Paul VI appropriately called 'the civilization of love.'[66]

Conversion, or spiritual rebirth, by God's grace, into Trinitarian communion is distinct from and yet linked to the social dimensions of solidarity. We may not reduce Trinitarian communion to social solidarity and yet there is a social dimension to conversion that is the fruit of communion. Communion is the uncreated interpersonal life of the Father, Son and Holy Spirit, into which man has been invited and in which, through Christ, he can truly share. 'I am the way, and the truth, and the life; no one comes to the Father, except through me' (John 14.6). It is a supernatural gift of God's grace that presupposes union with the Holy Spirit. 'Conversion leads to fraternal communion, because it enables us to understand that Christ is the head of the Church, His Mystical Body; it urges solidarity, [moreover,] because it makes us aware that whatever we do for others, especially for the poorest, we do for Christ Himself.'[67]

By its very nature, then, our sharing in Trinitarian communion requires the immense gift of self-offering. Because solidarity goes beyond the sharing of material goods and, therefore, leads to the service of our neighbours in all their needs, material and spiritual, the sharing of the great gift of communion between God and man, which is made possible by Jesus Christ who first gave himself for love of us on the cross, is nothing other than the outward expression of the very same gift of self in solidarity. '"Truly, I say to you, as you did it to one of the least of these my brethren, you did it to me" (Matt. 25.40; cf. 25.45). The awareness of communion with Christ and with our brothers and sisters, for its part the fruit of conversion, leads to the service of our neighbours in all their needs, material and spiritual, since the face of Christ shines forth in every human being.' Communion is not reduced here to solidarity; rather, 'solidarity is the fruit of communion,' and, John Paul II adds, 'that is grounded in the mystery of the triune God, and in the Son of God who took flesh and died for all. It is expressed in Christian love that seeks the goods of others, especially of those most in need.'[68]

Finally, the encounter with the living Jesus Christ is the path to conversion, communion and solidarity, because he is the only true answer to overcoming self-alienation. This alienation affects man's ability to become a fully developed self-transcending subject who finds himself only by self-giving in an authentic human community. Most important, man's self-alienation, which inhibits his capacity for self-transcendence

---

66 *Ecclesia in America*, nos. 7, 10.
67 *Ecclesia in America*, no. 26.
68 *Ecclesia in America*, no. 52.

toward others, also renders him unable to give himself 'ultimately to God, who is the author of his being and who alone can fully accept his gift [of self-donation].'[69] As Jesus said to his disciples: 'If anyone desires to come after Me, let him deny himself, and take up his cross, and follow Me. For whoever desires to save his life will lose it, but whoever loses his life for My sake will find it' (Matt. 16.24–25). By this act of real self-giving to God, or as Wojtyła puts it, 'by abandoning himself wholly to God,'[70] the individual comes to know himself truly, being transformed so that he can now say with St Paul, 'It is no longer I who live, but Christ who lives in me' (Gal. 2.20). 'The revelation of the mystery of the Father and his love [revealed] in Jesus Christ [and through the Holy Spirit] reveals man to man, and gives the ultimate answer to the question, "What is man?"' Christ's revelation to man is not self-alienating; rather, it enables 'him to enter into himself more profoundly, to discover the whole truth of his own humanity and personality, which is the contrary of "alienation."'[71] Indeed, Jesus Christ not only reconciles man with the Father, transforming, enabling and healing human nature – 'If anyone is in Christ, *he is* a new creation; old things have passed away; behold, all things have become new' (2 Cor. 5.17) – so that man can enjoy Trinitarian communion, but he also reconciles man with himself and thus reveals his true nature, as well as the way that man can realize fully his true vocation.

For John Paul II, the key to transforming man's alienation is stated by the Second Vatican Council in *Gaudium et Spes* (no. 22): 'The truth is that only in the mystery of the incarnate Word does the mystery of man truly take on light. For Adam, the first man, was a figure of Him who was to come, Christ the Lord. Christ, the new Adam, in the very revelation of the mystery of the Father and of His love, fully reveals man to himself and brings to light his exalted vocation. It is in Christ, "the image of the invisible God" [Col. 1.15; 2 Cor. 4.4], that man has been created "in the image and likeness of the Creator." It is in Christ, Redeemer and Saviour [and Lord], that the divine image, disfigured in man by the first sin, has been restored to its original beauty and ennobled by the grace of God.'

Now, since the Church is the presence of Christ, that is, his self-communication to the world, it is essential that the Church be rediscovered as the place where we encounter the living Christ as Lord and Saviour. For this to happen, 'the Church must come to life in the souls of men,' to paraphrase Guardini. 'In her the great regeneration is already

---

69 John Paul II, Encyclical Letter, *Centesimus Annus*, no. 41.
70 Karol Wojtyła, *Sources of Renewal*, p. 140.
71 Karol Wojtyła, *Sources of Renewal*, pp. 75, 273.

beginning for which the entire creation "groaneth and is in travail."[72] Put differently, the Church is the Mystical Body of Christ, the reborn humanity in Christ, says Wojtyła, and this truth is best grasped when we understand the Church as *communio*.[73] We must avoid reducing the divine encounter with Christ to a pure 'I-thou' interpersonal relationship, in the sense discussed above, and instead understand the Church as a 'we' relationship, which is a dimension of communio, but now in light of the Trinitarian 'we' of God. As Ratzinger explains,

> In Christianity there is not simply a dialogical principle in the modern sense of a pure 'I-thou' relationship, neither on the part of the human person that has its place in the historical 'we' that bears it; nor is there such a mere dialogical principle on God's part who is, in turn, no simple 'I,' but the 'we' of Father, Son, and Spirit. On *both* sides there is neither the pure 'I,' nor the pure 'thou,' but on both sides the 'I' is integrated into the greater 'we.' Precisely this final point, namely, that not even God can be seen as the pure and simple 'I' toward which the human person tends, is a fundamental aspect of the theological concept of the person. . . . This Trinitarian 'we,' the fact that even God exists only as a 'we,' prepares at the same time the space of the human 'we.' The Christian's relation to God is not simply . . . 'I and Thou,' but, as the liturgy prays for us every day, 'per Christum in Spiritu Sancto ad Patrem' (Through Christ in the Holy Spirit to the Father).[74]

It is precisely this notion of the Church as *communio*, as a 'we' relationship, that enriches our understanding of the Christ-centred key to overcoming alienation. Says Ratzinger, 'If human alienation is to be overcome, if human beings are to find their identity again, it is indispensable that they again find the Church, which is not an institution hostile to humans but [rather] that new "we" in which the "I" can first secure its foundation and a place to stay' (*NSL*, p. 148). I turn now, in the final section of this essay, to sketch an overall picture of the relationship between the liturgy, Christian personalism, which Ratzinger's own reflections on theological anthropology lead him to speak of as a 'Eucharistic Personalism', and our participation in the eucharistic Church as the source of mission to the world.

---

72 Romano Guardini, *The Church and The Catholic and The Spirit of the Liturgy*, pp. 11, 23.
73 Karol Wojtyła, *Sources of Renewal*, p. 120.
74 Joseph Cardinal Ratzinger, 'Concerning the notion of person in theology', *Communio* 17 (Fall 1990), pp. 439–54, and for this quote, p. 453.

Eucharistic Personalism, Communion and Transformation

There are three points I want to make in this concluding section. First, there is an intrinsic connection between the Eucharist and ecclesiology. The Eucharist constitutes us as the Church, the unity of the many in and through the one Christ. In receiving the body and blood of Christ, we become the Church, 'all one in Christ Jesus' (Gal. 3.28), as a result of becoming one body with him. 'Is not the bread that we break a participation in the body of Christ? Because there is one bread, we, who are many are one body, we all partake of the one bread' (1 Cor. 10.16–17). This point leads us back to Ratzinger's earlier claim that the relationship between Christ and me is not merely an 'I-Thou' interpersonal relationship, but rather, through Christ in the Holy Spirit to the Father, a new 'we' community, a eucharistic communion, that binds me at once into the 'we' of God, Father, Son and Spirit, and into the 'we' of all who belong to Christ (cf. *PFF*, pp. 78–9).[75] Says Ratzinger, 'The Eucharist takes us out of ourselves and into him, so that we can say, with Paul, "It is no longer I who live, but Christ who lives in me" (Gal. 2.20).' 'I, yet no longer I,' adds Ratzinger, 'a new and greater self is growing, which is called the one body of the Lord, the Church ... Of course, this "being one body" has to be thought of along the lines of husband and wife being one: one flesh, and yet two; two, and yet one. The difference is not abolished but is swallowed up in a greater unity' (*PFF*, p. 103). This unity is a 'we' unity, *we are* one single body, which does not diminish or distort the 'I' – for Jesus Christ is the meaning and destiny of the lives of every single person who belongs to him and is a member of his body.

Second, the heart in its biblical sense is the root and centre of our whole human existence, in other words, the whole man, or, as Ratzinger says, 'the inner person, the entirety of the self' (*NSL*, p. 177). The heart is, in the words of the *Catechism of the Catholic Church*,

> the depth of one's being, where the person decides for or against God. The heart is the dwelling-place where I am, where I live; according to the Semitic or biblical expression, the heart is the place 'to which I withdraw.' The heart is the hidden centre, beyond the grasp of our reason and of others; only the Spirit of God can fathom the human heart and know it fully. The heart is the place of decision, deeper than our psychic drives. It is the place of truth, where we choose life or death. It is the place of encounter, because as image of God we live in relation: it is the place of covenant ... relationship between God and man in Christ. (*CCC*, nos. 2563–4)

---

75 Joseph Cardinal Ratzinger, 'Concerning the notion of person in theology', p. 453.

Thus, the whole man must offer himself up 'as a living sacrifice, consecrated to God and worthy of his acceptance; this is the worship due from you as rational creatures [this is for you the true and appropriate worship/the spiritual worship]' (Rom. 12.1). This is the *sursum corda* – lifting up our *whole life*, our heart, to God and uniting our sacrifice of praise and thanksgiving with the self-giving of Jesus Christ to the Father, with his atoning action of sacrificial love on the cross, a sacrifice of propitiation and satisfaction, which is as such the true worship of God. In other words, in this consecration to God, this radical self-giving, 'we are asking', says Ratzinger, 'that we ourselves might become a Eucharist with Christ and, thus, become acceptable and pleasing to God.' Ratzinger insists that, in order to be correctly understood, the notion that our Christian life should be a living sacrifice must be 'read in the context of the Eucharist and of the theology of the Cross' (*PFF*, pp. 116–17).

Most significant, this is *eucharistic personalism*: the radical self-giving, the giving away of oneself to God the Father, in Christ, the Logos, who is the Son, through the Holy Spirit. 'The man who tries to save his life shall lose it; it is the man who loses his life for my sake that will save it' (Matt. 15.25). In this radical act of self-giving, by grace, I am united with the Logos, Jesus Christ, who is the true sacrifice, which accomplished my redemption once for all; there is an inward change, a radical rebirth of my heart, so that we become 'sons in the sacramental fellowship in which we are living'. Ratzinger elaborates:

> And if we become sacrifices, if we ourselves become conformed to the Logos, then this is not a process confined to the spirit, which leaves the body behind it as something to be distanced from God. The Logos himself has become a body and gives himself to us in his Body. That is why we are being urged to present our bodies as a form of worship consistent with the Logos, that is to say, to be drawn into the fellowship of love with God in our entire bodily existence, in bodily fellowship with Christ (*PFF*, p. 117).

Third, the eucharistic sacrifice itself is 'the source and summit of the Christian life' aiming at a complete transformation of the whole of our life. It is important to recall here the third dimension of Ratzinger's high theology of the liturgy, namely, the Mass 'makes Christ's one definitive redemptive sacrifice always present in time'.[76] The eucharistic sacrifice re-enacts that past atoning event by joining with that event in the eternal

---

[76] Second Vatican Council, *Lumen Gentium*, Dogmatic Constitution on the Church, no. 11, and John Paul II, 2003 Encyclical Letter, *Ecclesia de Eucharistia*, no. 12, respectively.

present of God. As John Paul II puts it, 'The Church constantly draws her life from the redeeming sacrifice; she approaches it not only through faith-filled remembrance, but also through a real contact, since *this sacrifice is made present ever anew*, sacramentally perpetuated, in every community which offers it at the hands of the consecrated minister.'[77]

Now, it follows from our union with Christ, which is a supernatural gift of God's grace received through the sacrament of baptism, a union that is renewed and deepened in sharing the eucharistic sacrifice, that our lives are changed and made in a certain way, says John Paul II, 'completely "Eucharistic"'. Here there is a certain confluence of thought between Benedict XVI and John Paul II in their understanding of eucharistic personalism: we become one with the self-giving of Jesus Christ, with his atoning acts of redemptive love, which is as such the true worship of God. And because we draw life from him who, for our sake, became the Lamb of God and sacrificed himself for our sins, this makes the Eucharist itself the ground motive that shapes and determines our entire existence. This transfigured existence must reveal itself in the whole of our temporal life because the cosmic drama of the liturgy – creation, fall into sin and redemption by Jesus Christ – embraces everything in existence, the whole of reality. I conclude with the words of John Paul II about the cosmic character of the liturgy, words that echo the penetrating thought of Romano Gaurdini, who held that the whole creation is embraced in the relation with God established by the liturgy.[78]

> The Eucharist is always in some way celebrated *on the altar of the world*. It unites heaven and earth. It embraces and permeates all creation. The Son of God became man in order to restore all [fallen] creation, in one supreme act of praise, to the One who made it from nothing. He, the Eternal High Priest who by the blood of his Cross entered the eternal sanctuary, thus gives back to the Creator and father all [fallen] creation [now] redeemed. He does so through the priestly ministry of the Church, to the glory of the Most Holy Trinity. Truly this is the mysterium fidei which is accomplished in the Eucharist: the world which came forth from the hands of God the Creator now returns to him redeemed by Christ.[79]

---

77 John Paul II, Encyclical Letter, *Ecclesia de Eucharistia*, no. 12.
78 Romano Guardini, *The Church and The Catholic and The Spirit of the Liturgy*, pp. 29–31.
79 John Paul II, Encyclical Letter, *Ecclesia de Eucharistia*, no. 8.

6

Liturgies within the Liturgy

BRUCE E. HARBERT

In the first chapter of Luke's Gospel we read that Zacharias, having been struck dumb in the Temple, returned home. The New Revised Standard Version translates the verse thus, 'When his time of service was ended, he went to his home.'[1] The New American Bible's translation of the same verse is, 'Then, when his days of ministry were completed, he went home.'[2] The Greek word translated in these versions as 'service' and 'ministry' is *leitourgia*, the direct ancestor of our English word 'liturgy'. So we could no less accurately translate the verse thus, 'When the days of his liturgy were completed, he went home.'

This translation would sound strange to modern ears, accustomed, as we are, to think of liturgy as belonging to a community, not to an individual. The two modern versions cited above reveal this prejudice, for whereas in the Greek, 'his' is more closely linked with *leitourgia* ('his liturgy'), they translate the phrase as though 'his' belonged with *hēmerai* ('his days'/'his time').

Another passage in early Christian literature that speaks of liturgy as proper to a single person is in the First Letter of Clement, where the author expounds the concept of hierarchy in the Church:

> The High Priest (i.e. the bishop) has been given his own liturgies . . . Let each of you, brethren, give thanks to God in his own rank, being of a good conscience, not transgressing the rule that has been laid down for his liturgy, and acting with reverence.[3]

Modern English versions, influenced by the notion that a 'liturgy' can-

---

[1] Luke 1.23, *The Holy Bible Containing the Old and New Testaments with the Apocryphal/Deuterocanonical Books*. New Revised Standard Version (Oxford, New York: Oxford, 1989); New Revised Standard Version (New York: HarperCollins, 2007).

[2] Luke 1.23, *New American Bible* (Washington, DC: USCCB, 2002).

[3] 1 Clement 40.5–41,1, *Apostolischen Väter*, eds K. Bihlmeyer and W. Schneemelcher, 2nd edition (Tübingen: Mohr, 1956), p. 57.

not belong to an individual, avoid using 'liturgy' here as a translation of *leitourgia* on its two occurrences, preferring such words as 'service' or 'ministry'.

A particularly interesting comment on this passage from Clement is to be found on the first two pages of Gregory Dix's *The Shape of the Liturgy*.[4] Dix begins his book with this sentence, '"Liturgy" is the name given ever since the days of the apostles to the act of taking part in the solemn corporate worship of God by the "priestly" society of Christians, who are "the Body of Christ, the church"'. Dix cites in his support Acts 13.2a, 'While they were worshipping the Lord and fasting . . . ,'[5] where 'worshipping' translates the participle *leitourgountōn*. Despite Dix's claim, there is no reason to assume that the 'worshipping' referred to here was a communal act, with all five participants gathered in a single place. The verb *leitourgeo* can equally well be used of a service performed alone, as we shall see in the case of Samuel.

Having begun with a flourish, Dix finds himself in difficulties when, further down his first page, he confronts the First Letter of Clement, which uses *leitourgia* for the act of an individual, not of a community. Dix gets round the problem by putting 'liturgy' in inverted commas, as though the word was not being used in its correct sense.

Turning the page, we find him recognizing that Clement uses *leitourgia* to refer to the duties of an individual, 'Clement in the preceding context seems to imply that these "appointed rules" for the "liturgies" of the different "orders" are of divine institution, apparently from our Lord Himself.'[6] But the evidence will not put him off his thesis, and he persists, 'Be this as it may, here in the first century the eucharist is emphatically a corporate action of the whole Christian body . . .'[7]

Dix's book has been widely read and highly influential for over 60 years, and must surely have contributed to the widespread assumption that a liturgy is a corporate act.

Another influential theological work of the twentieth century that helped spread this use of the word 'liturgy' is Gerhard Kittel's *Theological Dictionary of the New Testament*.[8] Hermann Strathmann, discussing the use of *leitourgeo* and its cognates in the New Testament,[9]

---

4 Gregory Dix, *The Shape of the Liturgy* (Westminster: Dacre Press, 1943), p. 1.
5 This is the translation found in both the Revised Standard Version and the New American Bible.
6 Dix, *Shape*, p. 2.
7 Dix, *Shape*, p. 2.
8 *Theological Dictionary of the New Testament*, ed. Gerhard Kittel, tr. Geoffrey W. Bromiley (Grand Rapids, MI: Eerdmans, 10 vols, 1964–74); (*Theologisches Wörterbuch zum Neuen Testament*, ed. Gerhard Kittel (Stuttgart: Kohlhammer, 10 vols, 1934–48)).
9 H. Strathmann, s.v. 'leitourgeia', in Kittel ET, Vol. 4, pp. 226–31 (German, Vol. 4, pp. 221–38).

sees there a movement away from a cultic view of *leitourgia* towards a 'spiritualised' one. The crucial text for him, as for Dix, is Acts 13:2, where in the participle *leitourgountōn* he finds a reference to 'a fellowship of prayer on the part of the five.' This need not involve any formality, or even the gathering of the participants in a single place. That is to say, it need not involve anything that we should now call 'liturgy'. The author, writing from within the Protestant tradition, insists that there is no differentiation of roles among the participants:

> The messengers of Christ and leaders of individual congregations do not have to fulfill a *leitourgia* for the community. Their task is to proclaim in the word of the crucifixion of Christ the *leitourgia* which has been fulfilled once and for all. . . The new community had no priests, for it consisted of priests.[10]

Though coming from an entirely different standpoint from Dix, Strathmann agrees with him that a Christian *leitourgia* is always the activity of a group. In pre-Christian Greek, *leitourgia* was used for any public service. The word itself is derived from *laos*, 'the people' and *ergon*, 'a work'. A person who had the duty of performing a work for the people was a *leitourgos*, and the verb for his action was *leitourgein*. (Note that *leitourgia* was used to mean a work *for* the people, not, as modern liturgists so often use it, a work *of* the people.) The meaning of the word was also extended to denote any service, including service of the gods, and indeed any kind of function. When Aristotle is discussing the function of the mouth in the bodies of animals, he calls it the 'liturgy' of the mouth.[11]

In the Septuagint, *leitourgia* is used in several different ways. Often it is used in relation to cultic activity performed by a group, for instance, 'Thereafter the Levites went in to do [or 'to liturgize' – *leitourgein*] their liturgy in the tent of meeting . . .'[12] Though here the Levites are spoken of collectively, as sharing a single *leitourgia*, elsewhere each Levite is said to have his own liturgy, 'and give them to the Levites, to each according to his *leitourgia*.'[13]

Leitourgia can also be used with a genitive to indicate, not the person

---

10 Strathmann, s.v. 'leitourgeia', in Kittel ET, Vol. 4, p. 228. (Die Boten Christi und die leitenden Männer der einzelnen Gemeinden haben keine *leitourgeia* für die Gemeinde zu vollziehen, sondern die ein für allemal geschehene *leitourgeia* in dem Wort vom Kreuz Christi zu verkündigen . . . Die neue Gemeinde hatte keine Priester, weil sie aus lauter Priestern bestand, 235).

11 Aristotle, *De Partibus Animalium* 2, 3.

12 Numeri 8.22, *Septuaginta*, ed. A. Rahlfs (Stuttgart: Deutsche Bibelgesellschaft, 1979), p. 229.

13 Num. 7.5, *Septuaginta*, ed. Rahlfs, p. 224.

or persons who perform the service, but the person or thing in whose honour the service is performed, 'And the Levite himself shall liturgize the *leitourgia* of the tent of meeting...'[14] ... 'the works of the *leitourgia* of the house of God.'[15] ... 'for all the *leitourgia* of the Lord and the service of the king.'[16] The solitary service in the Temple of the boy Samuel is thrice denoted by the verb *leitourgeo*,[17] a fact that casts doubt on Dix's claim that *leitourgeo* in Acts 13.2 refers to a corporate act.

In patristic Greek, the meanings given to *leitourgia* and its cognates by classical authors and the Septuagint survive, and are joined by new senses linked to the Christian ministry, both in its cultic and non-cultic aspects. Clement of Rome, whose use of *leitourgia* in a cultic context has already been discussed, uses the word also of the office of bishop more broadly considered, from which, he maintains, some have been unjustly dismissed, 'You, however, as we notice in more than one instance, have turned men out of a *leitourgia* in which they were serving honourably and without the least reproach.'[18]

Saint Athanasius speaks of the service offered by Christ in his humanity as a *leitourgia*.[19] According to Saint John Chrysostom, the *leitourgia* referred to in Acts 13.2 was not, *pace* Dix, a celebration of the Eucharist, but the ministry of preaching: the disciples were proclaiming the word of God as they fasted.[20] Those who wish to pursue further the use of *leitourgia* and its cognates in the patristic period may consult Lampe's Lexicon.[21]

When we turn to the history of *liturgia* in Latin, we encounter a surprising fact: the word was hardly known before the twentieth century. This is clear from the Library of Latin Texts database,[22] which indicates that the documents of the Second Vatican council use *liturgia* 69 times and *liturgicus* 94 times, but that in all the preceding centuries *liturgicus* was never used, and *liturgia* was used only once, by Saint Augustine,[23] who speaks of it as a Greek word.

---

14 Num. 18.23, *Septuaginta*, ed. Rahlfs, p. 248.

15 Paralipomenon 1, 1 Chron. 23.28, *Septuaginta*, ed. Rahlfs, p. 799.

16 Paralipomenon 1, 1 Chron. 26.30, *Septuaginta*, ed. Rahlfs, p. 805.

17 Regnorum 1, 1 Sam. 2.11; 2.18; 3.1, *Septuaginta*, ed. Rahlfs, pp. 505, 506, 507.

18 1 Clement 44.6, *Apostolischen Väter*, eds Bihlmeyer and Schneemelcher, p. 59.

19 Athanasius, *Contra Arianos* 3.44, ed. J. P. Migne (PG 26) (Paris: Migne, 1857), pp. 101–4.

20 John Chrysostom, *Homilies on Acts* 27.1, ed. J. P. Migne (PG 60) (Paris: Migne, 1862), p. 205.

21 *A Patristic Greek Lexicon*, ed. G. W. H. Lampe, 14th impression (Oxford: Clarendon Press, 2000), pp. 795–6.

22 CLCLT-5, *Library of Latin Texts*, 3 CDs (Turnhout: Brepols, 2002).

23 Augustine of Hippo, *Enarrationes in Psalmos* 135, 3rd edition (CCL 40) (Turnhout: Brepols, 1956), 1991: *ministerium uel seruitium religionis, quae graece liturgia uel latria dicitur.*

CLCLT-5, though vast, makes no pretence to be complete, and the picture it gives can be refined somewhat. *Liturgia* seems to appear first in the sixteenth century, the title of Erasmus's *Virginis matris apud Lauretum cultae liturgia* of 1523[24] being the earliest instance I have found. In this and similar usages, *liturgia* is used to mean 'a form of public worship' or 'a collection of formularies for the conduct of divine service'. These are definitions given by the Oxford English Dictionary for the English word *liturgy*, which also occurs first in the sixteenth century. As F. Cabrol remarked, they are 'not very ancient'.[25]

The sudden irruption of the word 'liturgy' and its cognates into ecclesial discourse in the West is illustrated by the fact that in Pope Leo XIII's Encyclical Letter on the Eucharist, *Mirae caritatis* of 28 May 1902, *liturgia* is not found, but 18 months later, in Pope Pius X's *Motu proprio* on sacred music, *Tra le sollecitudini* of 22 November 1903,[26] it occurs (in Italian) seven times.

In his encyclical *Mediator Dei*, Pope Pius XII proposed a definition of liturgy that shows a fine awareness of the Greek tradition behind the word,

> The sacred liturgy is, consequently, the public worship which our Redeemer as Head of the Church renders to the Father, as well as the worship which the community of the faithful renders to its Founder, and through Him to the heavenly Father. It is, in short, the worship rendered by the Mystical Body of Christ in the entirety of its Head and members.[27]

In this definition, the Pope speaks of the liturgy as the action first of an individual (Christ), then of a group (the Church) in relationship to that individual, and finally of the individual united with the group, the *totus Christus*.

The influence of *Mediator Dei* can be seen in the definition of liturgy given by the Second Vatican Council. It speaks first of Christ in relation-

---

24 Erasmus of Rotterdam, *Virginis matris apud lauretum cultae liturgia* (Basel: Frobenius, 1523), retrieved 7 March 2008. http://swissbib.org/spez/poeba/poeba-002935758.htm. For fuller discussion, see A. G. Martimort, 'Definitions and Method', in *Principles of the Liturgy*, ed. A. G. Martimort, trans. Matthew J. O'Connell (The Church at Prayer: An Introduction to the Liturgy 1), 2nd edition (Collegeville, MN: The Liturgical Press, 1986), pp. 7–8.

25 F. Cabrol, s.v. 'Liturgie', in *Dictionnaire de Théologie Catholique*, vol. 9, ed. E. Amann (Paris: Letouzey et Ane, 1926), Vol. I, p. 787: 'La liturgie, dans son acception actuelle... n'est pas fort ancienne.'

26 'Tra le Sollecitudini', *Acta Sanctae Sedis* 36 (1903–4), pp. 329–41.

27 'Mediator Dei', *Acta Apostolicae Sedis* 39 (1947), pp. 521–95.

ship to the Church, then of Christ alone, then of Christ united with the Church:

> Christ indeed always associates the Church with Himself in the truly great work of giving perfect praise to God and making men holy. The Church is His beloved Bride who calls to her Lord, and through Him offers worship to the Eternal Father . . .
> . . . Rightly, then, the liturgy is considered as an exercise of the priestly office of Jesus Christ. In the liturgy the sanctification of man is manifested by signs perceptible to the senses, and is effected in a way which is proper to each of these signs; in the liturgy full public worship is performed by the Mystical Body of Jesus Christ, that is, by the Head and His members.[28]

Later, the document stresses the corporate aspect of Christian worship thus, 'Liturgical services are not private functions, but are celebrations of the Church, which is the "sacrament of unity", namely, the holy people united and ordered under their bishops. Therefore liturgical services pertain to the whole body of the Church; they manifest it and have effects upon it.'[29]

Then the role of individuals and groups is touched on, 'but they concern the individual members of the Church in different ways, according to their differing rank, office, and actual participation. The individual dimension is stressed again a little later, 'In liturgical celebrations each one, minister or layperson, who has an office to perform, should do all of, but only, those parts which pertain to that office by the nature of the rite and the principles of liturgy.'[30]

Despite the clarity and nuances of magisterial teaching, it would be fair to say that the post-conciliar period has seen an explosion of the corporate, collectivist understanding of worship with a corresponding neglect of the part played in it by individual action and devotion. The title of a symposium published in 1972, *Liturgy: Self-Expression of the Church*,[31] edited by Herman Schmidt, the Professor of Liturgy at the Gregorian University whose influence began to be felt in the early 1950s with the reform of the rites of Holy Week,[32] and continued into the post-conciliar

---

28 *Sacrosanctum Concilium*, no. 7, *Decrees of the Ecumenical Councils* 2, ed. N. Tanner (Georgetown: Sheed and Ward, 1990), p. 822.
29 *Sacrosanctum Concilium* no. 26, ed. N. Tanner 2, p. 826.
30 *Sacrosanctum Concilium* no. 28, ed. N. Tanner 2, p. 826.
31 *Liturgy: Self-Expression of the Church*, ed. H. A. P. Schmidt (Concilium: Religion in the Seventies) (New York: Herder and Herder, 1972).
32 H. A. P. Schmidt, *Hebdomada Sancta*, 3 vols (Rome, Freiburg im Breisgau and Barcelona: Herder, 1956–7).

period, exemplifies the trend. One rarely hears talk of 'my liturgy', 'her liturgy' or 'the Bishop's liturgy', traditional though such expressions are. The collectivist view of liturgy is vividly manifested when a congregation joins in the doxology of the eucharistic prayer, or a priest or bishop reads the Gospel in the presence of a deacon. It has repercussions in the field of liturgical language, to which I now turn.

In the revision of the Latin Missal, which followed the Council, prayers where the priest speaks in the first person singular were for the most part abandoned. In his opening words, the antiphon 'I will go to the altar of God', has been replaced by the greeting 'The Lord be with you'. He no longer confesses his sins alone in the *Confiteor*, but joins the people in reciting it. His prayer over the bread which contained the singular form *offero*, 'I offer', was replaced with one containing *offerimus*, 'we offer'. Luis Maldonado offered a rationale for this change:

> ... all the presidential prayers (the formularies of the priest, in preconciliar parlance) are written in the plural. They must also be endorsed and 'received' by the assembly through its 'Amen'. Formularies written in the singular were creations of the Middle Ages when ... the sense of the assembly was lost.[33]

But not all the prayers in the liturgy are 'we' prayers. They cannot be. Sometimes the assembly must pray for others, for the sick, for example, or for the dead. Sometimes prayer must be made for a group within the assembly, such as candidates who receive one of the sacraments during the celebration. Then a 'they' prayer is in order. Furthermore, in the prayers of the Roman Rite, the priest often prays for the people as 'them' rather than 'us'. But English translators have become reluctant to reproduce this feature. I shall illustrate the growing preference for first-person forms over third-person ones by means of the history of translation of a single prayer, first found in a manuscript of the early ninth century,[34] which for many centuries before Vatican II was used at the end of the

---

33 Luis Maldonado, 'Liturgy as Communal Enterprise', in *The Reception of Vatican II*. eds Giuseppe Alberigo, Jean-Pierre Jossua and Joseph A. Komonchak. tr. Matthew J. O'Connell (Washington, DC: Catholic University of America Press, 1987), pp. 315–16.

34 MS Cambrai 164, the 'Hadrianum'. *Le Sacramentaire grégorien*, vol. 1, ed. J. Deshusses, (Spicilegium Friburgense 16), 3rd edition (Fribourg: Éditions Universitaires, 1992), no. 327. The prayer is subsequently found in many sacramentaries, for example, *Liber sacramentorum Gellonensis* eds A. Dumas and J. Deshusses (CCL 159) (Turnhout: Brepols, 1981), no. 587; *Liber sacramentorum Engolismensis*, ed. P. Saint-Roch (Turnhout: Brepols, 1987), no. 590.

Mass of Wednesday in Holy Week,³⁵ and is now the Prayer over the People for the end of the Mass of Palm Sunday.³⁶

The earliest English translation of this prayer that I know is by Cranmer, who adopted this text for his liturgy of Good Friday:

> Almighty God, we beseech thee graciously to behold this thy family, for the which our lord Jesus Christ was contented to be betrayed, and given up into the hands of wicked men, and to suffer death upon the cross.³⁷

The earliest English translation for Catholic use seems to be from an eighteenth-century Holy Week Manual:

> Look down, we beseech thee, O Lord, on this thy Family, for which our Lord Jesus Christ was pleased to be delivered into the Hands of the Wicked, and to suffer the Torment of the Cross.³⁸

In the nineteenth century, Frederick Charles Husenbeth published a pioneering hand-missal for the use of the laity, in which he translated our prayer thus:

> Look down, we beseech thee, O Lord, upon this thy family, for which our Lord Jesus did not hesitate to be delivered up to the hands of the wicked, and to undergo the torments of the cross.³⁹

Adrian Fortescue's translation of the Missal contains this version:

> Look down, we beseech thee, O Lord, upon this thy family, for which our Lord Jesus Christ hesitated not to be delivered up into the hands of wicked men and to undergo the torment of the cross.⁴⁰

---

35 *Missale Romanum ex decreto SS. Concilii Tridentini Restitutum Summorum Pontificum cura recognitum*, editio typica (Città del Vaticano: Typis Polyglottis Vaticanis, 1962), p. 151: 'Respice quaesumus, Domine, super hanc familiam tuam, pro qua Dominus noster Iesus Christus non dubitavit manibus tradi nocentium, et crucis subire tormentum . . .' which has reversed the words '*quaesumus*' and '*Domine*' of the more ancient manuscripts.

36 *Missale Romanum ex decreto Sacrosancti Oecumenici Concilii Vaticani instauratum Auctoritate Pauli PP. VI promulgatum Ioannis Pauli PP. II cura recognitum*, editio typica tertia (Città del Vaticano: Typis Vaticanis, 2002), p. 284.

37 *The Collects of Thomas Cranmer*, ed. C. Frederick Barbee and Paul F. M Zahl (Grand Rapids, MI: Eerdmans, 1999), p. 46.

38 *The Office of Holy Week, The Office of the Holy Week*, ed. tr. J. P. Coghlan, 8th edition (London: Keating, Brown and Keating, 1780), p. 149.

39 *The Missal for the Use of the Laity*, ed. tr. F. C. Husenbeth (London: Charles Dolman, 1847).

40 *The Missal: The Liturgy for Layfolk*, ed. tr. Adrian Fortescue (London: Burns Oates & Washbourne Ltd, 1926), p. 281.

In 1948 the Dominicans in England published a facing-page translation for use by lay people attending Mass in the Dominican rite, which also contained our text:

> Look down, we beseech thee, O Lord, upon this thy family, for which our Lord Jesus Christ did not refuse to be delivered into the hands of the wicked, and to endure the torment of the cross.[41]

By this time the Liturgical Movement was beginning to have an impact in Rome, evidenced by the publication in 1947 of Pius XII's Encyclical *Mediator Dei* and by the subsequent reform in the early 1950s of the liturgy of Holy Week. In 1951 a new Holy Week book was published with translations by Ronald Knox who, though justly famed as a translator, published few versions of liturgical texts. He seems to have been the first English translator to introduce first-person forms into our prayer:

> Lord, on this household of thine look down with mercy! For our sakes, our Lord Jesus Christ thought it no shame to die, given up into the hands of sinners, racked on a Cross.[42]

From Knox's published reflections on the task of translating Scripture, it is clear that he wrote for individual readers who would read his texts in solitude.[43] He was not concerned with public proclamation of his work, and this brought him into controversy. He was not in sympathy with the reform of Holy Week. His is a devotional translation, designed to help the lone worshipper in the pew, heightening the emotions by its exclamatory style. Vivid and arresting as it is, it lacks the sobriety of the Roman original, and few would now consider it suitable for public liturgical use.

Other hand-missals published in the immediate pre-conciliar period preserve third-person forms in our prayer. The first is by J. O'Connell and H. P. R. Finberg:

> Look favourably, Lord, we beg thee, upon this family of thine, for whose sake our Lord Jesus Christ did not hesitate to be betrayed into the hands of the wicked and to undergo the torment of the cross.[44]

---

41 *The Dominican Missal in Latin and English*, rev. ed. (Oxford: Blackfriars Publications, 1948), p. 388.
42 R. A. Knox, *Holy Week* (London, Burns Oates & Washbourne, 1951), p. 91.
43 R. A. Knox, *Trials of a Translator* (New York: Sheed and Ward, 1949).
44 *The Missal in Latin and English*, ed. tr. J. O'Connell and H. P. R. Finberg (London: Burns Oates & Washbourne Ltd, 1952), p. 350.

LITURGIES WITHIN THE LITURGY

Elsewhere, these translators frequently replace the third person with the first.[45] Their work indicates the direction that liturgical translation into English would take after the Council, and both of them were influential in liturgical circles soon after the Council.

Our next example comes from a hand-missal greatly esteemed in the twentieth century, which originated in Belgium and did much to prepare the ground for reception of the liturgical reforms of the Council:

> Look down, we pray You, Lord, on this Your family, for which our Lord Jesus Christ did not hesitate to be betrayed and to be delivered into the hands of wicked men and suffer the torment of the cross.[46]

Even after the Council, the National Liturgical Commission of England and Wales translated this prayer with third-person forms:

> O God, look kindly on this your family for whom our Lord Jesus Christ allowed himself to be betrayed into the hands of wicked men, and to undergo the torment of the Cross.[47]

However, the version published in 1973 by the International Commission on English in the Liturgy used the first person:

> Father,
> look with love upon your people,
> the love which our Lord Jesus Christ showed us
> when he delivered himself to evil men
> and suffered the agony of the cross.[48]

This is the style to which English-speaking Catholics have become accustomed. Let me demonstrate it with three further examples, comparing by means of italicization, the translations of Husenbeth with the current texts.

The first contains an assertion about human nature in general, which the current version obscures by making the prayer refer only to 'us':

---

[45] See their versions of the Collects for the Second Sunday of Lent, the Second Sunday after Easter, and the Fourteenth and Twenty-third Sundays after Pentecost.
[46] *Saint Andrew Daily Missal*, ed. tr. Gaspar Lefebvre (Bruges: Biblica, 1962), p. 311.
[47] *Saint Michael's Daily Missal* (Alcester: Goodliffe Neale, 1973), p. 405.
[48] *The Roman Missal Revised by Decree of the Second Vatican Council and Published by Authority of Pope Paul VI: Official English Texts* (London: Collins and Goodliffe Neale, 1974), p. 382.

| Preserve thy Church, we beseech thee, O Lord, with perpetual mercy: and since without thee *mortal man* goes astray, may *he* be ever withheld by thy grace from what is hurtful, and directed to what is profitable. | Lord, watch over your Church, and guide it with your unfailing love. Protect *us* from what could harm *us* and lead *us* to do what will save *us*. Help *us* always, for without you *we* are bound to fail. |

The next example, which occurs in Easter Week, is best understood as a prayer for those newly baptized. By applying it to 'us', the current version removes this allusion:

| O God, who dost ever multiply thy church by a new progeny, grant to thy servants, that they may retain in their lives the mystery they have received by faith. | Father, you give your Church constant growth by adding new members to your family. Help us to put into action in our lives the baptism we have received with faith. |

Our third example, which at least from the eighth century onwards was associated with the Easter season but has now been moved into Ordinary Time, also probably contains a reference to the recently baptized who have turned from error to justice,[49] but the use of the inclusive terms 'us' and 'all' hides this:

| O God, who dost shew to those that go astray the light of thy truth, that *they* may return to the way of justice; grant to all who are numbered in the profession of Christianity, to reject those things, which are inimical to this name and to pursue those that are becoming. | God our Father, your light of truth guides *us* to the way of Christ. May all who follow him reject what is contrary to the Gospel. |

---

49 *cunctis qui christiana professione censentur*, 'all who are counted as Christian for the faith they profess,' (author's translation).

Two causes have contributed to this preference for first-person forms. The first is the growing influence of the collectivist view of liturgy outlined above. The second is a desire to make liturgical texts more usable by the solitary reader of a hand-missal, that is, to turn liturgical texts into devotional ones. We have already seen this tendency operating in the case of Knox. It is also to be found much earlier.

The first translator into English for Catholic use of a substantial quantity of prayers from the Roman Missal seems to have been John Gother (c.1650–1704). He wrote voluminous prayers for Sundays and feast days for the use of those who could not attend Mass. They were intended to arouse devotion in the user, and so are overwhelmingly 'we'-prayers. But Gother incorporated into these devotions the Collect for the Day, usually translated fairly literally, so it is not surprising that occasionally he allowed the style of the liturgical prayers to be assimilated to that of his other material, transforming a liturgical text into a devotional one. I give two examples. The first is the Collect for the Fourteenth Sunday after Pentecost, of which I have already given Husenbeth's more literal rendering above:

> Preserve thy Church, O Lord, we beseech thee, by thy perpetual mercy; and, because without thee, *our* nature is always frail, by thy help may it be delivered from all that is sinful, and directed in the way of salvation.

The second is the old Collect for Whit-Monday, which was not included in the post-conciliar Missal:

> O God, who didst send down the Holy Ghost upon the apostles; hear the prayer of thy people, that we, who, through thy grace have the gift of a true faith, may enjoy true peace.

Husenbeth's more literal translation runs:

> O God, who didst give the Holy Spirit to thy Apostles, grant to thy people the effect of their pious prayers, that on those to whom thou hast given faith, thou mayest also bestow peace.

But even Husenbeth, who usually follows the Latin closely, occasionally introduces first-person forms not in the Latin, as in the Post-Communion for Sexagesima:

> We humbly beseech thee, O Almighty God, that thou wouldst graciously grant us to serve thee in a manner pleasing in thy sight, whom thou refreshest with thy sacraments.[50]

---

50 *The Missal for the Use of the Laity*, ed. tr. Husenbeth, p. 111.

Fortescue's version is more literal:

> We humbly beseech thee, almighty God, that thou wouldst grant that those whom thou refreshest with thy sacraments may serve thee worthily by a life well pleasing to thee.[51]

The Instruction *Liturgiam authenticam*, issued by the Congregation for Divine Worship and the Discipline of the Sacraments in March 2001, introduced new stipulations for the fidelity of translations prepared for liturgical use. The title of this document is sometimes misunderstood, for *authenticam* is taken to mean 'authentic' in the modern English sense of 'real', 'true' or 'genuine'. This is not what *authenticus* means in Latin. Applied to documents, as it most frequently is, it means 'in accord with the original'. Applied to people, it means 'authoritative' or 'worthy of belief'. For liturgy to be *authentica*, it must be faithful to the tradition from which it derives.

Faithful translation of the texts of the Mass necessarily involves using the third person where the Latin uses it. So accustomed are we to the ubiquity of first-person forms that this can produce some surprises, as the texts discussed above would lead us to expect.

One group of texts in which this feature is likely to be particularly noticeable is the Prayers over the People, in nearly all of which the people are referred to as 'they'. An example is the Prayer over the People for Palm Sunday, discussed above. The original function of these orations is disputed, but the most likely view seems to be that they were originally said by a bishop on his way out of church at the end of Mass, as he passed the place where the penitents were gathered. Since penitents were not fully part of the worshipping assembly, it may have seemed natural to avoid the use of first-person plural forms to refer to them. The pre-conciliar Missal had a Prayer over the People for each day in Lent, and in the third edition of the post-conciliar Missal this provision has been restored. There are also 30 *Orationes super populum* for use at other times of the year. Their use is always optional, but if they are used, we shall often hear the priest calling the people 'they', especially in Lent.

A strict interpretation of *Liturgiam Authenticam* would also require the replacement of first-person forms with third-person ones in the Roman Canon. Here is the current version of the sections of that prayer numbered 81 and 82 in the 1970 Missal:[52]

---

51 *The Missal: The Liturgy for Layfolk*, ed. tr. Fortescue, p. 121.

52 *Missale Romanum ex decreto Sacrosancti Oecumenici Concilii Vaticani instauratum Auctoritate Pauli PP. VI promulgatum*, editio typica (Città del Vaticano: Typis Vaticanis, 1970), pp. 447–8. In the *Missale Romanum*, editio typica tertia, 2002, these paragraphs are numbered 85 and 86, p. 572.

LITURGIES WITHIN THE LITURGY

Remember, Lord, your people,
especially those for whom we now pray, N. and N.
Remember all of us gathered here before you.
You know how firmly we believe in you
and dedicate ourselves to you.
We offer you this sacrifice of praise
for ourselves and those who are dear to us.
We pray to you, our living and true God,
for our well-being and redemption.

In union with the whole Church
we honour Mary,
the ever-virgin mother of Jesus Christ our Lord and God.
We honour Joseph, her husband,
the apostles and martyrs
Peter and Paul, Andrew,
(*a list of saints follows*) . . .
and all the saints.
May their merits and prayers
gain us your constant help and protection.
[Through Christ our Lord. Amen.]

The first point to notice is punctuation. For centuries, in both printed and manuscript missals, paragraphs 81 and 82 have been separated by the rubric *Infra Actionem*, indicating that on certain occasions extra words are to be added at this point. This separation led scribes, printers and editors to assume that the two sections are syntactically separate, and consequently to end paragraph 81 with a period and begin paragraph 82 with a capital letter. In fact, they form a single syntactic unit. In the earliest manuscript we have of the Roman Canon in anything like its modern form, the Old Gelasian Sacramentary, and in many other manuscript copies,[53] the two paragraphs are written as one. Moreover,

---

53 The following is a transcription of the relevant text as it appears in the Old Gelasian Sacramentary (*Liber Sacramentorum Romanae Ecclesia ordinis anni circuli*, ed. L. C. Mohlberg, (RED, Series Maior, Fontes 4), 3rd edition, Rome, 1981, 316-17, lines 180-1). The capitals and periods represent similar punctuation in the manuscript.
Memento domine famulorum famularumquae tuarum. et omnium circumadstantium. Quorum tibi fides cognita est. et nota devotio. Qui tibi offerunt. Hoc sacrificium. laudis. pro se suisque omnibus pro redemptione. animarum suarum pro spe salutis. et incolumitatis suae. tibi reddunt uota sua. aeterno deo uiuo et uero. Communicantes. et memor iam uenerantes. In primis gloriosae. semper uirginis. mariae. genetricis dei et domini nostri iesu. christi. sed et beatorum. apostolorum. ac martyrum tuorum. Petri. pauli . . . et omnium. sanctorum tuorum. Quorum meritis praecibusque. concedas. ut in omnibus protectionis tuae muniamur auxilio. per christum dominum nostrum.
Note that in the earliest manuscripts of the Roman Canon, the words 'for whom we offer

in the earliest manuscripts of the Roman Canon, the words 'for whom we offer you' do not occur. Before their addition in the ninth century, there were no first-person verbal forms at all in paragraph 81.

English translators have tended to translate these two paragraphs as a single syntactic unit, but to adopt the punctuation of the Latin printed text, thus putting a period and a capital letter in the middle of a sentence. The first known English translation of the Roman Canon is printed in the introduction to the 1684 edition of John Foxe's *Acts and Monuments* (often known as 'Foxe's Book of Martyrs'),[54] where it is attributed to Miles Coverdale (*c*.1488–1568), translator of the version of the Psalms that was incorporated into the *Book of Common Prayer*:

> Remember, Lord, thy servants and handmaids N. and N., and all that stand hereby round about, whose faith and devotion to thee is known and manifest; for whom we offer unto thee, or which themselves offer unto thee, this sacrifice of praise for them and theirs: for the redemption of their souls, for the hope of their salvation and health, and render their vows unto thee, the eternal living and true God.
>
> Communicating and worshipping the memorial, first of the glorious and ever Virgin Mary the mother of our God and Lord Jesu Christ, and also of thy blessed Apostles and Martyrs, Peter, Paul, ... and of all thy Saints: by whose merits and prayers grant thou, that in all things we may be defended with the help of thy protection, through the same Christ our Lord. Amen.

The earliest translation of the Roman Canon into English by a Catholic author that I know is by James Dymock (died 1718):[55]

> Be mindful, O Lord of all thy servants, Men and Women, N. and N. And of all those, especially that are here present, whose Faith and devotion is known unto thee, for whom we offer, or who offer up to thee this Sacrifice of praise for themselves, and for all theirs, for the Redemption of their Souls, for the hope of their Salvation, and pay their vows unto thee, the Eternal, Living and true God.
>
> Being made partakers of the same Communion, and honouring the Memory especially of the ever glorious Virgin Mary Mother of our

---

you' do not occur. Before their addition in the ninth century, there were no first-person verbal forms at all in paragraph 81.

54 J. Foxe, *Acts and Monuments of Matters Most Special and Memorable Happening in the Church*, 9th edition (London, 1684), Preface.

55 J. Dymock, *The Great Sacrifice of the New Law, Expounded by the Figures of the Old*, 6th edition (London, 1687).

Lord God Jesus Christ; as also of they blessed Apostles and Martyrs, Peter and Paul, Andrew, . . . and of all thy Saints, by whose merits and prayers, grant that we may in all things be strengthned [sic] by the help of thy protection. Through the same Christ our Lord. Amen.

These early translations set a pattern that persists until the mid-twentieth century. Translators recognize that the priest prays for those present as 'they', and reproduce the punctuation of the Latin text, allowing a period and capital letter to come in the middle of a syntactic unit.

The earliest version I have found that changes 'they' into 'we' was published in New York in 1936:[56]

> Remember, O Lord, thy servants and handmaids, N. and N. and all here present whose faith and devotion are known to thee; for whom we offer, or who offer up to thee this sacrifice of praise for themselves and all pertaining to them, for the redemption of their souls, for the hope of their salvation and well-being, and who pay their vows unto thee, the eternal, living and true God.
> We pray in union with and honour the memory, especially of the glorious ever Virgin Mary, Mother of our God and Lord Jesus Christ; as also of thy blessed apostles and martyrs, Peter and Paul, Andrew, . . . and of all thy saints; by whose merits and prayers grant that we may in all things be defended by the aid of thy protection. Through the same Christ our Lord. Amen.

Here, the priest prays for the people as 'they' in the first paragraph and then begins a new sentence in the second with 'we' as subject. This pattern is followed by several translations in the succeeding years.[57]

Translations of the Roman Missal prepared in accordance with the directives of *Liturgiam authenticam* will need to follow the Latin of this passage more closely than most recent versions. In doing so, they will not only be reinstating a traditional form of words, but also returning to an understanding of Christian worship more securely grounded in tradition than the collectivist one that has found favour in recent years. The spectacle of the priest setting himself apart from the people and praying for them, as well as with them, will remind us of a truth that has sometimes been overlooked in recent years, namely that within the liturgy there are many liturgies.

---

56 *The Catholic Sunday Missal*, ed. Charles J. Callan, tr. John A. McHugh (New York: P. J. Kennedy & Sons, 1936), pp. 75–7.

57 A selection: *My Sunday Missal*, ed. Stedman, 1942, pp. 49–50; *I Pray the Mass: Sunday Missal*, ed. tr. Hoever, 1951, pp. 37–8; *Daily Missal*, ed. tr. Gannon, 1953, pp. 723–4; *The Roman Missal for Sundays and Feast Days*, ed. Caraman and Walsh, 1961, pp. 237–8; *Saint Andrew Daily Missal*, ed. tr. Lefebvre, 1962, pp. 590–2.

Bibliography

Biblical

The Holy Bible Containing the Old and New Testaments with the Apocryphal/ Deuterocanonical Books. New Revised Standard Version, New York and Oxford: Oxford University Press, 1989.
New Revised Standard Version, New York: HarperCollins, 2007.
New American Bible, Washington, DC: USCCB, 2002.

Liturgical

The Catholic Sunday Missal, ed. Charles J. Callan, tr. John A. McHugh, New York: P. J. Kennedy & Sons, 1936.
Daily Missal, ed. tr. Robert I. Gannon, Birmingham, UK: Goodliffe Neale, 1953.
Decrees of the Ecumenical Councils, 2 vol. ed. N. Tanner, Georgetown: Sheed and Ward, 1990.
The Dominican Missal in Latin and English, rev. edn Oxford: Blackfriars Publications, 1948.
I Pray the Mass: Sunday Missal, ed. Hugo H. Hoever, New York: Catholic Book Publishing Co., 1951.
Liber Sacramentorum Romanae Aeclesiae ordinis anni circuli, eds Leo Cunibert Mohlberg, Leo Eizenhoefer and Petrus Siffrin (Rerum Ecclesiasticarum Documenta, Series Maior: Fontes 4) Rome: Herder, 1960.
Missale Romanum ex decreto SS. Concilii Tridentini Restitutum Summorum Pontificum cura recognitum, editio typica, Città del Vaticano: Typis Polyglottis Vaticanis, 1962.
The Missal for the Use of the Laity, ed. tr. F. C. Husenbeth, London: Charles Dolman, 1847.
The Missal: The Liturgy for Layfolk, ed. tr. Adrian Fortescue, London: Burns Oates & Washbourne Ltd, 1926.
The Missal in Latin and English, ed. tr. J. O'Connell and H. P. R. Finberg, London: Burns Oates & Washbourne Ltd, 1952.
My Sunday Missal, ed. Joseph F. Stedman, Brooklyn, NY: Confraternity of the Precious Blood, 1942.
The Office of the Holy Week, ed. tr. J. P. Coghlan, 8th edition, London: Keating, Brown and Keating, 1780.
The Roman Missal for Sundays and Feast Days, ed. Philip Caraman and James Walsh, London: The Caxton Publishing Co. Ltd, 1961.
The Roman Missal Revised by Decree of the Second Vatican Council and Published by Authority of Pope Paul VI: Official English Texts. London: Collins and Goodliffe Neale, 1974.
Saint Andrew Daily Missal, ed. tr. Gaspar Lefebvre, Bruges: Biblica, 1962.
Saint Michael's Daily Missal, Alcester: Goodliffe Neale, 1973.

Studies

Barba, Maurizio, '*Le orationes super populum* della *editio typica tertia* del *Missale Romanum*', Ecclesia Orans 19 (2002), pp. 189–240.

Callewaert, C., 'Qu'est-ce que l'*Oratio Super Populum?*', *Ephemerides Liturgicae* 51 (1937), pp. 310–18.

The Collects of Thomas Cranmer, eds C. Frederick Barbee and Paul F. M Zahl, Grand Rapids, MI: Eerdmans, 1999.

Dix, Gregory, *The Shape of the Liturgy*, Westminster: Dacre Press, 1943.

Dymock, James, *The Great Sacrifice of the New Law, Expounded by the Figures of the Old*, 6th edition, London, 1687.

Eizenhöfer, Leo 'Untersuchungen zum Stil und Inhalt der Römischen *Oratio Super Populum*', *Ephemerides Liturgicae* 52 (1938), pp. 258–311.

Foxe, John, *Acts and Monuments of Matters Most Special and Memorable Happening in the Church*, 9th edition, London, 1684.

Gother, John, *Prayers for Sundays, Holidays, and Other Festivals, from Low-Sunday to the Twenty-First Sunday after Pentecost*, London, 1704.

Jungmann, J. A., '*Oratio super populum* und altchristliche Büssersegnung', *Ephemerides Liturgicae* 52 (1938), pp. 77–96.

Knox, Ronald A., *Holy Week*, London: Burns Oates & Washbourne, 1951.

Knox, Ronald A., *Trials of a Translator*, New York: Sheed and Ward,1949.

Library of Latin Texts. Turnhout: Brepols, 2002. 3 CDs.

Liturgy: Self-Expression of the Church, ed. Herman Schmidt (Concilium: Religion in the Seventies), New York: Herder and Herder, 1972.

Maldonado, Luis, 'Liturgy as Communal Enterprise', in *The Reception of Vatican II*. eds Giuseppe Alberigo, Jean-Pierre Jossua and Joseph A. Komonchak. tr. Matthew J. O'Connell, Washington, DC: Catholic University of America Press, 1987, pp. 309–21.

Principles of the Liturgy, ed. A. G. Martimort, tr. Matthew J. O'Connell (The Church at Prayer: An Introduction to the Liturgy 1) Collegeville, MN: The Liturgical Press, 1986.

Schmidt, H. A. P., *Hebdomada Sancta*, 3 vols, Rome, Freiburg im Breisgau and Barcelona: Herder, 1956–7.

Theological Dictionary of the New Testament, 10 vols, ed. Gerhard Kittel, tr. Geoffrey W. Bromiley, Grand Rapids, MI: Eerdmans, 1964–74.

7

The Human Person at Play: A Model for Contemporary Liturgical Understanding

ZSOLT ILYÉS

(translated by Daniel McCarthy)

Preface

In the course of the twentieth century numerous scholars dedicated themselves to the study of play and to an understanding of reality as playful. The study of play has also sparked the interest of contemporary theologians and liturgists. Among the best known we number R. Guardini, H. Rahner, J. Moltmann, H. U. von Balthasar, A. N. Terrin, A. Paus and F. Euvé.[1] One may wonder why these theologians are interested in the study of play, only to discover that the majority are well acquainted with practical reality both in its cultural and ritual aspects. While they write on play and present its relationship to theology or liturgy, they are ever mulling over what is wrong with liturgical life and praxis and ever hopeful that their reflections might contribute to their revisioning.[2]

Recent studies on the character of play and the interpretation of reality as playful have focused both on the liturgical experience itself and on the human person, specifically one's attitudes toward liturgy and behaviour during ritual. This article departs from an initial consideration of liturgy as playful and presents certain consequences, which emerge from such an initial consideration.

---

1 See the bibliography.

2 J. Huizinga, *Homo ludens*, with introduction by U. Eco (Turin: Einaudi, 2001), pp. 229–51; H. Rahner, *Der spielende Mensch* (Einsiedeln: Johannes Verlag, 1952), pp. 10, 44; J. Moltmann, *Die ersten Freigelassenen der Schöpfung. Versuche über die Freude an der Freiheit und das Wohlgefallen am Spiel*, 5th edition (Munich: Chr. Kaiser Verlag, 1976), pp. 7, 19–20; R. Caillois, *I giochi e gli uomini. La maschera e la vertigine*, (Nuovo Portico 25), (Milan: Bompiani, 1981), pp. 75–9; H. Cox, *The Feast of Fools* (Cambridge, MA: Harvard UP, 1969), pp. 3–6.

Introduction

Playful activity and interpreting reality as playful are universally shared, independent of whether or not any given culture possesses the vocabulary that refers to this concept.

Play is present in diverse societies in various forms and functions and is often used in ritual activity or even in worship itself. Although the importance of play was recognized only in fairly recent times, nevertheless, we have come a long way in obtaining a theoretical and practical appreciation of play in modern Western culture, for example by reinforcing the right to play of children and adults alike, by affirming the educative and formative values of play and by giving adequate space to play.[3]

The concept of play is a persistent theme when reflecting on our humanity. We find it in mythology,[4] Greek philosophy[5] and in the Bible.[6] It is found not only in the writings of ancient Christian authors[7] and medieval saints and mystics,[8] but also in modern philosophy[9] and human sciences,[10] and even in modern times in social sciences[11] and

---

3 Since the eighteenth century there has been an increasing interest in the phenomenon of play. The concept has gained most ground in the discipline of philosophy. Schiller accentuated the importance of play, 'A human plays only when he is human in the full sense of the word and is a complete human only when he plays' (Schiller, *Briefe über die ästhetische Erziehung des Menschen*, ed. A Reble (Bad Heilbrunn: J. Klinkhardt, 1960)). But we must also note Sartre, who also emphasizes play when he defines it as a manifestation of freedom. (J.-P. Sartre, *L'essere e il nulla* (Milan: Il Saggiatore, 1975), p. 729). In the human sciences play is even more studied, and here we note the work of David L. Miller: *Gods and Games. Toward a Theology of Play* (New York: World, 1970), pp. 17–91. From the first quarter of the twentieth century the theme of play appears more and more often also in theological treatises.

4 Gods who play and dance (Dionysius, Hermes, Apollo and Zeus) are presented as 'children' who play, thereby creating the world; and play constitutes an integrating element in the metaphysics of many cosmologies; the image of the nymphs who dance (for example, in Homer: *Odyssey* 6).

5 For example, Heraclitus (*Aion* as a child who plays); Plato (he is the first who develops in a clear way the idea of play as a vision of life, of mankind and of a God who plays); the Neoplatonics (Plotinus, Philo of Alexandria); Aristotle (*eutrápelos*, the ideal man).

6 Gen. 26.8; 2 Sam. 6.1–5; Prov. 8.26–27a, 30–31; Wisd. 32.15–16; Ezek. 1.4–6, 11–12, 14–15, 17, 20, 24; Zech. 8.4–5; Matt. 18.3; 1 Cor. 7.29–32a.

7 Early Christian writers have very different ideas and positions on the subject of games and play. On the one hand some develop a mystical theology based on the idea of play (Tertullian, Clement of Alexandria, Origen, Eusebius, Gregory Nazianzen, Maximus the Confessor, Jerome, Augustine and Cyril of Alexandria); on the other hand we find severe injunctions against the games found in the surrounding society (Tertullian, Augustine, John Chrysostom).

8 For example, Saint Francis of Assisi in Italy; Margery Kempe in Norfolk and St Godric of Finchdale near Durham in England.

9 Kant, Schiller, J.-P. Sartre, F. Nietzsche.

10 In, for example, psychology and education theory.

11 Social sciences, mathematics, economics (J. Von Neumann and O. Morgenstein,

theology.[12] The continuing interest in play evident in such diverse disciplines demonstrates its universality, its steadfastness and the fruitfulness of play itself.

Recent authors interested in the study of play and the idea of reality as playful warn that in our own time we face a dramatic loss in the authentic capacity to play.[13] These authors caution that this problem is general, serious and profound. Some of them even ask whether the post-modern person is still capable of performing ritual acts, which of their nature are ludic. Indeed, their well-founded suspicion remains, as Guardini and Huizinga have already said, that ours is the era to have abolished the meaning of true play.

Among those who have diminished our sense of play I number various groups of people. Some, whether philosophers or not, are completely if not exclusively given to knowledge, and are exclusively dedicated to research and the contemplation of the true. Some desire to understand all things, to know-it-all. Some are exactingly scientific and want to demonstrate everything, to seize every opportunity to 'understand' and delimit all reality in definitions. Others wholeheartedly seek the goals of education and insist on attaining a certain pedagogy. Finally, some people, armed by holy zeal, search everywhere for moral absolutism to be slavishly followed.

Because all of these people have turned to 'holy' utilitarianism, they find themselves in serious difficulty before the reality of play and the perception of reality as play. Consequently they are disturbed by certain legitimate aspects of the liturgy,[14] because once the sense of play is lost, the very possibility of the liturgical act is inevitably diminished. The equation seems inevitable: a loss of play means a loss of the liturgical.

Clarifications on the Idea of Play

The Definition of Play

Approaches to the study of play are as complex as their respective disciplines are diverse: anthropology, sociology, pedagogy, psychology, philosophy, theology and mathematics. The study of play may seem a mere

---

Theory of Games and Economic Behavior, 1944), linguistics (Wittgenstein 'linguistic games': *Ricerche filosofiche*).

12 Dogmatic theology (H. U. von Balthasar; F. Euvé); pastoral theology, homiletics, exegesis, catechesis, liturgical science.

13 Huizinga, *Homo ludens*, p. 243; Rahner, *Der spielende Mensch*, p. 10; P. A. Bagyinszki, *Az Isten, az ember és a játék (Il Dio, l'uomo e il gioco)* (Szeged: Agape, 1998), p. 122.

14 R. Guardini, *Lo spirito della liturgia. I santi segni* (Brescia: Morcelliana, 2000), p. 113.

ruse because that which each discipline studies in the name of play is at times so diverse as to seem unrelated.[15] Often the results and affirmations of the learned seem to be, and even are, contradictory. Play is considered diversely as 'forgetting reality' (Durkheim, Huizinga) or 'sticking to reality' (Frobenius, Kerényi, Jensen). One defines play as 'venting unused energy' (H. Spencer), while another, to the contrary, as the 'massing and mobilization of energy' (P. Janet). One characterizes play as certain infantile behaviours, both mimic and competitive, behaviours certainly not becoming of adults, while another considers the useful purposes for play. Caillois opposes coercing play for its useful pedagogy when he says that play is not exercise, competition nor gallantry, except additionally so; the skills that play develops certainly benefit from this additional honing but the goal of play is play itself.[16] Some authors see in play the source and summit of all other forms of human activity and of social institutions (Huizinga, Moltmann); others, instead, give temporal priority to cult rather than to play (Kerényi, Jensen). According to some interpretations, play functions as a 'release valve' or as a means of realizing some desires which otherwise would not find a place in daily life. A differing line of interpretation understands the behaviour of play as a form of pleasure or recreation, and some even speak of a 'hedonistic' element of play.

As we cannot present all these interpretations here, this study will limit itself to two 'definitions' of play, which summarize well its fundamental characteristics. They are given by two noted authors: J. Huizinga and R. Caillois. Huizinga says:

> In summary, considered as a form, play may be called a free action, as it is consciously not taken 'seriously'; it is outside of ordinary life, still, it may completely engross the player. As an action, play does not comprise any material interest; it derives no advantage. One engages in play within a predetermined time and space. It unfolds in an ordered fashion according to given rules, and provokes social relationships, which are easily surrounded in mystery or accentuate by ruse their diversity from the ordinary world.[17]

> Play is an activity, or a voluntary engaging, carried out within certain defined limits of time and space according to a rule voluntarily assumed. Play, nevertheless, is all absorbing, an end in itself. It

---

15 See Caillois, *I giochi e gli uomini. La maschera e la vertigine*, [Nuovo Portico 25], (Milan: Bompiani, 1981), p. 188.
16 Caillois, *I giochi e gli uomini*, p. 195.
17 Huizinga, *Homo ludens*, p. 17.

is accompanied by a double sense of tension and joy, and from the realization of 'being diverse' from 'ordinary life'.[18]

Caillois defines play on the basis of its formal quality as:

> Play is a carefree activity: a person at play cannot be obligated, without play loosing straightaway its engaging and pleasurable amusement. It is set apart: play is circumscribed within precise limits of time and space determined in advance. It is undetermined: the progressive development inherent in play cannot be determined nor its result acquired before hand; the need to imagine requires that a certain freedom be left to the initiative of the one at play. It is not productive: play does not create goods or wealth, nor any other new thing; apart from a transfer of property within the circle of players, play is such as to return to a situation identical to that at the beginning of the session. It is regulated: play is subject to conventions that suspend ordinary laws and establish for its duration a new system of rules, which alone is in force. Play is fictitious: it is associated with a specific awareness of a different reality or of complete unreality in contrast to normal life.[19]

Play as Transition Between Liturgy and Rite: The Festive and Gratuitous Attitude of Disinterest[20]

Throughout the course of human history, cultic ritual has been strongly identified with utilitarian means. Cultic rites were a means to achieve a determined end, such as forgiveness, favour, mercy from the Gods, healing or victory over an enemy.[21] The liturgy, however, has a gratuitous dimension, as liturgy is also a feast, a dance, a form of play. The liturgy is more than the simple execution of a rite. The liturgical participant almost forgets the goals, and simply feasts, celebrates, expresses proper gratitude and joy for redemption, and for the love of God.[22] In this sense liturgy is essentially a playful rite. A liturgy celebrated exclusively for

---

18 Huizinga, *Homo ludens*, p. 35.

19 Caillois, *I giochi e gli uomini*, p. 26.

20 Many studies treat the question of the relationship between play and rite. Let us note two significant books in this area; C. Lévi-Strauss, *Il pensiero selvaggio*, 4th edition, (Milan: Il Saggiatore, 1970), and G. Agamben, *Infanzia e storia. Distruzione dell'esperienza e origine della storia*, [Piccola Biblioteca Einaudi 78] (Turin: Giulio Einaudi editore, 2001), esp. p. 78.

21 E. Durkheim, *Le forze elementari della vita religiosa* (Rome: Newton Compton, 1973), p. 383; B. Malinowski, *Magia, scienza e religione e Baloma. Gli spiriti dei morti nelle isole Trobriand* (Rome: Newton Compton, 1976), p. 47.

22 S. Marsili, 'Teologia della celebrazione dell'eucaristia' in *Anamnesis 1: La Liturgia, momento nella storia della salvezza*, ed. B. Neunheuser, S. Marsili, et al., (Genoa: Marietti, 1990), p. 105.

utilitarian motives, to achieve certain ends would be reductive to the point of (utilitarian) ritual. This reduction or deficiency of the gratuitous ludic dimension is evident in liturgies that are reduced to their bare essentials however valid they may be: for example the rite of penance or baptism reduced to its bare essentials.

When is a rite performed? When one wants to achieve an end. When is a liturgy celebrated? When one is free from ends, from utilitarianism; when the rite is carried out for its own sake (for the sake of play) and is not seen merely as a means for achieving other ends. Celebrating for the sake of play, for itself, occurs when the ritual elements are valued in and of themselves. A liturgical celebration involves actions such as confessing sin, giving absolution or offering the eucharistic prayer that have intrinsic meaning and value, and are not used as a means to some other end. Because the rites are taken seriously, they involve space, colour, movement, structure and rules, but these promote true celebration, rather than achieve other ends.

Play And Rite: Complementary Dimensions for an Adequate Liturgical Celebration

From the preceding reflection it is clear that a balanced liturgical celebration comprises both ludic and ritual dimensions. These are complementary in regard to both the meaning and the goal of a celebration (Guardini); both are indispensable. In addition, O. Seydel insists on the importance of this complementarity.[23]

Liturgical celebration is composed, then:

1 of a ritual order, which follows a predefined structure with fixed meaning (preserving the liturgy from anarchy) and which has well defined goals. The ritual assures that both the horizontal and vertical dimensions support communal expression and communication.
2 of ludic behaviour which affords levity, gratuity and the festive air of play at liturgy (protecting the liturgy from absolutism, from an

---

[23] 'Im christlichen Gottesdienst sollten sich Spiel und Ritual "komplementär zueinander verhalten, indem sie sich vor ihren jeweiligen Pervertierungen schützen. Dabei lösen sie sich nicht ineinander auf, denn dann könnten sie ihre jeweilige positive Funktion nicht mehr erfüllen. Spielerisches Verhalten kann das Ritual als Ordnungsmuster vor einer Verabsolutierung schützen, indem die festgefügten Interaktionsmuster durchbrochen, die Eindeutigkeit des Symbols in Frage gestellt und der Individualität des einzelnen Raum gegeben wird. Und umgekehrt kann ritualisiertes Verhalten Spiel als freie Kombination von Möglichkeiten vor anarchischer Auflösung schützen: durch die Schaffung gemeinsamer Interaktionsmuster werden gemeinsame Handlungen einer Gruppe ermöglicht, durch die Schaffung gemeinsamer Symbole kann eine Gruppe ihr Selbstverständnis formulieren und mitteilbar machen."' O. Seydel, 'Spiel und Ritual. Überlegungen zur Reform des Gottesdienstes', *WPKG* 60 (1971), pp. 507–15, 513.

austere and excessive severity). The ludic element lays the foundation for the free play of the individual, for personal creativity. In this the inner meaning of the liturgical act shines forth, and human activity approaches God's manner of acting.

That the liturgy is a ludic act and that such playfulness is the most pertinent aspect of the liturgy and the truest and most interesting complement of the rite, has already been well documented (Terrin). Anthropologists have provided many examples that demonstrate this. Playfulness is not a secondary characteristic of the liturgy, but is at its essence (Guardini, Tagliaferri).

Rite and play, then, are conjoined in the same event; they resemble one another, they have a common origin and roots; they are not separable (part of ritual remains ever playful, and play ever draws from ritual); if they are separated, both die; nevertheless they remain distinct.

Two mysterious acts, human play and ritual, are wed in a third, the liturgy, to become mystery itself. In the Liturgy, they find their true complement and realization by expressing in all its fullness the richness of their proper contribution. The degeneration of one provokes the exaggeration of the other, thereby injuring the balance and truth of the celebration.

Certain Aspects of The Fruitful Interplay Between Liturgy and Play

Because of its ludic character, liturgy is called by some theologians 'holy play'. Liturgy is celebrated playfully, or rather, it requires a playful disposition for its celebration. Liturgy expresses and celebrates the playfulness of life. In contrast, the play one engages in in daily life is imperfectly realized and this in an often unconscious manner; daily play, however, finds its full and complete expression in the liturgy, which raises play to a conscious celebration of, for example, joyful thanksgiving for the meaning of the world, of life, of suffering and death; for freedom or for order. Thus, play in liturgy helps one to consciously recognize, accept, celebrate and realize the gifts of God, whereas play in daily life celebrates and manifests these gifts in a veiled and incomplete way in as much as daily play anticipates and prefigures the playfulness of liturgy.

Celebrating Meaning: Life Given and Accepted

One of the principal motives for studying the relationship between liturgy and play is the desire to emphasize the importance of meaning in a world suffused by a utilitarian mentality, all the authors are convinced of this.

Meaning is evident when the value of something consists in being what it is. The comprehensibility or rationale for some thing or some action lies in itself and is not extraneous. To highlight the meaning of something is to affirm its very existence, that its meaning consists simply in being what it is. With Guardini[24] we can affirm that meaning arises from existence; something that merely exists is already a reflection of God, the infinite. A living being finds its proper meaning in living and thus realizing its proper and intimate essence as the flowering of the natural revelation of the living God. Science and art realize their meaning as the 'splendour of truth'.

In his book on play, Moltmann speaks in eloquent terms about the creation of the world and of human life.[25] He affirms that God created the world that God may be glorified and rejoice in creation. God creates to manifest a proper richness of meaning, and not for any ulterior motive. Humanity was created that its very being may glorify its creator and that it may rejoice in God and in its own existence. The meaning of life consists in accepting and rejoicing in one's own existence, and then expressing this joy in gratitude.[26] God gives meaning to human existence that we may accept and celebrate our existence.

Scholars use two basic examples to illustrate how ludic activity is full of meaning, yet without purpose: the movement of the cherubim and the play of children. First, the cherubim surrounding God are pure movement, powerful and majestic,[27] that wish nothing other than to express the interior being of the spirit, to manifest its innate activity and impetuous force. Second, the activity of a child at play manifests without impediment, as its activity flows directly from the current of life in a disinterested way. The meaning of the action is manifested in an activity that is not motivated by necessity, desire or ends, but is done for its own sake. They are acts of self-expression and self-representation (expressing and manifesting what we are) in all joy and freedom.[28]

---

24 R. Guardini, *Lo spirito della liturgia. I santi segni*, pp. 71–3.
25 J. Moltmann, *Die ersten Freigelassenen der Schöpfung*.
26 'Darum ist der Mensch geschaffen, um "Gott zu verherrlichen" ... und sich an Gottes und seinem eigenen Dasein freuen, denn das ist sinnvoll genug in sich selbst. Freude ist der Sinn des menschlichen Lebens, Freude im Dank und Dank als Freude. ... Die Antwort auf die Frage, wozu denn einer da sei, liegt nicht in nachweislichen Zwecken, für die einer gebraucht wird, sondern liegt in der Annahme seines Daseins selbst und in dem ... "demonstrativen Seinwert".' Moltmann, *Die ersten Freigelassenen der Schöpfung*, pp. 25–6.
27 Exod. 1.4ff. and 10.9ff.
28 Moltmann, *Die ersten Freigelassenen der Schöpfung*, pp. 25–31.

The very idea of an end, on the contrary, posits the centre of gravity of a thing or action outside itself. The thing or activity is considered merely as a means, even if decisive and obligatory, to achieve an objective.

Concerning the liturgy, we ought to distinguish two moments: the liturgy as an activity full of meaning and without utilitarian purpose (the ludic aspect), and the liturgy as a celebration of meaning (the celebration of the ludic).

Liturgy is a cherubic activity (Guardini) during which we cease 'to do' and simply 'are'; we pass from becoming to being. The liturgy expresses the essence of the Christian's existence, that one stands before God, is revealed in the presence of God, is inserted into God's life and thus one's own proper being is confirmed. Thus, the opportunity is offered of realizing one's own intimate and proper meaning, of one's due and desired being in conformity with the divine calling as a 'daughter or son of God'. Liturgical meaning, therefore, is realized properly in its celebration. The liturgical celebration doesn't require anything other than to recognize and accept the meaning of human existence, especially the redeemed existence of the Christian and thus to be and to celebrate that which we are (actually and potentially). The most authentic form of prayer or of a liturgical act is not realized in praying or celebrating for any purpose, such as to be heard in time of need or to receive thanks. Rather, we pray and celebrate both because we have been created for dialogue and communion with our Creator, and because we wish to unite ourselves to the Mystical Body of Christ to praise and give thanks to God, uniting our voices with the head, our Saviour, and with all the saints.

On the other hand, liturgy is the play of wisdom[29] (of the Son), which is displayed in church before the heavenly Father. Guardini says that only those who are not scandalized by this are capable of understanding the liturgy. Liturgical action involves putting into practice the words of the Lord to become as children; it involves dedicating oneself to play.

To be sure, those who write on the meaning of the liturgy do not deny its purpose. They advise, however, that its purpose is achieved only as its essence is realized. Excessive focus on its purpose endangers realizing its essence, and, consequently, its purpose as well. In this sense, then, the liturgy must be playful.

Liturgy is a celebration of meaning. Christ, who is both subject and object of every liturgical celebration, is the meaning and end of all creation, of human existence, and in Christ and through him even suffering and death find their meaning. Thus, in the liturgical act, we celebrate not only the love and mercy of God, but also the reality of suffering and death; these are celebrated properly through useless play, because in

---

29 Prov. 8.30–31.

Christ we find their meaning. Such meaning realized in Christ renders our celebration, in turn, both joyful and hopeful. Without this meaning, one could not even celebrate.

Celebrating Freedom: Freeing Oneself to Dedicate Oneself

Huizinga says that all play is free, and indeed is freedom itself. Play is the origin of freedom (Pannenberg) and an activity in and of freedom (Moltmann). According to these authors, freedom is presented as a condition for play and a characteristic of players. Play presupposes a certain distance, a certain freedom from instincts, from needs (Pannenberg), from preoccupations and daily problems (Paus) and from fear (Moltmann). Then Cardinal Ratzinger, in the first chapter of his book entitled, *The Spirit of the Liturgy*,[30] affirms that play possesses in itself a therapeutic and liberating character, which he characterizes as an oasis of freedom, because it takes us outside of this world and its daily preoccupations, and leads us to gratitude, thereby freeing us for whatever instant from the full weight of the world. J.-P. Sartre also notes the close relationship between play and freedom and affirms that when one becomes free, one begins to play. He asserts that as soon as one understands oneself as a free being and intends to use one's proper freedom, even if oppressed by one's proper distress, the activity is transformed into play.[31]

Both play and the liturgy require a certain interior freedom (Paus).[32] Such interior freedom is realized when one separates oneself from the desires and obligations of daily life and from every internal disturbance and dedicates oneself, with full attention and without self-preoccupation, to play or to the religious event. Joined to this interior freedom is a certain exterior freedom, which includes a tranquil environment, free from every external disturbance, fit for recollection or play. Both internal and external freedom are indispensably necessary (*unabdingbar notwendig*, Paus)[33] if the religious event in its objective reality (the unfolding of a rite independently of the observer) is also to embrace the subjective experience, the personal encounter. It is necessary to distance oneself from daily life to be able to enter body and soul into another world (self-freedom for self-dedication). The saying of Jesus as recorded in the Gospel of Matthew is fitting: 'No one can serve two masters; for a slave

---

30 Joseph Cardinal Ratzinger, *The Spirit of the Liturgy* (San Francisco: Ignatius, 2000) (trans. John Saward from *Einführung in den Geist der Liturgie*, Frankfurt: Herder, 2000), pp. 13-14.

31 J.-P. Sartre, *L'essere e il nulla* (Milan: Il Saggiatore, 1975), p. 729.

32 A. Paus, 'Liturgie als Spiel?' *Communicatio Fidei. Festschrift für Eugen Biser zum 65. Geburtstag*, ed. H. Bürkle, G. Becker (Regensburg: Verlag Friedrich Pustet, 1983), pp. 295-304, 297.

33 Paus, 'Liturgie als Spiel?', p. 297.

will either hate the one and love the other, or be devoted to the one and despise the other' (Matt. 6.24, NRSV).

H. Rahner, Caillois and Huizinga speak about freedom in the context of play. The player must be fully free to decide whether to play or not, for play on command is no longer play. One plays if, when and for as long as one wishes. Play lives solely by delight wherein it proves itself, and not from obligations or moral impulses. In asking whether such freedom is applicable to the liturgy, we must first respond that, due to the ludic character proper to the liturgy, the disposition of the celebrants must be noted for such freedom. Were one's presence at the liturgy motivated merely by obligation or moral precept rather than freely given, participation would be impoverished and the lived experience injured.

At this point we also ought to emphasize the freedom of God in regard to creation and ritual. All acts of creation by God, all God's works are free acts. God is absolute freedom. Creation, redemption, the election of Israel, of the Apostles and of the saints not by merit but by the sovereign freedom of God and God's self-manifestation in the liturgy, are all free acts of God.[34] The free presence of Christ in the liturgy guards it from magic and emphasizes its gratuitous character as a gift ever renewed in freedom. Thus emerges the difference between the liturgy and play. In play the realization of the imaginary world is due to the playful activity and disposition of the one at play, who accepts the rules and gives oneself freely to play and to the 'imaginary' world.

The liturgy, in contrast, requires three elements for its efficacious celebration: the disposition of the participant, the efficacy of the rite, and the gratuitous and free action of God. A well-celebrated liturgical rite is capable of a rousing spiritual effect and of arousing the emotions, because the rite itself is efficacious. This does not, however, 'obligate' God's self-manifestation. The efficacy of the liturgy is greater than that of a rite. In this sense the realization of the transcendent ever remains a gift, a free act of God and not simply the effect of the ritual act or of the disposition of the participant. Were it not so, were the liturgy identical to play in this regard, then the liturgy would be reduced to magic. Such freedom of itself does not provoke chaos, confusion or uncertainty, but, when guided by love, it constitutes the framework for the free encounter between God and humanity.

One may speak of free participation, a voluntary compliance with 'something other'. Both in liturgy and play one complies with some 'other' such as other people, other rules or another world. Willingly accepting the rules of play is necessary. There may be no rationale for the rules as they are; nevertheless, either they are freely accepted or one

---

34 See also Rahner, *Der spielende Mensch*.

does not play. The liturgy also requires such an attitude (Paus, Guardini); the rules may be disputed both before and after the liturgy, but to participate fully in the liturgy, one must accept the rules without hesitation during the celebration itself. Moreover, valuing a religious event positively is also a free act. No one and nothing can oblige the observer (or participant) to consider the rite either as a religious or sacred event or as an encounter with the Holy One. Such insight is a choice, a free human act, an act of faith.

The word 'play' also evokes the idea of limited freedom, a fitting but not excessive freedom, freedom within proper limits. By analogy we say that in the interplay among a mechanism's various elements that function in unison, 'freedom' contributes to good inter-workings and prevents the mechanism from blocking or breaking down. But this freedom is necessarily limited (Caillois). Paus applies this concept to the liturgy, which is simultaneously liberation and limitation of freedom. Without such a polarity (freedom – limitation) the celebration proper does not exist.

Again it needs to be said here that for the liturgy to be playful, one must engage in it freely. In fact, the liturgy is the celebration of freedom. In every liturgical act the Church celebrates our liberation from the slavery of sin, and from death; by every liturgical act the participant is freed from the customary world, realizes personal freedom, celebrates that freedom as the gift of God and as a self-offering in love. This divine freedom is celebrated as the manifestation of the greatness of God's love (redemption, election, encounter in the liturgical act). The child at play begins to learn how to act freely, which achieves its fulfilment in the liturgy, when it becomes a blessing. Freedom is a condition *sine qua non* for a full and proper fruition of the liturgical celebration. Freedom is both the promise and hope, font of joy and experience of love. Freedom is celebrated and experienced as grace, and at the same time it bears the offer of love.

Celebrating Order: Framing and Guaranteeing

Most games have rules, and are regulated. Here we shall not consider games without rules, which Caillois calls '*paidia*'. Such rules are completely obligatory and incontestable. They are arbitrary conventions, commanding without recourse to appeal. As soon as the rules are broken, the spell of play is broken. Some rules establish order in the otherworld of play, others regulate the concrete practice of play itself. As closely as play is linked to rules and to order, all the more so is ritual. In fact, the etymology of the word 'rite' brings us to two concepts: rule and order.[35]

---

35 According to Benveniste (E. Benveniste, *Le vocabulaire des institutions indo-européennes* (Paris: ed. de Minuit, 1969, p. 100) the word 'rite' comes from the Latin

There is no rite that does not have rules and that does not institute some order.

Rules are constitutive of both play and liturgy. The usual rules of daily life, the rules of habit, are temporarily suspended and replaced by other norms, which facilitate the opening of and engaging in another world. These rules establish a new and stable order in a universe without laws. In his article, Paus affirms that without this ludic aspect, that is without regulated structure, the otherworld of play would not impinge on this one, not even in the liturgy, nor would a sacred space be created, on which depends the very existence of the religious event.[36]

Let us briefly consider, then, the relationship between freedom and rules. One at play feels the freedom of expression, because the rules do not oppress the player. While playing, one does not feel weighed down by the rules established; one obeys the rules, which nevertheless coincide with gratuity. Kant says that only at the level of artistic play does one experience the possibility of reconciliation between world and spirit, between laws and freedom. Schiller, following in the wake of Kant, repeats and develops these ideas along the same lines. A human being is not exclusively material, nor exclusively spirit, nor exclusively law, nor exclusively freedom, but seeks to unite each with the other. Moreover, in his book on festivity and fantasy, Cox also seeks to reconcile these two realities in the ritual act.[37] It seems, however, that he still considers rules as obstacles to freedom and fantasy. It seems that play and feast, nevertheless, manage to reconcile in some way both body and spirit, law and freedom (Schiller, Rahner) with an agile levity, lively with an ephemeral elegance arising from their internal character, thus affording the possibility of anticipating and foretasting their eschatological reconciliation and unity (Rahner).

Let us now turn to explore the attitudes possible in regard to the rules of play. Huizinga, Caillois and Paus speak of two possible attitudes: the swindler and the killjoy. We, however, hold that there are four basic attitudes possible, spurred from four different approaches to the rules. (1) Some refute the rules and every limitation to freedom, and to free and spontaneous creativity however differing their motives; these are

---

ritus which indicates the established order, and links with the Greek *artys* meaning 'prescription, ordinance'. Benveniste thinks that the origin of this word is the Indo-European *ar* which indicates an ordained way of being, and the harmonious organization of the parts of a whole. Other authors think that the root of the word 'rite' may be *ri*, which means 'to flow' and so is linked with 'rhythm', 'rhyme', 'river'. It connotes an ordained flow of actions.

36 Paus, 'Liturgie als Spiel?', pp. 298–9.
37 H. Cox, *The Feast of Fools. A Theological Essay on Festivity and Fantasy* (Cambridge, MA: Harvard UP, 1969), pp. 70–5.

the spoilsports. (2) Others accept the rules and observe them out of obedience, but in reality they simulate, treating them as merely external ritual acts. They follow the form but not the reality; they speak mere words and do empty acts (Guardini). These are the swindlers or hypocrites. (3) Another group of persons are of the opinion that the rules have to be observed because they are sacred, or of great intrinsic worth, because of tradition or for devotional motives, or because the rules are unchangeable for various reasons. These are excessively rigid and serious in regard to the norms or rubrics. (4) Finally, others celebrate the liturgy as play, or rather they manage to strike an equilibrium between what is serious and playful. They observe the rules not out of obedience, not because they are held as unchangeable or sacred, but as one at play. Thus for them, and only for them, the norms, rubrics and rules are a true help.

With P. Berger we affirm that each act of play affirms a greater order as an act of faith and hope, a sign of transcendence. Play indicates that already from the foundations of creation there is order. Indeed, playing according to rules creates new universes, new order. Granted that in their infantile games babies merely put together (Terrin) or reproduce (Pannenberg) the order of the world already realized by adults (while the liturgy transfers), but from the perspective of the child it is a matter of intuition and unfolding of the true order of things, as in worship, even if the child is not capable of ordering the world according to its deeper reality. In other words, the same function is partially realized in the play of children, developing within them the power of play-ritual, which is realized in its full form during worship, which in turn helps us better to understand and recognize it even in the play of children.

In the liturgy we celebrate the order of the new creation, our redemption; accordingly the rules function less to create the new world as to express and constitute it. Liturgical order serves to frame our lives in the new creation and serves to guarantee the realization of the new order and none other. Liturgy's 'other world' is not imaginary, nor merely desired, but real; it is truly present, and with every celebration the order of that other world is ever more realized as the order of this one. The new order rendered present in every celebration guarantees our lives, our salvation, peace and joy.

Life, the Two-Faced Janus: Both Serious and Not-Serious

Many consider that the opposite of play is seriousness. According to their way of thinking, life and human activity are serious, while play is not. Because it does not produce, it is without real consequences for life. Because it is opposed to the seriousness of daily life, play is dismissed as frivolous, as time wasted. By 'seriousness', however, such people understand useful activity that produces results in daily life; play, of course, does not lend itself to such results.

Some scholars try to restore the honour of play by pointing out its fruitfulness especially as seen in a child at play, but also in adults at play. These scholars value play as therapy, as a privileged place of experience and self-knowledge. All who study play, however, are convinced that, understood properly, play is a serious activity, but not in the same sense as a useful activity. Plato, surprisingly, inverts the order by affirming that play is more serious than life; nothing is more serious than play. If play, then, is the most serious of human activities, then life has to be lived by playing certain games to win the favour of the gods. Even Huizinga, as one of the first in the twentieth century to take play seriously, asserts that the opposition playfulness–seriousness is neither conclusive nor stable. He admits that playfulness is not the negation of seriousness, then immediately adds that as soon as we say that play is not serious, we have erred. Indeed, even the authentic and spontaneous mindset of play can be profoundly serious. The player can wholly give oneself to play, and the awareness of merely playing may be almost entirely lost.

How, then, to clarify or resolve the ambiguity of play? Is it serious or not? At the root of the two faces of play is the perception from without that play is not serious, but from within that play is 'holy serious' – as it is called by A. Paus. Other authors such as J. Huizinga (referring to Plato), H. Rahner and H. Cox begin from this characteristic – serious from within: not serious from without. Cox's entire treatment of the comic addresses this very aspect of life and events. Rahner's reflections on the earnestly playful person (*ernstheiter Mensch*) also addresses this same topic. They both assert that this double dimension characterizes not only play, but all of human life in every aspect. They do not set these two perspectives of play as either serious or not serious in opposition to one another, but as complementary, characterizing the same reality from diverse perspectives. The complementarity of perspective colours all of creation and allows one to affirm that both life and liturgy are games, at one and the same time serious and not serious. Play is taken seriously by the player, but may seem ridiculous to the observer. Faith, likewise, is taken seriously by the believer, but may seem ridiculous to a non-believer. Liturgy too is taken seriously by one fully engaging in its beauty and affective power, but may seem a child's trifle to the observer. Even our earthly life is taken seriously by those living it from within, but just perhaps from without, from the heavens, it is considered with a smile for the play that it is.

Playfulness as fundamental condition

Beyond the aspects common to both play and liturgy, which we have already examined, the liturgy has other elements, which are fundamentally ludic. Gratuity or uselessness is such a ludic characteristic of the liturgy. E. Terrin observes that this ludic dimension properly expresses the transcendence of God. He departs from the idea that God, in fact, is uselessness par excellence, because God does not tend toward another. Consequently such a gratuitous experience or such an experience of useless activity, which, however, ought to be full of meaning, is a religious experience of an aspect of the divine. In my own words, it is not that the useless tends towards usefulness, but that usefulness tends towards uselessness, as work tends towards play and the world towards God. Thus, we do not celebrate rites primarily to realize the usefulness of daily life; to the contrary, the usefulness of daily life divulging its radical insufficiency provokes the freedom of the useless activity in play and in the liturgy.

Play is characterized by an isolation or distance from daily life. To be able to play one must set aside daily life. Terrin rightly notes that the liturgy also requires this ludic aspect, namely, a certain distance is necessary for celebration, a certain isolation, which Paus calls 'internal and external freedom'. Only in this way can we fully immerse ourselves in the other world of the liturgy, which also implies religious experience.

Play and liturgy also share the characteristic of being infinite. Some games have a beginning and a goal, as, for example, the game of chess. Certain liturgies as well have an internal dynamic that tends toward an end, for example the liturgy of penance. But such a resolution of an end is different than achieving the purpose of other human actions.

In some cases, however, the aspect of the infinite is fundamentally determinative, as Paus observes. Examples include football, many children's games, the liturgy of the Hours, the liturgy of the Word and the Eucharist. Accordingly liturgical participation requires a mentality different than that of other human activities. Liturgy is not a task to do, a work to finish or an action to bring to a conclusion; rather it is play to engage in. In this earthly life we may cease playing or celebrating the liturgy, but the eternal life will be a perennial liturgy; play will correspond to its internal dynamic, its capacity to be infinite.

It often happens at play that things like toys become other realities; this involves role changes or a form of death and rebirth. In fact, death is none other than a transformation in the continual realization of one's mystical self. This transformation of life in death and of death into new life pertains also to play and the liturgy. Such transformation happens while at play so easily that it can occur a hundred times an hour. Toys easily lose their essence, receiving another in its place. Such transformation happens in reality only with great difficulty and slowly over time. Changing roles is also proper to the liturgy; suffice it to consider the changing roles of the presider in the eucharistic assembly as president, mediator, simple faithful and representative of Christ or of the Church. To discover in the liturgy the transformation of life in death and of death unto life, one need only consider the baptismal rites, the Eucharist or funerals.

In a certain sense worship is the fulfilment of play. Play is representative of its complete form in worship because its representative function is rendered fully explicit in worship. In play one understands one's very self from without oneself, from an eccentric perspective. This begins in the symbolic play of children and finds its fulfilment in worship and adoration.

The Eschatological Aspect of Play

Play is, in a certain way, the anticipation of salvation. Play is a prelude of eternal life, as the then Cardinal Ratzinger noted.[38] Is this not, then, the most profound and radical meaning of liturgical festivity? Not infrequently children's play anticipates, works out and teaches an activity or a form of life that will be realized in adulthood. The roles adults play are determined by what impressed the child. In this way, play is a foretaste of future roles, and the satisfaction of desire undoubtedly intensifies the experience.

Beyond anticipation, play itself is an eschatological symbol, an image of eternal life. Beginning with Plato, numerous authors describe eternal life in terms of play, as even does the Bible. These agree that play itself is the human reality that most resembles eternal life. Our specific experiences of play are drawn to their transcendent realization in eternal life precisely through their quality of freedom, meaning, unity and of going beyond the merely moral.

The same qualities also characterize the liturgy, both as it anticipates and images eternal life. One need only to recall the affirmation of *Sacrosanctum Concilium*: 'In the liturgy on earth, we are sharing by anticipation in the heavenly one, celebrated in the holy city Jerusalem, the goal towards which we strive as pilgrims, where Christ is, seated at God's right hand, he who is the minister of the saints and of the true tabernacle' (no. 8 in Tanner, p. 822).

The difference between the liturgy as play and play in itself lies in that during the liturgy we share in another reality and not merely in its

---

38 Ratzinger, *The Spirit of the Liturgy*, pp. 13–14.

possibility. Nevertheless, this reality is perceived as the eschatological possibility into which we have already crossed.

God at Play

We could not conceive of the mystery of human play if we had not already profoundly understood God as at play, for whom even the most charming gesture of a human person at play is nothing other than an infantile and maladroit imitation of the Word at play from eternity to eternity.

In his book entitled *De arte celebrandi* [*On the Art of Celebrating*], W. Hahne examines certain aspects of God at play.[39] He compares the divine world with play on the basis of these characteristics: free activity, gratuity, contingency; an expression of oneself; joy, levity. The sum total is that the life and activity of God and even the entire work of salvation has a ludic character; some authors describe this as play.

K. Hemmerle describes the life of the Trinity as play. He even speaks of 'Trinitarian play' (*dreifaltiges Spiel*).[40] We have seen how the book of Proverbs in the Old Testament speaks of Wisdom that plays before the eternal Father (*die spielende Weisheit*), an image that will be reiterated by many scholars describing the life of the Word as play.

Not only divine life, but even the creative work and redemption are presented by many authors who speak of creation as play (*Schöpfungsspiel*), incarnation as play, redemption as play (also in the sense of 'new creation' as a new game – Moltmann) and the play of grace (*Gnadenspiel*).

Finally, we ought to add that even the Church and the liturgy as the work of God are described in terms of play (for example by Guardini, H. Rahner, E. H. Erikson, W. Hahne, H. B. Meyer, B. Lang). Both the world and the Church are described as the 'terrain for play' (*Arena für freies Zusammenspiel*) where the players are both human persons and God or Christ. In such a vision, where God is God at play, who creates by playing, and where the human person is the person at play, naturally, then, the liturgy is understood for the play that it is, because in this way alone does it correspond to the nature of God and to human nature (W. Hahne).

---

39 W. Hahne, *De arte celebrandi oder Von der Kunst, Gottesdienst zu feiern. Entwurf einer Fundamentalliturgik*, 2nd edition (Freiburg, Basel and Wien: Herder, 1991), pp. 283–94.

40 'Ja, dreifaltiges Leben ist Spiel. . . . Nirgendwo ist mehr Spiel, ursprünglicher Spiel als im Urspiel dreifaltigen Lebens.' K. Hemmerle, *Vorspiel zur Theologie. Einübungen* (Freiburg, Basel and Wien: Herder, 1976), p. 146.

Conclusion: On the Ludic Spirit of the Liturgy

In the past century the profound importance of play has emerged and has even become a theological category in the heart of Christian theology and praxis. Play opens the human person up to what is universal, to transcendence, to the expression of the divine.

Complementing its transcendental character, play also has a descending character in that we are created in the image and likeness of God at play (*Deus ludens*). Because all divine activity is sealed with playfulness, there is no human activity nearer to the divine than the play of a child. Therefore, the one who wishes to imitate God must play and has to become a child to enter into the reign of God.

From a theological and transcendental perspective, all of life seems to be playful. The authentic Christian, then, is the earnestly playful person (*ernstheiter Mensch*) for whom play is serious and the solemn is playful. Such a one knows how to live seriously and playfully at the same time.

Without doubt, then, liturgy is necessarily ludic, and every celebration a playful act wherein playfulness is a supreme theological, even divine quality, and is not something that diminishes the liturgical act.

With H. Rahner we affirm that the modern person needs the all too human and Christian wisdom of the person at play (*homo ludens*), which can unite both the serious and the playful in the person's self. This balance between play and sobriety may err in exclusive emphasis of either element. A person who only plays, who denies the tragic in life, is as self-deceptive as a person in despair seeking to hide or to camouflage one's own despair. On the other hand, a person who is always serious may place an excessive emphasis on earthly things or may suffer from a excessively weak sense of hope and trust in the love and the providence of God. The truly balanced person is earnestly playful (*ernstheitere Mensch*). Such a person has found a balance in a dialectic tension between heaven and earth, severity and joking, comedy and tragedy. The playful person is conscious of the profound sense of one's own existence with a corresponding sense of one's own contingency.

Rahner says that only a religious person is capable of such play, because to be able to play one must be inwardly secure, protected, loved.[41] A person who has an excessively serious or capricious view of the world, and thus a world devoid of a loving God, is no longer capable of play, nor is one for whom the world is all important, and thus devoid of a transcendent God, or for whom the world is only a frivolous reality lack-

---

[41] '... es will uns scheinen, als sei erst durch den Glauben an die wahre Menschwerdung Gottes überhaupt die Möglichkeit gegeben, jene "heitere Sicherheit und Freiheit" zu gewinnen, ohne die ein gelöstes Spiel nicht möglich ist.' Rahner, *Der spielende Mensch*, p. 35.

ing in meaning and value, and thus devoid of a God who gives meaning and value.

In contrast, a religious person and specifically a Christian considers the world at one and the same time both a light little game and a serious creation full of meaning.[42] Believers find their hope in being playful persons (*ernstheitere Mensch*), they place their trust in God, knowing that they live under the protection of God and that everything that happens in this world is nothing other than Wisdom at play (*spielender Logos*).

The disposition of a truly playful person, and, thus, of one who participates in the liturgy, is characterized by the same distinctive elements as that of an athlete: serenity, joy, ease, lightness, happiness, dedication, spirit, rhythm, dance and beauty. Such a person has the desire and the longing to imitate God, to become like God in one's own way of acting, because God is truly at play (*Deus vere ludens*). Thus one comes to human fullness as a child truly at play, in short a child of God (*filius Dei*) engaging in the eternal play.

Therefore, the spirit of the liturgy is, in a certain sense, the spirit of play. However, the playful spirit must not be confused with pleasure, desire or simple entertainment. The Christian at liturgy is a royal dancer like David before the ark. Ambrose appreciated the dance of David and said that his dance, in relation to our sacred duty to God, is worthy of respect, such that the one who reproves him loses his own soul in the pits of reprobation.[43] The liturgy, therefore, is the place where believers respond with their whole heart and mind to the wonderful play of grace by entering the play of the sacraments and of the entire liturgy. The liturgy is, therefore, certainly the gift of grace, but one suited to those attentive to play.

If one substitutes play with moral admonition or pedagogical instruction, play easily slips away and one can no longer grasp or appreciate it. To enter into and truly appreciate the liturgy, one must not co-opt the liturgy for ulterior purposes or be overly conscious of its immediate usefulness or be hyper-prudent as to never let oneself go. It is important not be too precocious and permanently adult.

---

42 'So darf denn eigentlich nur der in Gottes Wirklichkeit eingegründete Mensch dieses Erdenleben ein Spiel und eine Schattenfigur nennen. Denn nur ihm, dem an das schöpferische Hervorgehen eben dieser Welt aus der Seinsfülle Gottes Glaubenden, ist es gegeben, unmittelbar mit diesem Ja auch das Nein auszusprechen, das heißt, die eben liebend bejahte und als Gotteswerk umarmte Welt (sich selbst eingeschlossen) wegzuwerfen als ein müßiges Kinderspiel, um sich aufzuschwingen zu dem "seligen Ernst", der da ist Gott allein.' Rahner, *Der spielende Mensch*, p. 39.

43 Ambrose of Milan, 'Non erubuit igitur David femineas opiniones nec obprobria apud mulieres pro religione obsequio verecundatus est... Denique illa quae saltationem huiusmodi repraehendebit, ... non dedit subolem regiam, ne superbos crearet ...', *Epistolae et Opera*, ed. O. Faller, [CSEL 82/1] Vienna 1986, Epistola 27.6–7, 182–3.

Instead, one is called to be generous to the point of largesse and wasteful of time, not in the hurry of the 'said and done'! To engage in holy play one must not stumble by speculating about what useful purpose the proclamations, prayers and rites serve. If we rebel against the tyranny of what is useful, if we learn how or at least if we don't forget to play, then we will learn to act in freedom, beauty and holy joy before God who regulates the play of the liturgy (R. Guardini).

Work Cited in Translation

Decrees of the Ecumenical Councils, 2 vols, ed. N. Tanner, Georgetown: Sheed and Ward, 1990.
The Holy Bible Containing the Old and New Testaments with the Apocryphal/ Deuterocanonical Books. New Revised Standard Version, Oxford, New York: Oxford, 1989.

Bibliography

Berger, P. L., *A Rumour of Angels. Modern Society and the Rediscovery of the Supernatural*, New York: Anchor Books, 1969.
Caillois, R., *I giochi e gli uomini. La maschera e la vertigine*, (Nuovo Portico 25), Milan: Bompiani, 1981.
Casel, O., 'Zur Idee der liturgischen Festfeier', *Jahrbuch für Liturgiewissenschaft* III (1923), pp. 93–9.
Casel, O., *Fede, Gnosi e Misteso. Saggio di teologia del culto cristiano*, (Caro Salutis Cardo. Studi/Testi, 14), Padua: Messaggero di S. Antonio, 2001.
Cox, H. G., *The Feast of Fools*, Cambridge MA: Harvard UP, 1969. Italian translation: *La festa dei folli. Saggio teologico sulla festività e la fantasia*, (La ricerca religiosa – Studi e Testi 11), Milan: Bompiani, 1971.
Di Nola, A. M., 'Gioco e religione' in *Enciclopedia delle religioni* 3, eds A. M. di Nola, M. Adriani et al., Florence: Vallecchi, 1971, pp. 223–53.
Euvé, F., *Penser la création comme jeu*, (Cogitatio Fidei 219), Paris: Cerf, 2000.
Fink, E., *Spiel als Weltsymbol*, Stuttgart, Berlin and Cologne: W. Kohlhammer, 1960.
Frobenius, L., *Kulturgeschichte Afrikas. Prolegomena zu einer historischen Gestaltlehre*, Zürich: Phaidon, 1933.
Guardini, R., *Vom Geist der Liturgie*, 5th edition, Freiburg, Basel and Vienna: Herder, 1961. Italian translation by M. Bendiscioli, *Lo spirito della liturgia. I santi segni*, Brescia: Morcelliana, 2000.
Hahne, W., *De arte celebrandi oder Von der Kunst, Gottesdienst zu feiern. Entwurf einer Fundamentalliturgik*, 2nd edition, Freiburg, Basel and Vienna Herder, 1991.
Handelman, D., 'Mito, rito e attività ludica' in *Enciclopedia delle religioni* 2, (Il rito. Oggetti, atti, cerimonie) ed. M. Eliade, Milan: Jaca Book, 1994, pp. 252–7.

Handelman, D., 'Play and Ritual. Complementary Frames of Meta-Communication' in *It's a Funny Thing, Humour*, eds H. C. Foot, A. J. Chapman, Oxford: Oxford University Press, 1977.
Hemmerle, K., *Vorspiel zur Theologie. Einübungen*, Freiburg, Basel and Vienna: Herder, 1976.
Huizinga, J., *Homo ludens, con introduzione di U. Eco*, Turin: Einaudi, 2001.
Lang, B., *Heiliges Spiel. Geschichte des christlichen Gottesdienstes*, Munich: Beck, 1998.
Meyer, H.B., 'Die Messfeier als heiliges "Spiel"', *Heiliger Dienst* 44, n. 1/2 (1990), pp. 63–71.
Moltmann, J., *Die ersten Freigelassenen der Schöpfung. Versuche über die Freude an der Freiheit und das Wohlgefallen am Spiel*, 5th edition, Munich: Chr. Kaiser Verlag, 1976.
Padinjatummury, J., *Play in Religion. A Means for Catechesis and Evangelization*, Doctoral Dissertation in the Faculty of Missiology, Pontifical Urban University, Rome, 1985.
Pannenberg, W., *Antropologia in prospettiva teologica*, (Biblioteca di teologia contemporanea 51), Brescia: Queriniana, 1987.
Paus, A., 'Liturgie als Spiel?' in *Communicatio fidei. Festschrift für Eugen Biser zum 65. Geburtstag*, eds H. Bürkle and G. Becker, Regensburg: Verlag Friedrich Pustet, 1983, pp. 295–304.
Plato, 'Leggi. Sulla legislazione', in *Tutti gli scritti* ed. G. Reale, Milan: Rusconi, 1991.
Rahner, H., *Der spielende Mensch*, Einsiedeln: Johannes Verlag, 1952.
Ratzinger, Cardinal J., *The Spirit of the Liturgy*, San Francisco: Ignatius, 2000 (trans. John Saward from *Einführung in den Geist der Liturgie*, Frankfurt: Herder, 2000); *Introduzione allo spirito della liturgia*, Cinisello Balsamo: San Paolo, 2001.
Tagliaferri, R., 'Il progetto di una scienza liturgica', in *Celebrare il Mistero di Cristo. Manuale di Liturgia*, ed. Associazione Professori di Liturgia, vol 1, (BEL Subsidia 73, Collana 'Studi di liturgia', Nuova Serie/25), Rome: CLV-Ed. Liturgiche, 1993, pp. 45–120.
Terrin, A. N., 'Esperienza di Dio e ritualità. Prospettiva antropologico-funzionalista e tesi fenomenologica' in *Liturgia. Soglia dell'esperienza di Dio?* ed. A. N. Terrin (Caro Salutis Cardo 1) Padua: Messaggero, 1982.
Terrin, A. N., *Il rito. Antropologia e fenomenologia della ritualità*, Brescia: Morcelliana, 1999.

8

St Thomas Aquinas on Eucharistic Ecstasy†

PETER A. KWASNIEWSKI

St Thomas Aquinas's scriptural and patristic theology of the sacraments offers precious insight into what Guardini and Ratzinger call 'the spirit of the liturgy', as well as into the ambiguous and indigent subjectivity or selfhood with which the liturgy has to reckon as it feeds fallen men with the bread of angels. For Aquinas, we will argue, the dissolution and re-creation of the 'I' is shown forth in sacramental signs through which the Eternal High Priest touches bodies and souls with his power, effecting in the recipient a share in his life, death and resurrection. It is in this way that the Mass typifies and prepares for a mystical incarnation of the Word of God in the womb of the Christian whose ego is humbled like the Virgin's. In these pages, we will sketch some of the ways in which Thomas's sacramental theology tracks the complexity of our human experience and advocates, as part of the cure for our woundedness, a zealous eucharistic worship rooted in faith and tending toward the ecstasy of love.

Now, although we do not find in Thomas a formal discussion of the 'ego' as found in Cartesian or post-Cartesian sources, we do find a highly developed analysis of interiority, of self-knowledge and self-love, of the different aspects or elements of oneself, deriving from rich resources – among them, Aristotle's penetrating study of friendship in the *Nicomachean Ethics,* Augustine's pilgrimage inward and upward in the *Confessions* and, most of all, the Johannine and Pauline writings.[1] In harmony with these sources, we find his liturgical, sacramental and

---

† Unless otherwise noted, translations are my own, and Scripture quotations are from the RSV. Section numbers refer to Marietti editions. A much more developed version of this paper is forthcoming in *Nova & Vetera* (English ed.) during 2008.

1 A good example of an analysis of 'self' is found in *Summa theologiæ* [*ST*] II-II, q. 25, a. 7, where Thomas explains the difference between good self-love and bad self-love on the basis of how one construes what is 'most oneself': the 'inward man' or the 'outward man'.

eucharistic doctrine shot through with motifs of self and other, of transformation, indwelling and ecstasy (*extasis*).

The teaching on *extasis* is particularly important. Thomas understands *extasis* as a standing-outside-oneself, a going beyond oneself or *exitus a se* that involves *alienatio* from what one has been in order to become different, literally 'altered'.² *Extasis* can be debasing or perfective – debasing when a man is driven downwards by worldly passion, perfective when he is taken out of himself and caught up in the virtuous love of a friend.³ For Aquinas, a friend is 'another oneself', *alter ipse*, not in the sense of a duplication of an already-existent *ego* as if the 'I' were mirrored, but an expansion and extension of the 'I' in reference to a fundamentally different existence that causes my own to be redefined, at times from the roots up.⁴ Once again, it is God's friendship, freely offered in Christ, that most radically redefines the 'I' by transplanting the lover's ground from himself to the Lord in whom he abides and who abides in him, whose face he seeks, whose footsteps he follows. Christian *alienatio a se* is the negative supposition, one could say, of positive transformation in Christ, of which the motto is the Apostle's cry: 'I am crucified with Christ; nevertheless I live, yet not I, but Christ lives in me; and the life I now live in the flesh I live by faith in the Son of God, who loved me and gave himself for me' (Gal. 2.19–20).⁵ Paul asserts that he is living *Christ's own life*, no longer a merely natural life he can call his own; he abandons himself in faith to the One who loves him to the utmost, who therefore attracts and unifies his whole love. And so the world is crucified to him and he to the world (Gal. 6.14).⁶

---

2 Thomas defines or comments on the term *extasis* in a variety of ways. Examples include *ST* I-II, q. 28, a. 3: 'Someone is said to suffer *extasis* when he is placed outside himself', *extra se ponitur*; in the same response he speaks of *exiens quodammodo extra seipsum* and *exit extra se*. In the commentary on *De divinis nominibus* he uses the same phrases *ponit extra se/seipsum* (ch. 4, lec. 10, §430 and §433), but adds *a se alienatum* (ch. 7, lec. 5, §739). At *In III Sent.*, d. 27, q. 1, a. 1 ad 4, he explains *extasis* as a placement outside oneself, *extra se positio*, and links it to *fervor*, 'since that which burns rises beyond itself and vanishes into smoke'. Perhaps the most helpful definition is found at *ST* II-II, q. 175, a. 2, ad 1: '*Extasis importat simpliciter excessum a seipso, secundum quem scilicet aliquis extra suam ordinationem ponitur*'.

3 See Peter A. Kwasniewski, 'St Thomas, *Extasis*, and Union with the Beloved', *The Thomist* 61 (1997), pp. 587–603; David Gallagher, 'Desire for Beatitude and Love of Friendship in Thomas Aquinas', *Mediaeval Studies* 58 (1996), pp. 20–7; Juan Cruz Cruz, *El Extasis de la Intimidad: Ontologia del Amor Humano en Tomas de Aquino* (Navarre: Ediciones Rialp, 1999).

4 See David Gallagher, 'Thomas Aquinas on Self-Love as the Basis for Love of Others', *Acta Philosophica* 8 (1999), pp. 23–44; Gallagher, 'Desire for Beatitude', pp. 20–39; James McEvoy, 'The Other as Oneself: Friendship and Love in the Thought of St. Thomas Aquinas', in J. McEvoy and M. Dunne (eds), *Thomas Aquinas: Approaches to Truth* (Dublin: Four Courts Press, 2002), pp. 16–37.

5 Adapted from the KJV.

6 On the theology expressed in Galatians 2.20, see François Amiot, *The Key Concepts*

In Aquinas's view the most basic function of the sacraments is to place man in vital contact with the crucified and risen Lord; they are, in the words of Romanus Cessario, 'graced instruments for restoring the image of God'[7] through assimilation to God's Son, who is the Father's perfect image and man's formative exemplar. By virtue of the God-man's sacrifice, each sacrament has power to originate, deepen or repair a direct relationship between man and God, a communion of like-minded friends having a shared beatitude for its goal. The mediation of the Son as head of mankind and head of the Church prepares for and establishes in souls an immediacy of divine indwelling for all who belong to him as his members. What is more, each of the sacraments configures one to Christ in a specific way by communicating the grace associated with the saving deeds and sufferings of the Lord. For each sacrament Aquinas identifies the past reality it stems from and evokes; the present sacramental encounter in its threefold aspect – mere sign, a reality that is also sign and a pure reality; and the future reality this encounter promises and accomplishes. The first of these, the past reality of the sacraments, is most worthy of attention here. The Eucharist brings us into contact with 'Christ in the state of bloody immolation', though the *mode* is unbloody;[8] baptism unites us with 'Christ dying and rising'; confirmation, with 'Christ as descended upon by the Holy Spirit'. Holy orders fuses the candidate with 'Christ offering sacrifice'; marriage conjoins spouses to Christ in the act of 'uniting to himself mankind and the Church'. When the sick are anointed, it is 'Christ strengthening those who are struggling'; he is the angel who visits them in their Gethsemane. The penitent sinner is made one with 'Christ efficaciously making satisfaction for us' – the sinner is nailed to an invisible cross where the Saviour meets him, and breathes out peace upon him.[9] In every case, it is Christ himself, in his sacred humanity, in his eternal divinity, who acts directly upon the recipient; it is he who bestows the healing and elevating effects of grace *through* the sacramental signs administered by others. 'The man who baptizes provides only exterior ministry', writes Thomas, 'but it is Christ who baptizes interiorly, who is able to use all men for whatever he wills'.[10] In another text the point is made forcefully:

---

of St. Paul (trans. John Dingle; New York: Herder & Herder, 1962), pp. 142–9, cf. pp. 133–41, 195–202.

7 Romanus Cesario, 'Aquinas on Christian Salvation', in Thomas Weinandy, Daniel Keating and John Yocum (eds), *Aquinas on Doctrine: A Critical Introduction* (London: T&T Clark, 2004), p. 129.

8 Cf. David Berger, *Thomas Aquinas and the Liturgy* (trans. Christopher Grosz; Naples, FL: Sapientia Press, 2004), pp. 27–41.

9 The phrases quoted are taken from André-Charles Gigon, *De Sacramentis in communi* (Fribourg: Typographia Canisiana, 1945).

10 *ST* III, q. 67, a. 5, ad 1.

It is evident that Christ himself accomplishes all the Church's sacraments: he it is who baptizes; he it is who forgives sins; he is the true priest, who offered himself on the altar of the cross, and by whose power his own body is consecrated daily on the altar. And yet, because he was not to remain bodily present to all the faithful, he chose ministers, that through them he might give that same body to the faithful.[11]

Thus, in and through the seven sacraments, Christians re-live mystically the life Christ lived when he dwelt among us full of grace and truth, and the risen life he is now living forever: we enter into his earthly ministry, his passion and death, his resurrection and ascension.[12] One can see these connections by attending to the relevant prologues in the *Summa theologiae*. Before *ST* 1, q. 2, Thomas says he will expound the science of sacred doctrine by treating of God, of the rational creature's advance towards God, and finally of Christ, who *as man* is our way to God. Having arrived at *ST* 3, q. 1, he then says it remains to consider the Saviour Jesus Christ who showed in his very person the way of truth whereby we may attain to eternal bliss by rising again, a consideration to be unfolded in three stages: the Saviour himself; the sacraments whereby we attain our salvation; the end of immortal life. At the start of the second stage (q. 60) he announces that the sacraments follow next in order *because they derive their efficacy from the very Word made flesh*. This truth is the key principle for the remaining questions (qq. 60–90) that Thomas completed before the mystical breakdown of December 1273.[13] Each sacrament has its power and operation immediately from Jesus Christ, whose glorified humanity is the inseparable instrument, the predestined channel, through which the divine Word pours out grace into souls. When a human being, properly disposed, receives one of the seven sacraments, he is at that moment in mystical contact with the person of the Saviour, who pours out as much grace as the soul is ready to receive.[14] This mystical contact attains an incomparable fullness and

---

11 *Summa contra Gentiles* IV, ch. 76; cf. *Super ad Eph.* 4, lec. 2, §200.

12 See John Saward, *Cradle of Redeeming Love: The Theology of the Christmas Mystery* (San Francisco: Ignatius Press, 2002), pp. 47–120. See also Jean-Pierre Torrell, *Saint Thomas Aquinas*, vol. II: *Spiritual Master* (trans. Robert Royal; Washington, DC: Catholic University of America Press, 2003), pp. 125–52.

13 On the significance of the saint's breakdown (and breakthrough) occurring in connection with celebrating Mass, see Peter A. Kwasniewski, 'Golden Straw: St Thomas and the Ecstatic Practice of Theology', *Nova et Vetera* [English] 2 (2004), pp. 61–89.

14 Thus, in regard to baptism, Aquinas teaches not only that we receive certain benefits from Christ's passion, but that it is Christ who baptizes us (cf. *ST* III, q. 66, a. 5, obj. 1 and ad 1), and Christ into whom we are baptized. Moreover, all the world's water acquires baptismal potency subsequent to the descent of the body of Jesus into the Jordan River (cf. *ST* III, q. 39, a. 1; q. 66, a. 3, ad 4).

immediacy in the Eucharist, which both symbolizes and accomplishes the intimate communion of the Saviour with the members of his body.[15] Here the sacramental encounter is no mere contact, but the context for an unreserved, mutual gift of self that can attain a unity and fecundity only hinted at in human marriage.[16]

Thomas's sacramental *realism* is in many ways astonishing. Without denying that they are social, symbolic celebrations for recalling important truths, Aquinas holds the sacraments to be, first and foremost, a real participation in Christ's own actions, sufferings and glory, for the sake of receiving into oneself the effect of those actions, the fruit of those sufferings, the vision of that glory. As Gilles Emery phrases it: 'They bear the historical event of the passion of Jesus, whence they procure the fruit of grace in the present moment, while announcing the fulfilment whose seed they possess'.[17] For example, when asking whether a man is freed from *all* guilt through baptism, Aquinas responds:

> Through baptism one is incorporated into Christ's passion and death, according to Romans 6.8, 'If we have died with Christ, we believe that we shall also live together with Christ'. From which it is clear that Christ's passion is communicated to every baptized person as a remedy, as though he himself had suffered and had died. Now Christ's passion . . . is sufficient satisfaction for all the sins of all men. And so the one who is baptized is freed from the debt of all the punishment due to him for sins, as though he himself had sufficiently satisfied for his own sins.[18]

---

15 Cf. *ST* III, q. 73, a. 1, ad 3; a. 5, ad 2. At *ST* III, q. 66, a. 9, ad 5, Aquinas makes an important comparison between baptism and Eucharist. 'Both sacraments . . . are representative of the Lord's death and passion, but not in the same way. For in baptism Christ's death is commemorated in so far as man dies with Christ, that he may be born again into a new life. But in the sacrament of the Eucharist Christ's death is commemorated *in so far as the suffering Christ himself is offered to us as the paschal banquet*, according to 1 Cor. 5.7–8, 'Christ our pasch is sacrificed; therefore let us feast.' And since man is only born once, whereas he eats many times, so is baptism given only once, but the Eucharist many times' (emphasis added).

16 For a synthesis of all these points, see Matthias Scheeben, *The Mysteries of Christianity* (trans. Cyril Vollert; St Louis: Herder, 1946), pp. 469–610, and Emile Mersch, *The Theology of the Mystical Body* (trans. Cyril Vollert; St Louis: Herder, 1951), pp. 546–93.

17 Gilles Emery, 'The Ecclesial Fruit of the Eucharist', *Nova et Vetera* [English] 2 (2004), pp. 43–60. See Berger, *Aquinas and the Liturgy*, pp. 61–87: sacraments are not merely symbolic occasions of grace but physical causes emanating from Christ and bringing men into contact with his personal saving work. This Thomistic theme is central to Colman O'Neill's *Meeting Christ in the Sacraments* (New York: Alba House, 1964; new edn, 1991) and *Sacramental Realism: A General Theory of the Sacraments* (Wilmington, DE: Michael Glazier, 1983; repr. Chicago: Midwest Theological Forum, 1998).

18 *ST* III, q. 69, a. 2. Cf. the same article, ad 1, and *ST* III, q. 68, a. 5.

In baptism the death and resurrection of Christ becomes *ours*; it becomes *our* paschal mystery, the origin of a new life with him. Thomas approvingly cites Origen: 'As we died with the dying Christ and rose up again with the rising Christ, so through Christ we are circumcised with a spiritual circumcision; and so we do not stand in need of a carnal one'.[19] The effect is the same as if *we*, become unblemished victims, had hung on the cross; as if *we* had suffered and died, though guiltless of all crime; as if *we* had risen again, forever beyond the reach of death and decay.[20] The Apostle never tires of declaring this gospel: 'You have died, and your life is hid with Christ in God' (Col. 3.3).[21] As Cardinal Ratzinger explains:

> What Paul is describing is an event of birth and death. I am wrested from my isolation and incorporated into the communion of a new subject; my 'I' is inserted into the 'I' of Christ and consequently joined to the 'I' of all my brothers. Only from such deep renewal of the individual does Church come into being as a communion that binds us together and sustains us in life and death.[22]

This 'incorporation', begun at baptism, is perfected by a man's being united in the power of the Spirit to the body of Christ – engrafted into his mystical body by way of his glorified body shared in the Eucharist, that we may no longer live for ourselves, but for him.[23] The Eucharist is thus 'the consummation of spiritual life, and the end of all the sacraments'.[24] It contains substantially the common spiritual good of the whole Church.[25] It is 'the sacrament of Christ's passion in so far as a man is perfected in union with the Christ who suffered'.[26] It is called

---

19 *ST* III, q. 37, a. 1, ad 2.

20 This 'as if' is not the *als ob* of Kantian philosophy – we must behave as if there is a God; we must view nature as if there is teleology; we must approach the beautiful as if beauty is an objective trait. It is the mystical 'as if': we have really done and suffered these things because we have been spiritually joined, even identified, with the one who really did and suffered them. Being true man, Christ could act and undergo as a creature acts and undergoes; being true God, he can, in the power of the Spirit, make *his* accomplishments *ours*. The 'as if' merely preserves the reverent distance of participant to source.

21 Cf. 2 Cor. 5.15; Rom. 14.7–9; Rom. 6.3–4; Gal. 3.27. The last two are often cited when Aquinas wishes to underline the bond between Saviour and sacrament, between the 'work' Christ accomplishes on the cross and the 'gift' of our justification. Cf. *ST* III, q. 61, a. 1, ad 3.

22 Joseph Cardinal Ratzinger, *Called to Communion: Understanding the Church Today* (trans. Adrian Walker; San Francisco: Ignatius Press, 1996), p. 153.

23 Cf. *ST* III, q. 68, aa. 1–2; q. 73, a. 3.

24 *ST* III, q. 73, a. 3; cf. q. 63, a. 6, citing Dionysius.

25 *ST* III, q. 65, a. 3, ad 1.

26 *ST* III, q. 73, a. 3, ad 3. But it is the *risen* Lord, too. At q. 80, a. 10, ad 1, Thomas recalls Augustine saying to the daily recipient of communion: 'Daily Christ rises for you'.

synaxis or *communio* 'because we communicate with Christ through it – both because we partake of his flesh and Godhead, and because we communicate and are united to one another through it'.[27] Feeding on this spiritual food, man is changed into Christ,[28] and so the Greeks also call it *metalepsis* or assumption, because in this sacrament 'we assume the deity of the Son'.[29]

The sacraments in fact simply *Christianize* us. The soul is not, of its nature, naturally or anonymously Christ.[30] We must be transformed in consciousness and conscience; we need to be given the gift of connaturality with Christ. This means, of necessity, being alienated from our 'own' life – the *propria vita* we regard as ours and *not* another's – in order to live *in and for* Christ, or rather, to become, more and more, Christ himself. According to Thomas, that is exactly what love does, and why the Eucharist is 'the sacrament expressive of Christ's charity, and productive of the same in us'.[31] Love conforms the lover to the beloved, shifting his centre from self to other: 'Charity makes a man give up his very self in a way and adhere to the beloved, since, as Dionysius says, "love places a man outside himself and places him in the one loved"'.[32] Charity brings about 'a spiritual union whereby the will is, in a way, transformed into that [divine] end'.[33]

> When the affection or appetite is wholly imbued by the form of a good that is an object for it, it finds the good suitable, and adheres to it as though fixed upon it; and then it is said to love it. Whence love is nothing other than a certain transformation of affection into the thing loved. And since anything that is made the form of something is made one with it, through love the lover becomes one with what is loved, which becomes the lover's form. And therefore the Philosopher says in *Ethics* 9 that 'a friend is another self'; and we read in 1 Corinthians 6.17: 'Whoever adheres to God is one spirit [with him]'.[34]

---

27 *ST* III, q. 73, a. 4, citing Damascene.
28 *ST* III, q. 73, a. 3, ad 2.
29 *ST* III, q. 73, a. 4, citing Damascene.
30 See Berger, *Aquinas and the Liturgy*, p. 49; cf. Ratzinger's remarks on the 'breaking in from the outside' character of Christianity (and of its Jewish root) that distinguishes it entirely from immanentistic religion or the 'mysticism' of illumination: *Truth and Tolerance: Christian Belief and World Religions* (trans. Henry Taylor; San Francisco: Ignatius Press, 2004), pp. 32–44, 85–9, et passim.
31 *In IV Sent.*, d. 8, q. 2, a. 2, qa. 3, ad 5; cf. *ST* III, q. 73, a. 3, ad 3.
32 *In III Sent.*, d. 29, a. 5, obj. 1, citing *On the Divine Names* IV, n. 13 (PG 3:711).
33 *ST* I-II, q. 62, a. 3.
34 *In III Sent.*, d. 27, q. 1, a. 1. For further discussion of the doctrine of love contained in this and related texts of the *Scriptum*, see Peter A. Kwasniewski, 'The Ecstasy of Love in Aquinas's *Commentary on the Sentences*', *Angelicum* 83 (2006), pp. 51–93.

The sacraments find us more or less pagan, more or less self-centred, and they evangelize and convert us to be centred on Christ, to have our centre *in* him – entailing the dissolution of self earlier spoken of, and leading the trustful disciple into a gradual rediscovery of his own paths and purposes *in relation to* the beloved. This means that a sacramental life, so far as the recipient's *experience* is concerned, will not consist of satisfying encounters between a well-defined self or subject and a securely apprehended object.[35] It will be a mirror, at times bright, at times blurry, in which I can glimpse the meaning of my life and the face of the one who seeks me out in love. 'Sacraments are proportionate to faith, through which the truth is seen in a mirror and in an enigma'.[36] For Thomas, one may thus say about the sacraments what Ratzinger says about the Christian faith as such:

> It never comes out of what we have ourselves. It breaks in from outside. That is still always the way. Nobody is born a Christian, not even in a Christian world and of Christian parents. Being Christian can only ever happen as a new birth. Being a Christian begins with baptism, which is death and resurrection (Rom. 6), not with biological birth.[37]

The catholic custom of baptizing infants is seen to be all the more fitting in that there is not even the possibility of a conscious interpersonal relationship; the infant, a silent preacher of the doctrine of St Paul, cannot even *appear* to be performing a work of righteousness, it only 'suffers the divine love'. The child of nature's womb has first of all to be re-formed in the Church's womb, elevated to the point of being *able* to have a relationship of love with Christ and through him with the whole human family. This is a dramatically anti-Pelagian gesture in which individual helplessness is met and mended in solidarity with others.[38]

It is almost invariably Galatians 2.20 that St Thomas quotes when he wants to illustrate scripturally the reality of *extasis*, the paradox of the 'I' whose life, without ceasing to be a life that is his (for the person is not annihilated), has been handed over and transformed by love into

---

[35] The experience, as such, may be empty and dry, or overfull and beyond words. But this is not the crux of the matter. The desire to equate faith or love with a subjective 'experience' of God, and the consequent tendency to spurn a God who eludes experience, is one of the chief temptations a Christian has to overcome if he is to get beyond 'self-cultivationism' into the maturity of spiritual marriage. On this point, see Denys Turner, *The Darkness of God: Negativity in Christian Mysticism* (Cambridge: Cambridge University Press, 1995).
[36] *ST* III, q. 80, a. 2, ad 2.
[37] Ratzinger, *Truth and Tolerance*, p. 87.
[38] Cf. *ST* III, q. 68, a. 9; cf. q. 73, a. 3.

another's life, so much so that he lives *out of* himself, *in* another. 'Divine love makes a man, so far as possible, live not his own life, but God's life'.[39] 'Some are alive, but have not life in themselves, such as Paul. . . . He was living, yet not in himself but in another by whom he was living, even as a body is alive, yet has not life in itself but rather has life in the soul by which it lives'.[40] To find out how Aquinas envisions the communion effected by charity, we would do well to look at part of his commentary on Galatians 2.19–20:

> A man is said to live according to that in which he chiefly establishes his affection, and in which he most of all takes delight. Hence men who take their greatest delight in study or in hunting say that this is their life. Now, each and every man has his own private affection by which he seeks that which is his own. When therefore someone lives seeking only what is his own, he lives only unto himself; but when he seeks the good of others, he is said to live for them. Accordingly, because the Apostle had set aside his self-directed affection through the cross of Christ, he said that he was dead so far as self-directed affection was concerned, saying that *with Christ I am nailed to the cross* (2.19), that is, through the cross of Christ my own self-directed or private affection has been removed from me. Hence he says below (6.14): 'God forbid that I should glory save in the cross of our Lord Jesus Christ [by whom the world is crucified to me and I to the world]'; and 2 Cor. 5.14: 'If one died for all, then all were dead. And Christ died for all, that they also who live may not now live to themselves, but unto him who died for them'. *And I live, now not I,* as if having in my affection my own good, *but Christ liveth in me,* that is, I have Christ alone in my affection, and Christ himself is my life. 'For me to live is Christ, and to die is gain' (Phil. 1.21).
>
> . . . Strictly speaking, those things are said to live which are moved by an inner principle. Now the soul of Paul was set between his body and God; the body, indeed, was made to be alive and was moved by the soul of Paul, but his soul by Christ. . . . Therefore he says, *I live by faith in the Son of God* through which he dwells in me and moves me: 'But the just shall live in his faith' (Hab. 2.4). And note that he says *in the flesh,* not 'by the flesh', because [to live like] this is evil. Second, he shows that he is nailed to the cross, saying: [I live by faith in the Son

---

39 *In III Sent.* d. 29, a. 3, ad 1.
40 *Super Ioannem* 5, lec. 5. In both this passage and the preceding, Thomas cites Gal. 2.20 for support. Passages that invoke Gal. 2.20 include *In IV Sent.* d. 12, q. 2, a. 1, qa. 1; *ST* II-II, q. 175, a. 2, ad 2; *De perfectione spiritualis uitae* 11; *In librum Beati Dionysii De divinis nominibus* 4, lec. 10; *Super Ps.* 21, n. 26 and Ps. 30, n. 1; *Super Ioan.* 1, lec. 12; *Super II ad Cor.* 5, lec. 3; *Super ad Gal.* 2, lec. 6, lec. 4.

of God] because the love of Christ, which he showed to me in dying on the cross for me, brings it about that I am always nailed with him. And this is what he says, *who loved me*: 'he first loved us' (1 Jn. 4.10). And he loved me to the extent of *giving himself* and not some other sacrifice for me: 'he loved us and washed us from our sins in his own blood' (Rev. 1.5); 'As Christ loved the Church and delivered himself up for it, that he might sanctify it, cleansing it by the laver of water in the word of life' (Eph. 5.25).[41]

This passage from the Galatians commentary is directly relevant to our theme, for it is an important aspect of Thomas's eucharistic theology that the Lord of glory present under the consecrated species is the Christ-who-suffered, *Christus passus*. As he writes in the *Commentary on John*:

Since this sacrament is of the Lord's passion, it contains within itself Christ who suffered. Hence whatever is an effect of the Lord's passion is wholly contained in this sacrament, for it is nothing else than the application of the Lord's passion to us. ... Hence it is clear that the destruction of death, which Christ accomplished by his death, and the restoration of life, which he accomplished by his resurrection, are effects of this sacrament.[42]

This is significant for many reasons. One reason that might be overlooked is psychological. In being made to confront symbols of the death we inflicted on Christ – the crucifix, the host, the chalice – we are brought face to face with the reality of our own malice or even simply our moral weariness, and our failure to 'solve' the problems of human existence. Christianity does not automatically rid people of all sin and every stain of sin; sincere Christians are not necessarily better behaved than their unbelieving neighbours, and they can at times be worse.[43] But they are

---

41 *Super ad Gal.* 2, lec. 6, §106 and §107. The translation is adapted from that of F. R. Larcher, *Commentary on Saint Paul's Epistle to the Galatians by St. Thomas Aquinas* (Albany, NY: Magi Books, 1966), pp. 62–3.

42 *Super Ioan.* 6, lec. 6, §964. See, e.g. *In IV Sent.*, d. 8, q. 1, a. 2, qa. 2; *ST* III, q. 66, a. 9, ad 5 and q. 73, a. 5, ad 2.

43 Edward Schillebeeckx discusses this issue in *Christ the Sacrament of the Encounter with God* (New York: Sheed and Ward, 1963), pp. 217–21; cf. Ratzinger, *Called to Communion*, pp. 61–5, 148–56. Geoffrey Preston speaks of the providential persistence of defects; see *God's Way to Be Man: Meditations on Following Christ through Scripture and Sacrament* (London: Darton, Longman & Todd, 1978), pp. 53–60. All the same, the truth and effectiveness of the Christian faith must in fairness be judged not by lukewarm practitioners or apostates (can one blame a medicine that was never taken for a sickness that was not thereby ameliorated?), but by the saints who have washed their robes white in the blood of the Lamb.

nevertheless *aware* of two things, if they are truly practising their faith: how bad they are in turning away from the Lord, 'every one to his own way' (Isa. 53.6); how good they are in being his creatures, sprinkled in the Lamb's blood. They seek forgiveness and healing, ultimately resurrection, from the very one they have killed, who has already died *for them* and only awaits their turning around to him (one might say, they need to 'turn themselves in'). It is this prevenient offering of the sinless for the sinner and its counterpart, the surrendering of assailant to victim, that the cross symbolizes and the Mass makes present in a mirror and in an enigma.[44] We can understand these connections better by turning for a moment to Dom Sebastian Moore's probing of the 'psychology of the cross'. For Moore, the mystery of evil can be described as the 'will not to be', the effort to *deny* that 'man is called to an ever-greater intensity of selfhood': 'The most passionately protected thing in us is our mediocrity, our fundamental indecision in respect of life. Its protection will require, and will not stop at, murder'.[45] We only experience the love that overpowers evil, and the acceptance of ourselves as failures, when we first realize that *we* have crucified Jesus; in the crucifixion, all man's frustration with and flight from himself are focused vindictively on one innocent victim. Here, with open eyes, we see explicitly what we really want – but we also see that God knows this and is ready to forgive us, that he wants to heal and convert our desire. Writes Moore: 'It is only by a total surrender that we come into our identity, a surrender whose dimensions embrace the deep mystery of our refusal and has required, for its being made, the full experience of that refusal'.[46] Thus the unintended confession in Pilate's cry '*Ecce homo*' is precisely that here, and here alone, is Man encountered, and our latent humanity awoken: 'I come before the crucified *as a non-person,* seeking to be awoken to the person I am'.[47] And why? '"I am" equals "I love". "I love" is the only way to say "I am".'[48] For that very reason, taking up again St Thomas's language, the 'sacrament of love' *must be* the 'sacrament of the cross', commemorating the Lord's sacrificial death.

But the process of reform does not stop with acknowledging one's guilt, or even with detachment from sin; the former is an obstacle to be overcome, the latter a precondition for growth. Christians pursue detachment only for the sake of deeper attachment. Borrowing the Apostle's words, Thomas describes the highest of the three degrees of charity as

---

44 Cf. *ST* III, q. 83, a. 1.
45 Sebastian Moore, *The Crucified Jesus is No Stranger* (New York: Seabury, 1981), p. 13.
46 Moore, *No Stranger*, p. 14.
47 Moore, *No Stranger*, p. 78.
48 Moore, *No Stranger*, p. 96.

a 'longing to be dissolved and to be with Christ'.[49] What the Lord seeks is the total gift of oneself, the passionate clinging of lover to beloved, of wife to husband, forming one flesh, sharing one breath.[50] If nothing less will do for human lovers in their frenzied possessiveness, will Christ settle for a lukewarm exchange of goods and services? 'I am come to cast fire on the earth, and would that it were already kindled!' (Luke 12.49); 'I have ardently longed to eat this Passover with you before I suffer' (Luke 22.15).[51] Unlike earthly spouses, Christ is able to effect a union of pure, total, permanent possession, in no way limited in its fullness, going to the abyss of one's being, there where 'the depths of God' (1 Cor. 2.10) are darkly known and sweetly loved, are touched and savoured. 'I shudder to feel how different I am from it', says Augustine of God's Word, 'yet in so far as I am like it, I am aglow with its fire'.[52]

Since the matter of the Eucharist is bread and wine, which are food and drink for man, its proper effect can be discerned from the effects of food and drink in the one who consumes them – namely, the restoration of lost matter and, should there be surplus, an increase of bodily substance.[53] But, Thomas goes on to say, there is a crucial difference between bodily food and spiritual food. Bodily food has its effect, to restore lost flesh and increase its quantity, by being converted or turned into the one fed. Spiritual food, on the contrary, is not converted into the one eating; the one eating is rather converted into *it*, for it acts upon *him*, so as to turn him into itself.[54] The notion of being changed into the food one eats might seem odd, since that would be the contrary of what happens with all other food and drink. Were the food in question mere food, it would be impossible to speak this way, as Jesus recognizes when he says: 'the flesh profits nothing' (John 6.64), that is, as the Church Fathers interpret the saying, mere flesh is lifeless, it cannot bring life to the spirit.[55] But if the food is the life-giving flesh of the living Son of God, a believer's contact with it leads to life, renewal, deification – a

---

49 *ST* II-II, q. 24, a. 9.

50 See Ratzinger, *Called to Communion*, pp. 33–40, esp. pp. 38–9; cf. M. V. Berdanot, *From Holy Communion to the Blessed Trinity* (trans. Francis Izard; London: Sands, 1925; repr. 1951).

51 Following the NJB.

52 *Confessions* 11.9 (trans. R. S. Pine-Coffin; New York: Penguin, 1961), p. 260.

53 *In IV Sent.* d. 12, q. 2, a. 1, qa. 1. To these effects Thomas likens the sacramental effects of an increase in 'spiritual quantity' by the strengthening of the virtues, and a restoration of wholeness through the forgiveness of venial sin or the repairing of any defect.

54 Aquinas says this many times; in the *Sentences* commentary alone, at *In IV Sent.*, d. 8, q. 1, a. 3, qa. 1; *In IV Sent.*, d. 9, a. 2, qa. 4; *In IV Sent.*, d. 12, q. 2, a. 1, qa. 1.

55 Typical of patristic exegesis of Jn. 6.64 is Augustine's interpretation quoted in *ST* III, q. 75, a. 1, ad 1.

truth central to the theology of St Cyril of Alexandria,[56] the first patristic *auctoritas* Thomas cites in the important question on the effects of the Eucharist: 'The life-giving Word of God, uniting himself to his own flesh, made it life-giving. It was becoming, therefore, that he be in a certain way united to *our* bodies through his sacred flesh and precious blood, which we receive in a life-giving blessing in bread and wine'.[57] As Mersch explains, 'union with food is effected in a mysterious exchange of life, in an assimilation by which one becomes the other. But in the Eucharist, the more vital of the two is the bread we receive, the 'bread of life.' This bread consumes and changes into itself the one who eats it'.[58] This it can do because it is none other than the Lord in person, under the appearances of bread and wine. United to Jesus through faith and love, the communicant 'is transformed into him and becomes his member', says Aquinas, 'for this food is not changed into the one who eats it, but turns into itself the one who takes it . . . This is a food capable of making man divine and inebriating him with divinity'.[59] In the *Sentences*, Thomas simply states: 'the proper effect of this sacrament is the conversion of man into Christ, that it might be said with the Apostle, 'I live, now not I, but Christ lives in me''.[60] He later adds: 'It belongs to charity to transform the lover into the beloved, because charity is such that it brings about ecstasy, as Dionysius says. And since the increase of virtues caused by this sacrament comes about through the changing of the one eating into the spiritual food eaten, therefore to this sacrament is specially attributed the increase of charity rather than an increase of other virtues'.[61] L. Gregory Jones summarizes it thus: 'For Thomas, to feed on Christ is gradually to lose the old, sinful self in order to be changed into a new self, a Christlike friend of God'.[62] And such a change has communal, cosmic implications, as Ratzinger brings out:

---

56 See Emile Mersch, *The Whole Christ: The Historical Development of the Doctrine of the Mystical Body in Scripture and Tradition* (trans. John Kelly; Milwaukee: Bruce, 1938), pp. 337–58.

57 *ST* III, q. 79, a. 1.

58 Mersch, *Theology of the Mystical Body*, pp. 590–1.

59 *Super Ioan.* 6, lec. 7, §969; cf. *ST* III, q. 73, a. 3, ad 2 (in both places citing *Confessions* 7.10). Commenting on Ps. 22.5, Aquinas writes: 'This cup is the gift of divine love which inebriates, since one who is drunk is not in himself . . . for he is made to be in ecstasy'; 'the cup means the blood of Christ, which ought to make us drunk' (*Super Ps.* 22).

60 *In IV Sent.*, d. 12, q. 2, a. 1, qa. 1.

61 *In IV Sent.*, d. 12, q. 2, a. 1, qa. 1, ad 3. Cf. a. 2, qa. 1: 'by the power of this sacrament there is a certain transformation of man into Christ through love . . . and this is its proper effect'.

62 L. Gregory Jones, 'The Theological Transformation of Aristotelian Friendship in the Thought of St. Thomas Aquinas', *New Scholasticism* 61 (1987), p. 389.

Normal food is less strong than man, it serves him, is taken into man's body to be assimilated and to build it up. But this special food, the Eucharist, is above man and stronger than man. Consequently the whole process involved is reversed: the man who eats this bread is assimilated *by it,* taken into it; he is fused into this bread and becomes bread, like Christ himself. 'Though many, we are one body, for we are one bread'. The result of this insight is quite clear: Eucharist is never merely an event *à deux,* a dialogue between Christ and me. The goal of eucharistic communion is a total recasting of a person's life, breaking up a man's whole 'I' and creating a new 'We'. Communion with Christ is of necessity a communication with all those who are his: it means that I myself become part of this new 'bread' which he creates by transubstantiating all earthly reality.[63]

That the Eucharist effects a transformation of eater into eaten, an ongoing conversion into Christ that parallels the increase of charity, is a view prevalent among scholastic authors. What is striking is how Thomas links it up with *extasis* in a way reminiscent of the eucharistic doctrine of St Gregory of Nyssa, whom Thomas never explicitly cites on the matter. Gregory teaches that the progress of the soul into God and at the same time into its own true nature is 'a transmutation toward the divine (*ektasis pros to theioteron*) accomplished by the Holy Eucharist', and that 'through the divine food and drink, change and ecstasy from worse things to better things enter together into the soul (*metaboles kai ekstaseos . . . suneisiouses*)'.[64] I have not been successful in finding a source in which Thomas might have encountered Gregory's views. But there does not need to be a source; we are likely dealing with a 'coincidence' proceeding from a mind similarly disposed, a heart similarly moved. This suggests we are getting near the centre of Thomas's own mind and heart. Faithful reception of the Eucharist pushes forward an ecstatic self-transformation into the soul's beloved, Jesus Christ. It causes accelerating alienation from a pseudo-self, to bring the healing of reintegration and divinization in the Lord. Among the patristic quotations in the *Summa*'s treatise on the Eucharist we find the following, from St John Damascene: 'The fire of that desire which is in us, taking ignition from the burning coal (that is, from this sacrament), will burn up our sins and illuminate our hearts, so that by partaking of the divine

---

63 Joseph Cardinal Ratzinger, *Behold the Pierced One: An Approach to a Spiritual Christology* (trans. Graham Harrison; San Francisco: Ignatius Press, 1986), p. 89.
64 Cited in Kevin Corrigan, 'Ecstasy and Ectasy in Some Early Pagan and Christian Mystical Writings', in William Carroll and John Furlong (eds), *Greek and Medieval Studies in Honour of Leo Sweeney* (New York: Peter Lang, 1994), p. 33.

fire we may be set on fire and deified'.⁶⁵ Thomas himself had noted earlier that Christ superabundantly fulfilled on the cross what was prefigured by the burning up of animals: 'In Christ's holocaust, instead of material fire [being present], there was the spiritual fire of charity'.⁶⁶ When we receive the Eucharist in a state of grace, we are feasting upon this fire of love, letting it permeate and burn into all the powers and passivities of soul and body. Hence, too, so far as ritual is concerned, 'the exterior sacrifice which is offered is a sign of the interior sacrifice by which one offers himself to God, as Augustine says in *On the City of God*'.⁶⁷ Here Thomas is at one with the monastic tradition, with Bernard's homilies on the Song of Songs, with the Victorines who speak of *extasis* in prayer. And here we catch a glimpse of that stout and often silent Dominican friar whose contemporaries testified far more often about his tears at Mass, his vigilant prayer and virginal purity, than of his disputations and publications.⁶⁸ As one of his early biographers, William of Tocco, writes:

> He was especially devoted to the most holy Sacrament of the Altar; since it had been granted him to write so profoundly of this, he was likewise given grace to celebrate it all the more devoutly. . . . During Mass he often would be seized by such strong feelings of devotion that he dissolved in tears, because he was absorbed in the holy mysteries of the great sacrament and invigorated by its offerings.⁶⁹

St Thomas gave himself body and soul to the holy mysteries because in them he found his beloved Lord, and through them feasted upon his love. He was convinced that of all the good things Jesus wants for us, foremost is an intimate friendship between him and each person who believes in him (cf. Jn. 15.13–15). Giving reasons in support of the real presence of the Lord in the Sacrament, Aquinas says:

> Such a thing befits Christ's love, out of which he took up a true body of our nature, for the sake of our salvation. And since 'to live together

---

65 *ST* III, q. 79, a. 8, sc.
66 *ST* III, q. 46, a. 4, ad 1.
67 *ST* III, q. 82, a. 4, referring to Book 10, ch. 5. On this Augustinian-Thomasian understanding of sacrifice, see Ratzinger, 'The Theology of the Liturgy', in Alcuin Reid (ed.), *Looking Again at the Question of the Liturgy with Cardinal Ratzinger* (Farnborough: Saint Michael's Abbey Press, 2003), pp. 18–31, esp. pp. 25–9.
68 All this is prominent in medieval biographical accounts: see Angelico Ferrua (ed.), *Thomae Aquinatis vitae fontes praecipue* (Alba: Edizioni Domenicane, 1968); cf. Jean-Pierre Torrell, *Saint Thomas Aquinas*, vol. I: *The Person and His Work* (trans. Robert Royal; Washington, DC: Catholic University of America Press, 1996), esp. pp. 278–89, and Kwasniewski, 'Golden Straw', pp. 79–85.
69 Ferrua, *Fontes praecipue*, n. 30, p. 73.

is most of all proper to friends', as the Philosopher says, he promises his own bodily presence to us as a reward . . . . Yet meanwhile, his bodily presence has not abandoned us in this sojourning; rather, he joins us to himself in this sacrament through the truth of his body and blood. Hence he himself says in John 6.57: 'he who eats my flesh and drinks my blood abides in me, and I in him'. Hence this sacrament is a sign of the greatest love, and the support of our hope, from so close a joining [*ex familiari coniunctione*] of Christ to us.[70]

Asking whether Jesus fittingly instituted the Eucharist at the Last Supper, Thomas lingers over the same theme. It was fitting, yes, 'because the things said last, and most of all by departing friends, are more committed to memory – especially because one's affection is then more inflamed toward the friends, while those things toward which we have more affection are imprinted more deeply on the soul'.[71] Charity, as Thomas teaches, is divinely given friendship with God.[72] The Eucharist is the divinely given sign and agent of charity.[73] Therefore this sacrament is the sacrament of friendship *par excellence*, the supreme embodiment of God's love for each soul. Since ecstasy, too, is one of the chief effects of love,[74] and above all, of friendship-love (*amor amicitiae*) for another person, we can see once again why the Eucharist brings to the soul that which it commemorates and signifies: the Lord's gift of himself on the cross, where he sealed an eternal covenant with his bride, the Church.

All of this takes place in the dark, the darkness of faith; it is with good reason that Aquinas insists on the cloudy, enigmatic nature of the sacramental event. God gives himself in limitless intimacy, but we comprehend neither him nor his gifts, for we can hardly come to grips with a love so unlike ours in its generosity and humility, yet so longed for by us in our solitude and poverty. Can it be true? The mind baulks; the response is often bewilderment. It is not possible that God should be 'mine' as if he ceased to be immense and purely unreachable, unfathomable. Yet he is indeed mine, for, as creator and sustainer, he enters into my being far more profoundly than I can enter into my own thoughts or volitions, he is more within, and more 'mine', than my own thinking and willing, my own actions and sufferings.[75] And that is not all; he delivers himself to death for me, hands over his very life to me, plants within me the seed of everlasting life: his true flesh, his inebriating blood, his

---

70 *ST* III, q. 75, a. 1; cf. q. 46, a. 3.
71 *ST* III, q. 73, a. 5.
72 *ST* I-II, q. 65, a. 5; II-II, q. 23, a. 1.
73 *ST* III, q. 78, a. 3, ad 6.
74 Cf. *ST* I-II, q. 28, a. 3; this and related texts are gathered in Kwasniewski, 'St. Thomas, *Extasis*, and Union with the Beloved'.
75 See *ST* I, q. 8, esp. a. 1 and a. 2, ad 3.

glorious humanity, 'the divine, holy, most pure, immortal, heavenly, life-creating, and awesome mysteries of Christ', as the Liturgy of St John Chrysostom chants. No wonder we are bewildered. We are torn apart by a love that defies our logic, that multiplies our longings and frustrates our desires, which are always too few and too small. God would have it this way, for unless he rends us and remakes us, we cannot enter into his rest, be one with him, be the temple of his glory, bear him in our bodies, become his sons in our souls. This is the 'merciful cruelty' of God, the 'blessed wounding' spoken of by the mystics, and like its exemplar, the 'wise folly' of the cross, it belongs to the heart of the Christian experience. In essence, to be a mystic is to believe in the mystery Paul announces in Galatians 2.20, and to strive to live it day after day with the help of God's grace – that and nothing else.[76] This is why Aquinas wept so often when celebrating Mass, and why he is a master and model for all of us.

Because he is a mystic of Christ Crucified, St Thomas is able to be an inspiring teacher of liturgical theology.[77] On Easter morning Mary Magdalene stooped to peer into the tomb. Aquinas sees a good reason for her behaviour: she

> give[s] us the example to look continually on the death of Christ with the eyes of our mind, for one glance is not enough for the one who loves, in whom the force of love multiplies the desire for seeking: 'Looking to Jesus the pioneer and perfecter of our faith, who for the joy that was set before him endured the cross, despising the shame' (Heb. 12.2).[78]

In his person no less than in his pages, the Angelic Doctor brings into sharp relief the primacy of contemplation, receptivity, timeless truth, over activism, performance, timely relevance. He demonstrates that no activity is more perfect than waiting on God, seeking his face; that no doing of mine is better than dying to my will, clinging to the cross; that nothing can be more pertinent to man here and now, nothing more liberating for the world, than yielding in silent faith to the hidden God. 'He who would search into the mysteries of Christ must go out, in a

---

76 As Louis Bouyer unfolds in *The Christian Mystery: From Pagan Myth to Christian Mysticism* (trans. Illtyd Trethowan; Edinburgh: T&T Clark, 1990); cf. Heather McAdam Erb, '"Pati Divina": Mystical Union in Aquinas', in Alice Ramos and Marie George (eds), *Faith, Scholarship, and Culture in the Twentyfirst Century* (Washington, DC: The Catholic University of America Press, 2002), pp. 73–96.

77 For further reflections along these lines, see Kwasniewski, 'Golden Straw', pp. 76–89; Kwasniewski, '"Divine Drunkenness": The Secret Life of Thomistic Reason', *The Modern Schoolman* 82 (2004), pp. 1–31, at pp. 18–19.

78 *Super Ioan.* 20, lec. 2, §2494.

way, from himself and from fleshly ways', states Thomas soberly.[79] Jesus knew what was in the heart of man, and he came not only preaching, but healing infirmities; not only healing bodies, but divinizing souls. It was to make us his intimates that he instituted the sacraments of the new law, chief among them the sacrament of his own flesh-and-blood love, the feast of the New Covenant which is simply, and incomprehensibly, the gift of himself. The only response worthy of him is the total gift of myself, remade in the beauty of his grace. If I do this, I will no longer suffer estrangement from myself or from anything real, because I shall be one with him who is supremely real, the source of all identity and difference. I can only fall on my knees and say: *Domine, non sum dignus . . . sed tantum dic verbo, et sanabitur anima mea.*

---

79 *Super Ioan.* 20, lec. 1, §2477; cf. 1 Cor. 2.14.

9

The Formation of the Ecclesial Person Through Baptismal Preparation and the Celebrations in the RCIA: the Collects for the Scrutinies

JAMES G. LEACHMAN AND
DANIEL P. MCCARTHY

Abbreviations		
AAS	= *Acta Apostolica Sedis*, Città del Vaticano	(1909 ff.)
CCL	= *Corpus Christianorum. Series latina*, Turnhout	(1953 ff.)
CSEL	= *Corpus Scriptorum Ecclesiasticarum Latinorum*, Vienna	(1866 ff.)
ICEL	= International Commission for English in the Liturgy	
LQF	= *Liturgiewissenschaftliche Quellen und Forschungen*, Münster	(1919 ff.)
PLS	= *Patrologia latinae Supplementum*, Paris	(1958 ff.)
SC	= *Sacrosanctum Concilium*	(1963)
SCh	= *Sources Chrétiennes*, Paris	(1971 ff.)

Introduction

In previous articles[1] James Leachman has examined the role of the Holy Spirit in the catechumenate and in the period of purification and enlightenment in the *Ordo Initiationis Christianae Adultorum*

---

[1] James G. Leachman, 'The Role of the Holy Spirit in the Catechumenal Preparation for Baptism in OICA', in *Spíritus spiritália nóbis dóna poténter infúndit* (Studia Anselmiana 139) (Rome: PIL, 2006), pp. 277–92; 'The Holy Spirit in the Period of Purification and Enlightenment in RCIA', *Studia Liturgica* 36 (2006), pp. 185–200. For a comparative study with the initiation rites of the Church of England, see: J. G. Leachman, 'The new family of "Common Worship" liturgical books of the Church of England (2): An introduction to the Initiation Services and their theology' *Ecclesia Orans* 21 (2004), pp. 67–97.

(*OICA*).² In this study we shall examine how the enquirer is prepared by a step-by-step process, *per ritus et preces*,³ for their initiation in the faith as a member of the catholic community, that, as they are born into a new ecclesial identity, they may come to participate in the divine–human exchange. We shall do this by examining the three collects from the scrutiny rites and extrapolate from them for the whole *OICA*.

The Constitution on the Sacred Liturgy of the Second Vatican Council well describes this process as, *ne . . . sed per ritus et preces id bene intellegentes, sacram actionem conscie, pie et actuose participent*, '. . . through the ritual and the prayers, they should share in the worshipping event, aware of what is happening and deeply involved.'⁴ The Church desires that the worshippers, including the elect, *participent*, 'they should take part' in the worshipping event composed of 'rites' and 'prayers' with full conscious and active participation.

When we read further in the same paragraph we find that the deep structure and whole purpose of the liturgy is to lead the worshipper, and thus the elect, to share in that 'final goal of unity with God and among themselves through the mediation of Christ',⁵ which we term 'divine–human exchange'. Thus the enquirers and catechumens in the *OICA*, who have initially responded to God's grace, are called to respond with an ever-deepening and self-transcending gift of themselves.

Following the method developed at the Pontifical Institute of Liturgy, Rome,⁶ we hope to show through a grammatical and source analysis of the collects for the three scrutinies, understood within the structure of the whole rite, that both the prayers and the whole *OICA* reveal our

---

2 *Ordo Initiationis Christianae Adultorum* (*OICA*) (Città del Vaticano: Typis Polyglottis Vaticanis, 1972).

3 The formula 'per ritus et preces' is found in *Sacrosanctum Concilium* (*SC* throughout), the Vatican II Constitution on the Sacred Liturgy, 4 Dec 1963. *Acta Apostolica Sedis* 46 (1964) 96–114, no. 48.

4 *SC* 48, 'And so the church devotes careful efforts to prevent christian believers from attending this mystery of faith as though they were outsiders or silent onlookers: rather, having a good understanding of this mystery, through the ritual and the prayers [*per ritus et preces*], they should share in the worshipping event, aware of what is happening and deeply involved' (*Decrees of the Ecumenical Councils, II*, ed. N. Tanner (London and Washington: Sheed & Ward and Georgetown Univ. Press, 1990), p. 830).

5 *SC* 48, Tanner, p. 830.

6 At the Pontifical Institute of Liturgy we have worked together on our methodology for the study of liturgical texts. It combines the detailed grammatical analysis of the Latin language by Fr Reginald Foster OCD and the textual hermeneutic of Prof. Renato de Zan. Using their methodologies has led to our insight regarding the divine–human exchange, as presented in this article, in the series in *The Tablet*, particularly in the articles, 'Self-transcending Gift', *The Tablet*, 10 February 2007, p. 18, and 'Giving as One and as Many', *The Tablet*, 17 February 2007, p. 15. An article by James Leachman and Daniel McCarthy on the preface of the fourth Sunday of Lent for the Second Scrutiny appeared in *Studia Liturgica* 38 (2008).

deepening participation in the divine–human exchange both by developmental steps and moments of transformation. We believe that such research has not been undertaken before.

The creation of the New Ordo

After the Second Vatican Council the twelve-member Study-Group 22[7] produced the new *Ordo Initiationis*,[8] revising ancient texts and creating new ones for both the catechumenate and the period of purification and enlightenment. As source material they used principally the *Apostolic Tradition*, commonly attributed to Hippolytus, and the *Old Gelasian Sacramentary* (*GeV* throughout).[9] The authors of the 1972 *Ordo* retained most elements of the *Apostolic Tradition*, although they shifted some rites from the period of purification and enlightenment to the catechumenate proper. In the 1972 *Ordo* the Lenten scrutinies sensibly have been reduced from seven in the *GeV* to three, and, while some of the ancient prayers of exorcism have been retained as optional minor exorcisms during the catechumenate,[10] which certainly deserve further attention from researchers, newly composed scrutinies are given in the main body of the text.

The structure of the new Ordo

The new *Ordo*[11] begins with the Rite of Reception into the period of the catechumenate, which leads through the Rite of Election into the period of purification and enlightenment during which the three scrutinies are celebrated. The process culminates in the sacraments of initiation, leading into the period of mystagogy and ongoing Christian life.

This developmental structure allows the elect to mature in their understanding and co-operation with the divine self-gift and to yield to its

---

7 Paul Turner, 'Balthazar Fischer: Educator and Chair', in *The Hallelujah Highway: History of the Catechumenate* (Chicago: Liturgy Training Publications, 2000), pp. 156–9.

8 Leachman, 'The Role of the Holy Spirit in the Catechumenal Preparation', pp. 280–1; 'The Holy Spirit in the Period of Purification and Enlightenment in RCIA', pp. 187–8.

9 For a further consideration of the source of these prayers see: A. Chavasse, *Le Sacramentaire Gélasien (Vaticanus Reginensis 316)* (Paris: Desclée, 1958), pp. 230ff.; H. A. P. Schmidt, *Introductio in liturgiam occidentalem* (Rome, Friburg and Barcelona: Herder, 1960), pp. 287–9.

10 Leachman, 'The role of the Holy Spirit in the Catechumenal Preparation', pp. 282–6.

11 Its full title is, *Rituale Romanum ex decreto Sacrosancti Œcumenici Concilii Vaticani II instauratum auctoritate Pauli VI promulgatum, Ordo Initiationis Christianae Adultorum*.

transformative power. As the elect develop and are transformed into Christians, and thus into a more accurate representation of themselves as the image of God, they are introduced into a Christian anthropology which is essentially theandric. This is to say that they grow in their ability to participate in the divine–human exchange. This self-gift of the candidates to God, which increases both through stages of maturation and transformative moments, reforms their behaviour, their thought patterns and life goals.

Admirabile commercium *as hermeneutic*

St Augustine of Hippo, when preaching on the first day of Easter, spoke to the neophytes concerning the mutual exchange (*admirabile commercium*) between Christ and believers in the Paschal mystery,

> *Quodammodo in silentio rebus ipsis loquens dominus noster Christus dicit: Unde morerer non habebam: homo, unde viveres non habebas. Assumsi de te unde morerer pro te: assume de me unde vivas mecum. Commercia celebremus: do tibi, da mihi. Accipio a te mortem: accipe a me vitam. Expergiscere: vide quid dem, quid accipiam.*[12]

In *The Confessions* he wrote of the change wrought in us through this divine–human exchange, *Cibus sum grandium: cresce et manducabis me. Nec tu me in te mutabis sicut cibum carnis tuae, sed tu mutaberis in me*,[13] 'I am food of sublime realities: arise and you will chew upon me. And you will not change me into you like the food of your flesh, but you will be changed into me'.

The divine–human exchange in both the incarnation and baptism is developed by St Ephrem the Syrian in his first Hymn on the Resurrection:

> From on high He came down as Lord,
> from within the womb He came forth as a servant;

---

12 'Our Lord Christ, speaking in a certain manner in silence by things themselves, says: "I used to not have that by which I would die: human, you used to not have that by which you would live. I received from you that by which I would die on your behalf: receive from me that by which you may live with me. Let us celebrate the exchanges: I give to you, give to me. I receive death from you: receive from me life. Wake up: see what I give, what I receive"' (Augustine of Hippo, 'Sermo Aurelii Augustini in die primo sancti paschae 5' [= Sermo 375 B in ed. P. P. Verbraken, *Études critiques sur les sermons authentiques de Saint Augustin*, (Instrumenta patristica 12) Steenbrugge: Abbatia S. Petri, 1976], in *Sancti Augustini sermones post Maurinos reperti*, ed. D. G. Morin [*Miscellanea Agostiniana. Testi e studi* 1] (Rome: Typis Polyglottis Vaticanis, 1930), p. 26, line 29).

13 Augustine of Hippo, *Confessiones*, VII, 10, 16, [CCL 27] (Turnhout: Brepols, 1981), pp. 103–4.

Death knelt before him in Sheol,
And Life worshipped Him at the Resurrection.
Blessed be His victory![14]

We choose the hermeneutic of the divine–human exchange both because it embraces the Christian West and East in St Augustine's and St Ephrem's mystagogical interpretations of the paschal mystery, and because this paper considers the formation of the new ecclesial person in the OICA to involve our coming to share in the divine life of Christ who came to share in our humanity. Thus the exchange takes place first of all between the humanity and divinity of Christ, in whom we are formed as ecclesial persons.

Now let us turn to the collects of the three ritual masses for the scrutinies, found in OICA 1972 and Missale Romanum 2002,[15] to elucidate the developmental dynamic.

The Structure of the Collects for the Scrutinies

The Collect for the First Scrutiny celebrated on the Third Sunday of Lent (OICA 377)

Lord, you call these chosen ones to the glory of a new birth in Christ, the second Adam. Help them grow in wisdom and love as they prepare to profess their faith in you. (*The Sacramentary*, 1985)	Da, quæsumus, Dómine, eléctis nostris digne atque sapiénter ad confessiónem tuæ laudis accédere, ut dignitáte prístina, quam origináli transgressióne perdíderant, per tuam glóriam reforméntur. (*Missale Romanum*, 2002)

Through this prayer the assembly petitions God to grant that the elect may approach worthily and wisely unto the confession of the faith, so

---

14 Ephrem the Syrian, 'Hymn on the Resurrection 1', stanza 8, in *Ephrem the Syrian, Select Poems*, tr., ed., S. P. Brock and G. A. Kiraz (Provo: Brigham Young UP, 2006), p. 85. See also p. 51, n.3: 'Since Christ's presence in the Jordan makes the Robe of Glory available again to humanity, his presence in Mary's womb is understood as constituting her baptism, thus providing her with her Robe of Glory . . . Mary's giving Christ "a body as a tiny garment" and receiving in return a "Robe of Glory" is one of the ways in which Ephrem brings out the idea of exchange involved in the incarnation; this is expressed . . . in epigrammatic form: "He gave us divinity, we gave Him humanity".'

15 *Missale romanum, ex decreto Sacrosanctum Oecumenici Concilii Vaticani II instauratum auctoritate Pauli PP.VI promulgatum, Ioannis Pauli PP. II cura recognitum*, editio typica tertia (Città del Vaticano: Typis Polyglottis Vaticanis, 2002).

that in their original dignity, which they had lost through original sin, they may be reformed on account of God's glory.

Source: This prayer first appears in its present form in the *GeV* (no. 193), originally composed between 628 and 715 for use in the presbyteral liturgies in the titular churches of Rome.[16] Then, as today, the prayer was offered as an opening prayer for the third Sunday of Lent, when the first scrutiny was celebrated. After the tenth century the prayer fell into desuetude due to the absence of adult baptisms, and only with the liturgical renewal mandated by Vatican II was the prayer restored through its inclusion in the *OICA* to the *Roman Missal*.

Analysis of the Literary Form

Invocation: The simple vocative address *Dómine*, is translated literally in the official English text as, 'Lord'.

Petition: The imperative petition is *da . . . eléctis nostris digne atque sapiénter ad confessiónem tuæ laúdis accédere*, 'Grant . . . to our elect, worthily and wisely to approach unto the confession of your praise'. The official English translation divides the one Latin sentence into two independent sentences, the second of which translates the Latin imperative by a corresponding imperative petition: 'Help them [these chosen ones] grow in wisdom and love as they prepare to profess their faith in you'.

In classical Latin the construction *da* (grant) followed by the dative, *eléctis nostris* (to our elect) and the infinitive *accédere* (to approach) is used only poetically. The use of this construction developed in later Latin to express purpose, which would have been rendered in classical Latin by an object sentence expressing purpose,[17] composed of *ut* (that) followed by the subjunctive. This petition therefore includes a latent purpose clause, which we reconstruct with the first subjunctive, *accédant*: *da ut elécti nóstri . . . accédant*, 'grant that our elect may approach.' What we ask God to grant is expressed by the entire object sentence *ut . . . accédant*, which, because it expresses purpose, indicates God's intent or design in granting, namely that the elect themselves may approach.

---

16 C. Vogel, *Medieval Liturgy. An Introduction to the Sources*, tr. and rev. W. Storey, N. Rasmussen (NPM Studies in Church Music and Liturgy) (Washington, DC: Pastoral Press, 1986) (tr. and rev. of *Introduction aux sources de l'histoire du culte chrétien au moyen âge* (Spoleto: Centro italiano di studi sull'alto medioevo, 1981)). 'The Gelasian Sacramentary (Vat. reg. 316) is a "mixed" book in two senses: a) the primitive substratum is purely roman but various Frankish liturgical elements have been added to it . . . b) the early Roman substratum itself is not entirely homogeneous but is the result of an intermingling of a variety of Roman libelli belonging to different periods and representing both papal and presbyterial usages . . .' (p. 66)

17 What we term here 'an object sentence expressing purpose' is called a 'complementary final sentence' in B. L. Gildersleeve and G. Lodge, *Gildersleeve's Latin Grammar* (Wauconda, IL: Bolchazy-Carducci, 2003), reprint of 3rd edition (1985), para 546, pp. 345–9.

Because Latin has no future subjunctive, this first (or present) subjunctive not only must be used to express what is contemporaneous, incomplete, unfinished, on-going, future and eternal relative to the main verb of the petition, *da,* but also the first subjunctive is patient of all of these time frames simultaneously. Thus, not only do the elect (*eléctis nostris*), during the period of purification and enlightenment, approach (*accédant*) unto the confession of God's praise (*ad conféssionem tuæ laudis*) in their baptismal promises, but furthermore, all of Christian life may be understood as an approach unto God's praise in the eschaton.

The word *accédere* elicits the idea of way (*via*), *sapiénter* the idea of truth (*véritas*) and *digne* that of life (*vita*). Thus, the elect's approaching by living worthily and wisely (*digne atque sapiénter . . . accédere*) is a growing into new life in Christ, who is *via, veritas et vita,* 'the way, the truth and the life,' (John 14:6; *Vulgate*,[18] NRS[19] throughout).

Furthermore, the adverbial form, *sapiénter,* reminds us that the elect are 'putting on Christ' (Romans 13.14), the 'Wisdom of God' (1 Corinthians 1.24, 30), like a garment. The Latin word *sapiéntia* translates the Greek *sophía* and the Syriac *ḥeqmāthā*, all feminine nouns which personify God's attribute of wisdom. In later Hebrew and early Christian (Greek and Syriac) theology, *sophía–sapiéntia–ḥeqmāthā* came to be identified with the Word of God, *logos–verbum–melthā* respectively. So Jesus, the Word of God incarnate, came to be understood as God's *sophía–sapiéntia–ḥeqmāthā*. Thus, the elect approach wisely (*sapiénter*) by hearing and responding to the Word of God proclaimed in the liturgy and reflected upon in catechesis.

Putting on Christ in baptism came to poetic expression in the Syriac tradition as being clothed in the Robe of Glory, which Adam and Eve enjoyed before the fall, and which Christ restored to the waters of baptism in the Jordan. Jacob of Serugh, for example, relates how Christ 'came to Baptism, went down and placed in the Baptismal water the Robe of Glory, to be there for Adam, who had lost it.'[20] If Adam is considered a synecdoche for the human race, then the Robe of Glory is first received in Christian baptism and finally in the eschaton.

The adverb *digne* refers to worthy behaviour in the world, as in the

---

18 *Vulgate* = *Biblia Vulgata*, ed. R. Weber (Stuttgart: Deutsche Bibelgesellschaft, 1994).

19 NRS = *The Holy Bible, New Revised Standard Version* (New York and Oxford: Oxford University Press, 1989).

20 Jacob of Serugh, Homily 94, 'On Faith', (*Acta martyrum et sanctorum*, ed. P. Bedjan, I–VII, Paris: 1890–7, III, 593); cited by S. Brock in *St Ephrem the Syrian: Hymns on Paradise* (New York: St Vladimir's Seminary Press, 1989), p. 70; T. Kollamparampil, *Select Aspects of the Economy of Salvation in Christ according to Jacob of Serugh*, excerpta ex dissertatione ad doctorandum (Instit. Patristicum Augustinianum: Rome, 1997), p. 52.

passage *tantum digne evangelio Christi conversamini*, 'Only, live your life in a manner worthy of the gospel of Christ' (Philippians 1.27). The elect approach (*accédant*) the Easter mysteries wisely (*sapiénter*) and worthily (*digne*), that is both ritually and ethically. As they incrementally learn to do this, they come to share by steps as they are enabled in their new identity in Christ.

Once the object sentence expressing purpose has been reconstructed (*ut elécti nostri . . . accédant*) we can discern the presence of a motive clause in the participial phrase *elécti nostri* (our ones having been elected). *Elécti* is an anterior passive participle. It is not only anterior to the subjunctive verb *accédant*, it is also anterior to the third Sunday of Lent, because the Rite of Election is celebrated on the first Sunday of Lent. Because *elécti* is a passive participle it is a divine passive, for God elects through the mediation of the Church. Furthermore, the participial phrase is a motive clause, expressing that God's motive for granting that they may approach is that they have already responded to the call of God, and through the mediation of the ecclesial rite God has elected them. The elect's motive for being so bold as to approach is that they have already co-operated with the divine action in their election by God.

In this short phrase we can see that the *admirábile commércium* between God and the elect consists in the self-manifestation of God and the self-transcending response of the elect. God's self-revelation is expressed in 'being for us' by granting or enabling (*da*) that the elect may listen to the Word of God in the liturgy and, by extension, to the wisdom of God in the Christian community (*sapiénter*), while practising the virtues in their daily lives (*digne*), thus coming to a self-transcending love as they approach the day when they will profess God's praise not only in baptism but ultimately with the entire community of faith in the eschaton.

The petition is notable for its emphasis on the active participation of the elect themselves who, most notably, approach (*accédant*). The way in which they approach expresses both an active engagement in liturgy and catechesis (*sapiénter*) and, according to their developing Christian identity, their active engagement in the world. The goal of their approaching is their active confession of God's praise, which is done not only through the recitation of the creed (*redditio*) and the baptismal profession of faith, but especially when they join the Christian community around the eucharistic table; all of which is expressive of the full, conscious and active participation in the rites and prayers and engagement in daily life that the church asks of the emerging ecclesial persons.

Second Petition: The standard parenthetical insertion, *quǽsumus*, 'please, we ask', expresses the role of the assembly petitioning God on behalf of the elect. It was the methodology of ICEL to move such parenthetical petitionary verbs to the beginning of the doxology, which typically begins a third sentence, 'We ask this through Jesus Christ our Lord . . .'

Purpose: The purpose clause, *ut dignitáte prístina . . . per tuam glóriam reforméntur,* 'that in the original dignity . . . they may be refashioned for the sake of your glory', is rephrased in English as a declarative statement in the first independent sentence: 'you call these chosen ones to the glory of a new birth in Christ, the second Adam.'

The prepositional phrase *per glóriam tuam,* is odd here. Literally it signifies instrumentality: 'through or by means of your glory'. Perhaps a more fitting interpretation is achieved if *per* is taken to express cause: 'on account of, for the sake of [your glory]', for here God's means or cause for reforming is God's glory itself. This connects with the Pauline doctrine of baptism, *consepulti enim sumus cum illo per baptismum in mortem ut quomodo surrexit Christus a mortuis per gloriam Patris ita et nos in novitate vitae ambulemus,* 'Therefore we have been buried with him by baptism into death, so that, just as Christ was raised from the dead by the glory of the Father, so we too might walk in newness of life.' (Romans 6.4).

According to Irenaeus of Lyons, the elect are coming to share in the glory of God for, 'The glory of God is a fully living person' (*gloria enim Dei vívens homo*).[21] In John's Gospel the glory of God is revealed most clearly in the crucified Jesus. Thus, in this prayer the elect are reformed (*reforméntur*) through the glory revealed in the crucified. The clause also alludes to Philippians 3.21, where *claritatis* is a synonym for *gloriae*: *qui reformabit corpus humilitatis nostrae configuratum corpori claritatis suae,* 'He will transform the body of our humiliation that it may be conformed to the body of his glory'.

If we take the petition as an object sentence expressing purpose, as we have explained, then with regard to *da* both purpose clauses, *ut accédant* and *ut reforméntur,* are contemporaneous, incomplete, unfinished, ongoing, future and eternal actions. Furthermore, with regard to one another the purpose clauses may be understood in two ways: contemporaneous or successive. However, even if the two clauses are contemporaneous, they are structurally successive because the purpose clause *ut reforméntur* is dependent upon the object sentence *ut accédant,* which in turn depends upon the imperative *da*. Because the sentences are structurally successive, this prayer suggests a more complex developmental struc-

---

[21] Irenaeus of Lyons, *Adversus Haereses* Book 4, Chapter 20, 7, in *Contre les Hérésies 4, Édition critique d'après les versions Arménienne et Latine, texte et traduction,* ed. A. Rousseau, B. Hemmerlinger, L. Doutreleau and Ch. Mercier [SCh 100,2] (Paris: Cerf, 1965), p. 648, line 180.

ture in Christian maturation, for not only does God desire that the elect approach (*accédant*), but God desires further that they approach with the intention of being refashioned (*reforméntur*). From the perspective of human development in the faith they actively approach their confession of God's praise consciously desiring that they may thereby be refashioned. Therefore, God's intention in enabling (*da*) is that the elect may approach (*accédant*). The elect's intention in approaching furthermore, is that they may be reformed (*reforméntur*). Thus, as God enables (*da*) the elect may approach with the intent of being reformed in the waters of baptism and throughout their Christian lives unto the eschaton.

Motive: God's motive for reforming the elect is expressed by the relative clause insinuated within the purpose clause: *quam origináli transgréssione perdíderant*, 'which they had lost by original sin,' which is alluded to in the English only as, 'Christ, the second Adam'. The prayer implies that at creation, when humanity hosted the glory of God (*tuam glóriam*), it enjoyed an unspoiled dignity, which was lost (*perdíderant*) by original sin. The prayer states that now, for the sake of the same glory, the elect are being reformed (*reforméntur*) in that original dignity (*dignitáte prístina*).

Chiasms: In the following schema we now juxtapose the four verbal forms of the motive and purpose clauses in the order in which they appear in the prayer.

	motive	purpose	
God's intent in enabling:	1. *elécti*	*accédant*	2.
The elect's intent in approaching:	3. *perdíderant*	*reforméntur*	4.

In the top row we see the two verbal forms of the object sentence expressing God's motive (*elécti*) and God's intent (*accédant*). In the second row we see the verbal forms of the purpose clause expressing both the elect's motive (*perdíderant*) and their purpose (*reforméntur*) in approaching. When we consider the diagonal relationships between these four verbal forms we note that both 1 and 4, *elécti* and *reforméntur* are divine passives, whereas 2 and 3, *accédant* and *perdíderant* are active verbs. Thus the two actions ascribed to humanity are that it had lost and now approaches, whereas God elects and reforms. It is of note that while *perdíderant* refers to the remote past, and *elécti* to the recent past, nevertheless, the effect of this chiasm is to sandwich our human activity between God's activity. Thus although the narrative line places human action temporally first, the chiastic inclusion begins and ends with divine action.

We can now add further elements to the schema. We have maintained the central box structure while adding a column on the left indicating phrases of instrumentality and one on the right indicating goals.

	instrument	motive	purpose	goal
God's intent in enabling:	*digne atque sapiénter*	*elécti nostri*	*accédant*	*ad confessiónem tuæ laudis*
The elect's intent in approaching:	*per tuam glóriam*	*quam origináli transgressióne perdíderant*	*reforméntur*	*dignitáte prístina*

The ideas form a double chiasm, albeit not expressed grammatically, in that God's (A) intent is that the elect (B) approach unto the confession of God's (A) praise, whereas the elect's (B) intent in approaching the confession of God's (A) praise is to be reformed in their human (B) dignity: thus A–B–A : B–A–B. Both protagonists, furthermore, use their proper instruments in that the elect approach by a worthy and wise manner of living and God reforms through God's glory. Thus, God intends that the elect approach worthily and wisely to the confession of God's praise, whereas the elect's intent in approaching is to be reformed through God's glory in their original human dignity.

Summary: It is striking that *perdíderant* in the pluperfect tense recalls a remote event, but there is no past event, apart from their election (*eléctis*), for this pluperfect to precede. The effect is to make the loss through original sin even more remote, whereas everything else is made contemporary. In fact, even our original dignity is not referred to primarily as that which we enjoyed before the fall, rather it is that in which the elect are now being reformed. Thus *anàmnesis* in this prayer is not expressed as the recovery or memory of a past event, but as the naming and celebration of a present gift or grace,[22] which humanity had enjoyed before the fall.

By examining the chiasms we may come to understand the divine–human exchange expressed in the very structure of this prayer. The simplest form of the chiasm is that between the active and passive verbs, contrasting our explicit human action and God's implicit action. The

---

22 'Il memoriale sacramentale è più che un semplice ricordo, che come passato deve essere lasciato al passato. ... Il memoriale fa entrare nel Mistero della Memoria-sacramentale, communione profonda col sacrificio di Cristo, per aver parte alla sua presenza di Risorto' (Joseph Cardinal Ratzinger, 'Presentazione', in *Passione per l'unità e contemplazione del mistero*, ed. M. F. Richter and M. Russotto (Città del Vaticano: Libreria Editrice Vaticana, 1996), p. 7.)

double chiasm expresses God's (A) intention that the elect (B) should glorify God (A), and the elect's (B) intention in glorifying God (A) is to be restored in their original human (B) dignity. In the incarnation the Word of God assumed our humanity in its perfection, thereby bringing humanity to its full stature, therein our humanity in Christ came to share in the self-manifestation of divine love. Thus, in terms of the second chiasm of this prayer, God became human to bring us unto God, and by our approaching God our humanity is restored; and all of this is seen in the elect on their way to baptism.

We can now show the correspondence between the sequence of the events in this prayer with those of salvation history in general, and of the *OICA* in particular. In the beginning, after the creation of all that is good, humanity lost its original dignity (*dignitáte prístina*) in the fall (*origináli transgréssione perdidérant*). Our redemption dawned when 'The Word became flesh, he lived among us, and we saw his glory' (John 1.14), and in him we became the glory of God, human beings fully alive (Irenaeus). The elect came to share in this redemption in the rite of election celebrated two weeks previously. Proleptic of the Gospel of the Samaritan woman proclaimed on this Sunday, the Church prays that the elect may co-operate with the gift of God (*da*) by their approaching (*accédere*) worthily (*digne*) and wisely (*sapiénter*) unto the future profession of God's praise (*ad conféssionem tuæ laúdis*) with the intention that they may be reformed in their original dignity (*dignitáte prístina*) already at work within them, all for the sake of God's glory (*per tuam glóriam*). The polyvalence of the first subjunctive allows us to say further that, once fully initiated, the elect, by their co-operation with God's continued self-gift (*da eléctis túis*) and continued conversion of life and thought (*digne atque sapiénter*), may be transformed (*reforméntur*) by the eschatological vision of God's glory and ever sing God's praise (*conféssionem tuæ laudis*). In Christ our humanity is brought thus into its fullness as it comes to share in the divine life of the Trinity.

This collect expresses the transformation of the elect into new ecclesial persons by developmental stages and transformative events. Thus, as the elect approach worthily (*digne*) and wisely (*sapiénter*), they are gradually transformed until they arrive at the confession of God's praise (*ad confessiónem tuæ laudis*) in the Easter Vigil, when they are decisively transformed (*reforméntur*) by the sacraments of initiation. Thus, even as they gradually come to co-operate with the divine self-revelation and gift, they also become new ecclesial persons and mediate to the world the union of God and humanity. Thereafter, the whole of their Christian life is understood as an approaching unto the eschatological consummation.

The Collect for the Second Scrutiny celebrated on the Fourth Sunday of Lent (OICA 381)

Almighty and eternal God,	*Omnípotens sempitérne Deus,*
may your Church increase in true joy.	*Ecclésiam tuam spiritáli iucunditáte multíplica,*
May these candidates for baptism, and all the family of man, be reborn into the life of your kingdom.	*ut, qui sunt generatióne terréni, fiant regeneratióne caeléstes.*
(*The Sacramentary*, 1985)	(*Missale Romanum*, 2002)

Through this prayer the assembly asks God to multiply the Church with spiritual joy, that those who are earthly by birth may be made heavenly by rebirth.

Source: Like that of the first scrutiny, this prayer first appears in the *GeV* (no. 225), and then disappears from liturgical books until the prayer is restored in the Vatican II renewal. The only change from the *GeV* text is that *caelestis* was corrected to read *caeléstes*.

Analysis of the Literary Form

Invocation: The address is complex with a noun and two adjectives: *Omnípotens sempitérne Deus*, translated literally as 'Almighty and eternal God'. Here, the adjective *omnípotens* refers particularly to God's power to create and generate life, as we shall see.

Petition: The imperative petition is, *Ecclésiam tuam spiritáli iucunditáte multíplica*, 'increase your Church with spiritual joy.' The English prayer has divided the Latin prayer into two sentences, the first of which renders the imperative petition as an exhortative subjunctive, 'may your Church increase in true joy'.

In our prayer, 'Almighty God' (*Omnípotens Deus*) is asked to increase (*multíplica*) the Church (*Ecclésiam tuam*), with spiritual joy or delight (*spiritáli iucunditáte*). '*Multiplicáre* itself has the connotation of giving with abundance.'[23] God's increasing the Church in number (*multíplica*) alludes to the passage: *et verbum Dei crescebat et multiplicabatur numerus discipulorum in Hierusalem*, 'The word of God continued to spread; the number of the disciples increased greatly' (Acts 6.7; cf. Acts 12.24). The community is associated with an increase in love in 1 Thessalonians 3.12, *vos autem Dominus multíplicet et abundare faciat caritatem in*

---

[23] Gerard Moore, *Vatican II and the Collects of Ordinary Time: A Study in the Missal (1975)* (San Francisco, London and Bethesda: International Scholars Press, 1998), p. 520.

THE FORMATION OF THE ECCLESIAL PERSON

invicem et in omnes, 'And may the Lord make you increase and abound in love for one another and for all.'

There are strong parallels too, between the vocabulary of this collect with that of the first optional collect of Ascension Day,[24] which contains related phrases such as, *Fac nos . . . sanctis exultáre gáudiis,* 'Enable us to rejoice with holy joys' and, *pía gratiárum actióne laetári,* 'and to rejoice with holy thanksgiving.' This common vocabulary indicates a theme linking both the generative joy requested in Lent and the regenerative joy of the Resurrection realized in those born again in the waters of baptism.

This common theme of generative and regenerative joy, expressed in this prayer by the three ablatives, *iucunditáte, generatióne* and *regeneratióne,* alludes to the numerous biblical narrations in which joy is connected with conception, pregnancy and child-bearing. When Sarah was told she would conceive a child she laughed, *quae rísit Sarra occulte,* 'Sarah laughed to herself' (Genesis 18.12). In the narrative of the birth of Christ, Mary came to joy by steps. First, when the archangel Gabriel announced to her that she would conceive, he not only told her not to be afraid, but even more that she was favoured by God: *ait Angelus ei ne timeas Maria invenisti enim grátiam apud Deum,* 'The angel said to her, 'Do not be afraid, Mary, for you have found favour with God' (Luke 1.30). Then in the visitation, the child rejoiced in Elizabeth's womb: *et factum est ut audívit salutatiónem Mariae Elisabeth exultávit infans in utero eius,* 'When Elizabeth heard Mary's greeting, the child leaped in her womb,' (Luke 1.41). Then finally Mary rejoiced: *et ait Maria magníficat anima mea Dóminum,* 'And Mary said, "My soul magnifies the Lord"' (Luke 1.46). Moreover, Jesus himself spoke of his second coming in terms of the joy of giving birth: *cum autem pepererit puerum iam non meminit pressurae propter gaudium quia natus est homo in mundum,* 'But when her child is born, she no longer remembers the anguish because of the joy of having brought a human being into the world' (John 16.21). These allusions reinforce the connection between Almighty God's (*omnípotens Deus*) increasing (*multíplica*) the church (*Ecclésiam tuam*) with spiritual joy (*spiritáli iucunditáte*) and God's generativity (*generatióne*), given in abundance (*regeneratióne*). We would like to add that as the reality of giving birth is fraught with difficulties, so is the reality of coming to mature Christian faith.

Motive: There is a subtle relationship between the petition clause and the motive and purpose clauses which form a couplet, in that the petition is expanded in the couplet which expresses both God's motive and design (purpose) when increasing the Church in spiritual joy. Nestled within the

---

24 *Missale Romanum* 2002, p. 425.

purpose clause, the relative clause, *qui sunt generatióne terréni,* 'those who are earthly by birth', expresses God's motive for acting. The clause does not appear in translation, but finds an allusion in the phrase 'and all the family of man'.

Purpose: The purpose clause *ut . . . fiant regeneratióne caeléstes,* 'in order that . . . they may become heavenly by rebirth', is rendered as a second exhortative petition, 'may these candidates for baptism . . . be reborn into the life of your kingdom'. The subjunctive verb *fiant* means 'may they become, may they be made.' Its form is the divine passive indicating that the action is performed by God.

As we have noted the motive and purpose clauses form a couplet. Our motive for praying is that we are earthly, which is God's motive for acting. Our goal (purpose) in praying is to become heavenly, which is God's design (purpose) in acting. The substantive plural *terréni,* 'earthly people', is opposed in this prayer to *caeléstes,* 'heavenly people'. Such contrasts in the New Testament include: *primus homo de terra terrenus secundus homo de caelo caelestis,* 'The first man was from the earth, a man of dust; the second man is from heaven' (1 Corinthians 15.47; cf. 15.49). *Terréni* and *caeléstes* are again contrasting yet complementary in Philippians 2.10: *ut in nomine Iesu omne genu flectat caelestium et terrestrium et infernorum,* 'so that at the name of Jesus every knee should bend, in heaven and on earth and under the earth'. Their complementarity here gives the idea that no one and nothing is outside the purview of glorifying God.

The couplet continues in the pairing of *generatióne* which yields to *regeneratióne*. *Regeneratióne* alludes to, *Benedictus Deus . . ., qui secundum magnam misericordiam suam regeneravit nos,* 'Blessed be the God . . . by his great mercy he has given us a new birth' (1 Peter 1.3). Both *regeneratióne* and *caeléstes* find resonance both in Philippians 3.20–21, where Paul wrote of this rebirth or transformation into the life of heaven, and in John 3.5, where Jesus talked of new birth in the Spirit: *respondit Iesus amen amen dico tibi nisi quis renatus fuerit ex aqua et Spiritu non potest introire in regnum Dei,* 'Jesus answered, "Very truly, I tell you, no one can enter the kingdom of God without being born of water and Spirit"'.

In John's Gospel, according to J. K. Barrett's imagery,[25] when Jesus 'the stranger from heaven' instructs his hearers with the words, *vos de deorsum estis ego de superna sum. Vos de mundo hoc estis ego non sum de hoc mundo,* 'You are from below, I am from above. You are of this world; I am not of this world' (John 8.23), there are obvious allusions to our prayer, especially to the binary *caeléstes – terréni.* Like that Gospel

---

25 J. K. Barrett, *The Gospel according to St John: An Introduction with Commentary and Notes on the Greek Text* (London: SPCK, 1978).

passage, our collect plays on the contrasts between heavenly (*caeléstes*) and earthly (*terréni*) and between birth (*generatióne*) and rebirth (*regeneratióne*); accordingly, the elect, though still belonging to the earth, will soon be reborn as heavenly ones (*caeléstes*).

This being made heavenly by rebirth (*fiant regeneratióne caeléstes*), relative to God's generous giving (*multíplica*), is contemporaneous, incomplete, unfinished, ongoing, future and eternal; it is present because as we co-operate with God's giving, we are even now being made heavenly by rebirth in the liturgy we celebrate; it is future, because the elect will be regenerated in the waters of baptism; it is eternal in that at the end of time we who are reborn in water and the Spirit will see God face to face (cf. 1 Corinthians 13.12).

In the purpose clause the word *caeléstes* parallels the spiritual joy (*spiritáli iucunditáte*) in the petition clause, because the spiritual joy (*spiritáli iucunditáte*) of the Church is a mark of the ones who are heavenly by rebirth (*regeneratióne caeléstes*).

Summary: In contrast to the chiasm in the first prayer which highlighted the developmental process and active approaching of the elect with the intention of being reformed, the couplet in this prayer turns on an axiological change of state whereby one earthly by birth becomes heavenly by rebirth.

The passive undergoing of rebirth in Christ at the hand of God, regrettably often overlooked, is described in James Alison's book, *Undergoing God*, where he writes, 'how tiring and tedious is the business of being brought into being without excitement!' and '. . . to allow myself to be brought quietly into being, trusting that I will be given to be someone, that that being will be of worth, and that I don't have to do anything special in order to be given that being.'[26]

The elect during this period of purification are called to relinquish any obstacles to their full participation in this divine–human exchange, and in this period of enlightenment come to see how profound will be their share as they undergo the active-passivity of being reborn as *caeléstes*, a rebirth sacramentalized once in baptism, yet an ongoing transformation throughout the Christian life. Thus are the elect initiated into the mutual self-gift between God and humanity, the nuptial covenant that they who were born earthly and reborn as heavenly may mature to the full stature of spouse, image of God's generativity.

The *Leitmotif* of heavenly joy and generativity both on God's part and the assembly's, and the active-passive rebirth of the elect in the baptismal waters is emphasized in other ways; for example, by the context of the celebration on the fourth Sunday of Lent whose introit, *Laetare*

---

26 James Alison, *Undergoing God: Dispatches from the Scene of a Break-in* (London: DLT, 2006), p. 89; see also pp. 88, 173.

Sion, et conventum facite, omnes qui diligitis eam; gaudete cum laetitia, qui in tristitia fuistis, ut exultetis, et satiemini ab uberibus consolationis vestrae,[27] refers to our mother Jerusalem. Whenever this scrutiny is celebrated, this collect also precedes the Gospel pericope of the cure of the man born blind, John 9, who in his blind state is an example of those who are earthly by birth, and after his healing comes to faith and thus comes to share in rebirth as heavenly. Thus the Gospel adds to this prayer another level of meaning, that as we pass from earthly to heavenly, we pass from blindness to sight, darkness to illumination, sadness to joy.

Omnípotens Deus (when imaged as father) increases *Ecclésiam tuam* (when imaged as mother) with joy (*iucúnditate*) in their fecund nuptial union that brings forth as the fruit of their intimate exchange the 'heavenly ones' (*caeléstes*), newly reborn of the Spirit in the Easter waters. The Church's joy (*iucúnditate*), when tested, is found to be of the spirit (*spiritáli*) and thus eternal. The elect, like the man born blind, come to faith by stages even as they approach their rebirth in the waters of baptism. God's nature as bountiful source of joy and generativity encounters our humanity which knows that nothing but this nuptial union with God can satisfy our deepest needs and desires.

The Collect for the Third Scrutiny celebrated on the Fifth Sunday of Lent (OICA 385)

Lord,	Concéde, Dómine,
enlighten your chosen ones with the word of life.	eléctis nostris, ut, sanctis edócti mystériis,
Give them a new birth in the waters of baptism and make them living members of the Church.	et renovéntur fonte baptísmatis et inter Ecclésiæ tuæ membra numeréntur.
(*The Sacramentary*, 1985)	(*Missale Romanum*, 2002)

Through this prayer the assembly petitions God to grant to the elect that they, having been thoroughly formed in the holy mysteries, both may be renewed by the waters of baptism, and be numbered among the members of the Church.

Source: This prayer first appears in its current form in the *GeV* (no. 254). Like the other two collects, this one also disappeared from use

---

27 Rejoice with Jerusalem, and [call an assembly] be glad for her, all you who love her; rejoice with her in joy, all you who mourn over her, that you may nurse and be satisfied from her consoling breast; that you may drink deeply with delight from her glorious bosom. (NRS)

when adult baptism was no longer the norm. Similarly, it now accompanies the third scrutiny during Lent, as it did in eighth-century Roman practice.

Analysis of the Literary Form

Invocation: The simple vocative address *Dómine*, is translated literally as, 'Lord.'

Petition: The imperative petition is, *Concéde . . . eléctis nostris*, 'Grant . . . to our elect'. The official English translation divides the prayer into two sentences, the first of which expresses the Latin imperative petition with a corresponding English imperative petition, 'enlighten your chosen ones with the word of life'. The choice of the imperative 'enlighten' and the addition of the phrase 'the word of life' is perhaps informed by the motive clause, as we shall see.

In ecclesiastical Latin *eléctis* means 'to ones having been chosen of God' or 'to ones having been destined to be saved'. It alludes to the scriptural passages, *sicut elécti Dei sancti et dilecti*, 'As God's chosen ones, holy and beloved,' (Colossians 3.12) and *multi autem sunt vocati pauci vero elécti*, 'For many are called, but few are chosen' (Matthew 22.14). Not only does *eléctis nostris* serve as the dative complement of the imperative *concéde*, but as an antecedent passive participial phrase it also serves as the first of two motive clauses in this prayer: they shall be considered together below.

Purpose: What the Church asks God to grant to the elect is given in an object sentence expressing purpose, composed of *ut* (that) followed by two subjunctive verbs *renovéntur* and *numeréntur,* which establish a double purpose clause thus: *ut . . . et renovéntur fonte baptísmatis et inter Ecclésiæ tuæ membra numeréntur,* 'so that . . . they may both be renewed in the font of baptism and numbered among the members of your Church', which is rendered in the second English sentence by a double imperative, 'Give them a new birth in the waters of baptism and make them living members of the Church.'

Renovéntur alludes to Colossians 3.10: *et induentes novum eum qui renovatur in agnitionem secundum imaginem eius qui creavit eum,* 'and have clothed yourselves with the new self, which is being renewed in knowledge according to the image of its creator.' *Numeréntur* alludes to Wisdom 5.5: *quomodo conputati sunt inter filios Dei et inter sanctos sors illorum est,* 'Why have they been numbered among the children of God? And why is their lot among the saints?'

Relative to *concéde* (grant), both present subjunctives, *renovéntur* (may they be renewed) and *numeréntur* (may they be counted), are grammatically contemporaneous, incomplete, unfinished, ongoing, future and eternal, and this full polyvalence is applicable in various ways to this prayer. Accordingly, *fonte baptísmatis* indicates that both *renovéntur* and *numeréntur* find privileged expression at the Easter font. But, not only are the elect renewed and numbered as members of the Church in baptism, at the end of an entire Christian life of being renewed in their baptismal vows, they also hope to be numbered among the saints.

Thus, what the Church asks God to grant to the elect is that they actively undergo their own being renewed (*renovéntur*) at the hand of God and thus their being numbered (*numeréntur*) among the members of the Church.

Motive: Nestled at the beginning of the purpose clause is the second participial phrase expressing motive, *sanctis edócti mystériis,* 'ones having been thoroughly instructed in the holy mysteries,' which informs the first imperative petition, 'enlighten your chosen ones with the word of life', as mentioned above.

The implied subject of both *eléctis* and *edócti* is *ii*, (the ones), the subject of *renovéntur* and *numeréntur* of the purpose clause. As anterior passive participles, both *eléctis* and *edócti* are antecedent to both subjunctive verbs. Because both *renovéntur* and *numeréntur* have particular relevance to the Easter Vigil, accordingly, while *edócti* refers to the entire period of formation leading up to the Easter Vigil including both the catechumenate and the period of purification and enlightenment, *eléctis* refers specifically to one moment within this period of formation, the rite of election. More broadly, while *renovéntur* also refers to an ongoing process throughout the Christian life, so *edócti* also refers to the period of mystagogy and to our lifelong formation. This interpretation is supported by two biblical allusions, *renovéntur* referring to the ongoing renewal of Christians after baptism in the passage *Renovamini autem spiritu mentis vestrae*, 'and be renewed in the spirit of your minds' (Ephesians 4.23), and *edócti* also referring to post-baptismal instruction in the passage *hic erat edoctus viam Domini*, 'He had been instructed in the way of the Lord' (Acts 18.25). Similarly, *numeréntur* refers to the Church's being numbered among the elect (*eléctis*) in the eschaton.

The pairing of two anterior passive participles expressing motive with two first subjunctive verbs expressing purpose suggests the following schema:

nostris	*eléctis*	*edócti*	*sanctis mystériis*
fonte baptísmatis	*renovéntur*	*numeréntur*	*inter Ecclésiæ tuæ membra*

In the top row we see the two participles expressing motive, *eléctis* and *edócti*. Both participles begin with the prefix *e-* or *ex*, meaning, in the case of *eléctis*, 'to ones having been chosen out from a number', and in the case of *edócti*, 'ones having been taught "out to the end"' and thus 'thoroughly'. We have placed the other words of each participial phrase in columns to the left and right. In the bottom row we see the two subjunctive verbs expressing purpose, with their related phrases again to the left and right. When arranged in this way, the chiasm between the four verbal phrases becomes apparent in the relationships among their related phrases, in that *sanctis mystériis* is related to *fonte baptísmatis* and *nostris* to *inter Ecclésiæ tuæ membra*. This chiasm is further strengthened in that *eléctis* refers to 'choosing out from a number', and *numeréntur* to 'numbering as one's own'. Unfortunately, a relationship between *edócti* and *renovéntur* is not readily apparent. However, we can conclude that this chiasm unites the Church and the sacred mysteries with God, the unseen protagonist.

Furthermore, the phrase *sanctis mystériis* alludes to Mysterium quod absconditum fuit a saeculis et generationibus nunc autem manifestatum est sanctis eius 'the mystery that has been hidden throughout the ages and generations but has now been revealed to his saints' (Colossians 1.26). The catechumens and elect participate in this mystery, who is 'Christ among you', as they, by steps, come to give themselves in response to the divine self-gift in the divine–human exchange.

Summary: The prayer begins with God's direct action, as the Church petitions God to grant (*concéde*). The elect's four actions all appear in the passive voice: *eléctis* (to ones having been chosen), *edócti* (ones having been thoroughly instructed), *renovéntur* (may they be renewed) and *numeréntur* (may they be numbered). All four verbal forms are divine passives, for God is the one who has elected them, who has thoroughly instructed them and who renews and numbers them.

In each of these divine passives the Church mediates God's action, for through the rites and prayers of the Church (*OICA*) God calls the elect, thoroughly instructs them for baptism and renews and numbers them among the members of the Church. The action of the Church, furthermore, is made explicit in several ways. First of all the assembly prays to God on behalf of the elect for whom it owns responsibility by calling them 'our' elect (*eléctis nostris*). The Church facilitates the renewal of the elect (*eléctis nostris*) by engaging them in catechetical preparation (*sanctis edócti mystériis*) until they pass through the waters of baptism (*fonte baptísmatis*), are anointed with chrism and are made one with the Church in the eucharistic feast, and so are renewed (*renovéntur*) and numbered among the members of God's Church (*inter Ecclésiæ tuæ membra numeréntur*). Thus 'our elect' become 'part of us', the Church.

The deep structure of the prayer reveals the mutual self-giving in love between God and those who respond to their election (*eléctis*), that as God's self-gift (*concéde*) is mediated through the mysteries, and as they give themselves to being formed (*edócti*) by God in the mysteries, they may be renewed (*renovéntur*) and numbered (*numeréntur*) by God among the chosen ones.

This mutual self-gift is accurately represented in the love shared among the circle of Jesus and his friends, Lazarus, Martha and Mary in the Gospel assigned to this mass each year (John 11.1–44), which images the active-passivity of the elect in this prayer. On the one hand, Lazarus was passive because he was dead (vv.14, 17), and he was actively passive in being raised by Jesus. Moreover, he was dependent on the faith of his sisters at whose request Jesus raised him up (vv. 21–22, 24, 27, 32). On the other hand, Lazarus co-operated actively in his response to Jesus' command, 'Lazarus, come out!' (v. 43), and in his struggle to liberate himself from his grave-clothes (v. 44). Accordingly, in Lent the elect are called out (*elécti*) and instructed for a new life (*edócti*); they are actively passive in pursuing their transformation both for baptism and for their future life as Christians.

The larger liturgical context of the prayer further interprets the paschal mystery according to the bivalent Pauline *Leitmotif* of dying and rising. The introit, *Iudica me Deus, et discerne causam meam de gente non sancta; ab homine iniquo et doloso eripe me, quia tu es Deus et fortitudo meo*,[28] (Psalm 42.1–2) asks for rescue from the unholy and the wicked, and the Gospel of the Raising of Lazarus from death (John 11.1–42) emphasizes the Pauline *Leitmotif* of suffering, death and resurrection, thus preparing the elect for the Easter sacraments. On the one hand, in baptism we share in the suffering and death of Jesus, imaged in being buried in the waters of the font, and on the other hand we undergo an active-passive rising to new life from the tomb, imaged in our emerging from the waters of the font. This Pauline *Leitmotif* complements and contrasts with the Johannine imagery which emphasizes resurrection as new birth.

The deep structure and theology of these prayers

Sources of the prayers: The three prayers we have examined are original to the *GeV*, which was composed between 628 and 715 for presbyteral liturgy in the titular churches of Rome. They are drawn from the corresponding masses of the third, fourth and fifth Sundays of Lent when the

---

28 Vindicate me, O God, and defend my cause against an ungodly people; from those who are deceitful and unjust deliver me! For you are the God in whom I take refuge ... (NRS).

scrutinies were celebrated. All three prayers fell out of use when adult baptism ceased to be the norm. With the renewal of the *OICA* all three have been reclaimed with only one spelling correction.

Invocation: God is addressed both as *Dómine* (Lord) and as *Omnípotens sempitérne Deus* (Almighty and everlasting God). The vocabulary and grammar establish a playful dynamic between the transcendence of the titles and the direct address of the vocative case, between formality and immediacy. God's omnipotence is evoked not to overpower, but to empower us both to act and to yield. God's actions are often hidden, implied in the divine passives.

Amplification: None of our prayers includes an amplification of the address, which typically expresses the anamnetic element of the prayer, yet we have identified only one phrase pertaining to anamnesis, *dignitáte prístina quam origináli transgressione perdíderant*. Only the loss by original sin, however, is referred to in the past tense, whereas the previous original dignity is considered only in the present tense as that in which the elect are currently being reformed (*reforméntur*).

Petition: The petitions are of two types. The simplest form is the parenthetical *quæsumus* (we ask, please), which is the only verb in the first person plural in these three prayers, and thus belongs explicitly to the entire assembly.

The other form of petition is the imperative, which still indicates the role of the assembly in petitioning God. The use of the imperative involves the direct address of Almighty God, using, astoundingly, the simple command form which accentuates the immediacy of the transcendent. Fundamentally, the Church petitions the gift of God's self, yet God's self is always given according to our ability to receive, and so our three imperative petitions specify the gift of God petitioned. Each prayer presents its own grammatical structure and challenges: we begin with the simplest.

In the second prayer the petition is straightforward. The Church asks God, *Ecclésiam tuam spirituáli iucunditáte multíplica* (increase your Church with spiritual joy). In the more complex third prayer the imperative verb *concéde* has the indirect complement *eléctis nostris*. Furthermore, what the Church petitions God to grant to our elect is expressed in the double object sentence,[29] *ut . . . et renovéntur . . . et numeréntur*, which is to say that the church is not asking God to grant the gift as if it were a 'thing', but rather that our co-operating with God's generous self-gift is an essential part of God's mode of giving. In the first prayer, more complex yet, the imperative *da* (grant) is followed by the indirect complement *eléctis nostris*. What the Church asks God to grant to our

---

29 Or 'complementary final sentence', see Gildersleeve and Lodge, *Gildersleeve's Latin Grammar*, para 546, pp. 345–9.

elect is the whole phrase *digne . . . accédere*, which is to say once again that the elect's co-operating with God's generous self-gift is an essential part of God's mode of giving.

The epicletic element is typically expressed in the petition in which the Church invokes God as both giver and gift; yet again we see that God's mode of self-gift is part of God's gift, bringing us to share in God's life. The epicletic element is nowhere more manifest than in the second prayer's baptismal imagery of being reborn (Galatians 4.29) and in its latent marital imagery.

Because both object sentences *ut . . . et renovéntur . . . et numeréntur* and *ut . . . accédant* are also purpose clauses, we shall examine them in the next section.

Purpose: In order to make sense of the variety of grammatical structures, let us begin with the second prayer in order to distinguish between what God gives and the purpose for which God gives it. In this prayer the assembly petitions God to multiply the Church, thus what God multiplies is the Church, *Ecclésiam tuam*, expressed as a simple, direct object in the accusative case. Distinct from what God multiplies (the Church) is the purpose for which God multiplies the Church, expressed in a two-line couplet composed of both the motive and purpose clauses, *ut . . . fiant*. Thus, God's purpose for multiplying the Church is that people earthly by birth may become heavenly by rebirth. Accordingly, our purpose for offering this prayer is that God may do for the elect what God has done for us.

In the third prayer we find that what God gives and the purpose for which God gives it are expressed in the same object sentence, *ut . . . renovéntur et . . . numeréntur*. Which is to say that the gift given contains the goal desired by God, that the elect be renewed (*renovéntur*) and be numbered (*numeréntur*); but this comes about only by the free co-operation of the elect themselves, and thus the gift given is their capacity and desire freely to yield to their own transformation. In preparation for discussing the following prayer it is helpful to note that in this prayer the two subjunctive verbs are simply juxtaposed (*et . . . et*: both . . . and).

In the first prayer we find a more complex structure. Like the prayer just considered we find that what God gives and the purpose for which God gives it are expressed in the same object sentence. God's intention in granting (*concéde*) furthermore, is more clearly seen when the object sentence is reconstructed as a purpose clause, as we have said above: *ut elécti nostri . . . accédant* (in order that our elect may approach). In contrast to the prayer just considered, however, where both passive verbs (*et renovéntur et numeréntur*) highlight the active-passivity of the elect, here the verb is active, *accédant*, indicating the active co-operation of the elect themselves. Thus, God's intent in granting is that the elect may actively approach: this is to say that the gift given contains the goal desired by God. Unlike the previous prayer where the single object sentence juxtaposes two verbs, this one follows the object sentence *ut accédant* with the successive purpose clause *ut . . . per tuam glóriam reforméntur*. Thus the object sentence *ut accédant* expresses God's intention in granting that the elect may approach with the intention expressed in the purpose clause *ut reforméntur*.

Before considering the motive clauses let us recapitulate the use of the subjunctive. Because Latin has no future subjunctive, the first subjunctive must be used to express what is contemporaneous, incomplete, ongoing, unfinished, eternal and future relative to the main verb of the petition, in our cases, *da, multíplica* and *concéde*. Thus, in regard to these three imperatives, the five first subjunctives, *accédant, reforméntur, fiant, renovéntur et numeréntur*, even if these verbs are particularly applicable to certain stages of the elect's incorporation into the body of Christ, they also are more generally applicable to their ongoing preparation for, and subsequent celebration of baptism, and to their continuing Christian life and its realization in eternity.

This polyvalence of the Latin first subjunctive has the effect of uniting both our eschatological hope with its partial realization in our current lives, and our developing participation in the divine life with its full realization in eternity. The grammatical structure of the prayers, therefore, is easily patient of an interpretation that favours both this gradual but realized incorporation into the divine–human exchange (*admirábile commércium*).

Motive: As we have seen, the three prayers have four object sentences expressing purpose; they also have five motive clauses. These latter are composed according to two different grammatical constructions; two are relative clauses and two participles; and, as it happens, the motive clauses are used in a variety of ways. Typically, the motive clause is nestled within its respective purpose clause.

Let us begin by examining the two motive clauses that are constructed as relative clauses. They are, in the first prayer, *quam origináli trangressióne perdíderant*, 'which they had lost by the first sin' and in the second prayer, *qui sunt generatióne terréni*, 'who are earthly by birth'. They both refer to the given state of humanity either as fallen or simply 'born', which is to say that our process of human development begins here. That these motive clauses are nestled within their respective purpose clauses establishes a polarity between the given state of humanity and our desire (purpose). Thus, we note this contrast between *perdíderant* (they had lost) and *reforméntur* (may they be reformed), and between *sunt* (are) and *fiant* (may they become).

Furthermore, the motive clause in these prayers is used not only to establish the given state of human development, but is also used to express God's motive for granting what we desire in the prayer. Thus, in the first prayer, God's motive for reforming (*reforméntur*) the elect is because they had lost (*perdíderant*) their original dignity by sin. In the second prayer God's motive for making (*fiant*) people heavenly is because they are (*sunt*) earthly by birth. It is helpful to point out that neither of these motive clauses implies human co-operation.

The first prayer has both an object sentence and a purpose clause, and each has a corresponding motive clause. Were the object sentence to be rendered classically, as we have said, it would read, *ut elécti nostri . . . accédant* and the participial phrase *elécti nostri* would be the motive clause. Like the previous two motive clauses then, *elécti* refers to the current state of the elect, but unlike those clauses, here their election by God has already come to its maturity, and the elect are no longer at the beginning, but are well advanced in their developmental formation as new ecclesial persons.

As we turn now to the motive clause of the third prayer we notice that the same phrase *eléctis nostris* appears here as well, and thus forms the first of two motive clauses in this prayer. Although *eléctis nostris* lies outside the purpose clause, the elect are the subject of both subjunctive verbs of the purpose clause, for the elect are renewed and numbered. Thus, what we have said above also applies here.

The second motive clause in this prayer is the participial phrase, *sanctis edócti mystériis* (ones having been taught well in the holy mysteries), which is nestled within the purpose clause. Rather than expressing a given state of humanity or of the elect as in the other motive clauses, this motive clause expresses an intermediate stage of the elect's co-operation with the divine gift. Because *edócti* is anterior to the two subjunctive verbs of the purpose clause, *renovéntur* and *numeréntur*, it has particular reference to the period of formation prior to baptism. In that this prayer is offered on the fifth Sunday of Lent, the elect are in the process of being taught well and yet this developmental process has not yet come to its maturity prior to baptism. Thus we pray that God be present to them now as they are co-operating in their formation, that after they have been fully taught they may be ready to be renewed in the font.

Whether the motive clause expresses the original state or their ongoing preparation, in each case it expresses the developmental character of Christian maturation, and the divine motive for acting.

Verbal Forms: As we have seen, the three prayers include two verbal forms which belong to the whole of humanity, *perdíderant* (they had lost) and *sunt terréni* (they are earthly). They indicate the state of humanity on whose behalf the Church invokes God's action. The three prayers also include three imperatives, by which the Church petitions God to act on behalf of the elect. Furthermore, only one active verb belongs to the assembly, the parenthetical *quǽsumus*.

Moreover, only one active verb belongs to the elect, the infinitive *accédere* (*accédant*, may they approach). This is the one properly active task assigned to the elect, who approach first of all through their full, conscious and active participation in the liturgical assembly, through its rites and prayers of Christian initiation, as mandated by *SC* 48, which thereby mediate their participation in the divine–human exchange. This is further elucidated in the third prayer where the implied protagonist in the chiasm between our full conscious and active participation in the sacred mysteries and our being numbered among the members of the Church is latent[30] in the divine passives. This is because the process of becoming a Christian combines both our active co-operation with the divine enabling and our actively yielding to divine transformation, as the chiasm in the first prayer also suggests.

Accordingly, all the other verbal forms belonging to the elect are divine passives: two are anterior participles, *eléctis* (to ones having been elected) and *edócti* (ones having been thoroughly instructed), and the rest are passive subjunctives, *reforméntur* (may they be reformed), *fiant* (may they be made), *renovéntur* (may they be renewed) and *numeréntur* (may they be counted). These six divine passives indicate forcefully that God is the latent protagonist bringing the elect to rebirth in baptism by reforming them, renewing, numbering, instructing, choosing and making them new ecclesial persons. The elect are actively passive as they undergo God. This is seen clearly when, for example, after the scrutinies the catechist leads them out of the assembly to a place where they will continue in quiet prayer and reflection on the Scriptures. Only after their Christian initiation will they, as neophytes, assume their rightful ministry of full, conscious and active participation in the liturgical assembly. Yet even now in the three scrutinies their liturgical and ecclesial participation already mediates their developing mutual participation with God in the divine–human exchange.

Conclusion: The vocabulary of the three collects presents a microcosm of the entire *OICA* process; the collects refer both to specific moments of axiological change of status and to developmental processes of Christian maturation. For example, the word *eléctis* refers to the rite of election, and thus a change of state from catechumens to the elect. *Accédere ad* refers to the entire period leading up to baptism, and the phrase, *sanctis edócti mystériis* refers to their ongoing formation in the mysteries. *Digne* and *sapiénter* refer more broadly to their whole manner of life,

---

30 'Adoro te devote, latens Deitas/Quae sub his figuris vere latitas: Tibi se cor meum totum subiicit,/Quia te contemplans totum deficit,' ascribed to St Thomas Aquinas (1225 + 1274).

public and ecclesial in approaching baptism. The phrase *confessiónem tuæ laudis* refers to the sacraments of Christian initiation, as do *regeratióne* and *renovéntur fonte baptísmatis*: the axiological change *par excellence*. Then *inter Ecclésiæ tuæ numeréntur* refers to the neophytes' new state after baptism, as do *fiant caeléstes* and *per tuam glóriam*. In each of the prayers then, the Church petitions God to act now, which is to say to give God's self to the elect that they may act and yield.

A grammatical and source analysis of these three prayers has revealed in each of them a developmental structure drawing the elect into the divine–human exchange. Augustine describes our mutual participation with God in his Guelferbyternus sermon, *Mirum proinde nobiscum egit mutua participatione commercium: nostrum erat, unde mortuus est; illius erit, unde vivamus*,[31] (Hence he accomplished with us a wonderful exchange by mutual participation: the death was of us from which he died; in order that from his life we may live). The divine–human exchange is no more clearly expressed than in the double chiasm of the first prayer, where God's intention for the elect's approaching to the confession of God's praise is that the elect intend in coming to confess God's praise that they be reformed in their original human dignity.

Our deepening participation by developmental stages in the divine–human exchange, *admirábile commercium* (Latin), *synergía* (Greek) and *shawtaputā* (Syriac), while lying at the heart of every orthodox and catholic prayer, is also the model for the entire rite of Christian initiation. The developmental structure of the collects, and of the entire *OICA* process, with its constituent rites and prayers, leads the candidates, step by step, as they are enabled, into the mutual participation with God in the divine–human exchange, thus creating the new ecclesial person.

Bibliography

Sources

Augustine of Hippo, 'Sermo in die primo sancti paschae 5' (= Sermo 375 B in ed. P. P. Verbraken, *Études critiques sur les sermons authentiques de Saint Augustin*, (Instrumenta patristica 12), Steenbrugge: Abbatia S. Petri, 1976), in *Sancti Augustini sermones post Maurinos reperti*, ed. D. G. Morin (*Miscellanea Agostiniana*. Testi e studi 1), Rome: Typis Polyglottis Vaticanis, 1930.

Augustine of Hippo, *Confessiones*, VII, 10, 16, (CCL 27), Turnhout: Brepols, 1981.

---

[31] Augustine of Hippo, *Sermo Guelferbyternus* 3, ed. A. Hamman (PLS 2) (Paris: Garnier, 1960), pp. 545–6; *Liturgia Horarum: Tempus Quadragesima et Tempus Pasquale*, II (Città del Vaticano: Libreria Editrice Vaticana, 2000), Hebdomada sancta, Feria secunda, p. 347.

Augustine of Hippo, *Sermo Guelferbytanaus 3*, ed. A. Hamman (PLS 2), Paris: Garnier, 1960, p. 546 lines 2–5; *Liturgia Horarum II: Tempus Quadragesima et Tempus Pasquale*, Città del Vaticano: Libreria Editrice Vaticana, 2000, 'Hebdomada sancta, feria secunda', 347.

Biblia Vulgata, ed. R. Weber, 4th edition, Stuttgart: Deutsche Bibelgesellschaft, 1994.

Coetus a studiis 22: De Sacramentis. Consilium ad exsequandam constitutionem de sacra Liturgia. Schemata, *Rite of Christian Initiation of Adults. 1965–69*. Archives care of Hesburgh Library, University of Notre Dame, IN, USA.

Cyril of Jerusalem, *Mystagogical Catechesis*, ed. F. L. Cross, London: SPCK, 1951.

Decrees of the Ecumenical Councils, II, ed. N. Tanner, London and Washington: Sheed & Ward and Georgetown University Press, 1990.

Ephrem the Syrian, *Hymns on Paradise*, tr., ed. S. P. Brock, New York: St Vladimir's Seminary Press, 1989.

Ephrem the Syrian, *Select Poems*, tr., ed., S. P. Brock and G. A. Kiraz, Provo: Brigham Young UP, 2006.

Irenaeus of Lyons, *Adversus Haereses 4, Édition critique d'après les versions Arménienne et Latine, texte et traduction*, eds A. Rousseau, B. Hemmerlinger, L. Doutreleau and Ch. Mercier (SCh 100, 2), Paris: Cerf, 1965.

Jacob of Serugh, Homily 94, 'On Faith' (*Acta martyrum et sanctorum*, ed. P. Bedjan, I–VII, Paris: 1890–97, III).

Jacob of Serugh, *Homilies of Mar Jacob of Serugh*, tr., ed. S. P. Brock, Piscataway, NJ: Gorgias Press, 2006.

La Tradition Apostolique de Saint Hippolyte: Essai de reconstruction, ed. B. Botte (LQF 39), 5th edition, Münster: Aschendorff, 1989.

Les Ordines Romani du haut moyen âge. Tome II: Les textes (Ordines I–XIII), ed. M. Andrieu (Spicilegium Sacrum Lovaniense 23), Louvain: 1948.

Liber Sacramentorum Romanae Aeclesiae ordinis anni circuli. Cod. Vat. Reg. Lat 316 (*Sacramentarium Gelasianum*), eds L. C. Mohlberg, L. Eisenhöfer and P. Siffrin (Rerum Ecclesiasticarum Documenta, Series Maior, Fontes, IV), 3rd edition, Rome: Herder, 1981.

Missale Romanum ex decreto Sacrosanctum Oecumenici Concilii Vaticani II instauratum auctoritate Pauli PP. VI promulgatum, editio typica altera, Città del Vaticano: Typis Polyglottis Vaticanis 1975.

Missale Romanum ex decreto Sacrosanctum Oecumenici Concilii Vaticani II instauratum auctoritate Pauli PP. VI promulgatum, Ioannis Pauli PP. II cura recognitum, editio typica tertia, Città del Vaticano: Typis Polyglottis Vaticanis, 2002.

Ordo Initiationis Christianae Adultorum (OICA), Città del Vaticano: Typis Polyglottis Vaticanis, 1972.

Translations

NRS = *New Revised Standard Version*, Oxford and New York: OUP, 1989.

The Roman Ritual, Rite of Christian Initiation of Adults, approved for use in England and Wales, Scotland, prepared by the International Commission on English in the Liturgy, London: Geoffrey Chapman, 1987.

The Roman Ritual, Rite of Christian Initiation of Adults: Study Edition. International Commission on English in the Liturgy and US Bishops' Committee on the Liturgy, Chicago IL: Liturgy Training Publications, 1988.

The Sacramentary, New York: Catholic Book Publishing Company, 1985.

Instruments

Gildersleeve, B. L. and G. Lodge, *Gildersleeve's Latin Grammar*, Wauconda IL: Bolchazy-Carducci, 3rd edition 1985, reprinted 2003.

Lewis, C. T. and C. Short, *A Latin Dictionary*, Oxford and New York: OUP, 1879, reprinted 1995.

Corpus Orationum, eds E. Moeller and J. M. Clément, B. Coppieters 't Wallant (Corpus Christianorum, Series Latina 160), Turnhout: Brepols, 1992–2004.

10

The influence of Anthropology on the development of Baptismal Rites: up to and including the Mystagogical Catechists of the Fourth Century

ENRICO MAZZA

(translated by Daniel McCarthy)

The influence of anthropology on the development of the baptismal rites up to the end of the fourth century is difficult to formulate given that we do not know what the Christian anthropology of that era might have been. Christianity of that time probably had not yet articulated its own proper anthropology. Thus, we do not know if the baptismal rites might have contributed to a general understanding, amply diffuse, or if they might have had a specific meaning, proper to the rite as such.

In this essay we shall examine certain moments in the development of the baptismal rites, to see if they contribute to a particular understanding of the human person. We shall find that there are two principal elements that influence the birth of pre-baptismal rites: Gnostic anthropology with its opposition between the devil and the Lord, and Greek anthropology with its opposition between slave and free.

It is not possible to examine here every element of the baptismal liturgy, from the New Testament to the great liturgical books of both East and West. Rather, in this essay, we shall limit ourselves to examining certain texts, which clearly witness the turning points in the development of the baptismal liturgy.

The Structure of the Baptismal Rites

A great exchange of ideas, information and ritual uses among various churches is evident in antiquity. At the end of the fourth century, in fact, in spite of the differences between the various liturgies,[1] the structure of the baptismal rite is common and is composed of three fundamental stages:

1. pre-baptismal rites composed of the renunciation of Satan, the profession of Christ and, eventually, the anointings, which can be joined to an exorcism;
2. baptism proper, which includes the immersion in water accompanied by a verbal *formula*, which is not identical in all the churches, as each has its own; moreover, the formula undergoes change in the various eras, even within a single church;
3. And post-baptismal rites, which may include one or more anointings, or the imposition of hands, or only a *sealing*.

The Origins of the Pre-baptismal Rites

At the end of the fourth century the first stage of the baptismal rites, as described in the mystagogical homilies, centres on the exorcisms, which conclude with the renunciation of Satan and are followed by professing Christ. These homilies stress the great importance of these two rites. Why such importance? Baptism, strictly speaking, is composed of only the water rite accompanied by the formula. The witness of the Apostle Paul is clear: there are neither pre- nor post-baptismal rites. Only with the passage of time are the pre- and post-baptismal rites developed.

In this study we hope to demonstrate the influence of anthropology, present in the surrounding culture, on the baptismal liturgy.

The Oldest Attestation of Anointing

The most ancient witnesses come from the Orient. The archaic structure of the baptismal rites includes the pre-baptismal anointing, the water rite accompanied by its formula and no baptismal anointing.[2] For a more

---

[1] The mystagogical homilies present on the same stage diverse churches, distant and differing from one another. They present the churches of Milan and Jerusalem, the churches of Antioch and Constantinople, which are neighbouring churches in regard to the development of the rites. They also present the churches of Cilicia, which perhaps witness the development of the ancient liturgy of Syria. With Augustine we have the witness of the church in North Africa, even if, perhaps, a definite Roman influence is already present.

[2] The most recent form has evolved to include two pre-baptismal anointings, the blessing of the water, the water rite accompanied by the passive formula ('N. is baptized in the name . . .') and, finally, a post-baptismal anointing with a meaning ever pneumatological.

ample treatment of this structure we defer to the studies of Gabriele Winkler.[3]

In the *Acts of Thomas* five baptisms are recounted. The accounts most relevant to our topic are found in chapters 25–27 and 132–133. In both texts baptism is preceded by an anointing, which consists in *pouring* the oil on the head of the one being baptized: this action, which is the sole anointing in the rite, is called a *sign* and by synecdoche[4] gives its name to the entire baptismal rite. Thus the entire baptismal rite comes to be called a *sign* from the name of the pre-baptismal anointing.[5] Here is one text:

> Then he ordered them to present the oil that they may receive the seal by means of the oil. They presented the oil and lit many lamps, as it was night. The Apostle, having taken the oil, poured it on their head and, after having anointed and coated them, began to say: 'Come, O Holy Name of Christ, high above every name. Come, O Power of the Most High and Perfect Compassion. Come, O Sublime Chrism. ... Come, O Holy Spirit and purify their loins and their hearts and sign them in the name of the Father and of the Son and of the Holy Spirit'.[6]

A revealing characteristic may be noticed both in this text and in that of chapter 132:[7] the anointing is linked to the name of Christ who is praised.

Two other texts speak to us about baptism. They are important because, in place of the single pre-baptismal anointing, there are two: the first is an anointing of the head alone, while the second is of the entire body of the one being baptized. The reason for the development from one anointing to two pre-baptismal anointings is explained:

> ... I wish only one cup of wine, one whole loaf, and bring me also a little oil, even if in a lamp. When Narses had gathered these things,

---

3 G. Winkler, 'The Original Meaning and Implications of the Prebaptismal Anointing', *Worship* 52 (1978), pp. 24–45; and above all: G. Winkler, *Das armenische Initiationsrituale: Entwicklungsgeschichtliche und liturgievergleichende Untersuchung der Quellen des 3. bis 10. Jahrhunderts*, (Roma: Orientalia Christiana Analecta 217, 1981).

4 Translator's note: synecdoche is a figure of speech whereby the name of a part names the whole, or vice versa.

5 M. Erbetta (ed.), *Gli apocrifi del Nuovo Testamento: Atti e leggende*, vol. II (Torino: Marietti, 1966), p. 322 (cf. note 18); cf. p. 362.

6 Ch. 26–27 (Erbetta, *Gli apocrifi*, pp. 322–3).

7 This text gives the same witness as the one already mentioned: 'Then he poured the oil on their head, saying: 'Glory to you O Compassionate Charity. Glory to you, Name of the Messiah (= Anointed). Glory to you O Power placed in the oil' (or *in the Messiah?*). He made a basin to be brought in and there he baptized in the name of the Father, and of the Son and of the Holy Spirit' (Erbetta, *Gli apocrifi*, pp. 362–3).

Mygdonia came before the Apostle with her head unveiled. He took the oil; in the act of pouring it on her head he exclaimed: 'Holy Oil, given to us for anointing; O Hidden Mystery in which the cross is revealed: you are the rectifier of crooked limbs! You are our Lord Jesus, our Life, our Health and the Remission of our Sins. May your power come and dwell in this oil. May your health dwell in it'. . . . Then, after having poured the oil on her head, he ordered his nurse to anoint her.[8]

The second text[9] gives us the same witness without adding anything new, at least not in the text of the prayer.

The Anointing Belongs to the Baptismal Rite as Such and Not to the Pre-Baptismal Rites

From these earliest texts we may draw a conclusion about the origin of the pre-baptismal anointings.

In both texts above there are two anointings. In the second text the second anointing (of the entire body) emerges with greater clarity as none other than the development and continuation of the first anointing, which consists of pouring the oil on the head. The difference between the two anointings appears more evident when women get baptized. In the case of the man, the Apostle begins by anointing the head and continues anointing his entire body; in the case of the women, however, the Apostle begins by anointing the head, then halts, and entrusts the rest of the anointing to a woman, who anoints the entire body. It is not fitting, indeed, that a man anoint the women. The single pre-baptismal anointing, thus, is duplicated in two distinct rites: an anointing of the head and one of the entire body.

---

8 Ch. 120-121 (Erbetta, *Gli apocrifi*, p. 359).

9 '". . . Be the doctor of their bodies and give life to their souls: transform them into your holy temples, and may your Holy Spirit dwell within them". Then after the prayer, the Apostle says to Mygdonia: "Undress your sisters". After their robes were removed, she wrapped them with loincloths and presented them. But Vizan had preceded them and they came after him. Judah took some oil in a silver cup and spoke this invocation: "O Good Fruit you who were worthy to ferment by means of the holy word, that humans *would clothe you* again and by you they would conquer their enemies, after they have been purified of their base works. Yes, my Lord, come, live in this oil as you lived on the wood, and those crucifying you were unable to endure your word. May your gift come which you blew against your adversaries, those who retreated and fell on their faces, and may you dwell in this oil upon which we invoke your name". This said, he poured the oil first on the head of Vizan, then on those of the women, saying: "In your name, O Christ Jesus, may it be useful for these souls as the remission of debts and sins, unto the destruction of the adversary and for the healing of their souls and bodies". And he ordered Mygdonia to anoint the women; he, however, anointed Vizan. After they had been united, he made them to descend into the water and baptized them in the name of the Father, of the Son and of the Holy Spirit' (Ch. 157; Erbetta, *Gli apocrifi*, p. 370).

The explanation for this duplication is simple. The anointing is not made with an ointment, but with oil, which, if it is poured on the head of a person, tends to run and descend on the entire body, all the more because those being baptized are nude in preparation for the imminent baptismal immersion. The anointing of the head, then, becomes an anointing of the whole body. The second anointing, then, happens automatically and the minister has only to manage it and accompany it in such a way that it becomes a structured part of the rite.

Here the anointing – with the theme of the Holy Spirit – precedes and is closely joined to baptism. It is, moreover, a constitutive element of baptism, given that it is called *sign* and by synecdoche gives its name to the entire baptismal rite. The rationale for this anointing is found in the Acts of the Apostles 10.38,[10] where the baptism of Jesus is interpreted as an *anointing*, because the Holy Spirit descended on Jesus during his baptism in the Jordan's water. As the baptism in the Holy Spirit is not some other reality, but is identified with the water baptism, so this pre-baptismal anointing gets interpreted in the same way. Baptism bestows the Holy Spirit, which is made evident in the anointing preceding the water rite. The baptism of Jesus was defined as an *anointing*, in Acts 10.38. In the same way, this ancient Syriac baptismal rite is defined as a *sign* because this is the name of the anointing that precedes it.

Thus the origin of the correlation *anointing-baptism* is theological. The reasons for the development of the pre-baptismal anointings, however, are different than those of the post-baptismal anointings. This difference is attributed to then cultural *understanding of the human person* and not to the theology of baptism.

The First Indications of Baptismal Exorcisms and their Meaning

The oldest witnesses to baptism, then, included the anointing and the water baptism with its formula, but did not include any rite of exorcism. These witnesses arise in the region of Syria and were brought to light by G. Kreschmar.[11] Let us see now how this gives way to a succession of exorcisms.

---

10 'God anointed (*echrisen*) in the Holy Spirit and power (*dunamei*) Jesus of Nazareth, who went about doing good and healing all those who were under the power of the devil, because God was with him'.

11 G. Kretschmar 'Nouvelles recherches sur l'Initiation chrétienne', *La Maison-Dieu* 132 (1977), pp. 7–32; cf. also G. Kretschmar, 'Die Geschichte des Taufgottesdienstes in der alten Kirche', in K. F. Müller and W. Blankenburg (eds), *Leiturgia: Handbuch des evangelischen Gottesdienstes* 5, (Kassel: Johannes Standa, 1970), pp. 1–348. Thereafter he brought to the table the methodological question for research in the context of Christian initiation: G. Kretschmar, 'La liturgie ancienne dans les recherches historiques actuelles', *La Maison-Dieu* 149 (1982), pp. 57–90.

The Excerpts of Theodotus *by Clement of Alexandria*

Elizabeth A. Leeper correctly states that the first attestations of exorcisms are in the so-called *Apostolic Tradition* from the third century, after which she wonders when and how the exorcisms entered into the baptismal rites.[12] The most interesting indications are found in the *Excerpts of Theodotus* from the second century as transmitted by Clement of Alexandria,[13] which remain an important source of understanding of Valentinian Gnosticism. Theodotus was active in Alexandria between 140 and 160, and as a proponent of Christian Gnosticism was a disciple of Valentinus, who had already left Alexandria to return to Rome around the year 138, where he taught and was active between 138 and 160.[14]

According to Theodotus every human being is subject to fate, from birth, for better or for worse. Only the Saviour can break the chains of fate, bringing the human being from the power of the devil[15] to that of Christ.[16] Fate acts upon a human person, not only by the influences of the stars and external elements but especially by the body, which has been claimed by slavery.[17] With baptism the candidate receives the seal, in the name of the Father, of the Son and of the Holy Spirit. The seal is a sign of belonging to Christ. *Excerpts* 67–86[18] give a clear witness to this baptismal practice interpreted according to the Gnostic anthropology and soteriology common to Valentinus and Theodotus: (1) human beings are possessed by the devil; (2) only the Lord is able to liberate the human person from evil spirits (*dunameis kakopoioi; akathara pneumata*).[19] The baptismal rites described in *Excerpts* 67–86 conform to this anthropology, which provides the logical basis and the meaning for the baptismal exorcisms whether performed on a person or over the water. Clement of Alexandria clearly states that he does not agree with this anthropology, which understands the human person as a dwelling place for the devil. The rites of exorcism, whether of a person or over the water, were practised in Alexandria but they must have not been a widespread liturgical practice, otherwise Clement's argument would be inexplicable, given that he was speaking against the baptismal rites of his own church.

---

12 E. A. Leeper, 'From Alexandria to Rome: the Valentinian Connection to the Incorporation of Exorcism as a prebaptismal Rite', *Vigiliae christianae* 44 (1990), pp. 6–24.

13 F. Sagnard (ed.), *Clément d'Alexandrie: Extraits de Théodote*, (Sources chrétiennes 23; Paris: Les Editions du Cerf, 1948, reprinted 1970).

14 Leeper, 'From Alexandria', p. 12.

15 *Excerptum* 77 (Sagnard, *Clément d'Alexandrie: Extraits*, p. 200).

16 Leeper, 'From Alexandria', p. 7.

17 *Excerptum* 73, 1 (Sagnard, *Clément d'Alexandrie: Extraits*, p. 196; for comment cf. *Appendice F*, p. 231).

18 Sagnard, *Clément d'Alexandrie: Extraits*, pp. 190–212.

19 Leeper, 'From Alexandria', p. 17.

In the *Excerpts of Theodotus*, we find a description of the baptismal rite. There are some preparatory rites, described as 'fasts, supplications, prayers, impositions of the hands, genuflections'.[20] These rites[21] serve to purify the spirit and to liberate it from demons before the human person enters into the baptismal water and receives the seal by the invocation of the name.[22] There is, however, a problem: if several evil spirits enter into the water together with the one being baptized, they also receive the seal and, in consequence, become so strong that it is impossible to cast them out. For this reason it is necessary to exorcize the water as well with a prayer that invokes the Name of God.[23] If the Spirit already lives in the water, the demons will not be able to enter it and take up residence there. Here is the text in which Theodotus states this problem:

> It would be normal to approach baptism with joy, but because the impure spirits often enter (into the water) at the same time as those (being baptized), accompanying the one being baptized and obtaining the seal with her or him – rendering the spirits resistant to every remedy for the future – then the joy is mixed with fear, such that only the one who is pure is able to descend into the water.[24]

From this it follows that the blessing prayer for baptismal water also belongs with the exorcisms. It supposes, indeed, that the devil invades and is master of all reality, including baptismal water. Thus it is necessary to cast the devil from the water and make sure that the Holy Spirit takes its place in such a way that Satan can no longer turn to dwell in that water.

---

20 *Excerptum* 84 (Sagnard, *Clément d'Alexandrie: Extraits*, p. 208; for comment cf. Appendice F, p. 234). The enumeration of these rites, separated from the description of baptism (and anointing), led me to think that they are preliminary rites, which have a place – not yet in an institutionalized way – in the life of those to be baptized as they prepare themselves for baptism, and which rites do not yet constitute a precise grouping, namely the first part of the baptismal rite.

21 E. Segelberg maintains that the order of the rites mentioned in the *Excerpts of Theodotus* is confirmed in the document *Evangelium Veritatis* (E. Segelberg, 'The Baptismal Rite according to Some of the Coptic-Gnostic Texts of Nag-Hammadi' (Papers Presented to the Third International Conference on Patristic Studies Held at Christ Church, Oxford, 1959, part III, Liturgica Monastica et Ascetica, Philosophica, in: F. L. Cross (ed.), *Studia Patristica* 5, [= Texte und Untersuchungen 80], Berlin: Akademie-Verlag, 1962), p. 120; especially p. 123 f.).

22 The invocation of the Name consists of pronouncing the Trinitarian formula.

23 'The bread and oil are also sanctified by the *dynamis* [power] of the Name of God: the bread and oil, while remaining themselves, by all outward appearances as they were when they were received, were transformed into a *dynamis pneumatica* (= active spiritual power). In the same way the water, by becoming exorcised water, and baptism not only separates the lower element, but also acquires sanctification' (*Excerptum* 82, in: Sagnard, *Clément d'Alexandrie: Extraits*, p. 206).

24 *Excerptum* 83 (Sagnard, *Clément d'Alexandrie: Extraits*, pp. 206–7).

We can conclude, then, that the meaning of the exorcisms is closely linked to the anthropology and soteriology of the Gnostics. Theirs is an age in which the rites are not yet fixed with the same precision as in the fifth century and are still linked to the phenomenon of liturgical *creativity*. Therefore, we need not be surprised that someone was able to introduce into baptism several preparatory rites derived from exorcisms in various forms. According to V. Saxer, the *Excerpts of Theodotus* exhibit a certain disjunction between the pre-baptismal rites and the preceding catechesis. Thus, Saxer maintains that these rites were developed in a second phase, when the form of the catechesis had already been codified.[25] Moreover he offers this interesting observation: after having said that the baptismal rites of Valentinian Gnosticism are described in the *Excerpts of Theodotus*, he adds that, in all probability, these rites had been part of the baptismal practice of the Great Church in Alexandria some fifty years previously.[26] Clement, furthermore, documents a Gnostic ritual formula, which accompanies the imposition of the hands:

For this [reason], during the imposition of the hand(s) (*keirothesia*), these people say towards the end:

'for angelic redemption (*lutrosin*)',

that is for the redemption, which even the angels share. They say this that the person baptized may have redemption (*lutrosin*) in the same Name in which even the person's own angel was baptized before her or himself.[27]

His observation deserves a study dedicated both to the use of the term *lutrosis* and to the function of the term *keirothesia*. This later term might designate either a rite of the imposition of the hands, or that the imposition of a hand is functional for immersing the one being baptized in the water. My reading of Irenaeus leads me to think that *keirothesia* refers to the imposition of a hand by which the one being baptized gets immersed. In any case, we affirm that this text ought not be relegated to secondary consideration, because even in Irenaeus we find something similar, which documents the same formula.

---

25 V. Saxer, *Les rites de l'initiation chrétienne du IIe au IVe siècle: Esquisse historique et signification d'après leurs principaux témoins*, (Spoleto: Centro italiano di studi sull'Alto Medioevo 7, 1988), p. 68.
26 Saxer, *Les rites de l'initiation chrétienne*, p. 76.
27 *Excerptum* 22, 5 (Sagnard, *Clément d'Alexandrie: Extraits*, p. 102).

The Description of Valentinian Baptism in Irenaeus of Lyons

Irenaeus of Lyons says that the Gnostics have a great variety of baptismal practices, on account of which it is difficult to explain their baptism in an organic way. Nonetheless he manages to pass on some of these uses and formulae. Irenaeus cites the entire text of such a formula, only the last words of which are found in the *Excerpts*. Irenaeus quotes:

> The name, which was hidden from every divinity, domination and truth, that Jesus the Nazarene has put on in the lives of the light of Christ. I mean of Christ who lives by the Holy Spirit, for the redemption of the angels.[28]

Thus, both Clement of Alexandria and Irenaeus of Lyons know the same Gnostic baptismal formula. In the above text of Irenaeus, baptism is constituted by the anointing and by a water rite, which as a rule is an immersion. These two elements are constant, even when a proper immersion may not be evident. Irenaeus, in fact, recounts that some Gnostics don't immerse, rather they mix oil with water and thus wash and anoint in a single gesture.[29] I find this practice telling. Moreover, Irenaeus adds that at the conclusion of the rite, after exchanging the greeting of peace (*Pace*), there is an anointing with perfumed ointment: 'then they anoint the initiated with the ointment made from balsam. And this ointment, they say, is the figure (*typum*) of the fragrance that surpasses all things'.[30] Even when baptism is celebrated with oil mixed with water, the rite concludes with the anointing with balsam.[31] According to Segelberg a post-baptismal anointing is also attested in the *Evangelium Philippi* (67–69).[32]

---

28 A. Rousseau and L. Doutreleau (eds), *Irénée de Lyon: Contre les hérésies. Livre I*, Tome II, (Sources chrétiennes 264; Paris: Les Editions du Cerf, 1979), p. 300.

29 'Some of them say that it is superfluous to bring them to the water, rather they mix oil and water in one container and by an invocation similar to those which we have mentioned before, they pour it on the head of those who are initiated. They even claim that this is the redemption. They also anoint them with the basalm' (Rousseau, *Irénée de Lyon*, p. 302. English is from the Italian translation by E. Bellini, *Ireneo di Lione: Contro le eresie*, p. 96).

30 Rousseau, *Irénée de Lyon*, p. 302.

31 I think sufficient evidence exists to say that the *vexata quaestio* of the origin of the post-baptismal anointing (which we call *cresima*) has to be seen from a different perspective, given that its first attestation is in the Gnostic baptismal rites.

32 This text actually suggests an anointing that follows baptism: 'The Lord has accomplished everything in one mystery: one baptism and one chrism, one Eucharist and one redemption and one nuptial chamber' ('Gospel of Phillip', n. 68 in M. Craveri (ed.), *I Vangeli apocrifi* (Turin: Einaudi Editore, 1969), p. 525). Nevertheless, the matter is not settled, given that the second binary ought to be understood as an hendiadys [translator's note: a hendiadys is the use of two words to express one idea], the first term also ought to be understood in the same way.

The anointing is so central to the ancient baptismal rite, attested since the *Acts of Thomas*, that it gives its name to the entire rite, but in this case the anointing is pre-baptismal. Equally central is the anointing in the baptismal rites of *Evangelium veritatis* and *Evangelium Philippi*.[33]

We may conclude, therefore, that a correlation exists between the testimony of Irenaeus and Clement concerning Gnostic baptism, which was based on and had conformed to the teaching of Valentinus,[34] namely to his Gnostic anthropology and soteriology, as we already have said citing the words of Elizabeth A. Leeper.

When treating the origins of Gnosticism, C. Jouco Bleeker maintains that one cannot affirm that Gnosticism was born in Egypt, but that, nevertheless, one must agree that it has drawn deeply from Egyptian culture and religion. One of the elements that arises here and is of great interest to us, concerns the tendency to *express in the cult* the ideas that made up the myths expressing the anthropology and religion of these people. Bleeker states this when speaking of the mystery rites celebrated in Egypt for initiates alone, which focused on the themes of death and life.[35] Nevertheless, this tendency expresses a mentality that can be shown also in the Alexandrian baptismal rites, given that the Egyptian culture prefers the rite to complicated formulations of the myth. When speaking of Egyptian religion one must keep in mind that 'in Egypt, myth plays a modest part. Egyptian religion is expressed above all in the rites, in the cult'.[36] In this context the myth comes to be translated into ritual language.

Finally we must note that these rites are clothed in the thought and anthropology of Gnosticism. Thereafter, in fact, these rites were received everywhere, even in regions where Theodore of Mopsuestia and John Chrysostom attest to the liturgy.

The Development of the Anointings According to the Mystagogical Homilies of the Fourth Century

Cyril of Jerusalem

In the baptismal and mystagogical catechisms of Cyril (understood as a single *corpus* given that they concern the liturgy of the same City, even if

---

33 Segelberg, 'The Baptismal Rite', p. 127.

34 'We have noted the presence of developed anti-demonic rites both in Alexandria and in Rome, in the circles where Valentinus was active and where he would have been in such a position that he could influence liturgical changes so they would reflect his teaching (Leeper, 'From Alexandria', p. 16).

35 C. J. Bleeker, 'The Egyptian Background of Gnosticism', in U. Bianchi (ed.), *Le origini dello gnosticismo*, (Colloquio di Messina [13–18 aprile 1966], [Studies in the History of Religions – Supplements to 'Numen' 12], Leiden: E. J. Brill, 1967, reprint 1970), p. 232.

36 Bleeker, 'The Egyptian Background', p. 233.

THE INFLUENCE OF ANTHROPOLOGY

in two successive eras), there are two points of contact with the Gnostic ritual practice we have just described.

1. There exists a post-baptismal anointing, as in the rites attested by Irenaeus, and this anointing is described as a perfume.[37] Greater emphasis is placed on the anointing as *perfume*, than as *oil*. We note that the post-baptismal anointing is new and that other elements are not present to explain its origin.
2. The sanctification of the baptismal water, effected by the invocation, is described in the same way as in the *Excerpts* (see table on p. 225). In Theodotus it is said that the bread and the wine are sanctified by the *dynamis* [power] of the *Nome* [Name], because these elements receive a *dynamis pneumatica* [spiritual power]. Likewise does the water receive the sanctification. The synoptic table (on p. 225) shows the parallel use of *dynamis* in line six of Theodotus and line thirteen of Cyril. Furthermore, the thought of both authors is identical in line three of Theodotus and line fifteen of Cyril, differing only in their formulation in that Cyril explicitly cites the invocation of the *Holy Spirit, the Son and the Father*, while Theodotus limits the reference to the *Name of God*. In both cases the theology of the *Name* is present. It must be borne in mind that in this era the invocation of the *Name* simply means the proclamation of the name of the Father, Son and Holy Spirit,[38] in the baptismal context.

Having pointed out above a certain continuity between the Gnostic baptismal rites and those practised in Jerusalem during the time of Cyril, let us now pass to another vantage point. We shall examine the elements of the baptismal rites (from the end of the fourth century), that are closely related to classical culture. We shall do this by considering specifically the exorcisms and the various pre-baptismal rites, which already then were interpreted in terms of exorcism.

In the mystagogical catecheses of Cyril of Jerusalem there is only one pre-baptismal anointing, this of the whole body, and it is made with the

---

37 Cyril knows the term *myros* (Catechesi mistagogica III, 3, in A. Piédagnel (ed.), *Cyrille de Jérusalem: Catécheses mystagogiques*, [Sources Chrétiennes, 126], Paris: Les Editions du Cerf, 1966, p. 124); this text has to be compared with *Adversus haereses* I. 21. 3: '*ointment unguent sacrato opobalsamo (to opo to apo balsamou)*', namely with the *perfume* (the term *balsamos* is equivalent to the Greek *myros*).

38 I have illustrated this fact in 'La formula battesimale nelle omelie catechetiche di Teodoro di Mopsuestia', *Ephemerides liturgicae* 104 (1990), pp. 23–34. This study of mine cannot be understood without an understanding of the dispute between Connolly and Tyrer: R. H. Connolly, 'On the meaning of *epiklesis*', *The Downside Review* 41 (1923), pp. 28–43; J. W. Tyrer, 'The meaning of *epiklesis*', *The Journal of Theological Studies* 25 (1924), pp. 139–50; R. H. Connolly, '"The meaning of *epiklesis*": A Reply', *The Journal of Theological Studies* 25 (1924), pp. 337–64.

oil of exorcism. While this fact is clearly stated, nevertheless, its effects are described by setting aside the idea of exorcism: indeed, the anointing places those being baptized 'in communion with the good olive Jesus Christ. ... in the communion of the abundance of the true oil'. The exorcized oil, then, was a symbol of communion in the abundance of Christ, being a 'refuge against every trace of adverse energy'.[39] Then, the argument advances by dropping the reference to communion with Christ to refer only to its exorcistic quality, proper to the power of the oil because of the expulsion 'of the invisible powers of the evil one'.[40] Thus, the emphasis is on the exorcism, and this emphasis prevails in Cyril. The evidence constrains us to conclude that Cyril of Jerusalem shifts between emphases, and that this oscillating indicates that the rite was pre-existing, but his interpretation is still fluid. Thereafter the emphasis on exorcism received by Cyril is decisive in that not only does the anointing get its meaning from the exorcism that precedes it, but, as we shall see, the emphasis on exorcism will prevail hereafter and the anointing comes to be understood as the conclusion of the exorcisms.

We may conclude then that Cyril interprets the pre-baptismal rites according to an anti-demoniac preoccupation. The Gnostics shared this interpretation and understood it in terms of a devil *indwelling* in the human being, while this aspect is absent in Cyril. We may attribute this development, then, to classical culture – with its opposition between slavery and freedom – as an examination of the following authors will show.

Theodore of Mopsuestia

Theodore is aware of two pre-baptismal anointings: one of the head and the other of the entire body. He also shows an awareness of the pneumatological meaning of the pre-baptismal anointing,[41] even if, when commenting on the two anointings, he offers interpretations that are not pneumatological. The text of the ritual says: 'The pontiff signs you on

---

39 Catechesi mistagogica II. 3 (Piédagnel, *Cyrille de Jérusalem*, p. 106 f.).

40 Piédagnel, *Cyrille de Jérusalem*, p. 108; it is helpful to see R. G. Coquin, 'Le thème de la parresia et ses expressions symboliques dans les rites d'initiation à Antioche', *Proche-Orient chrétien* 20 (1970), pp. 1–19.

41 Theodore demonstrates his awareness of the pneumatological character of the pre-baptismal anointing when he says that Jesus, coming up from his baptism, received the grace of the Holy Spirit and was called *anointed* of the Spirit 'to show that the Holy Spirit absolutely will not leave Jesus; as also happens for those who are anointed by humans with the anointing of oil, the anointing adheres and does not leave again' (R. Tonneau and R. Devreesse (eds), *Les homélies catéchétiques de Théodore de Mopsueste*, [Studi e testi 145: Città del Vaticano: 1949], p. 457). In this passage Theodore speaks of an anointing with oil, which, however, cannot refer to the post-baptismal sealing because the ritual he cites does not involve the use of oil.

the forehead with the oil of the anointing and says: "N is sealed in the name of the Father and of the Son and of the Holy Spirit".[42] Theodore explains this passage saying that this anointing means that one belongs to Christ, whether as a sheep of Christ's flock, or as a soldier in Christ's army.[43] Continuing with the commentary, Theodore adds the idea of the *parousia* to conclude by emphasizing the eschatological meaning of the 'ineffable service'[44] to which those being baptized are called. The second pre-baptismal anointing is of the entire body with the oil of the anointing and is accompanied with the same formula as the preceding anointing. Theodore comments, saying 'you are clothed anew by the anointing, sign of an incorruptible garment that you anticipate receiving with baptism.'[45] The meaning of the anointing is simply to envelop the entire body in the image of a garment from which Theodore develops his baptismal symbolism: what is symbolized by this anointing comes about in reality at baptism. At baptism 'the grace of the Holy Spirit'[46] is conferred. According to Theodore of Mopsuestia the gift of the Holy Spirit is associated with the baptismal immersion as such, not to the pre-baptismal anointings or to the post-baptismal sealing. Even in the case of Theodore, the two pre-baptismal anointings lend themselves to differing interpretations: the meaning oscillates. The anointings first arise for reasons noted above when commenting on the *Acts of Thomas*. The meaning attributed to the anointings, however, arises from the interpretative skill of the bishop giving the catechesis, in the cultural milieu, given the ability of the people to understand.

John Chrysostom

John Chrysostom has left us various series of catecheses from various years; the oldest series, edited by Papadopoulos and Kérameus,[47] was collected in the year 388[48] while that of codex *Stavronikita* probably

---

42 Tonneau, *Les homélies catéchétiques*, p. 369.

43 Tonneau, *Les homélies catéchétiques*, p. 397. The theme of the *seal* as a seal of belonging is common to all these authors and is present also in the Gnostic texts already examined (*Excerptum* 86. 2 in Sagnard, *Clément d'Alexandrie: Extraits*, p. 210).

44 Tonneau, *Les homélies catéchétiques*, p. 401.

45 Tonneau, *Les homélies catéchétiques*, p. 419.

46 Tonneau, *Les homélies catéchétiques*, p. 429.

47 Papadopoulos and A. Kerameus (eds), *Varia Graeca Sacra*, (collection of unedited Greek theological texts from the fourth to the fifteenth century: St. Petersburg: 1909 [in Russian]). These catecheses of Chrysostom are now edited under the direction of A. Piédagnel and L. Doutreleau (eds), *Jean Chrysostome: Trois catéchèses baptismales* (Sources chrétiennes 366: Paris: Les Editions du Cerf, 1990).

48 A. Wenger (ed.), *Jean Chrysostome: Huit catéchèses baptismales inédites* (Sources chrétiennes 50 bis: Paris: Les Editions du Cerf, 1970), p. 64. Piédagnel accepts and re-presents the arguments of Wenger (Piédagnel, *Jean Chrysostome*, p. 39).

dates from 390.⁴⁹ The disassociation of the rite from its interpretation rings clear in the catecheses of Chrysostom. During the era of Chrysostom and Theodore of Mopsuestia the baptismal rite was still fairly fluid; in consequence it was able to undergo various transformations, as is already evident in the exorcisms and the baptismal formula.⁵⁰

From this difference one can see that the rite used in the years 388 and 390 is different from the rite of the year 372, when Chrysostom was baptized. The catechism in codex *Stavronikita* continually refers to a rite no longer in use, that of 372.⁵¹ The preceding rite, indeed, emphasized the oath sworn by the one being baptized after renouncing Satan, an oath that obliges for the rest of one's life.⁵² Previously – and yet still in 372 when Chrysostom was baptized⁵³ – the renunciation of Satan and the profession of Christ occurred immediately before baptism. This is also in full accordance with the witness of Theodore of Mopsuestia. In the rite in use in 388, however, things have already changed: in the third catechesis of the series by Papadopoulos and Kérameus, the rejection of Satan and profession of Christ took place on Good Friday at 3.00 p.m. (the hour of Christ's death). The first pre-baptismal anointing served as a conclusion to the rite. On Holy Saturday at a *fitting time of night*, they celebrated the anointing of the entire body and then baptism.

Having described these differences between the two rites, let us turn now to the meaning of the pre-baptismal anointings, remembering that Chrysostom ignores any post-baptismal anointing.

The first pre-baptismal anointing functions as an exorcism: the sign of the cross, made with the *myron* on the forehead of the candidate, is to instil the fear of the devil.⁵⁴ This recalls the image of the athlete for Christ led into the arena. Nevertheless, it must be remembered that the explanation given by the second Catechesis by Stavronikita develops the image of the sign conferred on the soldier as a badge of belonging.⁵⁵ The second anointing, made over the entire body, is made with spiritual oil: 'to fortify all your members and make them invulnerable

---

49 Wenger, *Jean Chrysostome: Huit catéchèses*, pp. 63–5.

50 Cf. E. Mazza, 'L'uso di *sacramentum* nella Lettera 10, 96 di Plinio jr.: Un confronto con la liturgia battesimale', *Ephemerides liturgicae* 113 (1999), pp. 466–80; cf. also E. Mazza, 'La formula battesimale nelle omelie catechetiche di Teodoro di Mopsuestia', *Ephemerides liturgicae* 104 (1990), pp. 23–34.

51 In this rite Chrysostom explicitly cites his own baptismal experience.

52 I illustrated this problem in my article: 'L'uso di *sacramentum* nella Lettera 10, 96 di Plinio jr. . . .'

53 Wenger, *Jean Chrysostome: Huit catéchèses*, p. 80.

54 Catechesi II. 22–23 in the series by Stavronikita (Wenger, *Jean Chrysostome: Huit catéchèses*, p. 145 f.).

55 Catechesi II. 22 in the series by Stavronikita (Wenger, *Jean Chrysostome: Huit catéchèses*, p. 145).

to the onslaughts of the adversary';[56] this explanation takes the part of the struggle against Satan, like the explanation of the first anointing. Here we no longer have references to the Holy Spirit. It speaks of the Spirit when describing the baptismal immersion done by the hand of the priest on the head of the one being baptized. It concerns a simple gesture that serves the immersion, but which gets emphasized, equal to the words of the baptismal formula, as filled with a certain importance: 'It is in this moment that, by the words and by the hand of the priest, the descent of the Holy Spirit comes about, and the one who then rises up is a new human being.'[57] The hand that the priest places on the head of the one being baptized is definitively – even if the gesture is functional for *immersing* – an imposition of the hand.

Effects of Baptism

Cyril speaks of baptism from a particular point of view dependent on the biblical texts he quotes and explains. Cyril strongly emphasizes the struggle against the devil, but his explanation of baptism is much fuller and cannot be reduced to the question of liberation from sin and from the devil:

> He comes with a heart of fraternal love. He comes, indeed, to save, cure, teach, admonish, strengthen, console and illumine the mind, first of all [the mind] of the one who welcomes him, then through this one also the others. And as for one who was first in darkness, then having suddenly seen the sun, the appearance of the body becomes luminous and sees clearly that which one previously did not see, so also to the one who was made worthy by the Holy Spirit, the Spirit gets illuminated and, beyond every human possibility, sees the things [that] it did not know. The body is on the earth, but the spirit contemplates the heavens as in a mirror.[58]

This text serves as a plan and an indicator of that which gets treated thereafter: in successive paragraphs, indeed, each of these points gets developed as a theme unto itself. From this it is clear that, for Cyril, the specific function of the Holy Spirit is positive, namely to illumine those

---

56 Catechesi II. 24 in the series by Stavronikita (Wenger, *Jean Chrysostome: Huit catéchèses*, p. 147).

57 Catechesi II. 24 in the series by Stavronikita (Wenger, *Jean Chrysostome: Huit catéchèses*, p. 147).

58 Catechesis 16. 16 (G. Maestri and V. Saxer (eds), *Cirillo e Giovanni di Gerusalemme: Catechesi prebattesimali e mistagogiche* (Testi 18: Milan: Edizioni Paoline, 1994), pp. 499–500).

to be illuminated, rather than negative, namely to cast out Satan.[59] For Cyril, indeed, there is a type of identification between the water and the Holy Spirit. We find the motive in the baptismal catecheses when he says:

> The Holy Spirit will surely place the seal on your spirits.... Draw near to the bath not as to ordinary water but as to the grace of the Spirit, which is conferred through the water. As, indeed, things brought to the Altar, which by their nature are ordinary, become stained by the invocation of idols, so, in a contrary sense, ordinary water acquires the power to sanctify upon receiving the invocation of the Holy Spirit, of the Son and of the Father.[60]

The effect of all this is the definition of baptism as baptism in the Holy Spirit;[61] as a result, there is a formal definition of the relationship water–Spirit: 'For what reason does the grace of the Spirit come to be called water?'[62] Despite this specific pneumatological understanding of baptism, the reference to idols, nevertheless, also merits our attention. The reference concerns the transformation of ordinary water into baptismal water on account of the invocation of the divine Names. This text is analogous to a text by Theodotus, as we have already seen at the beginning of the previous section. I find it surprising that Cyril explains the transformation of the water without looking for a theological basis, but in an analogy with pagan rites of invoking the names of idols. From this it is evident that the mentality of that era was open to these analogies. His cited reason does not pertain as much to Christian theology, as to the culture of the time. It concerns the understanding of the human person in relation to the idols; more specifically it concerns questions that arise from the anthropology characteristic of that time and culture.

Let us turn now to another factor, which considers the human person according to another characteristic of the classical world also present in late antiquity: the binary *slavery–freedom*.

---

59 We may also cite a verse of the mystagogy, where the positive value of baptism is clearly evident: 'Let no one, therefore, believe that baptism obtains only the grace of the remission of sins and of becoming daughters and sons of God, as happened by the baptism of John, which procured only the forgiveness of sins. May one understand baptism, rather, just [as it is]: in the same way that baptism is the remission of sins and procures the gift of the Holy Spirit, so it is also the antitype of the sufferings of Christ' (Catechesi 2. 6 in A. Piédagnel, *Cyrille de Jérusalem*, p. 114).

60 Catechesi 3. 3 (Maestri, *Cirillo e Giovanni di Gerusalemme*, p. 190).

61 Catechesi 17. 14 (Maestri, *Cirillo e Giovanni di Gerusalemme*, p. 528).

62 Catechesi 16. 12 (Maestri, *Cirillo e Giovanni di Gerusalemme*, p. 494).

From Slavery to Freedom, in the Mystagogical Homilies

Many texts of the mystagogical catecheses describe Christian initiation as a passage from slavery to freedom. Let us cite a few of them here. Chrysostom, speaking of exorcism, says:

> As those, who suffer this corporal prison, even by their posture, express the pain of the calamity that has befallen them, so likewise do those, who became prisoners of the devil, when they are on the point of being freed from his tyranny to come under the benevolent yoke; initially by their posture they call to mind their former condition, although they recognize by his hands the one who liberated them, to whom they draw close, and this reality becomes their motive for greater thanksgiving and good position.[63]

The same speech is given for the renunciation of Satan:

> See in this the posture of a prisoner: the priests, who are initiating you, first order you to pray in this way, by bending the knee and raising your hands to heaven, and to recall in such a posture the one by whom you have been freed and to whom you are about to dedicate yourselves.[64]

The anointing, carefully detailed,[65] receives the same interpretation, as a passage from slavery to freedom:

> The adversary ... seeing that they, who once were under his tyranny, turn as one against him, renounce him, pass over to Christ and demonstrate that they have enlisted with Christ; on account of this the priest anoints the forehead and imposes the seal, that the adversary may avert his gaze.[66]

---

63 Catechesi II. 14 in the series by Stavronikita (Wenger, *Jean Chrysostome: Huit catéchèses*, p. 141).

64 Catechesi II. 18 in the series by Stavronikita (Wenger, *Jean Chrysostome: Huit catéchèses*, p. 143-144).

65 'Following after this covenant, after the renunciation and the promise, because you have confessed his sovereignty and by the words of the tongue you have put yourself under Christ, now as a soldier and one destined to the spiritual arena, the priest anoints your forehead with spiritual oil imposing on you the seal and saying: "N. is anointed in the name of the Father, of the Son and of the Holy Spirit"' (Catechesis II. 22 in the series by Stavronikita in: Wenger, *Jean Chrysostome: Huit catéchèses*, pp. 145-6).

66 Catechesi II. 23 in the series by Stavronikita (Wenger, *Jean Chrysostome: Huit catéchèses*, p. 146).

Thereafter John Chrysostom emphasizes the themes of slavery and freedom, stressing by whom they were freed and drawing a parallel between the state of freedom and that of daughters and sons:

> The actions that follow suffice to teach us from whom they have been freed and what they have obtained, who have been deemed worthy of this mysterious initiation. Straightaway after rising from the sacred waters, all present embrace them ... because these, who before were slaves and prisoners, in an instant have become free, daughters and sons, and have been invited to the royal table.[67]

The interpretation of the third catechesis by Papadopoulos and Kérameus differs but only apparently:

> It is proper therefore that all of you now as one body, once initiated, hands raised to heaven, give thanks to God for this gift. The sacred laws ordain to kneel and thus to confess even by one's posture the sovereignty; concerning the fact that bending the knee is proper to those who acknowledge their slavery, listen to what Paul says: 'To [Jesus] every knee shall bend of heavenly beings, terrestrial and those under the earth' (Phil. 2.10). Now those who introduce you to the mysteries call for bending the knees and saying these words: 'I renounce you, O Satan'.[68]

I said *apparently* because, even if the binary slavery–freedom is not explicitly present, the idea is the same, as is evident in the following paragraph:

> 'I renounce you, O Satan.' What happens? How is this strange and paradoxical? Did you fearing and trembling rebel against the tyrant? Do you disdain his cruelty? Who pushed you to such folly? Whence came your courage? 'I have a powerful weapon,' you say. Which weapon, which help? Tell me. 'I am allied with you, O Christ' you say. 'For this I am courageous and rebel: I possess a powerful refuge.'[69]

The task of liberating from slavery to the devil to attain freedom is not attributed to one particular rite of Christian initiation alone. Time and again it is associated with various ritual moments. For this reason

---

67 Catechesi II. 27 in the series by Stavronikita (Wenger, *Jean Chrysostome: Huit catéchèses*, p. 148).
68 Catechesi III. 4 in the series by Papadopoulos and Kérameus (Piédagnel, *Jean Chrysostome*, p. 231).
69 Catechesi III. 6 in the series by Papadopoulos and Kérameus (Piédagnel, *Jean Chrysostome*, p. 232).

one may affirm that baptism gets properly interpreted as liberation from slavery to the devil to arrive at freedom, although Chrysostom himself attributes to baptism various interpretations far richer than this. Indeed the theme of belonging to Christ is associated with the rites of profession and anointing. Anointing in the form of a cross is a *sign* placed on the forehead of the faithful to manifest one's belonging to the flock of Christ, or being Christ's soldier. It expresses a highly traditional image, clearly present both in Theodore of Mopsuestia[70] and Theodotus.[71] Otherwise, the Pauline image is also present in Chrysostom of being crucified and buried with Christ that one may rise with him. Nevertheless, he immediately adds the image of slavery and freedom to illustrate the rite:

> Wishing to remind you of the former tyranny of the devil, by the garment [you wear] return to the memory of your ignoble birth. This is why you were not only nude and barefoot, but even holding your hands facing behind you, to confess even in this way the lordship of God whom now you approach. All of you are a prize and booty.[72]

As we have seen, the pre-baptismal anointings belong to the baptismal rite as such. They serve, indeed, to emphasize that the water baptism as such is the anointing of the Holy Spirit. We cannot say that baptism transmits the Holy Spirit because of the anointings that are performed; to the contrary, we have to say that the anointings are present precisely because baptism, giving the Spirit, is the anointing of the Holy Spirit. None of this concerns the logic of the exorcisms and the renunciation of Satan. Nevertheless, John Chrysostom, after having commented on the rite of renunciation and profession, concludes by linking the anointing to the rationale of the exorcisms and the *renunciation–profession*: 'For this reason the priest anoints the forehead and places the seal, that the adversary may avert his gaze'.[73] The second anointing – that of the entire body – undergoes the same interpretation derived from the exorcisms and renunciation of Satan, given that Chrysostom compares it to the athlete in the arena who is anointed to combat better against the enemy. In our case the faithful receives the anointing to fight with the devil:

> Following this rite, at the proper hour of the night, having taken off all your clothes to initiate your very self into heaven itself by the rites which are performed, you prepare to anoint your entire body

---

70 Tonneau, *Les homélies catéchétiques de Théodore de Mopsueste*, p. 397.

71 *Excerptum* 86. 2 in Sagnard, *Clément d'Alexandrie: Extraits*, p. 210.

72 Catechesi II. 6 in the series by Papadopoulos and Kérameus (Piédagnel, *Jean Chrysostome: Trois catéchèses*, p. 190).

73 Catechesi II. 23 in the series by Stavronikita (Wenger, *Jean Chrysostome: Huit catéchèses*, p. 146).

with that spiritual oil, such that all your members are strengthened by the anointing and become invulnerable to the arrows cast by the adversary.[74]

In conclusion, the pre-baptismal rites are above all exorcisms, and the pre-baptismal anointings – which did not originate with this perspective – have also been drawn into the orbit of the exorcisms and acquired new meaning. When the exorcisms were separated from the baptismal rites and associated with Good Friday, the first pre-baptismal anointing became the conclusion of the *renunciation–profession* rite, and was interpreted as conferring the strength necessary to struggle against Satan. At a certain point on Holy Saturday night the entire body was anointed then baptized: the same interpretation was given to this anointing as was given to the first, although it is unrelated to the exorcisms. One gets the clear impression that the entire baptismal rite has been interpreted by this preoccupation with the devil. If John Chrysostom were the only witness, the explanation would be easy, because he is particularly sensitive to the problem of Satan's activity. Suffice it to recall that even the Eucharist is interpreted from this perspective, an interpretation that is truly startling. Nevertheless, lest we consider that all this depends on the particular position of John Chrysostom, let us recall that we are not talking about his idea, but of the structure of the baptismal rites themselves. This preoccupation hostile to the demoniac is proper to the baptismal rites, which results not only in the witness of Chrysostom, but also that of Theodore of Mopsuestia and Cyril of Jerusalem. These are witness to the baptismal rites of diverse churches, but the anti-demoniac concern is shared. The following is a good description of the devil's power on a human person, which V. Saxer cites from the catechesis of Cyril:

> Satan is a cruel tyrant and no legitimate sovereign; he is the cunning serpent of the Bible, the crafter and accomplice of every evil, prefigured by the Pharaoh and his army cast down into the Red Sea. His works are sin in all its forms; his pomp is the theatre, races at the horse track, combat at the racecourse; his cult, the idols, the idolaters, the prayer in the temples just like private and domestic magic are, as is well seen, the common topics of ecclesiastical preaching on this subject.[75]

In a word, by baptism a person passes from the state of slavery to one of freedom: slavery to the devil, freedom of the daughters and sons of

---

74 Catechesi II. 24 in the series by Stavronikita (Wenger, *Jean Chrysostome: Huit catéchèses*, p. 147).

75 Saxer V., *Les rites de l'initiation chrétienne du IIe au IVe siècle: Esquisse historique et signification d'après leurs principaux témoins* (Spoleto: Centro italiano di studi sull'Alto Medioevo 7, 1988), pp. 202–3.

God in Christ. Clearly this interpretation conveys a certain theological truth: nevertheless, I believe that a fuller explanation is found in the dialogue between nascent Christianity and classical culture still influential in late antiquity. What is slavery? What is a free person?

The Free and Slaves in the Classical World

The binary *freedom–slavery* was of great importance in ancient Greece; we may even call it a *leitmotiv*. It is well articulated in *The Persians*, by Aeschylus, who succeeds in giving a synthetic definition of Athens and the Athenians; he says it all in one simple phrase: 'These are not called slaves of anyone, these do not owe obedience to anyone' (v. 242). A Greek person, indeed, did not obey another person, but the law, which is the expression of the will of the people: and the Greek's self is the people.[76] As a result, a Greek person is proud of one's proper freedom possessed in the city.[77]

Ancient Greek society was composed of slaves and the free, be they poor or rich. The structure of Greek society was based on these two possibilities, even if many differences existed among the various types of free people, types of slavery and the various forms of work done by the slaves. Nevertheless, one is either free or a slave: there is no other possibility. Only the free are citizens of the *polis*. 'In *Politics*, Aristotle defined the Greek person with the noted formula *zoon politikòn* or *political animal*'.[78] The citizen of the Greek *polis* is a free person; the slave is not a citizen – not even of secondary stature – even if the slave performs a highly valued service. The idea of freedom is closely tied to the life of the *polis* and matures with the concept of the *polis*, which dominates the entire classical Greek period, because freedom is the foundation of democracy.[79] All of this generates a culture that is not exhausted in classic Greece or Hellenism, but continues to make itself felt even in late antiquity.

Giuseppe Cambiano, of the University of Turin, sketches the situation of a slave in a few words:

> To be a slave in Greek cities meant exclusion from participation in the political life, from many civil rights and from a good part of the religious feasts of the city, and even from the sporting centres and training schools, where the education of future citizens took place.

---

76 Festugière A.-J., *Liberté et civilization chez les Grecs* (Initiations 14: Paris: Editions de la Revue des jeunes, 1947), p. 19.

77 Festugière, *Liberté et civilization*, p. 4.

78 C. Mossé, 'L'uomo e l'economia', in J.-P. Vernant (ed.), *L'uomo greco* (Storia e società: Rome: Editori Laterza, 1991), p. 25.

79 Festugière, *Liberté et civilization*, p. 4.

And again:

> If the adjective *andràpodon* meaning *foot person* and used to designate a slave, tended to lower a slave to the state of a *four legged animal* called a *tetràpoda*, the term *pais* [slave, servant, male or female of any age], by which a slave was frequently called, emphasized the ongoing minority status of the slave. As Aristophanes says in *The Wasps*, 'It is proper to call one who takes blows a slave, even if of advanced years.' In Athens corporal punishment could legitimately be meted out only to slaves and children, not to free adults.[80]

In the ancient world the ideas of *douleia* [slavery, bondage] and *eleutheria* [freedom, liberty] are mutual correlatives:

> Freedom – slavery: for those who conferred the full and precise meaning to these terms in the context of the *polis*, these terms appear so reciprocally exclusive that they cannot both be applied to the same individual. One who is free cannot be a slave, or better could not be a slave without immediately ceasing to be free.[81]

This concerns political freedom in the Greek *polis*, not spiritual freedom.[82] At this point, we ought to define more clearly the idea of freedom. In what does freedom consist? From what is the citizen of the *polis* liberated? From the bonds of slavery and subservience to tyrants.[83] The fundamental laws – already in 600 BC with Solon – concerned themselves with safeguarding freedom from debtors' slavery: this is the baseline. Subsequently, with Pericles, freedom is enriched with a new element: freedom from submission to a tyrant.[84] With the passing of centuries, however, things change, such that with the monarchy of the Diadochi, freedom takes flight to the interior life.[85] Then, from this moment on for centuries to come, freedom is purely a concern of philosophy.[86]

A free person possesses the fullness of rights, while the slave is kept outside the rights of a citizen and the operations of public institutions. Corresponding to the opposition between *slavery* and *freedom* is the opposition *kurios* and *tyrannos*. These two antonyms describe a state of affairs: they describe a social institution characteristic of the ancient

---

80 G. Cambiano, 'Diventare uomo', in Vernant, *L'uomo greco*, p. 90.
81 J.-P. Vernant, 'Introduzione', in Vernant, *L'uomo greco*, p. 10.
82 Festugière, *Liberté et civilization*, p. 3.
83 Festugière, *Liberté et civilization*, p. 10 f.
84 Festugière, *Liberté et civilization*, p. 8.
85 Festugière, *Liberté et civilization*, p. 5.
86 Festugière, *Liberté et civilization*, p. 5.

world, a manifest institution that perpetuates itself and as such that no one contests. It is an understanding of the classical world familiar to all from time immemorial. Society is constructed in this way, and there are no means by which one may think of society in a different way even if, from a spiritual perspective, Christianity has overcome the opposition between freedom and slavery.[87] This opposition was resumed in the New Testament and by the early church.

These two opposing binaries, indeed, are presented en masse in the baptismal and mystagogical catecheses. But even before they appeared in the mystagogical catecheses, these two oppositions were present in the baptismal rites, in both the exorcisms and the renunciation of Satan and profession of Christ.[88] All these rites are built upon the opposition between slavery to the devil and freedom in Christ. It is necessary to choose between slavery and freedom, between the tyrant and the Lord. During the exorcism those to be baptized kneel while renouncing Satan. The posture of kneeling is a sign of enslavement to Satan, to whom those to be baptized are bound by a debtor's contract. I consider it necessary to strongly emphasize that the debtor's contract with the devil is the contract with which one is bound to Christ when entering into Christ's service. With the renunciation of Satan, the one to be baptized tramples underfoot the contract that bound one to the devil and stands upright to profess Christ. In the rite of profession, the one to be baptized stands upright as a sign of freedom. At this point it is necessary to reveal that the one to be baptized, by renouncing the pomp of the devil and professing Christ, assumes a new role, that of service to Christ. Strictly speaking, if now a servant of Christ, the one to be baptized should remain kneeling because slavery to the devil has been substituted with the service of Christ. However, this does not happen. The one to be baptized has to stand upright because the opposition is not between service to the devil and service to Christ, but between slavery[89] and liberty. The commentary in the catecheses also develops the theme of the service of Christ, but this is understood as a fruit of the freedom that Christ gives to human beings, not as a new enslavement, analogous to the previous one. An important observation of Vernant explains well the rationale of this rite:

> To emphasize one's proper difference from the barbarian, the Greek proudly affirms one's status as free, *elèutheros*, and the expression

---

87 Paul writes to Philemon concerning the slave Onesimus: 'Perhaps for this reason he was separated from you for a time that you may have him again for ever; no longer, however, as a slave, but as much more than a slave, as a brother beloved in the first place by me, but how much more by you, both as a human being, and as a brother in the Lord' (Phil. 15–16).
88 At times this *profession* takes the form of a profession of faith.
89 In the sense of service to the devil and obedience to him.

slave of God, generally attested by other peoples, is not used, and this not only in the then current cultural practice.[90]

Conclusion

We have seen that the entire first stage of the rites of baptism, more precisely the exorcisms, the renunciation of Satan, the profession of Christ and the anointings, are based on the opposition between Christ and Satan. The whole world is dominated by Satan and all human beings are subjected to him. One who becomes a Christian abandons Satan and his dominion by professing the lordship of Christ. During the fourth century the rites that preceded the water bath had this meaning and function. Moreover, in the catechetical teachings of Theodore of Mopsuestia, there are some elements that lead one to consider that this might have been the fundamental import of baptism.[91] All of baptism, then, is interpreted as a passage from slavery to the devil to the lordship of Christ, including the blessing of the water over which the Holy Spirit is invoked, as we have seen above. All this has nothing to do with the simplest and oldest form of the baptismal rite, as described in the *Acts of Thomas*. Here the anointing precedes and specifies the baptismal water, which, accompanied by the invocation (*epiclesis*) of the three divine Names, is defined as an *anointing* of the Holy Spirit. In its successive development, the anointing comes to be duplicated and, as we have seen, interpreted as the conclusion of the exorcism, from which it receives its interpretation.

We have examined how this entire understanding of baptism developed, namely how the interpretation given in the mystagogical catecheses shows the development of baptism as an exorcism.

I believe that the only possible explanation is found in the anthropology prevalent where Christianity was practised.

We may conclude, then, that the development of the rites of baptism as exorcisms had as a particular cultural background the anthropology of Valentinian Gnosticism and, in turn, the fundamental elements of the anthropology of classical antiquity: the understanding of the human person – slave or free – was as familiar to people in the classical world even in late antiquity, as it guided the development of the rites which precede the baptismal immersion. In this way the rites handed on the theology of baptism in anthropological and social categories known and familiar to all.

---

90 Vernant J.-P., 'Introduzione', in Vernant, *L'uomo greco*, p. 10.
91 As already said, I have examined this data in 'L'uso di *sacramentum* nella Lettera 10, 96 di Plinio jr . . .'.

Appendix: Comparison of Theodotus with Cyril of Jerusalem

	Theodotus	Cyril
	Excerptum 82, in Sagnard, *Clément d'Alexandrie: Extraits*, p. 206.	Catechesi 3.3 in Maestri, *Cirillo e Giovanni di Gerusalemme: Catechesi*, p. 190.
1	Also the bread	As indeed the things brought to the altar
2	and the oil are sanctified by the *dynamis*	
3	of the Name of God	
4	remaining the same, in outward appearance, as when they were taken	which in their own nature are ordinary things
5		they become soiled (*memolusmena*) by the invocation made to the idols,
6	but by the *dynamis*, they are transformed into a *dynamis pneumatica*.	
7	In the same way	thus,
8		on the contrary
9	the water	ordinary water
10	becomes exorcized water, and baptism	
11	not only sheds the inferior element, but also	
12	acquires	acquires
13		a power (*dynamin*)
14	the sanctification	sanctifying
15		in receiving the invocation of the Holy Spirit, Son and Father.

11

The Holy Trinity and the Liturgical Subject

SIMON OLIVER

> ... [A] relationship to the Logos, who was at the beginning, brings salvation to the subject, that is, to the person. At the same time it puts us into a true relationship of communion that is ultimately grounded in trinitarian love.[1]
> *Joseph Cardinal Ratzinger*

The doctrine of the Trinity frames Christian worship and the liturgical subject in certain obvious ways. The gate into the liturgical life of the Church and the beginning of a new subjectivity is through baptism in the divine name, Father, Son and Holy Spirit. We commonly begin our particular liturgical acts by placing our worship under the protection of the Trinity in praying that we may speak in the name of the Father, Son and Holy Spirit while making the sign of the cross over our bodies.[2] At the Eucharist, collects – that is, the collective prayers of the people – are addressed to the Father, through the Son, in the Holy Spirit. In the Church of England's most recent liturgical revision, *Common Worship*, the intercessory petitions of the people are invoked with the phrase 'In the power of the Spirit and in union with Christ, let us pray to the Father.' The Trinity structures the eucharistic prayer. Our principal liturgical celebrations are concluded with the blessing of the congregation in the name of the Trinity. While it is clear that the formation of liturgical action and prayer by the doctrine of the Trinity is very evident in the texts of the liturgy, one might also suggest that the doctrine of the Trinity is at once a commentary upon, and exposition of, liturgical

---

1 Joseph Cardinal Ratzinger (trans. John Saward), *The Spirit of the Liturgy* (San Francisco: Ignatius Press, 2000), p.155.

2 Ratzinger, *Spirit of the Liturgy*, p.178: 'We connect the sign of the Cross with confession of faith in the triune God – the Father, the Son, and the Holy Spirit ... Whenever we make the sign of the Cross, we accept our Baptism anew; Christ from the Cross draws us, so to speak, to himself (cf. Jn 12.32).'

praxis. Following Cardinal Kasper, the Trinity might be regarded as 'the grammar of doxology'.[3]

Liturgy, however, is more than written text; it is also embodied and dramatized in gesture, action, speech, vesture, vessel, music, scent and food. How are we to understand the relationship between human corporeal subjectivity as it is constituted in the liturgy of the Church, and the doctrine of the Holy Trinity? How are the *vestigia trinitatis* to be discerned in God's people and the goal of their being, namely the work of divine praise?

Because the doctrine of the Trinity has become something of an abstract intellectual conundrum in the hands of some Christian theologians of modernity, it might be thought that the link between the doctrine of God and the inherently practical matters of Christian liturgy has become far from obvious.[4] One clear response to this issue might refer to the apparently social nature of God's Trinitarian life, and the concomitant social nature of the Christian liturgy. On this view, the worship of God is a corporate and social act. At the heart of the eucharistic mystery, towards which all liturgy points, is the gathering of God's people into one to receive the body and blood of Christ. The Church is formed through the shared receipt of these mysteries and it is constituted as a new form of relational society, which might also provide a model for a wider polity. The basis for such a polity is the social nature of God's inner life, for, according to a number of contemporary theologians who have sought to recover a relational ontology in the midst of modern nominalistic individualism, the Trinity might best be understood as a society or community of divine persons. By providing a 'model' for personal and relational being, the Trinity constitutes the basis for subjectivity constructed through the liturgy understood as the central expression of the society of the Church. Ultimately, the Trinity might become 'our social programme'.[5] Could we therefore understand the social nature of the Church and its liturgy as a participation in, or imitation of, the social nature of being itself, namely the eternal society of divine persons?

What I have thus far articulated is the bare bones of so-called social Trinitarianism. Such a doctrine of God – which comes in a variety of

---

3 Walter Kasper (trans. M. J. O'Connell), *The God of Jesus Christ* (New York: Crossroad Publishing Company, 1988), p. 311.

4 Indeed, pressing home an important point in Laurence Hemming's contribution to this collection, one might argue that the Trinity is regarded as an intellectual conundrum to be explained (or explained away) precisely because of a failure to understand the speculative enterprise of Christian theology as a commentary on the nature and form of the Church's prayer.

5 Miroslav Volf, '"The Trinity Is Our Social Programme": The Doctrine of the Trinity and the Shape of Social Engagement', *Modern Theology* 14 (1998), pp. 403–23.

forms but might be defined most essentially as the view that God is, in himself, a society of persons – could constitute a very obvious attraction in any attempt to draw together the doctrine of the Trinity with a social and relational understanding of liturgical subjectivity. Such an approach to Trinitarian theology was championed by Jürgen Moltmann in his *Trinity and the Kingdom of God*, and has been advocated very recently by, among others, Leonardo Boff, Miroslav Volf and the late Colin Gunton.[6] Moltmann draws an explicit connection between his own Trinitarian theology and the liturgy of the Church when he writes, 'The assertions of the immanent Trinity about eternal life and the eternal relationships of the triune God in himself have their Sitz im Leben, their situation in life, in the praise and worship of the church: Glory be to the Father and to the Son and to the Holy Ghost!'[7] For social Trinitarians, an emphasis on theological reflection beginning with the threefold nature of God (which they associate particularly with the Cappadocian Fathers against the supposed Western Augustinian and Thomist emphasis on the unity of the divine substance) is of great importance.[8] This argument suggests that to begin to talk about God in anything other than Trinitarian terms is already to have rendered the Trinity a logical or mathematical conundrum which supplements a more essential unitary substance. Furthermore, social Trinitarians are frequently committed to a certain view of subjectivity even within the Godhead. 'Person', they maintain, is a term too quickly discarded by Rahner and Barth in their discussions of the Trinity.

---

6 See especially Jürgen Moltmann (trans. M. Kohl), *The Trinity and the Kingdom of God: The Doctrine of God* (London: SCM Press, 1981); Leonardo Boff (trans. P. Burns), *Trinity and Society* (Tunbridge Wells: Burns & Oates, 1988); Colin Gunton, *The One, the Three and the Many* (Cambridge: Cambridge University Press, 1993); Miroslav Volf, *After our Likeness: The Church as the Image of the Trinity* (Grand Rapids, Michigan: William B. Eerdmans, 1998). While particularly popular among some Protestant theologians of the last 20 years, social Trinitarianism is also a prominent theme in some Catholic writing. See, for example, Catherine Mowry LaCugna, *God for Us: The Trinity and Christian Life* (New York: Harper Collins, 1992), ch. 4. To see the extent of the application of social Trinitarianism, see M. Douglas Meeks, 'The Social Trinity and Property' in Miroslav Volf and Michael Welker (eds.), *God's Life in Trinity* (Minneapolis: Fortress Press, 2006). The notion of a social Trinity has also become prominent among analytic philosophers of religion who are anxious to resolve what they regard as an intolerable mathematical contradiction at the heart of the Christian doctrine of God, namely the three-in-oneness of the divine. See, for example, Peter van Inwagen, 'And Yet They Are Not Three Gods But One God', in Thomas V. Morris (ed.), *Philosophy and the Christian Faith* (Notre Dame: University of Notre Dame Press, 1988). For a critique of this approach, see Brian Leftow, 'Anti Social Trinitarianism', in Stephen Davis, Daniel Kendall SJ and Gerald O'Collins SJ (eds), *The Trinity* (Oxford: Oxford University Press, 1999).

7 Moltmann, *The Trinity and the Kingdom of God*, p. 152.

8 See David Cunningham, *These Three are One: The Practice of Trinitarian Theology* (Oxford: Blackwell, 1998), ch. 1; Colin Gunton, 'Augustine, the Trinity and the Theological Crisis of the West', *Scottish Journal of Theology* 43 (1990), pp. 33–58.

In this essay I will first respond to this prominent trend in recent writing on the Trinity by examining the proposal that our relational, social subjectivity is constituted in the liturgical praise of God who is himself to be understood as social. I will suggest that such a view, while at first glance obvious and attractive, is problematic for a number a reasons. Most particularly, social Trinitarianism leads to a notion of liturgical participation which is reduced to *mimesis* (that is, mimicry at a distance) and which circumvents the necessary mediatory priesthood of Christ. Moreover, social Trinitarianism tends to erode a liturgical apophaticism which insists that it is only by divine grace that we are delivered from the impossibility of the finite addressing the infinite in praise. Such an apophaticism, I will suggest, must lie at the heart of Christian liturgy and subjectivity if idolatry is to be avoided. In contrast to social Trinitarianism, I will suggest that liturgical subjectivity is constituted in relation to the divine through the mediation of Christ who, by the Holy Spirit, is made corporeally present in the eucharistic sacrifice. In discussing this view I will refer particularly to Aquinas's theology of the sacraments, for here one finds the heart of liturgy and Christian subjectivity – baptism, Eucharist and the other sacraments – expounded with a different Trinitarian reference, namely a return to the Father by incorporation into Christ by the Spirit. This is the gateway into the life of the Trinity: a sharing in a liturgy that is first God's work – the Son's offering to the Father in the Holy Spirit – only to be rendered humanity's work by the operation of grace. Thus, as the Holy Father suggests, it is by a relationship first with the Logos – incarnate and sacramentally present – that we are put into a true relationship of communion (*koinonia*) within Trinitarian love.

Social Trinitarianism and Liturgy

Among those theologians of the twentieth century who sought to restore the doctrine of the Trinity to the heart of Christian reflection on the divine, the use of the word 'person' in relation to the Godhead seemed to present problems. In the wake of Descartes and the philosophers of the Enlightenment, the term 'person' was used to refer particularly to an individual centre of consciousness, or a unique will.[9] Applied to God without qualification, this would imply tritheism. This led Karl Barth, for example, to apply the similarly contentious term *Seinsweise* ('way of being', or 'mode of being') to the Father, Son and Holy Spirit in order to avoid any sense that, within God, there were three

---

9 See, for example, John Locke's definition in his 1690 treatise *An Essay Concerning Human Understanding* (abridged J. Yolton) (London: Dent, 1990), II.27, p. 171.

individuals.[10] More recently, and from a more Rahnerian perspective, Nicholas Lash has made a similar and forceful argument against the use of the term 'person' with reference to the Trinity.[11] However, those whose theology might be placed under the broad label of social Trinitarianism have pointed out that the term 'person' in relation to God is a nuanced and technical term, and that this traditional theology of the person in reference to the divine should not be jettisoned, but rather recovered in order to challenge modern individualistic conceptions of human subjectivity. For example, both Moltmann and Zizioulas offer historical accounts of the meanings of the Latin term *persona* and the Greek terms *prosopon* and *hypostasis*, pointing to the essentially relational meaning of the latter term. Moltmann writes, 'The three divine Persons exist in their particular, unique natures as Father, Son and Spirit in their relationships to one another, and are determined through these relationships. It is in these relationships that they are persons. Being a person in this respect means existing-in-relationship.'[12]

To say the least, referring to the persons of the Trinity as 'unique natures' seems to risk a tritheistic interpretation. Indeed, those who write in the vein of social Trinitarianism – particularly those in the analytic tradition of philosophy – risk tritheism and the proposal that in God there are three individuals, wills or centres of consciousness, albeit in perfect harmony. How is such an interpretation mitigated so as to preserve monotheism? Typically, the notion of *perichoresis* is deployed.[13]

---

10 Karl Barth (trans. G. W. Bromiley), *Church Dogmatics* I/1 (Edinburgh: T&T Clark, 1975), §9.1 and 2, especially pp. 351ff.

11 Nicholas Lash, *Believing Three Ways in One God: A Reading of the Apostles' Creed* (London: SCM Press, 1992), p. 31: 'There is no doubt whatsoever, to my mind, but that the arguments for ceasing to speak of "persons" in Trinitarian theology greatly outweigh those in favour of the term's retention. Let us take our bearings, once more, from Augustine. "Because the Father is not the Son and the Son is not the Father, and the Holy Spirit who is also called the gift of God is neither the Father nor the Son, they are certainly three . . . Yet when you ask 'Three what?', human speech labours under a great dearth of words. So we say three persons, not in order to say that precisely, but in order not to be reduced to silence."' (Quoting Augustine, *De Trinitate*, V.10.)

12 Moltmann, *The Trinity and the Kingdom of God*, p. 172; John Zizioulas, *Being as Communion* (London: DLT, 1985), ch.1. The analysis of the meaning of *hypostasis* and the general notion of the Trinity as 'social' is frequently attributed to the Cappadocian Fathers over and against the Western Augustinian tradition. In an important article, Sarah Coakley has established clear reasons for not interpreting the work of Gregory of Nyssa as an example of social Trinitarianism. See Sarah Coakley, '"Persons" in the "Social" Doctrine of the Trinity: Current Analytic Discussion and "Cappadocian" Theology' in Coakley, *Powers and Submissions: Spirituality, Philosophy and Gender* (Oxford: Blackwell, 2002), pp. 109–29. See also John Milbank, 'The Force of Identity' in Milbank, *The Word Made Strange: Theology, Language, Culture* (Oxford: Blackwell, 1997), pp. 194–216.

13 See Moltmann, *The Trinity and the Kingdom of God*, pp. 174–6. John 17.20–26 is frequently cited as the clearest Biblical exposition of this concept.

This patristic term, extending at least to John Damascene in the eighth century, refers to the coinherence, 'circumincession' or interpenetration of the divine persons of the Trinity. For social Trinitarians, this mutual indwelling is the principal strength of the Eastern, as opposed to Western, doctrine of God. It indicates the perfect loving unity of the persons of the Godhead, and a mutuality to be found only fleetingly in human relations.

In the midst of late modern anxiety concerning isolation, individualism, authoritarianism, threats to pluralism and the disintegration of community, the social doctrine of the Trinity has had obvious appeal. Yet in a clear and incisive article, Karen Kilby has provided a critique of social Trinitarianism on a number of fronts, focusing particularly on the notion of *perichoresis* and the deployment of this concept in contemporary writing on the doctrine of God.[14] Kilby points out that recent social views of the Trinity tend to describe the divine inner life in some considerable and unwarranted detail with the use of such terms as 'empathy', 'transparency', 'zestful community', 'mutuality' and 'verve' applied to God's inner life.[15] While such terms may be used speculatively and with more or less restraint, the key factor to which Kilby points is that the notion of *perichoresis*, and the doctrine of the Trinity more generally, is thought to have 'positive implications for that which is not God.'[16] For example, the social doctrine of the Trinity is believed to provide models for ecclesiology. There is considerable polemic against what is seen as a monarchical, centralized and clerical Western Church, which, it is supposed, reflects a tendency to emphasize the singular monarchy of God rather than Trinitarian unity-in-plurality that is better reflected in a more conciliar or Reformed ecclesiology.[17] Inferences are also drawn

---

14 Karen Kilby, 'Perichoresis and Projection: Problems with Social Doctrines of the Trinity' in *New Blackfriars* 81 (2000), pp. 432–45. I am greatly indebted to Dr Kilby's article and our discussions on this and other topics. While concurring with her analysis, her concluding suggestion that the Trinity might be understood as a 'second order proposition' (following the themes of Lindbeck) could be problematic (p. 443). I agree that Trinitarian language does not convey substantial information about God. However, following Gregory of Nyssa, one can maintain that God is literally Father, Son and Holy Spirit without understanding the meaning and implications of these terms. On this view, rather than divine 'Fatherhood' being a metaphor (or second order proposition), human 'fatherhood' would be understood analogically as referring primarily to God and, by attribution, secondarily to human relations. The ground of such language is revelation in Christ.

15 See, for example, Cornelius Plantinga, Jr, 'Social Trinity and Tritheism' in Ronald J. Feenstra and Cornelius Plantinga, Jr (eds), *Trinity, Incarnation and Atonement* (Notre Dame: University of Notre Dame Press, 1989), cited in Kilby, 'Perichoresis and Projection', p. 435.

16 Kilby, 'Perichoresis and Projection', p. 436.

17 See, in particular, Miroslav Volf, *After Our Likeness (passim)* and Moltmann, *The Trinity and the Kingdom of God*, pp. 200ff.

regarding human relationality and gender (Patricia Wilson-Kastner[18]) and human politics. Moltmann writes,

> If we take our bearings from the Christian doctrine of the Trinity, personalism and socialism cease to be antitheses and are seen to be derived from a common foundation. The Christian doctrine of the Trinity compels us to develop social personalism or personal socialism. For, right down to the present day, the Western cult of the person has allied itself with monotheism, whereas the basis of the socialism of the Eastern countries . . . is not so much atheistic as pantheistic . . . Today it is vitally necessary for the two to converge in the direction of a 'humane' society; and here the Christian doctrine of the Trinity can play a substantial role.[19]

What binds these accounts together is a largely uncritical assumption that relationality within the Godhead is a transparent concept which can be applied more-or-less univocally to the Church, human polity or liturgical subjects in a fashion which renders the doctrine of the Trinity relevant and practical.

I mention this recent approach to the doctrine of the Trinity (which claims for itself significant patristic precedence) because it appears to provide a very obvious resource for an understanding of liturgical subjectivity. The recovery of a relational ontology which is apparently not arbitrary or voluntaristic but grounded in being itself has clear force. The liturgy of the Church might be understood as a ritual and relational enterprise that is not only counter-cultural but redemptive in providing a model for overcoming the individualism of the Enlightenment and late modernity and, more acutely, the isolation of sin. The liturgical subject is therefore constituted as a person-in-relation who, in joining the prayer of the Church and sharing in a common meal at the altar, is expressing a more replete human nature which reflects the social nature of the Godhead. The supposed advantage to connecting the Trinity with the liturgy in this way is that it renders an otherwise abstract doctrine in some way relevant for liturgical subjectivity, theological anthropology, ecclesiology and Christian politics.

There are, however, significant problems with such an approach, and a number are highlighted by Kilby.[20] Social Trinitarianism involves a projection of human relationality onto the Trinity in a fashion which renders it, in the end, a form of natural theology. Because social Trini-

---

18 Patricia Wilson-Kastner, Faith, Feminism and the Christ (Philadelphia: Fortress Press, 1983), cited in Kilby, 'Perichoresis and Projection', p. 436.
19 Moltmann, *The Trinity and the Kingdom of God*, pp. 199–200.
20 See Kilby, 'Perichoresis and Projection', p. 442.

tarianism construes the persons of the Trinity as individuated, the concept of *perichoresis* is deployed in order to account for the divine unity. Yet *perichoresis* in the hands of the Eastern patristic Fathers is a technical term which is understood apophatically when applied to God. In the hands of more recent social Trinitarians, *perichoresis* is interpreted in terms of human interrelatedness and mutual dependence. It is then claimed that the relation between the divine persons is similarly relational, only infinitely more so through interpenetration. As Kilby points out, there is, however, a final crucial move: having interpreted the inner divine life in terms of *perichoresis* understood all-too-univocally as an infinitely accentuated form of human relationality, this concept is then reflected back on to humanity and 'presented as an exciting resource Christian theology has to offer the wider world in its reflections upon relationships and relatedness.'[21] It therefore comes as little surprise that, as Kathryn Tanner has observed, 'The closer Trinitarian relations seem to human ones, the less the Trinity seems to offer advice on how to move beyond them... Pushing imaginatively beyond those experiences to something better... would seem to be require the Trinity to be something more too. Without being more, the Trinity's potential for critical, informative commentary is simply deflated.'[22]

So how might relationality in the Trinity be understood differently? A glance at Aquinas's discussion of relationality within the Godhead reveals a far more apophatic doctrine, which is based more clearly on our analogical (rather than mimetic) participation in the divine life. In the midst of a complicated question concerning real relations in God, a key point for Aquinas is that, whereas in creatures relations are accidental and contingent, in God the relations of the persons are necessary and, as such, one with his nature.[23] A human person is not exhaustively or necessarily defined by any relationship into which she might enter; there is an individual integrity which enters into a variety of mediated and contingent relations. Whereas complete self-donation to another is not possible within created relations – there is always a remainder – a replete self-donation, for Aquinas, is precisely what characterizes the perfect and eternal relationality of the persons of the Trinity. The

---

21 Kilby, 'Perichoresis and Projection', p. 442.
22 Kathryn Tanner, 'Trinity', in Peter Scott and William T. Cavanaugh (eds), *The Blackwell Companion to Political Theology* (Oxford: Blackwell, 2004), p. 327.
23 Aquinas, *Summa Theologiae*, 1a.28.2: 'Quidquid autem in rebus creatis habet esse accidentale, secundum quod transfertur in Deum, habet esse substantiale, nihil enim est in Deo ut accidens in subiecto, sed quidquid est in Deo, est eius essentia. Sic igitur ex ea parte qua relatio in rebus creatis habet esse accidentale in subiecto, relatio realiter existens in Deo habet esse essentiae divinae, idem omnino ei existens. In hoc vero quod ad aliquid dicitur, non significatur aliqua habitudo ad essentiam, sed magis ad suum oppositum.'

Father is Father only through an eternal subsistent relation to the Son and Holy Spirit as the one from whom the Son is eternally begotten and from whom the Spirit eternally proceeds. The persons of the Trinity are, therefore, their relations without reserve. The Godhead is pure relationality.[24] Yet Aquinas says nothing more. He expounds his understanding of the Trinitarian relations within the logic of perfection with reference to divine simplicity and necessity, preserving a clear ontological difference between God and creation in the spirit of negative theology. We might suggest that 'relationality' is a perfection term that is predicated primarily of God and, by *analogia attributionis*, secondarily of creatures. This is to say that relationality belongs properly, primarily and literally to God in a manner that is consonant with eternal and necessary being. Humanity, by contrast, exhibits relationality only secondarily and 'after a fashion' in a way consonant with created being. In so far as *esse ipsum* and *esse commune* are sheerly different, so the relational nature of divine and created being will sheerly differ. Just as creation exists only by participating in the divine, so created beings only enter into relation in so far as they are constituted first by one relation that *is* necessary to their existence – a relation to the creator – and thereby participate in the eternal relationality of the Godhead. Crucially, however, this is not to suggest that we thereby gain significant information concerning the nature of the Trinitarian relations, for those relations are replete, eternal and necessary. An appropriate apophaticism must be observed lest we read into God what properly belongs to creatures.

What appears to be at issue in these accounts of the Trinity is the nature of our participation in divine being. Regarding our present concern, how does the liturgical subject, in and through the liturgy, participate in God? According to some varieties of social Trinitarianism, the form of this participation is *mimesis*, or mimicry. It is as if, from a distance, we 'copy' the Trinitarian relations in human relationality. Thus the Trinity becomes a 'model', a social programme, a political manifesto, or a cipher through which we might understand the nature of the liturgical subject as social.[25] As Kilby observes, however, such an understanding of relation is merely a projection of what we already observe in the best of human relationships. This is the result of a predominantly univocal doctrine of God which, in order to avoid anthropomorphism or pantheism, must maintain participation or *mimesis* 'at a distance' lest the divine collapse into creation. As Alan Torrance suggests, it is precisely an inadequate notion of participation that lies at the

---

24 For a more extensive discussion of Aquinas on real relations in God, see Thomas Weinandy, OFM Cap., *Does God Suffer?* (Notre Dame: University of Notre Dame Press, 2000), pp. 117ff.

25 See Kathryn Tanner, 'Trinity'.

heart of Moltmann's voluntaristic interpretation of Christian worship as essentially something that the human subject initiates and undertakes through mimicry of the divine society.[26] On such a view, the liturgical subject becomes merely an actor within a ritual game; the distinction between ceremony and liturgy is lost. Why? Because liturgy is understood to be exclusively 'our work', a mimicking of what God is supposed to be in himself. Moreover, because the univocal understanding of relationality tends to characterize many forms of social Trinitarianism, one also loses any sense of what one might call the impossibility of liturgy. Given the sheer difference between creator and creation, from the beginning one is confronted with how it might be possible for humanity to address the divine in worship. Why are our acts of praise directed towards infinite plenitude not hopelessly futile and meaningless?

To answer this question requires a proper understanding of the impossibility of the liturgy as twofold: a gift from God and a sacrifice to God.[27] Overcoming this impossibility is an act of divine grace by which we are drawn towards the divine. In order to understand how the liturgical subject is so incorporated into divine praise, it is necessary to offer a Trinitarian account not in terms of mimesis or 'society', but first through Christology and pneumatology. As Kilby comments, it is necessary to remember that the Trinitarian doctrine of God is the Church's profession because of what is also professed about Christ and the Spirit.[28] In the next section of this chapter, I therefore turn to the Christological and pneumatological aspects of liturgy as the proper routes towards a Trinitarian understanding of the liturgical subject.

The Liturgical Subject and Trinitarian Grace

The Church's liturgy is a hierarchy in which the Offices and occasional sacraments are ordered towards the celebration of the Eucharist; here, at the altar, all other acts of worship find their consummation. The pattern of worship is infused with the graceful power of the sacraments. At the beginning of his consideration of these liturgical sacraments in the *Summa Theologiae*, Aquinas comments that 'After studying the mys-

---

26 Alan Torrance, *Persons in Communion: An Essay of Trinitarian Description and Human Participation* (Edinburgh: T&T Clark, 1996), pp. 310ff.

27 Catherine Pickstock, *After Writing: On the Liturgical Consummation of Philosophy* (Oxford: Blackwell, 1997), p. 176.

28 Kilby, 'Perichoresis and Projection', pp. 442–3: 'The doctrine of the Trinity arose in order to affirm certain things about the divinity of Christ, and, secondarily, of the Spirit, and it arose against a background assumption that God is one. So one could say that as long as Christians continue to believe in the divinity of Christ and the Spirit, and as long as they believe that God is one, then the doctrine is alive and well; it continues to inform the way they read the Scriptures and the overall shape of their faith.'

teries of the incarnate Word, the next investigation is the sacraments of the Church, for it is from the Incarnate Word that they derive their efficacy.'[29] Thus, as Louis-Marie Chauvet points out, for Aquinas 'the sacraments are conceived as prolongations of Christology.'[30] Chauvet continues with an exposition of Aquinas on the sacramental incorporation of the human subject into the divine life with a critique of the scholastic emphasis on the hypostatic union. Aquinas comments that 'the principal efficient cause of grace is God himself, and the humanity of Christ stands to him in relation of a conjoined instrument, whereas a sacrament stands in relation of a separate one. Thus it is right that the power to bestow salvation should flow from the divinity of Christ through his humanity into the sacraments themselves.'[31] Thus the sacraments of the Church are secondary causes of grace (in the Neoplatonic sense as expounded in Aquinas's commentary on the *Liber de Causis*), the primary cause being God. The basis of divine power being conjoined to visible liturgical signs in the sacraments is the incarnation. Why? In answering this question, we must make a very brief excursus to examine the incarnation and the hypostatic union. This will also provide an indication of how the impossible liturgy is, by grace, made possible.

As John Milbank has argued at length with particular reference to the gift and forgiveness, the reconciliation of humanity to God seems to be impossible.[32] On the one hand, because it is humanity which has sinned and must make restitution, humanity must provide an atoning sacrifice. Yet any such sacrifice, because it is a human action, will always be tainted by sin, thus being wholly inadequate to the task of reconciliation with the divine. Only God, whose actions are replete and perfect, may provide such a sacrifice whereby humanity might be reconciled to its creator. The impossibility of this reconciliation is mirrored in the impossibility of liturgical subjects engaging in divine praise: how can the sinful finite creature address the infinite? St Paul teaches that in Christ, God is

---

29 Aquinas, *Summa Theologica* III.60: 'Post considerationem eorum quae pertinent ad mysteria verbi incarnati, considerandum est de Ecclesiae sacramentis, quae ab ipso verbo incarnato efficaciam habent.'

30 Louis-Marie Chauvet (trans. Patrick Madigan SJ and Madeleine Beaumont), *Symbol and Sacrament: A Sacramental Reinterpretation of Christian Existence* (Collegeville, Minnesota: The Liturgical Press, 1995), p. 453.

31 Aquinas, *Summa Theologiae* III.62.5.reponsio: 'Principalis autem causa efficiens gratiae est ipse Deus, ad quem comparatur humanitas Christi sicut instrumentum coniunctum, sacramentum autem sicut instrumentum separatum. Et ideo oportet quod virtus salutifera derivetur a divinitate Christi per eius humanitatem in ipsa sacramenta.' This text is cited and incorrectly referenced in Chauvet, *Symbol and Sacrament*, p. 454.

32 See John Milbank, *Being Reconciled: Ontology and Pardon* (London: Routledge, 2003), chs. 4–6. These comments are made in the context of the aporia of intra-human forgiveness.

reconciling the world to himself.[33] It is by a divine humanity that reconciliation is brought about, for in Christ's humanity a sacrifice is offered vicariously on behalf of all the sinful. Meanwhile, in Christ's divinity this action is singular, replete and perfect. In the hypostatic union, the unmixed human and divine natures make possible this sacrificial reconciliation.[34] Christ is both priest and victim – the one whose offering is replete, and the one offered who is without sin. Similarly, it must be with primary reference to Christology and the hypostatic union that the liturgical praise of God is made possible. In joining ourselves to Christ's humanity, we are at the same time incorporated into his divinity, namely the Logos, the second person of the Trinity. It is thus that the liturgical subject is drawn into the Trinitarian life through the mediatorial priesthood of Christ.

How are we incorporated first into Christ's humanity so that we might share in his divinity? For Aquinas, it is the power of God which flows from the divinity of Christ through his humanity into the sacraments and their recipients. Sacraments are material signs which are unconjoined[35] instruments of God's power. They are material because God delivers grace in a fashion that is orientated to our material and created natures.[36] The use of such material signs is a participation in the incarnation itself and, ultimately, in Christ's sacrifice on the cross. Therefore, the liturgical use of material things is part of the incorporation of the liturgical subject into the divine life. This reaches its apex in the liturgy of the Eucharist, for here Christ is corporeally and sacramentally present under the accidents of bread and wine.[37] Aquinas notes four effects of the sacrament.[38] First, the sacrament 'holds Christ' and thereby 'causes the life of grace'. Second, the Eucharist is the sacrament of the passion of Christ into which we are thereby literally 'incorporated' – that is, we are made corporeally part of the passion by receiving the body of Christ

---

33 2 Corinthians 5.19. Of course, this entails that we are not reconciling God to us, for God is, in himself, eternally reconciled. Likewise, in the liturgy we are not making God present to us. God makes us present to himself.

34 The unmixed natures of Christ are, of course, crucial. If Christ's natures were not distinct, he would be a hybrid – neither divine nor human, but some 'third thing' standing apart from the divine and human. In the unmixed natures of the hypostatic union, Christ truly holds together – and thereby reconciles – the divine and human in one person in being *fully* human and *fully* divine.

35 In contrast to Christ's humanity, which is a conjoined instrument of God's power.

36 See Aquinas, *Summa Theologiae*, III.60.2 & 4.

37 See Aquinas, *Summa Theologiae*, III.75–8. Elsewhere, I have argued in favour of Aquinas's understanding of transubstantiation in the Eucharist and provided a parallel critique of the lack of corporeality in Calvin's doctrine of the Lord's Supper and the consequent impoverishment of the liturgy. See Simon Oliver, 'The Eucharist before Nature and Culture', *Modern Theology* 15 (1999), pp. 331–53.

38 Aquinas, *Summa Theologiae*, III.79.1.responsio.

into ourselves. Third, 'this sacrament does for the life of the spirit all that material food and drink does for the life of the body, by sustaining, building up, restoring, and contenting.' Finally, by delivering this sacrament in the form of a unity derived from countless parts – namely bread from grain and wine from grapes – the unity of the mystical body of Christ and the union of the believer (body and soul) with Christ is thereby signified.[39]

The essence of this position is expressed succinctly by the Holy Father when he writes that

> The elements of the earth are transubstantiated, pulled, so to speak, from their creaturely anchorage, grasped at the deepest ground of their being, and changed into the Body and Blood of the Lord. The New Heaven and the New Earth are anticipated. The real 'action' in the liturgy in which we are all supposed to participate is the action of God himself.[40]

This is a crucial point: the liturgy is not simply 'our work', but is first God's work in Christ realized by the Spirit. Because God's work can only ever be an expression of God's very self, the self-offering *eucharistia* of Christ is that which pertains in eternity as the Son returns himself to the Father in the Holy Spirit. Thus the liturgical subject is, by grace, incorporated into this Trinitarian dynamic, but the only way in which to understand this is first and foremost through Christ our Redeemer. Our participation in that life is not, however, mimetic, voluntaristic or even merely spiritual (as it was for Calvin): the liturgical subject is incorporated into the Trinitarian mystery, body and soul.

In his investigation of sacramental theology, Chauvet makes a number of criticisms of this Thomist perspective, two of which I will address directly. First, he remarks that 'One of the most fundamental lessons of the Church liturgical tradition from its earliest antiquity is that the point of departure for sacramental theology is not to be sought in the hypostatic union, but in the Pasch of Christ . . .'[41] He points out that the *anamneses* of the ancient eucharistic prayers, in conformity with the Pauline theology of the Eucharist as an announcement of the Lord's death until he comes, do not mention the incarnation as such. Thus while the initial thanksgiving in the ancient prayers does recall the incarnation, the anamnesis is focused on Christ's sacrifice. This is perhaps significant, but Chauvet here points out the place of the doctrine of the hypostatic union in relation to the liturgy. While the hypostatic union

---
39 See also Aquinas, *Summa Theologiae* III.73.responsio.
40 Joseph Cardinal Ratzinger, *The Spirit of the Liturgy*, p. 173.
41 Chauvet, *Symbol and Sacrament*, p. 476.

is not the focus of the anamnesis, nevertheless it is a commentary upon that aspect of the liturgy. In other words, the doctrine of the hypostatic union, which I have suggested is crucial in understanding how the liturgical subject is incorporated into the Trinitarian dynamic of faith, finds its purpose as an exposition of the Pasch of Christ as this is recalled at the Eucharist. Aquinas would not disagree that we begin with the cross and the sacrifice of Christ. One must merely point out that the *Summa Theologiae* is not Aquinas's beginning. *Sacra doctrina*, as expressed in the Church's liturgy, is his beginning and end. Indeed, he remarks that 'From this it is manifest that the sacraments of the Church derive their power especially from the Passion of Christ, and that it is through receiving the sacraments that the power flowing from this becomes, in a certain way, united to us.'[42]

But what of the Spirit? Surely a proper incorporation of the liturgical subject into the divine life must contain an equally pneumatological perspective? Chauvet argues that Aquinas's focus on the hypostatic union with regards to grace and the liturgy of the sacraments – common among the Scholastic theologians – renders his account 'static' and, along with much of the Western tradition, somewhat Christomonistic.[43] With the more pneumatological perspective of the Fathers, one would glean a much greater sense of the dynamic motion of humanity towards God and concomitantly of that which enlivens the Church. Given the dynamic sense of movement within liturgical celebration culminating in the receipt of Christ, this is surely important. As Chauvet also notes, Aquinas's sacramental theology, and the related ecclesiology and doctrine of creation, are not without a clear account of the action of the Holy Spirit. Yet he sees a clear imbalance; Aquinas merely quotes, rather than expounds and develops, the relevant scriptural passages relating to the Spirit. As Chauvet points out, an adequate pneumatology is required in order to make clear that the liturgical sacraments are the sacraments of the Church. They are gifts offered by God and returned. What is offered is not a nondescript power, but the very power of God himself: the Holy Spirit.

Yet how is the Spirit related to the corporeal nature of liturgical subjectivity? Chauvet reminds us that 'Faithful to its biblical roots, ecclesial tradition has attempted to discern what is most "spiritual" in God on the basis of what is most "corporeal" in us. This is especially the case with the liturgy.'[44] The discernment of the work of the Spirit in the life of

---

42 See Aquinas, *Summa Theologiae*, III.62.5: 'Unde manifestum est quod sacramenta Ecclesiae specialiter habent virtutem ex passione Christi, cuius virtus quodammodo nobis copulatur per susceptionem sacramentorum.'
43 Chauvet, *Symbol and Sacrament*, pp. 456 and 463.
44 Chauvet, *Symbol and Sacrament*, p. 523.

the Church is a clear Pauline motif. It is the fruit of corporeal, existential behaviour – love, joy, peace, patience, kindness, goodness, faithfulness, gentleness and self-control – in which the action of the Spirit is to be discerned. With more specific reference to the liturgy, it is by baptism in the Spirit that we are incorporated into the Church, and it is by the agency of the Spirit that the elements of bread and wine are transformed into the sacramental presence of Christ by the invocation of the *epiclesis* during the eucharistic prayer: 'The Spirit is the agent of the enfleshment of the word',[45] both at the annunciation and, likewise, at the Eucharist. It is through the gift of the Spirit that the liturgical community of the Church is born at Pentecost.

Conclusion

The contrast I have drawn between social Trinitarianism and the sacramental theology of Aquinas with respect to liturgical subjectivity is, at heart, a difference of theological method. On the one hand, social Trinitarianism, while incorporating varied and variously subtle doctrines of God, has tended to suggest that the distinction between the economic and immanent Trinity is problematic and that implications for human subjectivity be drawn from the relational of nature of God's immanent self.[46] In this enterprise, speculation concerning God's inner life (which is frequently rife) is used to inform our understanding of, for example, liturgical subjectivity through mimetic participation. Liturgy follows speculative doctrine.

By contrast, John Milbank has argued that 'Properly speaking there is only an immanent Trinity, participated in by the creation. However, since the fall "entraps" the divine glory which is Trinitarian, an "economic" presence of the Trinity as such in creation (Incarnation, Spirit, Church) becomes tragically necessary.'[47] What this suggests is that our approach to the Trinity must not only take account of the difference between creator and the creation (which, we might suggest, implies an

---

45 Chauvet, *Symbol and Sacrament*, p. 526.

46 Moltmann, *Trinity and the Kingdom of God*, p. 160: 'In order to grasp the death of the Son in its significance for God himself, I found myself bound to surrender the traditional distinction between the immanent and the economic Trinity, according to which the cross comes to stand only in the economy of salvation, but not within the immanent Trinity.' Colin Gunton, another prominent proponent of social Trinitarianism, maintained the importance of the distinction between the immanent and economic. See his 'The Church as a School of Virtue? Human Formation in Trinitarian Framework', in Mark Thiessen Nation and Samuel Wells (eds), *Faithfulness and Fortitude: In Conversation with the Theological Ethics of Stanley Hauerwas* (Edinburgh: T&T Clark, 2000), p. 213.

47 John Milbank, 'The Second Difference' in *The Word Made Strange*, p. 183.

economic presence of the Trinity) but also that we are fallen, which leads to our encounter with God in the particular economy of salvation of which we are a part. This therefore places primary emphasis on the economy of salvation as the beginning of theological reflection, and we participate in that economy – and encounter God – as liturgical subjects within the Church by virtue of the incarnation and the gifts of the Spirit. That encounter, however, is not merely speculative, but is mediated sacramentally (that is, corporeally), supremely in the sacrament of the Eucharist to which all liturgical celebration is orientated. Thus our liturgical formation as subjects is not through speculative mimesis, which, in the end, may only be an idolatrous self-projection, but rather through incorporation into the body of Christ by the power of the Holy Spirit. The notion of a Trinitarian liturgical subject rests, therefore, on Christology and pneumatology – on an account of how, in the economy of salvation, the Trinitarian persons of God make the eternal work of praise also our work of praise, thus overcoming what, to us, must always be regarded as the impossibility of liturgy. Speculative theology – Christology and pneumatology, giving rise to a Trinitarian doctrine of God – therefore becomes a commentary on our liturgical and sacramental encounter with God: *lex orandi, lex credendi*.

This is not to suggest that relationality, a concept which recent writings on Trinitarian doctrine has returned to the heart of Christian theology, is not crucial to this understanding of liturgical subjectivity. A relational subjectivity must, however, begin with the restoration of the one relation that *is* necessary to created being, namely a relation to the creator. This relation is fractured by sin, and thereby taints all human relations. Restoration of right relation is not undertaken by a voluntaristic mimetic participation in what we speculate concerning the immanent life of God, but rather through the paschal mystery of Christ and its liturgical mediation to us in the Church. This sense of mediation (which one loses even in Barth's all-too-Hegelian notion of divine '*self-revelation*'), in which our Trinitarian liturgical subjectivity is constituted in the economic encounter with Christ and the Spirit, should always make us reticent about drawing conclusions concerning the direct and 'unmediated' implications of God's eternal Trinitarian life. The implications of Christian theology must begin with the teaching that God, in Christ, is reconciling the world to himself. That reconciliation is effected and celebrated in the liturgy.

12

Communio, Truth and the Preaching of John Henry Newman

DENIS ROBINSON OSB

Introduction

The Second Vatican Council has been described as the 'Council of the Church' and rightly so. The Council produced two major documents on ecclesiology and included countless other allusions to the nature of the Church in the 14 remaining documents. Reflections on the idea of the Church, its origins and goals, its present and future have, likewise, consumed theologians in the more than 40 years since the Council. Seemingly eschewing older 'hierarchical' or 'pyramidal' models of the Church prevalent over the past two centuries, Vatican II appropriated an image of the Church as 'People of God'. The question remains in the post-conciliar period, however, as to the exact meaning of the term and its implications in the life of the Church in the twenty-first century. Conflicts have arisen, based on ecclesiological interpretations. Parties have emerged, using one or the other image of the Church to ground their particular approach to Christian life and discipleship.

This chapter explores the possibility that a nineteenth-century thinker, namely, John Henry Newman, may offer some assistance to the Church of our time in resolving some of the conflicts that have caused division between the proponents of competing notions of Church since Vatican II. Like us, Newman lived in a time of theological controversy. Factionalism was rampant in the Anglican Church of Newman's early years. The Broad Church party (liberals) fought with the Evangelicals. Both of these factions were in opposition to the High Church ecclesiology. Furthermore, a rampant epistemological dualism was evident between those who sought evidence of God in reason (deists) and those who thought God could only be experienced through intensely personal emotions (evangelicals). Newman's attempt to find a middle way, a *via media*, between these extremes was the focus of his work. He lived in a world that was becoming increasingly secular in its self-perception and in which traditional ideas about God were increasingly seen as passé. Likewise, he lived in a time when the Christian subject, under the influence of thinkers like Schleiermacher, was becoming increasingly isolated. In this sense, Newman's age, one in which 'mistiness is the mother of Wisdom', was not so unlike our own.

The first part of this chapter briefly explores the theologies of the Church that emerged in explicit ways after the Second Vatican Council, particularly contained in the notion of '*communio*'. The second part looks at the question of Truth in Newman's thought and the way in which his ideas about Truth relate to resolving the crisis of subjective isolation in a Christian context. The third section explores Newman's preaching method for signs of a practical theology of Church that may assist in clarifying some ecclesiological questions for today. In the final section, some applications of Newman's ideas will be offered in reference to the questions about *communio* raised in the first section.

Competing Notions of *Communio*

Communio is a charged word in contemporary theology. It is a controversial and occasionally misunderstood concept in the post-Vatican II Church. In twentieth-century theological discourse at least three distinctive and somewhat contradictory meanings of the word are at play. The first is the sense of the word employed by theologians who have fixed on the image of the Church as the 'People of God' and '*Communio*' found in (but certainly not originating in) the conciliar documents, particularly *Lumen Gentium*.[1] Pope John Paul II noted that the idea of *communio* lies 'at the heart of the Church's self understanding'.[2] Arising from the Vatican II documents, this notion of *communio* emerged in post-conciliar ecclesiology as what might be described as a 'horizontal' ideal. The people of God in this image of the Church formed a community based upon natural bonds. Social orders, neighbourhoods, families and other relational ties were inherent in the human condition. According to this vision, the hierarchical model of the Church, represented by earlier theology, is supplanted by a vision of the Church in the world. This model views the ecclesiology of Vatican II as representing a distinctive break with that of the First Vatican Council. Strains of this approach can be found, for example, in the versions of 'correlation' theology in the Catholic Church. The political theology of Johann-Baptist Metz, in attempting to distance itself from what Metz perceived

---

[1] See: *Lumen gentium*, 4, 8, 13–15, 18, 21, 24–5: *Dei Verbum*, 10; *Gaudium et spes*, 32; *Unitatis redintegratio*, 2–4, 14–15, 17–19, 22.

[2] See Congregation for the Doctrine of Faith, *Communio Notis*, 4.

as the too-introspective (spiritual) focus of Karl Rahner's transcendental method, sought a more public, more 'secular' context for theology in the marketplace. This impetus was replicated in the versions of liberation theology that emerged in the 1970s. *Communio* represented the people of God in the world, with many concerns and natural affiliations. This 'people' was constituted by natural means, within cultures, societies, economic and political groups and was, secondarily 'of God' that is, engaged in a relationship with the divine.

This strict division of the sacred and the secular was called into question, particularly in the examination of liberation theologies by the Magisterium. It also led to particular questions related to the question of the role of the subject. As post-modern social and cultural critics began to question the reality of human social models, the 'horizontal' model of Church was increasingly eroded until only subjective churches remained. In other words, if cultures were not real, but constructed, they risked, in a post-modern epistemology, being reduced to subjective realities.

A second understanding of *communio* in post-Vatican II ecclesiology is what might be termed the 'vertical' ideal proposed by some neoconservative elements in the Church. Disdaining the 'horizontal' theories proposed above, these constituents favour a 'vertical' dimensionality to Church life that sometimes resembles the older, pyramidal models, but occasionally emerges as something more radical, the appearance of what might be termed an 'alternative' magisterium. Groups espousing these views have been highly critical of what they see as the 'worldly' elements advocated by the Fathers of the Council. Some have gone so far as to establish 'mirror' communities that look like small-scale Roman Catholic churches, but in keeping with their particular visions. Other groups, seemingly having profited at least from Vatican II's decree on social communications, *Inter Mirifica*, have taken their cases for a more conservative church to the media, offering plentiful critique of the Church's 'misguided' hierarchy and promoting a view of ecclesiology that looks suspiciously at times like the direct divine guidance favoured by some aspects of Protestantism. Ironically, many such groups are founded by or substantially supported by laity whose very voice in the Church may have been bestowed by the Council they so regret. Again the question of subjectivism raises its head. A strictly 'vertical' Church runs the risk of communicating its message in the form of privatized revelations, which, having no 'checks and balances' in the 'horizontal' Church may erode into isolationism.

A final understanding of *communio* emerging in the post-conciliar Church is that represented by the theological journal, *Communio*, founded in 1972, by a group of theologians including Joseph Cardinal Ratzinger, Hans Urs Von Balthasar and others. *Communio*, in Balthasar's vision sought an authentic understanding of the notion of the people of God presented by the Council. These theologians, by extension, sought to implement what they considered to be an authentic interpretation of the council documents. In their estimation, the ecclesiology represented in Vatican II was an extension of the model presented in Vatican I. It did not represent a radical departure from the earlier council. In this model, human *communio* is secondary to the relationship that exists between God and the human person but is, nevertheless, a constitutive element of Church life. Human communities are constituted and adjudicated in terms of their quality by their faithful representation of the relationship between God and humanity. While the vision of the *Communio* theologians does not discount the 'horizontal' nature of human communities, it does not see that 'horizontal' quality as primary, but as something interrelated with the divine relationship. In that sense, this vision is not strictly a 'vertical' view of *communio*; it is rather one in which the 'horizontal' dimension is necessarily constituted with and in some senses, by the 'vertical' dimension. This view of *communio* is more complex than the two presented above in the sense that, precisely in not being univocal, it necessitates a living context that is complex, multifaceted and relational. This plurivocity also assists ecclesiology in discarding the unwanted mantle of subjectivity. The third approach is subtle where the others are simple. It demonstrates a more nuanced epistemological perspective. It is imaginative where the others are analytical. This last notion of *communio* is similar to the vision of the Church espoused by Newman during the nineteenth century. In his estimation, all reality in the Church was predicated on an unswerving proclamation of the complexity of the Truth of Jesus Christ.

Newman and Truth

John Henry Newman made many significant contributions to the development of religious thought in the nineteenth century. In some ways, as Avery Dulles and others have observed, he was unappreciated in his own time, but has become the (often unnamed) source of many of the advancements that characterize twentieth-century theology, including the Second Vatican Council.[3] Newman's understanding of conscience, his appreciation of the role of the laity in Church life, his extensive writings on spirituality have all played an essential role in contemporary theological discourse. Arguably, however, Newman's most original and significant contribution to thought is his contribution to epistemology. Thought about Truth pervades all of the works of Newman. His great

---

3 A. Dulles, *John Henry Newman* (London: Continuum, 2002).

Catholic treatise, *An Essay in Aid of a Grammar of Assent,* is his most systematic, but certainly not his first contribution to this area of discourse.[4] As stated above, Newman's obsession with the idea of Truth originated in the competing understandings of Truth inherent in the Church of his time. Newman's concern, as a pastor, was how to resolve these conflicts in order to facilitate discipleship and the full expression of Church in the life of the faithful.

Newman's creative contribution to epistemology has four distinct components. The first is the somewhat simplistic insight that Truth is complex. The second is that the pursuit of Truth is always imbued with a moral aspect, a place in a life of action. In other words, knowledge is not passive; it has consequences. The third is that Truth is a product not of individual and isolated reflection but of the life and vigour of the community. And the fourth is that Truth, in its ultimate sense, is a particular Christian Truth.

The Complexity of Truth

First, Truth is complex. Truth, for Newman, begins with the insight (for him a *phenomenological* insight) that nothing comes to us immediately and directly; we have to work for what we know. This is his first direct challenge to the simplistic subjectivist epistemologies of Reason and Emotion. For Newman, there are no instantaneous enlightenments. There are no Newtonian 'Eurekas!' or Wesleyan 'Alleluias!' Coming to know something is a practice that involves a great intricacy of insights, some rational and scientific, some historical, some emotional, and some whose origin may remain cloaked in mystery. In other words: 'The idea which represents an object or supposed object is commensurate with the sum total of its possible aspects, however they may vary in the separate consciousness of individuals.'[5] For Newman, this development involves a kind of peripatetic process, that is, a *purposeful* consideration and reconsideration of various points of view and opinions from various disciplines.

> Ordinarily an idea is not brought home to the intellect as objective except through *this variety*; like bodily substances, which are not apprehended except under the clothing of their properties and results, and which admit of being walked round, and surveyed on opposite

---

[4] The best commentary on this seminal work is T. Merrigan, *Clear Heads and Holy Hearts: The Religious and Theological Ideal of John Henry Newman* (Louvain: Peeters Press, 1991).

[5] J. H. Newman, *An Essay on the Development of Christian Doctrine* (London: Longmans, Green and Co., 1845), p. 35.

sides, and in different perspectives, and in contrary lights, in evidence of their reality.⁶

Newman equates such knowledge to the construction of a cable, whose fibres, taken separately, could never be strong enough to support anything, but which combined together are very strong indeed.

> We conceive by means of definition or description; whole objects do not create in the intellect whole ideas, but are, to use a mathematical phrase, thrown into series, into a number of statements, strengthening, interpreting, correcting each other, and with more or less exactness approximating, as they accumulate, to a perfect image.⁷

Truth, then for Newman is always the product of an elaborate process of construction, which Newman names the illative sense.

There is no one aspect deep enough to exhaust the contents of a real idea, no one term or proposition which will serve to define it; though of course one representation of it is more just and exact than another, and though when an idea is very complex, it is allowable, for the sake of convenience, to consider its distinct aspects as if separate ideas.⁸

The illative sense constructs knowledge through practice, an active and pursued process of intellection, and, indeed, of the whole person and, ultimately, of the whole community. For Newman this was a natural instinct in the human person. It is a kind of truth, of education, that extends beyond cognition and presses on to a reality that cannot be reduced to the simplistic categories of argumentation. As Newman says in *The Idea of a University*:

> We know, not by a direct and simple vision, not at a glance, but, as it were, by piecemeal and accumulation, by a mental process, by going round an object, by the comparison, the combination, the mutual correction, the continual adaptation, of many partial notions, by the employment, concentration and joint action of many faculties and exercises of the mind.⁹

The theological and pastoral implications of this insight are as follows: If this is the way Truth is attained, the process of preaching and teaching in the Church must somehow emulate and facilitate this process. The

---

6 Newman, *Essay on Development*, p. 35.
7 Newman, *Essay on Development*, p. 56.
8 Newman, *Essay on Development*, p. 36.
9 J. H. Newman, *The Idea of a University* (London: Longmans, Green and Co., 1852), p. 152.

Church must *practise* Truth in this way. Truth as a complex assemblage is in proportion to what Newman refers to as the actual state of things, which is understood in contrast to the *simplicity* of theory. There is a subtlety in the construction of Truth that is illusive to those who strive for facile answers. 'Divine Truth should be attained by so subtle and indirect a method, a method less tangible than others, less open to analysis, reducible but partially to the forms of Reason, and the ready sport of objection and cavil.'[10] Truth is complex because the world is complex and the God who created the world is complex and therefore, it is not only foolish but also futile to seek simple answers in the face of overwhelming complexity. Indeed, all simple and straightforward answers will be intuited by the person as shallow. Newman writes:

> It seems incredible that any men, who were really in earnest in their search after truth, should have begun with theorizing, or have imagined that a system which they were conscious they had invented almost without data, should happen, when applied to the actual state of things, to harmonize with the numberless and diversified phenomena of the world.[11]

Patience, then, is an essential element in the pursuit of truth. 'Rashness of assertion, hastiness in drawing conclusions, unhesitating reliance on our own acuteness and powers of reasoning, are inconsistent with the homage which nature exacts of those who would know her hidden wonders'[12] Newman asserts: 'Accordingly the Poet makes Truth the daughter of Time. Thus at length approximations are made to a right appreciation of transactions and characters. History cannot be written except in an after-age.'[13]

The Active Nature of Truth

Second, the acquisition of Truth for Newman is never passive, as the writing on a *tabula rasa*. Rather its primary conduit is always a sense of *earnestness* in the seeker. 'It is obvious that to be in earnest in seeking the truth is an indispensable requisite for finding it.'[14] The pursuit of Truth produces restlessness in the seeker that cannot be satisfied and yet the perception of the object as something great, indeed ultimate, gener-

---

10 J. H. Newman, *Fifteen Sermons Preached before the University of Oxford* (London: Longmans, Green and Co., 1868) p. 216.
11 Newman, *Fifteen Sermons*, p. 9.
12 Newman, *Fifteen Sermons*, pp. 9–10.
13 Newman, *Essay on Development*, p. 48.
14 Newman, *Essay on Development*, p. 8.

ates the energy for further pursuit. For Newman authentic ideas and truths must be what he termed 'living': 'When an idea, whether real or not, is of a nature to arrest and possess the mind, it may be said to have life, that is, to live in the mind which is its recipient.'[15]

The acquisition of Truth is never a purely cognitive pursuit but one that unfolds in every aspect of the human person fully alive. The witness of experience, the vicissitudes of youth, the example of other people, the chance encounter with nature, a powerful experience of art, the poetic imagination, all of these have the same power to inform as the premises of an argument. All of these things are assimilated over time, often in ways we control, manipulate and understand, but often as a result of simply *being in the world*. 'As fresh and fresh duties arise, or fresh and fresh faculties are brought into action, they are at once absorbed into the existing inward system, and take their appropriate place in it.'[16]

The strength of proof generated by this convergence does not admit to any (at least successful or determinative) attempt at analysis: 'First, every part of the Truth is novel to its opponent; and seen detached from the whole, becomes an objection.'[17] In other words what is grasped by this pursuit is only understood in its assemblage and attempts at analysis yield only failure and doubt. Like Truth, faith, for Newman, is a principle of action:

> Faith is a principle of action, and action does not allow time for minute and finished investigations. We may (if we will) think that such investigations are of high value; though, in truth, they have a tendency to blunt the practical energy of the mind, while they improve its scientific exactness; but, whatever be their character and consequences, they do not answer the needs of daily life.[18]

In other words, there is the necessity of the maintenance of a kind of tension that becomes the very hallmark of the pursuit. What is gained by education, by the pursuit of Truth, rather than *satisfying*, impels the seeker to greater heights and depths. The horizons change and develop over time so that there is a constant desire to pursue further. Tension, indeed, is the essence of Truth. The resolution of tension is a sign of error. Christianity is defined by tension. The central principles of Christianity, the incarnation and the redemptive act of the cross exemplify this tensile property. Attempts to appreciate these central principles *necessarily* maintain tension by denying resolution to questions and maintaining

---

15 Newman, *Essay on Development*, p. 37.
16 Newman, *Fifteen Sermons*, p. 82.
17 Newman, *Fifteen Sermons*, p. 89.
18 Newman, *Fifteen Sermons*, p. 189.

an endless hermeneutic stance that mirrors the depth of the object of its intellection, for Newman, the divine reality.

> It is indeed sometimes said that the stream is clearest near the spring. Whatever use may fairly be made of this image, it does not apply to the history of a philosophy or belief, which on the contrary is more equable, and purer, and stronger, when its bed has become deep, and broad, and full.[19]

Truth, for Newman, is contained not in argument alone but in the power of the Truth to *generate* moral action precisely by means of tension:

> On the other hand, that its real influence consists directly in some inherent moral power, in virtue in some shape or other, not in any evidence or criterion level to the undisciplined reason of the multitude, high or low, learned or ignorant, is implied in texts, such as those referred to just now: – I send you forth as sheep in the midst of wolves; *be ye, therefore*, wise as serpents, and harmless as doves.'[20]

Indeed the shortcoming of pure reason is the inability to work, to propel, to generate, and to inspire. No one was ever inspired to devote his or her life to a mere argument. For Newman, then, nothing can be perceived as true that does not have a consequence. If I say for example that I believe in God, that I have perceived, at some level, the Truth of the Deity, then I must act upon that in some way. I cannot have a passive faith just as I cannot have a passive education. There are no truths that are good *simply* to know. The perception of Truth changes lives; it necessitates conversion and movement, which, in turn, propels the learner, the believer toward increasing knowledge and Truth. Perceptions that arouse complacency or a mere satisfaction in knowing are not really the Truth for Newman. Finally, all of these activities and pursuits instil in the person a commitment to their further pursuit, a habit of the mind and of the personality:

> Whereas in him who is faithful to his own divinely implanted nature, the faint light of Truth dawns continually brighter; the shadows which at first troubled it, the unreal shapes created by its own twilight-state, vanish; what was as uncertain as mere feeling, and could not be distinguished from a fancy except by the commanding urgency of its voice,

---

19 Newman, *Essay on Development*, p. 41.
20 Newman, *Fifteen Sermons*, p. 79.

becomes fixed and definite, and strengthening into principle, it at the same time develops into habit.[21]

The Communal Nature of Truth

Third, for Newman, the pursuit of Truth always takes place within the context of the community. Just as it is never isolated in the mental capacity of the person, Truth, for Newman, is never privatized. It needs the presence of others to inspire and augment its development. It only thrives in a critical and mutually corrective atmosphere. It rejects pure subjectivism as a mode of knowing the Truth. Just as the perception of Truth necessitates action, so this action necessarily has ramifications in the life of the community. Here his stance is in direct opposition to that of the enthusiastic religion of his Evangelical contemporaries. There is no privatized Revelation or Truth. 'Truth is not the heritage of any individual, it is absolute and universal; mankind ought to seek and profess it in common.'[22] Indeed, for Newman, Truth can only be acquired in a living context. 'And others, not being able to acquiesce in the unimportance of doctrinal truth, yet perplexed at the difficulties in the course of human affairs, which follow on the opposite view, accustom themselves gratuitously to distinguish between their public and private duties, and to judge of them by separate rules.'[23]

Therefore, in Newman's estimation there is always the need to in a sense 'grow where one is planted'. That is to say, the community provides the proper ground for growth, and there is no need to look beyond it for confirmation of the Truth, yet un-revealed.

The Context of Faith in the Discovery of Truth

Finally, the fullness of Truth is manifested in the active living of a life of faith. Secular learning and institutions of education can benefit from Newman's insights on epistemology only to a certain point because Newman was convinced that the fullness of Truth is not open to all. Indeed, 'She refuses to reveal her mysteries to those who come otherwise than in the humble and reverential spirit of learners and disciples.'[24] Truth, however, is instinctual in the hearts of those who believe and practise their faith. 'Nay, such confessors have a witness even in the breasts of those who oppose them, an instinct originally from God, which may indeed be perverted into a hatred, but scarcely into an utter disregard of the Truth,

---

21 Newman, *Fifteen Sermons*, p. 82.
22 Newman, *Essay on Development*, p. 51.
23 Newman, *Fifteen Sermons*, p. 131.
24 Newman, *Fifteen Sermons*, p. 10.

when exhibited before them.'[25] Faith, Christian belief *and* practice, however, are not to be understood as another aspect of knowledge, or even of the highest knowledge. For Newman, the insight of Christianity is the epistemological ground of knowledge. For Newman the object of pursuit in the context of Christian faith is the Truth of the divine reality, the central aspect of which is the matter and form of revelation. God as divine reality is, in Newman's estimation, not only the source of Truth but also the only goal of Truth finally worth pursuit. This in no way denigrates any other branch or discipline of learning, in fact it enhances the disciplines by making them essential components in the construction of the Great Truth, the divine reality. But herein lies the paradox for Newman. The nature of this divine reality is its very inexhaustibility, that is, what we know when we know God is the infinite itself and pursuit of God is the ultimate pursuit in that it can never be exhausted. What it yields is the same paradox one encounters in education. For the educated person, the more one knows, the more one knows what one does not know. The horizons shift and the pursuit is endless. The paradox of God is the same. The more the believer 'knows' God, the greater, deeper and broader the divine reality becomes. God is not something to be grasped, rather God is the energy, as it were, of grasping, one with which to be in relationship. '[This pursuit of God] becomes an active principle within [believers], leading them to an ever-new contemplation of itself, to an application of it in various directions, and a propagation of it on every side.'[26] The Truth here sometimes yields paradoxical and parabolic contradictions that can, nevertheless, be held in perfect tension because of the nature of the Truth pursued. In this way, the incarnation, with its inherent and irresolvable tension, becomes the central teaching of Christianity, the core of its life.

In this sense I should myself call the incarnation the central aspect of Christianity, out of which the three main aspects of its teaching take their rise, the sacramental, the hierarchical and the ascetic.

In the above we see the full force of Newman's complicated epistemology. I know that I know, an artistic or poetic knowing that is not reducible to easy categorizations. All Truth is poetical for Newman. Even the sciences are poetical in that they are supersaturated with meaning, a meaning that cannot be reduced to simple analyses or formulae.

The Truth that living a life of Christian faith yields is not the product of academic or even intellectual reflection alone. Rather, it is open and part of the faith *experience* of every Christian person. 'No irreligious man can know any thing concerning the hidden saints. Next, no one,

---

25 Newman, *Fifteen Sermons*, pp. 135–6.
26 Newman, *Essay on Development*, p. 37.

religious or not, can detect them without attentive study of them. But, after all, say they are few, such high Christians; and what follows? They are enough to carry on God's noiseless work.'[27]

Newman also requests that we:

> Next, consider the extreme rarity, in any great perfection and purity, of simple-minded, honest devotion to God; and another instrument of influence is discovered for the cause of Truth. Men naturally prize what is novel and scarce; and, considering the low views of the multitude on points of social and religious duty, their ignorance of those precepts of generosity, self-denial, and high-minded patience, which religion enforces, nay, their scepticism (whether known to themselves or not) of the existence in the world of severe holiness and truth, no wonder they are amazed when accident gives them a sight of these excellences in another, as though they beheld a miracle; and they watch it with a mixture of curiosity and awe.[28]

For Newman, all Christian theology begins with these fundamental epistemological insights. All *practice* in the Church must be faithful to them. In the next section, Newman's famed preaching style will be examined in relation to the above reflections in the hope that what emerges is a vision of Church that is faithful to the Truth it celebrates.

Newman the Preacher

Newman was, of course, one of the great preachers in the history of the Church. As an Anglican pastor, he preached almost every Sunday from the time he was ordained until his retirement to Littlemore in 1843. 'The church was full when Newman preached, thronged usually by not less than five or six hundred graduates, besides other members of the congregation.'[29] A pronounced sense of clarity defined Newman's homiletic style. 'Newman's sermons are distinguished not for vague platitudes and pious aspirations, but for their utter concreteness and definiteness.'[30] This is especially true of the imaginative way in which Newman handled his texts. He was quite calculating in the presentation of his images and the dependability of his structure. The sermons, in their attention to structure and the careful handling of language, had the quality of

---

27 Newman, *Fifteen Sermons*, p. 97.
28 Newman, *Fifteen Sermons*, p. 93.
29 Robert D. Middleton, 'The Vicar of Saint Mary's', in G. Wheeler (ed.), *Newman Centenary Essays* (London: Burns, Oates and Washbourne Ltd, 1745), p. 130.
30 Ian Ker, *The Achievement of John Henry Newman* (Notre Dame: University of Notre Dame Press, 1990), p. 76.

poetry.[31] This might be seen as a concrete expression of Newman's conviction that religion was primarily poetical.[32]

The Structure of Newman's Preaching

Newman invariably structured his sermons in the same way. The exposition section of every sermon presents a dilemma, a problem to be resolved in the context of the life of the Church. These dilemmas vary widely from sermon to sermon, but Newman was determined they must be made in some way *real* to the hearers. This presentation of a dilemma in the form of two terms or two images was Newman's starting point. In the second part of each sermon he expanded upon the basic dilemma using vivid word-pictures, which, although drawn from the biblical texts, were invariably set up to link the historical discourse with the situation in the Church of Newman's time. This was Newman's opportunity to demonstrate that he knew his hearers, sometimes uncomfortably well.

Approaching the sermons of Newman, one notices the number of linguistic devices he employed. These devices were engaged to lure the hearer into the parabolic discourse. They had the power not only to engage the hearer but at times even to shock. One of these devices was the *use of binaries and trinaries*. He placed two or three terms together, drawing dramatic images and inviting comparison, yet remaining vague about the way the terms actually fit together. In fact, almost all of Newman's sermons deal with an underlying primordial binary, the connection between the 'real' and the 'unreal'.[33] Often in Newman's sermons, these binaries and trinaries are introduced and are either left unresolved or they are resolved in the context of the introduction of a further confounding element. It remained the task of the hearers to discover how these elements were connected.

A second device Newman frequently employed was that of *hypertextuality*. He used a word in two different ways or chose a word that had a variety of meanings and which was likely to lead the hearer down completely different paths. He frequently employed an image that invoked a response and expanded the possible horizons of meaning for the hearer. For example, Newman may use the word 'novel' in a way that evokes both the idea of a written work and a new thing, leaving the hearer to work out the way in which the word is employed.

---

31 See Paul Vaiss, 'Art de la persuasion et rhétorique chez Newman', *Etudes Newmaniennes* 10 (1994), pp. 83–94.

32 'Revealed Religion should be especially poetical – and it is so in fact.' Newman, *Select Treatises of St. Athanasius*, 2 vols (London: Longmans, Green and Co., 1868–81), I, p. 23.

33 Ker, *Achievement*, p. 79.

A third device was Newman's use of *temporal adaptability,* that is, replacement of elements of the sermon by means of the evocation of a historical allusion that illustrated the sermon's purpose and which led the hearer into further parallels, particularly with contemporary situations, without the benefit of further development by the preacher. This was one of Newman's most frequently employed devices and was useful not only in the sermons but in the discursive writings as well. For example, Newman may employ the word 'Arian' in a certain way that means, *at one and the same time,* both the heretics of the fourth century and modern thinkers who deny the divinity of Christ.

Another device used by Newman was the persistent counsel for patience on the part of the hearers.[34] Indeed, patience and its concomitant theme of regularity became a significant theme in Newman's sermons. He counselled, 'Nothing is more difficult than to be disciplined and regular in our religion.'[35] Too much of religion, in Newman's estimation, was governed by 'fits and starts', themselves the products of a presumptuous 'Fancy' and emotionalism. The key to the right appropriation of religious truth was dissociation with all excitements. In patience and perseverance, religion has the opportunity to operate on the imagination. 'Is not holiness the result of many patient, repeated efforts after obedience, gradually working on us, and first modifying and then changing our hearts?'[36] Newman shunned every kind of immediate resolution to religious dilemmas, although he recognized the propensity of Christians to jump to conclusions and ready-made solutions. In the *Oxford University Sermons* he writes: 'Modesty, patience, and caution, are dispositions of mind quite as requisite in philosophical inquiries as seriousness and earnestness, though not so obviously requisite.'[37] Repeatedly in the sermons, Newman warns against too facile a concretization of the truths of Christianity.

A final and crucial device employed by Newman was one that cannot be gained from reading the sermons, namely Newman's frequent and purposeful use of *pauses,* '. . . which sometimes lasted long enough to thrill his hearers to an almost unbearable degree.'[38] It was an element that Ker

---

34 See Ramon Mas, 'Parole et silence chez Newman', *Etudes Newmaniennes* 10 (1994) pp. 43–52. See also R. Michael Olson, 'Newman's Patient Mind', *The Newman Rambler* 5, no. 2 (2001).

35 Newman, *Parochial and Plain Sermons,* 8 vols (London: Longmans, Green and Co., 1868–81), I, p. 252.

36 Newman, *Parochial and Plain Sermons,* I, p. 11.

37 Newman, *Fifteen Sermons,* p. 10.

38 Archbishop Temple quoted in Middleton, 'The Vicar of St Mary's', p. 131. See also Maurice Montabrut, 'Newman, éloquence du silence et fécondité de la parole selon Coventry Patmore', *Etudes Newmaniennes* 17 (2001), pp. 135–42. See also Olson, 'Newman's Patient Mind'.

ascribes to Newman's 'sheer intensity of thought.'[39] It was certainly not an element introduced by Newman for mere effect. Newman was almost immune to the impact of the dramatic gesture.[40] He was not interested in promoting the theatrical qualities of the preacher. He was consistently and doggedly interested in the impact of *words* on the hearer.[41]

Observing this complicated series of devices, it is possible to see how Newman inculcated a sense of involvement on the congregation's part in his homiletic technique. The role of the preacher in this method is the introduction of images real, rich and varied that at least initially might confound the hearer with their dizzying interplay of relationships. The preacher chooses the images carefully.[42] The insight of the preacher comes from a sense of pastoral involvement in the life of the community. In other words, the preacher knows how to approach the unveiling and realization of the images because there has been an investment in the life of the community. Preaching, for Newman did not take place in a generic setting and Newman's preoccupation with, and sense of inadequacy to his pastoral task offer keen insight into this assertion.[43] Having presented the various images, using a variety of techniques, Newman employed the pause to give his hearers the chance to process the material before the introduction of the next element. Finally, the sermons are, for the most part, left *open at the end*. Occasionally there is a sense in reading the sermons of Newman that there is an element missing. The hearer/reader must supply the missing element. Newman employed the image of an inventory to discuss the way in which the Church deals with religious ideas. 'All is given to us in profusion; it remains for us to catalogue, sort, distribute, select, harmonize, and complete.'[44] This 'inductive' methodology demonstrates that Newman placed a great deal of confidence in the community to manage and assimilate the images into a meaningful whole.[45] This is what Newman was later to describe as 'enlargement' or the development of the religious self.[46]

---

39 Ker, *Achievement*, p. 75.

40 See Jacques Coupet, 'Newman écrivain de sermons', *Etudes Newmaniennes* 10 (1994), pp. 5–22.

41 See D. M. Whalen, 'John Henry Newman: The Rhetoric and the Real', *Nineteenth-Century Prose* 8, no. 2 (1991), pp. 1–9.

42 For a complete treatment of economy and reserve in Newman see Robin Selby, *The Principle of Reserve in the Writings of John Henry Cardinal Newman* (Oxford: Oxford University Press, 1975). See also James Gaffney, 'Newman on the Common Roots of Morality and Religion', *The Journal of Religious Ethics* I (1988), pp. 143–59.

43 For Newman's various pastoral perspectives, see Dermot Fenlon, 'The Aristocracy of Talent and the Mystery of Newman', *Louvain Studies* 15 (1990), pp. 203–25.

44 Newman, *The Via Media* (London: Longmans, Green and Co., 1868–81), I, p. 23.

45 An excellent account of the inductive methodology in modern homiletic theory can be found in Fred B. Craddock, *Preaching* (Nashville: Abingdon Press, 1990).

46 Brinkman, 'Newman's Personal Principle at its Source', in Gerard Magill (ed.), *Per-*

The Centrality of Christology in the Sermons

All of Newman's homiletic devices and methodology were directed to a central purpose, to unveil the mystery of the Incarnation.[47] For him, 'the preacher's aim was to present the person of Christ not in an "unreal way – as a mere idea or vision," but as "Scripture has set Him before us in His actual sojourn on earth, in His gestures, words and deeds."'[48] It was to present Christ in the full crisis of his being God and Human at once.[49] In this way the incarnation is firmly wedded to the ongoing life of the Church. 'Henceforth He is the one principle of life in all His servants, who are but His organs.'[50] Three important expressions of the Christological imperative were interwoven in the sermons of Newman.

The first theme in Newman's sermons is the identity of Jesus as the God-Man. 'Several times in his writing Newman presented the humanity and divinity of Christ antithetically.'[51] Newman was eager to preach the full humanity of Jesus expressly as a soteriological truth. Newman perceived the mystery of the incarnation to be more overwhelming than that of the Trinity.[52] Language could not adequately express the mystery of the God-Man. It was a mystery that Newman considered as necessarily possessed of so many various and contrary attributes that it defied *definition* and invited *engagement*.[53]

A second significant theme in Newman's homiletic Christology is that of the cross of Christ. This can be discerned in the Lenten sermons of Newman found in the *Parochial and Plain Sermons*. In 'The Incarnate Son, a Sufferer and Sacrifice', Newman holds to his usual pattern. The initial dilemma is presented in the juxtaposition of the 'form of God' and the 'humbling of himself' found in Philippians 2.8. He uses this passage to make a few remarks 'upon that dreadful, yet most joyful event, that passion and death of our Lord'.[54] This use of the binary points to Newman's ultimate concern for *realizing* the irony of the cross in the life of believers. The cross presents for modern Christians the same dilemma of being 'folly and scandal' and, at the same moment, source of salvation.

---

sonality and Belief: Interdisciplinary Essays on John Henry Newman (Lanham: University Press of America, 1990), pp. 75–88.

47 See F. Morrone, 'L'incarnazione nel pensiero cristologico di Newman,' *Rassegna di Teologia* 33 (1992), pp. 315–32.

48 Ker, *Achievement*, p. 83.

49 Newman, *Parochial and Plain Sermons*, III, pp. 165ff.

50 Newman, *Lectures on the Doctrine of Justification*, (London: Longmans, Green and Co., 1868–81), p. 196.

51 Roderick Strange, *Newman and the Gospel of Christ* (Oxford: Oxford University Press, 1981), p. 55.

52 Newman, *Parochial and Plain Sermons*, III, pp. 165–6.

53 Newman, *Parochial and Plain Sermons*, III, p. 169.

54 Newman, *Parochial and Plain Sermons*, VI, p. 70.

However, for Newman the true nature of the human being was to live in the very tension and fecundity of this problem. To attempt to escape the tensile reality is a natural by-product of the fall. To live within the very *crisis* of the *cross* is to live a graced, if 'problematic' life. Such a life does not admit, in the final analysis, to the cold scrutiny of Reason nor the obviousness of evangelical enthusiasm. It is an assurance in no assurance, a certainty in the lack of certainty, an investment in a way of life that is fully *way* and not destination.

> And as the doctrine of the Cross, though it be the true interpretation of this world, is not prominently manifested in it, upon its surface, but is concealed; so again, when received into the faithful heart, there it abides as a living principle, but deep, and hidden from observation.[55]

The last way in which Newman expressed the Christological imperative inherent in the sermons was in his theme of the hiddenness of Christ. His Christmas sermon of 1837, 'Christ Hidden from the World', provides an eloquent exposé of this theme.[56] The sermon was developed in a prologue and four sections. The prologue relates the essential tension in the subject matter of the day, the incarnation of Christ. This was presented in terms of the binary found in the text from the prologue of John, 'The light shineth in the darkness, and the darkness comprehended it not.' The opening lines allude to the obscurity of Christ, which was a feature of his earthly sojourn. Although seen by all, he remained shrouded in mystery by virtue of his hiddenness. Furthermore, this hiddenness was an attribute Christ assumed deliberately. His hiddenness was a quality that baffled even those closest to him, that is, his family members and his disciples. 'Have I been so long time with you, and yet thou has not known Me, Philip?' Leaving the perplexity of this allusion in the balance, Newman then proceeds in the next three sections, to expound upon this parabolic situation by an appeal to the terms of the parable, the first being the humanity of Christ. Here he draws on the very ordinariness of the human term of the Incarnation, the poverty of Mary and Joseph, Jesus' lowly trade, and his obscurity from the public eye for 30 years of his life. Juxtaposed to these simple and homey images, Newman introduces the full force of the parabolic discourse. 'That little babe, so born, so placed, is none other than the Creator of heaven and earth, the Eternal Son of God.'[57] Newman allows the impact of this

---

55 Newman, *Parochial and Plain Sermons*, VI, p. 88. See Ian Ker, *Healing the Wound of Humanity: The Spirituality of John Henry Newman* (London: Darton, Longman and Todd, 1993).
56 Newman, *Parochial and Plain Sermons*, IV, pp. 239ff.
57 Newman, *Parochial and Plain Sermons*, III, p. 241.

assertion to exact its effect, and returns to expounding the theme of the confusion that surrounded the person of Jesus. This confusion was not limited to the years of his private life, but extended as well to his public ministry. Here Newman engages the device of temporal adaptability by drawing the contemporary audience into the parable by likening them to the apostles who '. . . had lived so long with Him, and yet did not know Him'.[58]

The various images and ways of approaching Christological *reality* for Newman amounted, in their variety, to an expression of the parabolic imperative. 'Here one image corrects another; and the accumulation of images is not, as is often thought, the restless and fruitless effort of the mind to *enter into the Mystery,* but is a *safeguard* against any one image, nay, any collection of images being supposed adequate.'[59]

Drawing Some Conclusions

Truth and the Incarnation

For Newman, Truth and the incarnation are intimately bound together. Truth is complex because the source of Truth, the incarnate Word is a complex reality that necessitates a relationship in order to delve into that complexity. Christian discipleship is not a matter of questions and answers or one-dimensional 'solutions' to existential or social problems, but, rather, a complex interaction between the divine and the human, between pastors and congregations, and between individuals and communities. The question of Church cannot be 'ironed out' for Newman. Rather, it must be lived out. Preaching, liturgy, catechesis and, indeed, all aspects of the life of the Church must replicate this complexity, using various devices (such as Newman's homiletic techniques) to instil in congregations the need to *be Church* rather than to understand the question of Church. This active being Church was what Newman termed the 'sense of the faithful', an idea that has often been misunderstood in post-conciliar theology. In Newman's estimation, the Truth about Christ could only be manifested when the faithful live their true vocations. It is important to note that by 'faithful' here, Newman is not implying the laity on their own, but rather, the laity living, praying, worshipping and serving *with their pastors and bishops*. The warrant for this communal sense comes from the Incarnation. The divine reality of Christ is the source of all human reality and community, even if unacknowledged. The full manifestation of this divine reality, however, is not something

---

58 Newman, *Parochial and Plain Sermons*, III, p. 242.
59 Newman, *Select Treatises of St. Athanasius*, II, pp. 444-5.

that is merely given from 'on high' by an act of private revelation or by the teachings of the hierarchy. Rather, it is 'worked out' in the messy context of all of these praying and thinking together to give witness to the Truth of God.

Communio in Newman's model is, therefore, akin to that of the third model provided in the first section of this chapter. For Newman, *communio* was the dynamic interaction of the vertical and horizontal manifestations of divine Truth, something given from above, yet fully realized below. In this model, human communities can never be understood apart from their divine origins. Likewise, the fruitful interaction of the people of God in their earthly realities is necessary to give more faithful witness to the divine gift. The radical subjectivity which is a danger of the extreme 'horizontal' and 'vertical' models of Church presented since Vatican II is overcome in Newman's model by a radical intersubjectivity, both human and divine that makes for a complex, sometimes mysterious, but always living and growing image of the Church.

Challenges for Today

As was the case in Newman's age, today we live very often in what seems like a Church of 'parties'. Points of view are seen as dogmatical. The 'liberal' party in the Church has slowly been evolving a particular vocabulary for speaking theologically. The authentic Magisterium of the Church has been challenged by an alternative 'conservative' magisterium. The result is that the authentic teachers of the Church (and, indeed, the majority of the faithful) have been relegated to yet another party in the cacophony of voices heard, but not listened to in contemporary Church life. The liturgical life of the local church is frequently the battleground upon which these internecine wars are waged, the pulpit a prominent bunker in this pocked landscape. As in Newman's time, the complexity of the Church as been reduced to simple categorisations, horizontal and vertical models. Ecclesiology has become isolated from other theological disciplines to the detriment of all.

Newman viewed the incarnation as the source of all Truth and reality. Nothing was real that did not take the incarnation into account. Furthermore, all aspects of the life of faith, including the nature of the Church, theology, worship, religious education, etc., must be faithful *in their individual natures,* to the nature of the divine reality from which they proceed and by which they are given life. In other words, all reality in the life of faith must replicate the tensile reality inherent in the incarnation, the need for a perpetual re-examination and fruitful, dynamic interaction between the vertical and the horizontal. Without the tension, individual and subjective isolationism will result. *The* Church becomes *my* Church. Some commentators have referred to this phenomenon as 'cafeteria Catholicism'. Newman's preaching took this danger seriously and this imperative into account. In its method and mode of presentation, preaching should inculcate the incarnation. It should engage the Church as a horizontal reality (hearers) in a living vertical relationship with God. Newman used an inductive preaching method to instil this reality. In his estimation, it lead the faithful, not to facile answers, which they would have intuited as somehow unsuited to the awesomeness of the Truth of God, but to a *relationship* with God, with Christ, with the Church, the Scriptures, doctrine and one another. This leads the faithful ever deeper into the mystery of God, not understood as something unknowable, but as a person who is infinitely knowable and with whom the Church is in relationship and from whom it takes its existence.

But one aspect of Revelation must not be allowed to exclude or to obscure another; and Christianity is dogmatical, devotional, practical all at once; it is esoteric and exoteric; it is indulgent and strict; it is light and dark; it is love, and it is fear.[60]

One of the problems of Church life in the period after the Council has been a pronounced lack of subtlety. This lack of subtlety has been experienced in many ways. Liturgically it has been experienced in a desire to make the liturgy 'relevant' in the context of the modern world. The employment of modern musical idioms, the removal of 'antiquated' ornaments in churches, the 'simplification' and 'explanation' of the rich symbolic language inherent in the liturgy, rather than making the worship of the Church more meaningful, seems, at times, to have had the opposite effect, removing a sense of contact with the transcendent reality that worship should create. Preaching is one dimensional, focusing horizontally on social issues or moral imperatives. The sacrificial language of the Eucharist has been completely dismissed in favour of a 'meal-based' approach. The Mass has become, in some places, a friendly Sunday picnic. The cult of relevance has created a situation in which the 'horizontal' dimension of *communio* crowds out the vertical. The public life of the Church has been sanitized of God, Mystery and the transcendent.

On the other hand, some who perceive this impoverishment of Church life since the Council have advocated a reversal of gears. They see the answer to the Church's current situation in a going back to older formulae and models of worship. Some even go so far as to criticize the authentic Magisterium in its attempts to re-align the Church's liturgical life in more contemporary forms. In this mode of thinking the 'vertical' and the sacrificial are the only authentic metaphors for liturgical reality. Preaching must be clear and dogmatic, telling congregations what they

---

60 Newman, *Select Treatises of St. Athanasius*, II, p. 37.

must believe and, in some ways, treating them as passive recipients of delivered dogmas.

Joseph Cardinal Ratzinger commented in the 1992 document of the Congregation for the Doctrine of Faith, *Communio Notis,* that, 'If the concept of communion, which is not a univocal concept, is to serve as a key to ecclesiology, it has to be understood within the teaching of the Bible and the patristic tradition, in which communion always involves a double dimension: the *vertical* (communion with God) and the *horizontal* (communion among men).'[61] Such a notion is in keeping with Newman's incarnational imperative. The question remaining for us is how to make it a living reality in the life of the Church's preaching, worshipping, praying and service. It will not happen if professional theologians and pastors continue to seek to present the faith in 'sound bites', in hyperbole, and in other easily media digested forms. It will only happen when the faithful, in all their complexity are determined to live the life of faith in its fullness. Newman, over a century ago offered a particular model that might be helpful for the struggling Church today.

---

61 *Communio Notis,* 3.

Index of Names

Abbot, Walter M. xvi n4, 17 n3
Adorno, T.W. and G. 6–8
Aeschylus 221
Altizer, Thomas J. J. xviii
Amiot, François 155 n6
Andronikof, Constantin 33
Anselm of Canterbury 26
Aquinas, Thomas xi, xii, 15, 19, 26, 27, 43, 154, 155–71, 197, 229, 233–40
Aristotle 20, 21, 116, 133 n5, 154, 221
Augustine of Hippo 22, 23, 117, 133 n7, 154, 159 n26, 165, 168, 175–6, 198, 199, 202 n1, 228 n8, 230 n11

Balthasar, Hans Urs von 24, 30, 132, 134 n12, 244
Barker, M. 14 n26
Barron, Robert 17–31
Barth, Karl xvii, 23, 24, 228, 229, 230 n10, 241
Beckett, C. 42
Bellah, Robert N. 102 n58,
Benedict of Nursia 61, 63
Berger, David 156 n8, 158 n17, 160 n30
Berger, Peter 145, 152
Bianchi, Ugo 210 n35
Bleeker, C. Jouco 210
Bolton, C.A. 5 n12
Bonaccorso, Giorgio 32 n2, 33 n6
Bonhoeffer, Dietrich xvii

Bourne, Cardinal F.A. 14 n27
Bouyer, Louis 170 n76
Brinkman 256 n46
Bruce, Steve xvii
Buhle, P. 32 n2
Busani, G. 32 n2

Caesarion, Romanus 156
Cambiano, Giuseppe 221, 222 n80
Caprioli, A. 37 n17
Carr, Ephrem 43 n41
Cardita, Angelo M.S. 32–56
Carmelo, L. 38 n20
Carrol, William 167 n64
Casel, Odo 2, 152
Chapman, Mark xviii n8
Chauvet, Louis-Marie 32 n2, 54, 55 n76, 236, 238–9
Clement of Alexandria 133 n7, 206, 209
Clerck, Paul de 32 n1
Connolly, Robert Hugh 211 n38
Coquin, René-Georges 212 n40
Corrigan, Kevin 167 n64
Coverdale, Miles 128
Cox, Harvey 144
Craddock, Fred B. 256 n45
Cravieri, M. 209 n32
Crosby, John F. 94 n51, 95
Cruz, Juan Cruz 155 n3
Cupitt, Donald 18
Cusa, Nicholaus of 26
Cyril of Jerusalem 199, 210–11, 220, 225

INDEX OF NAMES

Descartes, René 1, 10, 18, 39, 229
Devreesse, R. 212 n41
Dix, Gregory 137 n4-7
Dobszay, László 13 n25, 57-73
Dooyeweerd, Herman 87 n34, 101 n57, 102 n58-60
Dostoyevsky, Fyodor 24
Dulles, Avery 245
Joseph Dunne 17 n1
Dunne, M. 155 n4
Durkheim, Emil 135, 136 n21
Dymock, James 128, 131

Echeverria, Eduardo J. xi, 74-113
Emery, Gilles 158
Ephrem the Syrian 175, 176, 178 n20, 199
Erasmus of Rotterdam 118
Erbetta, M. 203 n5-7, 204 n8
Euvé, F. 132, 134 n12, 152

Fenlon, Dermot 256 n43
Festugière, André-Jean 46 n47, 221 n76, n77, n79, 222 n82-86
Feuerbach, L. 34-6
Finberg, H.P.R. 122, 130
Fink, Eugen 152
Fischer, Balthasar 174 n7
Fortescue, Adrian 14, 121, 126, 130
Foster, Reginald 173 n6
Foxe, John 128, 131
Fraijó, M. 35 n10
Frei, Hans 24
Frobenius, Leo 135, 152

Gaffney, James 256 n42
Gallagher, David 155 n3-4
George, Marie 170 n76
Gigon, André-Charles 156 n9
Giussani, Luigi 75 n4, 78 n13, 79 n16
Gother, John 125, 131
Gregory of Nazianzen 133 n7

Guardini, Romano 32 n2, 75 n4, 79, 80, 84, 109, 110 n72, 113 n78, 132, 134, 137-40, 145, 149, 152, 154
Guiver, George 48 n49

Hahne, Werner 149, 152
Handelman, Don 152, 153
Harbert, Bruce 114-31
Hemmerle, K. 149, 153
Hemming, Laurence Paul 1-16, 227 n4
Hobbes, Thomas 22
Huizinga, J. 132 n2, 134-5, 136 n18, 141-2, 144, 146, 153
Husenbeth, Frederick Charles 121, 123, 125, 130
Hyman, Gavin xviii

Ilyes, Zsolt 132-53
Irenaeus of Lyon 28, 180, 183, 199, 208-11

Jacob of Serugh 178, 199
John Chrysostom 117, 133 n7, 170, 210, 213-14, 215 n56-58, 217-20
Jüngel, E. 32 n1, 36 n1

Kant, Emmanuel 6-8, 18, 23, 133 n9, 144, 159 n20
Ker, Ian 253 n30, 254 n33, 255, 256 n39, 257 n48, 258 n55
Knox, Ronald 122, 125, 131
Kretschmar, Georg 205 n11
Kwasniewski, Peter A. 154-71

Leachman, James G. xiv-xx, 172-200
Leeper, Elizabeth A. 206, 210
Leo the Great 118
Lévinas, Emmanuel 18, 38, 39, 41-2 n36
Lindbeck, George 14, 37, 231
Little, Joyce 104

INDEX OF NAMES

Locke, John 22, 229 n9
Lubac, Henri de 79 n14, 87, 88 n36

McAdam Erb, Heather 170 n76
McCarthy, Daniel P. 132, 172–200, 201
McEvoy, James 155 n4
MacIntyre, Alistair 17 n2
Macquarrie, John M. xv–xix, 32 n2
Maestri, G. 215 n58, 216 nn60–2, 225
Marion, Jean-Luc 28 n18, 38–42, 42 n36
Maritain, Jacques 46 n47, 87
Mas, Ramon 255 n34
Mazza, Enrico 201–24
Merrigan, T. 246 n4
Mersch, Emile 158 n16, 166 n 56, 58
Maesneer, Yves De 6, 7 n14–16, 8 n 17–18
Metz, Johann-Baptist 243
Meyer, Hans Bernhard 149
Milbank, John xviii, 23 n12, 230 n12, 236, 240
Moltmann, Jürgen 132, 135, 139, 149, 228, 230, 231 n17, 232, 235, 240 n46
Montabrut, Maurice 255 n38
Montini, (Giovanni Battista) Pope Paul VI xviii, 123 n48, 130
Moore, Gerard 184 n23
Moore, Sebastian 164
Mossé, C. 221 n78
Mourão, J. A. 33 n5

Newman, John Henry 242–62
Nichols, Aidan ix, 5 n12, 74 n2, 81–3, 93 n50
Nietzsche, Friedrich 1, 7, 8, 18–19, 39, 133 n9
Nola, Alfonso M. di 172

Oliver, Simon 226–41

O'Connor, Flannery 21
O'Neill, Colman 158 n17

Padinjatummury, J. 153
Pannenberg, Walter 141, 145, 153
Parsons, Susan Frank ix
Paus, Ansgar 132, 141, 143, 144, 146–7, 153
Pius X, Pope (Giuseppe Sarto) 118
Pius XII, Pope (Eugenio Pacelli) 4–6, 8, 13 n25, 15, 118, 122
Plato 20, 21, 38, 133 n5, 146, 148, 153
Platten, Stephen xvii n8
Preston, Geoffrey 163 n43
Prosper of Aquitaine 15 n28

Rahner, Hugo 132, 134, 142, 146
Rahner, Karl 24, 36, 51–4, 144, 149–50, 151 n42, 228, 230, 244
Ramos, Alice 170 n76
Ratzinger (Joseph), Pope Benedict XVI ix, xix, xx, 1, 5, 6, 19, 25, 74–94, 110–12, 141, 148, 153, 154, 159–61, 163 n43, 165 n50, 182 n22, 226, 238 n40, 244, 262
Reali, N. 36 n15
Reid, Alcuin 168 n67
Ricci, Scipio de 5
Ricoeur, Paul 38–9
Robinson, Denis 242–62
Robinson, John xvii
Rousseau, A. 180 n21, 199, 209 n28–30
Rouvillois, Samuel 42–4

Sagnard, F. 206 n13, n15, n17, n18, 207 n20, n24, 208 n27, 213 n43, 219 n71, 225
Sartre, Jean-Paul 18–20, 85 n31, 133 n3, n9, 141
Saward, John xx n13, 74 n2, 141 n30, 153, 157 n12, 226 n1
Saxer, Victor 28, 215 n58, 220

265

INDEX OF NAMES

Scheeben, Mattias 158 n16
Schleiermacher, Edward 24, 34–5, 243
Schillebeeckx, E. 32 n2, 163 n43
Scruton, Roger 75, 85 n31
Segelberg, E. 207 n21, 209, 210 n33
Séguy, J. 32 n2
Shakespeare, William 24
Sokolowski, Robert 2, 26 n16, 90 n42, 91–2
Strange, Roderick 257 n51

Tagliaferri, Roberto 32 n2, 138, 153
Tena, P. 32 n2
Terrin, Aldo Natale 34 n7, 25 n9, 132, 138, 145, 147, 153
Theodore of Mopsuestia 210, 212–14, 219–20, 224
Theodotus 206–8, 211, 216, 219, 225
Thomas Aquinas, St 12, 15, 19, 26, 27, 43, 154–71, 197 n30, 229, 233–40
Tillich, Paul 23, 24
Tonneau, R. 212 n41, 233 n42–46, 218 n70

Torrell, Jean-Pierre 157 n12, 168 n68
Turner, Denys 161 n35
Turner, Paul 174 n7
Turner, Philip 82 n23
Tyrer, J. W. 211 n38

Ubbiali, S. 34 n7, 36 n15, 37

Vagaggini, Cipriano 32, 33
Vaiss, Paul 254 n31
Valentinus 206, 210
Verdeyen, Paul 3–5

Wahlen, D. M. 256 n41
Weinandy, Thomas 156–7, 234 n24
Wenger, A. 213 n48, 214 n49, 215 n56–58, 217 n63–66, 218 n67–69, 220 n74
Winkler, Gabrielle 203
Wittgenstein, Ludwig 17, 134
Wojtyla (Karol), Pope John Paul II xviii–xx, 72, 74–5, 79–80, 86–9, 93–6, 98, 103 n61, 105–13

Zan, Renato de 173 n6

Index of Scriptural References

Genesis
1—3   94
1.27   103
1.31   89
3.14–15   88, 89
18.12   185
26.8   133 n6

Exodus
26.26   76

Numbers
23.23   117 n14

Deuteronomy
6.4   25

1 Samuel
2.11   117 n17
2.18   117 n17
3.1   117 n17

2 Samuel
6.1–5   133 n6

1 Kings
17.13   28

1 Chronicles
23.28   117 n15
26.30   117 n16

Psalms
42   60, 192
135   117 n23

Proverbs
8.26–27a ??
30—31   133 n6

Song of Songs
168   ??

Ezekiel
1.4–6   133 n6
11—24   133 n6

Zechariah
8.4–5   133 n6

Wisdom
5.5   189
32.15–16 133 n6

Matthew
6.24   142
16.24–25 109
18.3   133 n6
22.14   189
25.40   108
25.45   108

Mark
4.28   77
10.47   19

Luke
1.23   114
1.29   185
1.41   185
1.46   185
12.49   165

John
1.14   183
3.5   186
6.64   165
6.57   169
8.23   186
9   188
11.1–42   142, 192
44   142, 192
12.32   226 n2
13.34   104
14.6   108, 178
14.9   107
15.13–15 168
16.17   107
16.21   185
17.20–26 230

Acts
6.7   184
12.24   184
13.2   117
17.23   11
18.25   190

Romans
5.5   104, 107
6.4–5   11 n21, 180
6.8   158
13. 14   178

1 Corinthians
1.1   18
6.7   160
7.29   133 n6

INDEX OF SCRIPTURAL REFERENCES

1 Corinthians *cont.*
1.24	30, 178
13.12	187
15.28	90
15.47	186
15.49	186

2 Corinthians
5.17	89
5.19	237

Galatians
2.(19–)20	109, 111, 155 n6, 161, 162, 163, 170
4.29	194

Ephesians
4.23	190

Philippians
1.27	179
2.8	257
2.10	186
3.20, 21	180, 186
3.21	180, 186

Colossians
2.13	89
3.10	189
3.12	189

1 Thessalonians
3.12	184

Philemon
15–16	223 n87

Hebrews
24.24	92

1 Peter
2.9	77
2.4–5	77
1.3	186

1 John
4.9–11	104, 162

Revelation
5.6–12	92